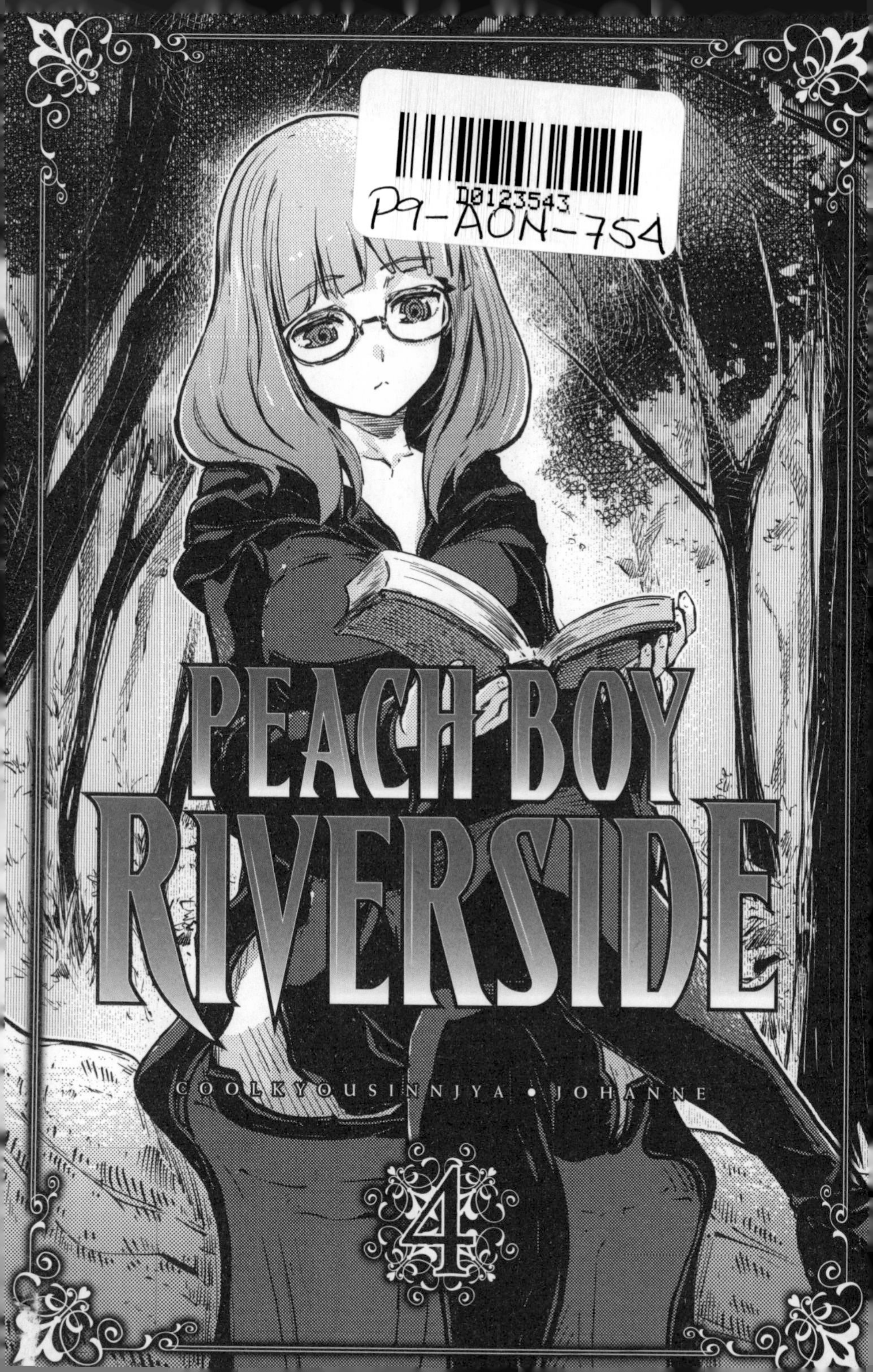
PEACH BOY
RIVERSIDE
COOLKYOUSINNJYA • JOHANNE
4

CONTENTS

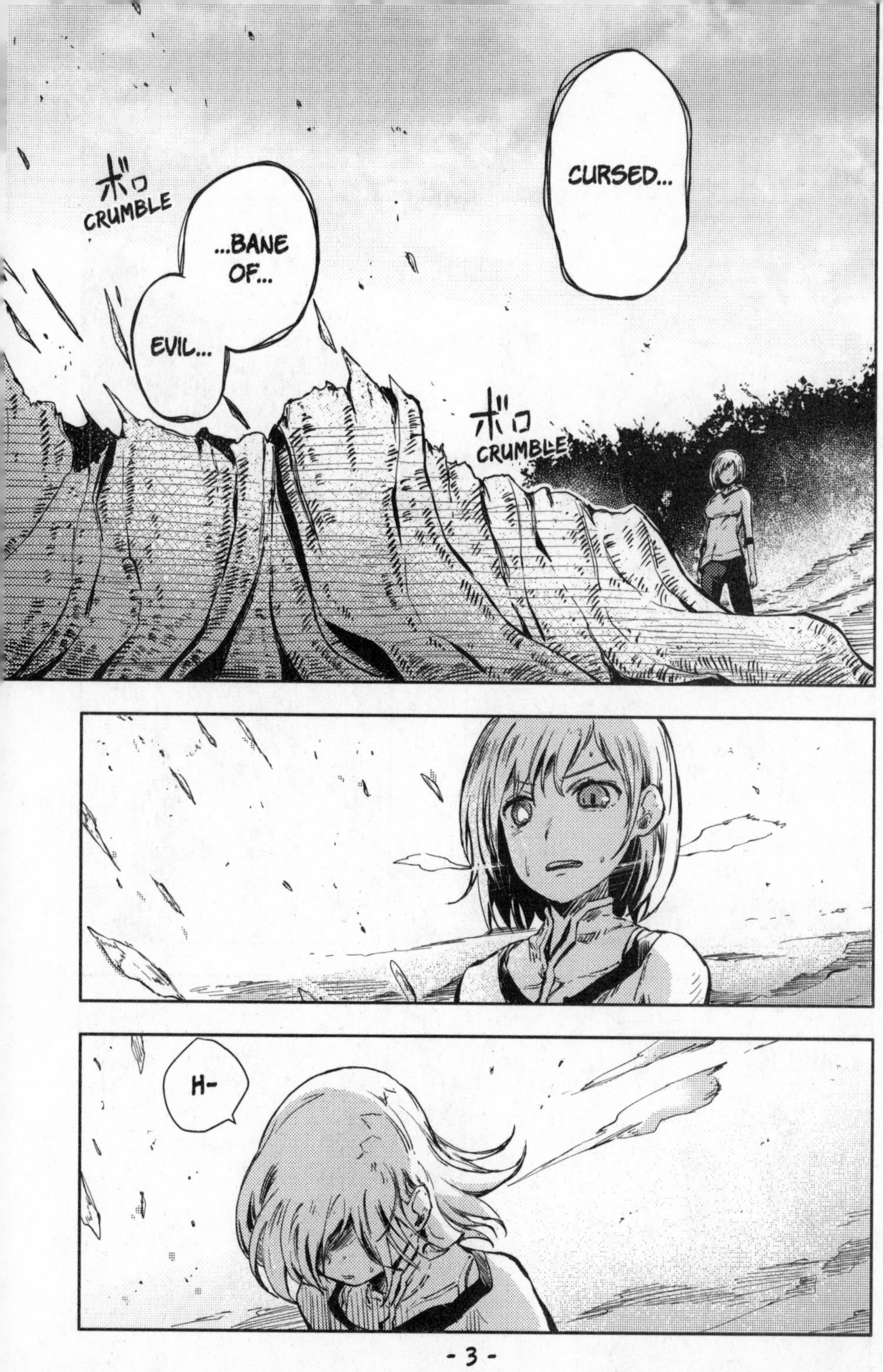
CURSED...
...BANE OF...
EVIL...
ボロ CRUMBLE
ボロ CRUMBLE
H-

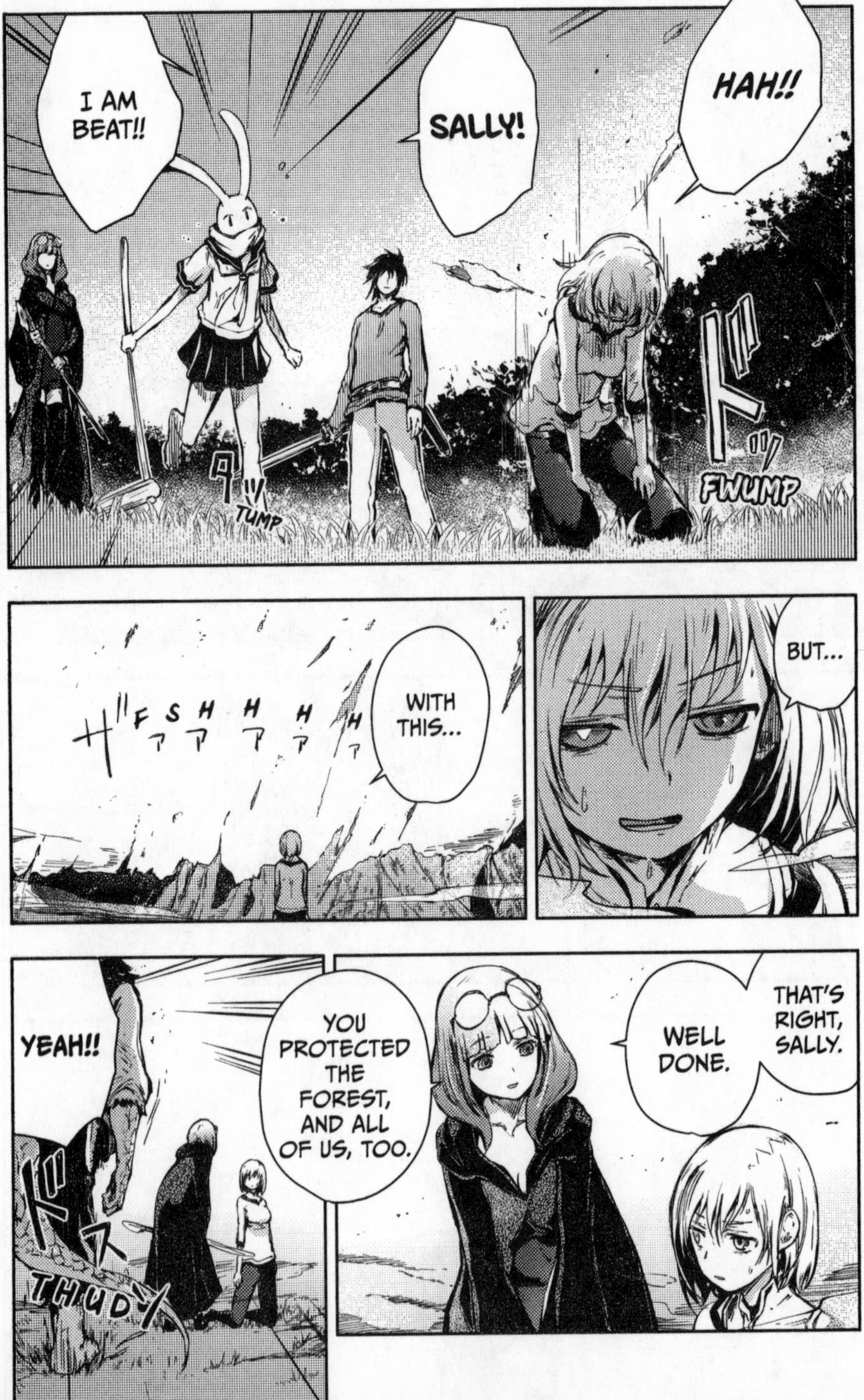
HAH!!
SALLY!
I AM BEAT!!
FWUMP
TUMP
BUT...
WITH THIS...
FSHHHH
THAT'S RIGHT, SALLY.
WELL DONE.
YOU PROTECTED THE FOREST, AND ALL OF US, TOO.
YEAH!!
THUD

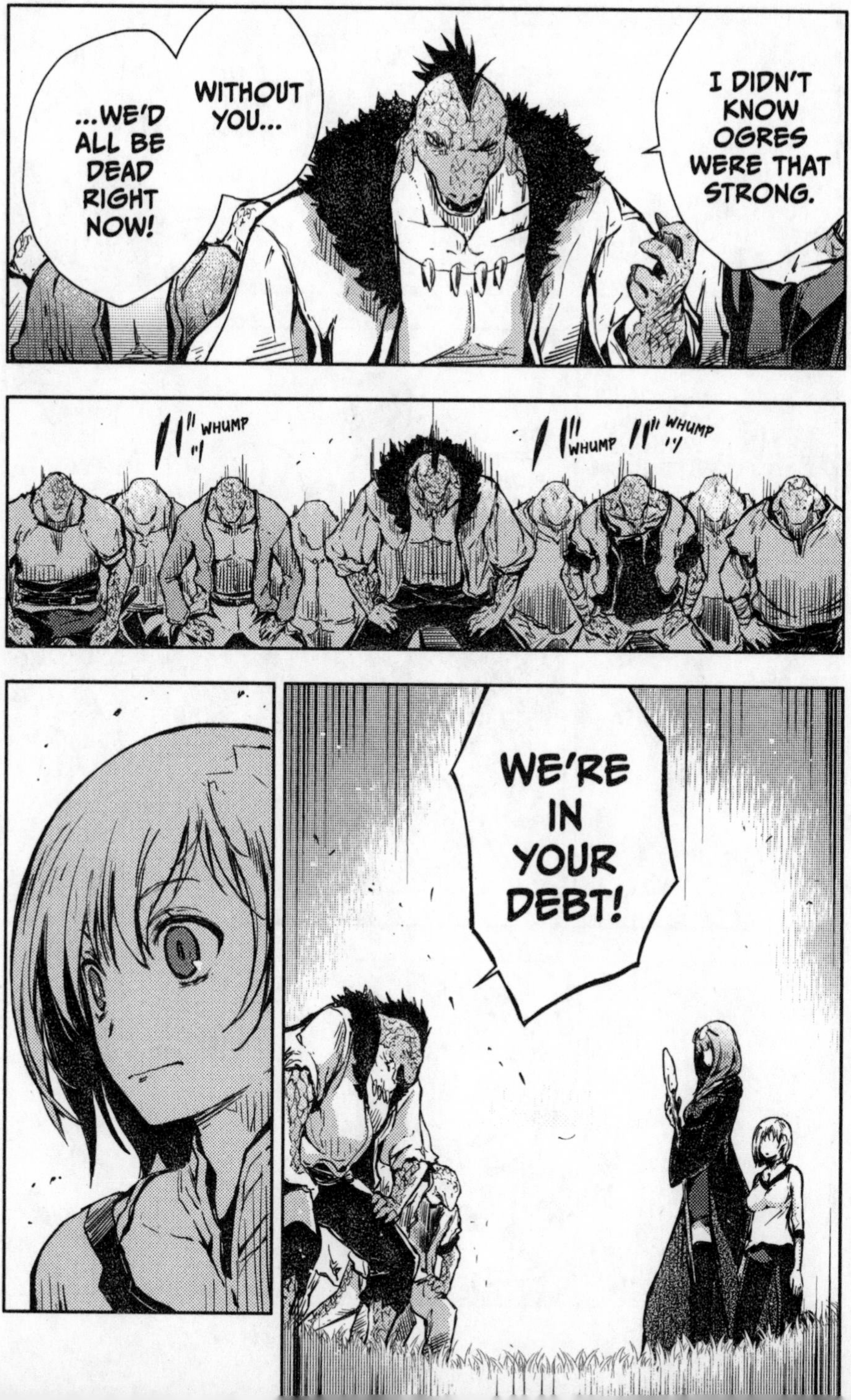
I DIDN'T KNOW OGRES WERE THAT STRONG.
WITHOUT YOU...
...WE'D ALL BE DEAD RIGHT NOW!
WHUMP
WHUMP
WHUMP
WE'RE IN YOUR DEBT!

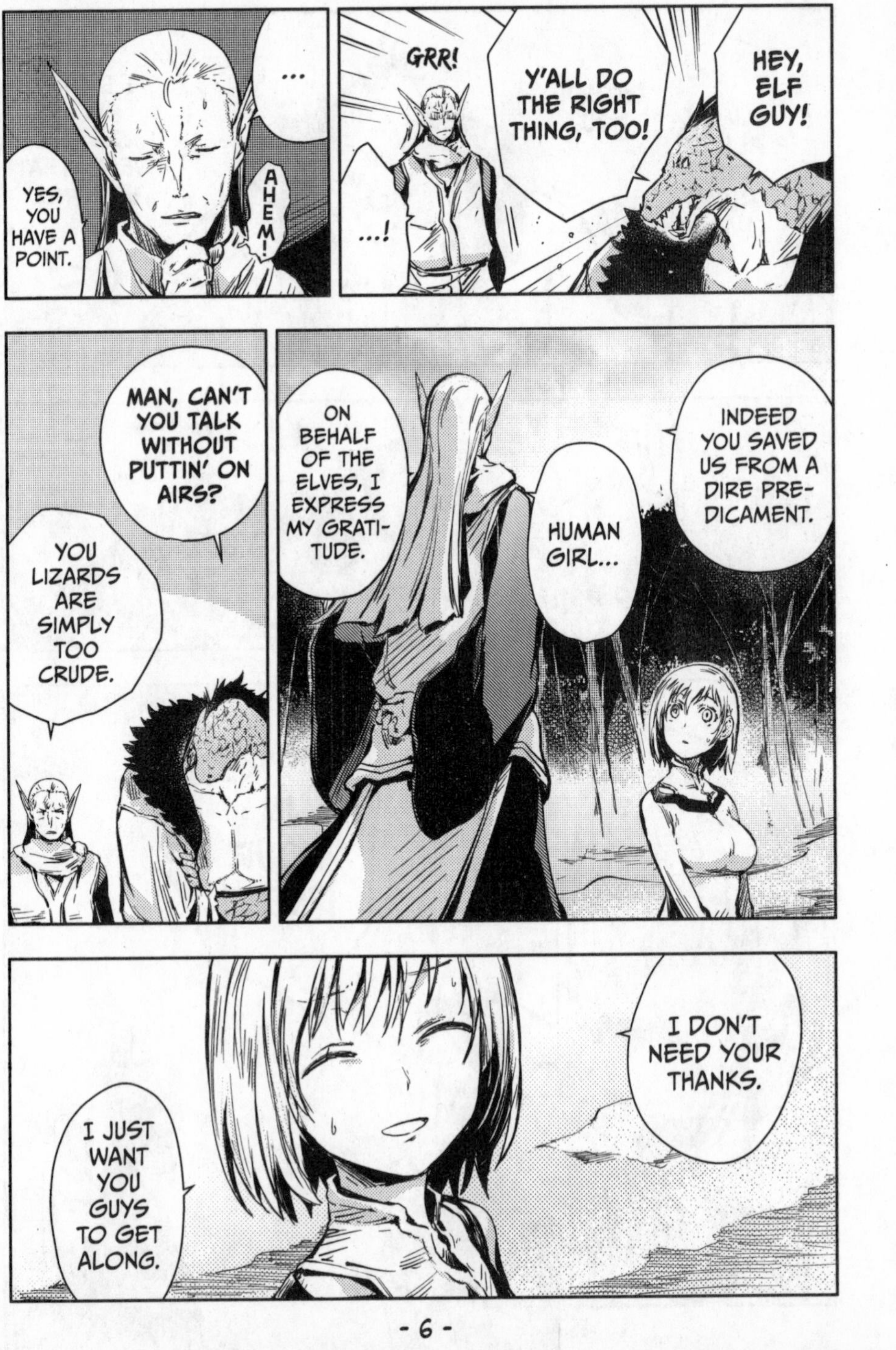
HEY, ELF GUY!
Y'ALL DO THE RIGHT THING, TOO!
GRR!
...!
...
AHEM!
YES, YOU HAVE A POINT.
INDEED YOU SAVED US FROM A DIRE PREDICAMENT.
HUMAN GIRL...
ON BEHALF OF THE ELVES, I EXPRESS MY GRATITUDE.
MAN, CAN'T YOU TALK WITHOUT PUTTIN' ON AIRS?
YOU LIZARDS ARE SIMPLY TOO CRUDE.
I DON'T NEED YOUR THANKS.
I JUST WANT YOU GUYS TO GET ALONG.

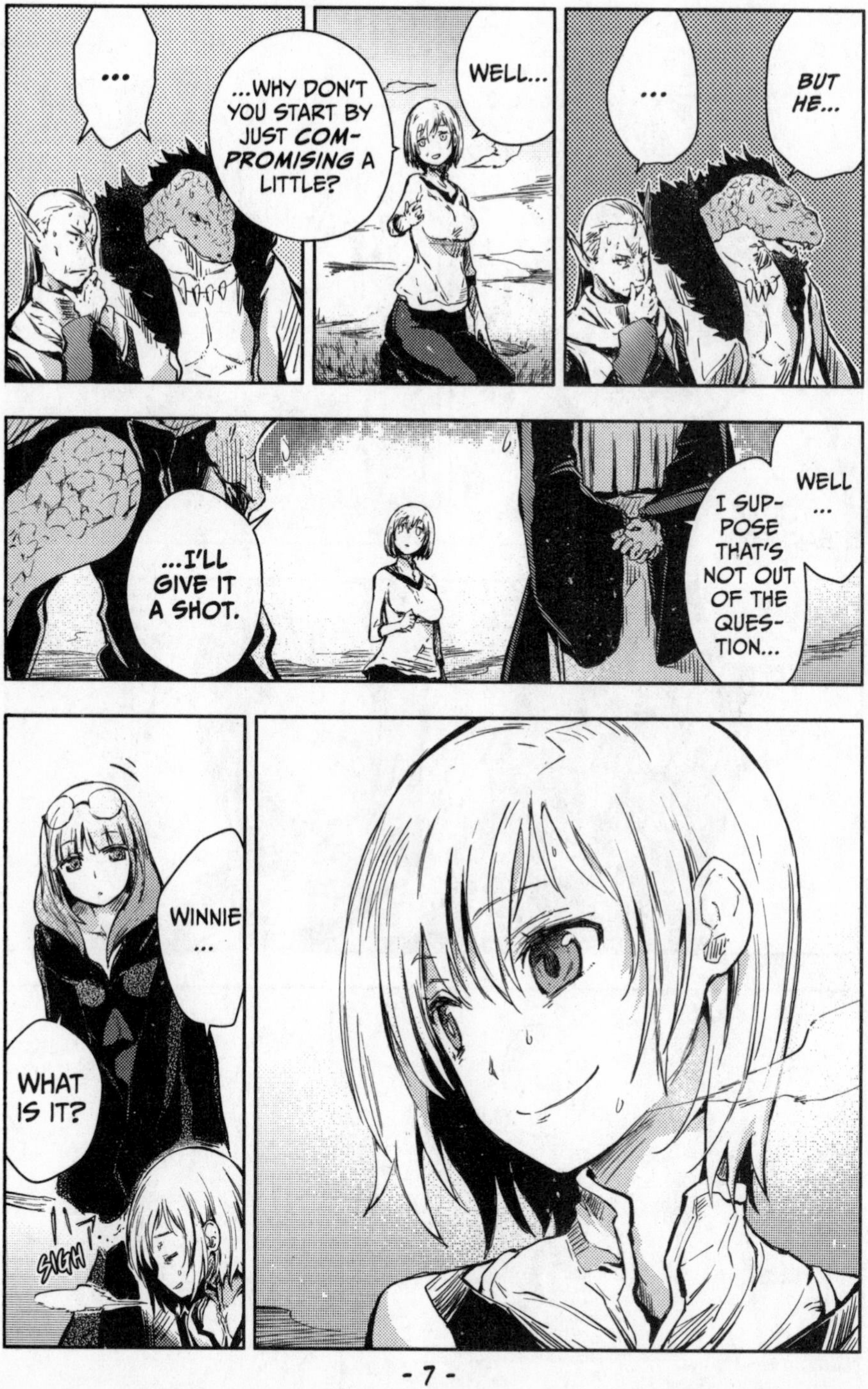
BUT HE...
...
WELL...
...WHY DON'T YOU START BY JUST *COMPROMISING* A LITTLE?
...
WELL ... I SUPPOSE THAT'S NOT OUT OF THE QUESTION...
...I'LL GIVE IT A SHOT.
WINNIE ...
WHAT IS IT?
ハア
SIGH

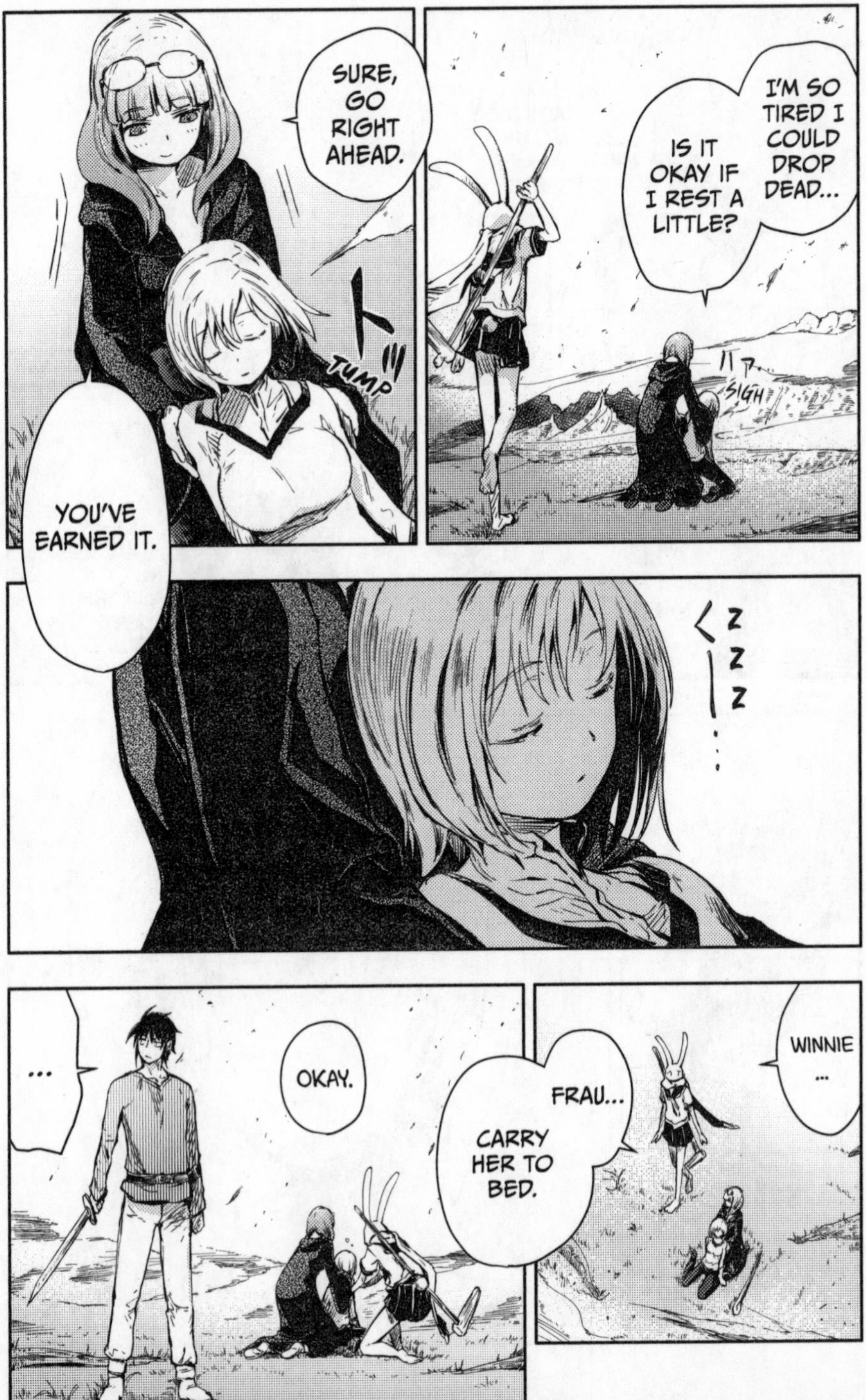
I'M SO TIRED I COULD DROP DEAD...
IS IT OKAY IF I REST A LITTLE?
SIGH
SURE, GO RIGHT AHEAD.
TUMP
YOU'VE EARNED IT.
ZZZ
WINNIE ...
FRAU... CARRY HER TO BED.
OKAY.
...

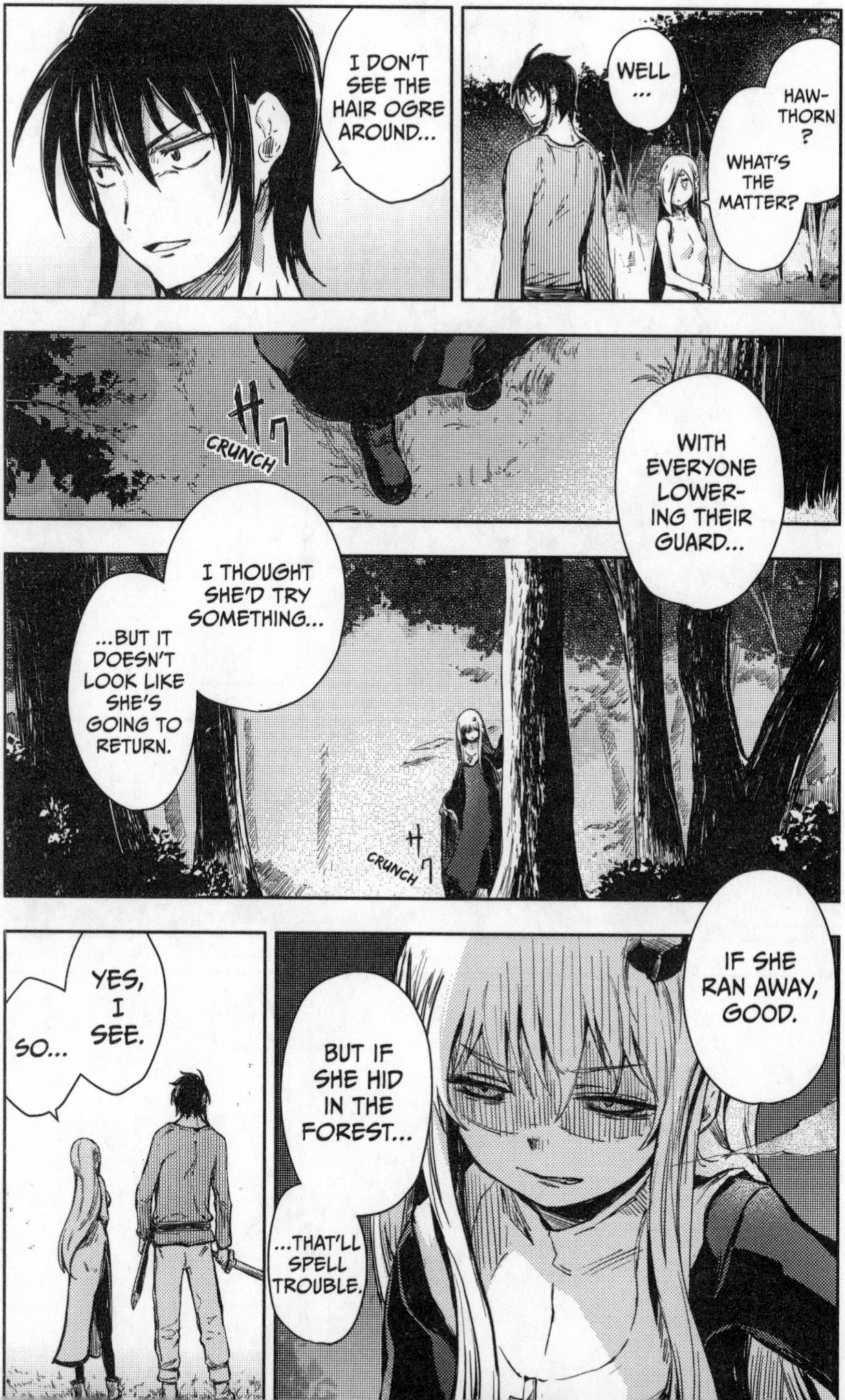
HAW-THORN? WHAT'S THE MATTER?
WELL...
I DON'T SEE THE HAIR OGRE AROUND...
CRUNCH
WITH EVERYONE LOWER-ING THEIR GUARD...
I THOUGHT SHE'D TRY SOMETHING...
...BUT IT DOESN'T LOOK LIKE SHE'S GOING TO RETURN.
CRUNCH
IF SHE RAN AWAY, GOOD.
BUT IF SHE HID IN THE FOREST...
...THAT'LL SPELL TROUBLE.
YES, I SEE.
SO...

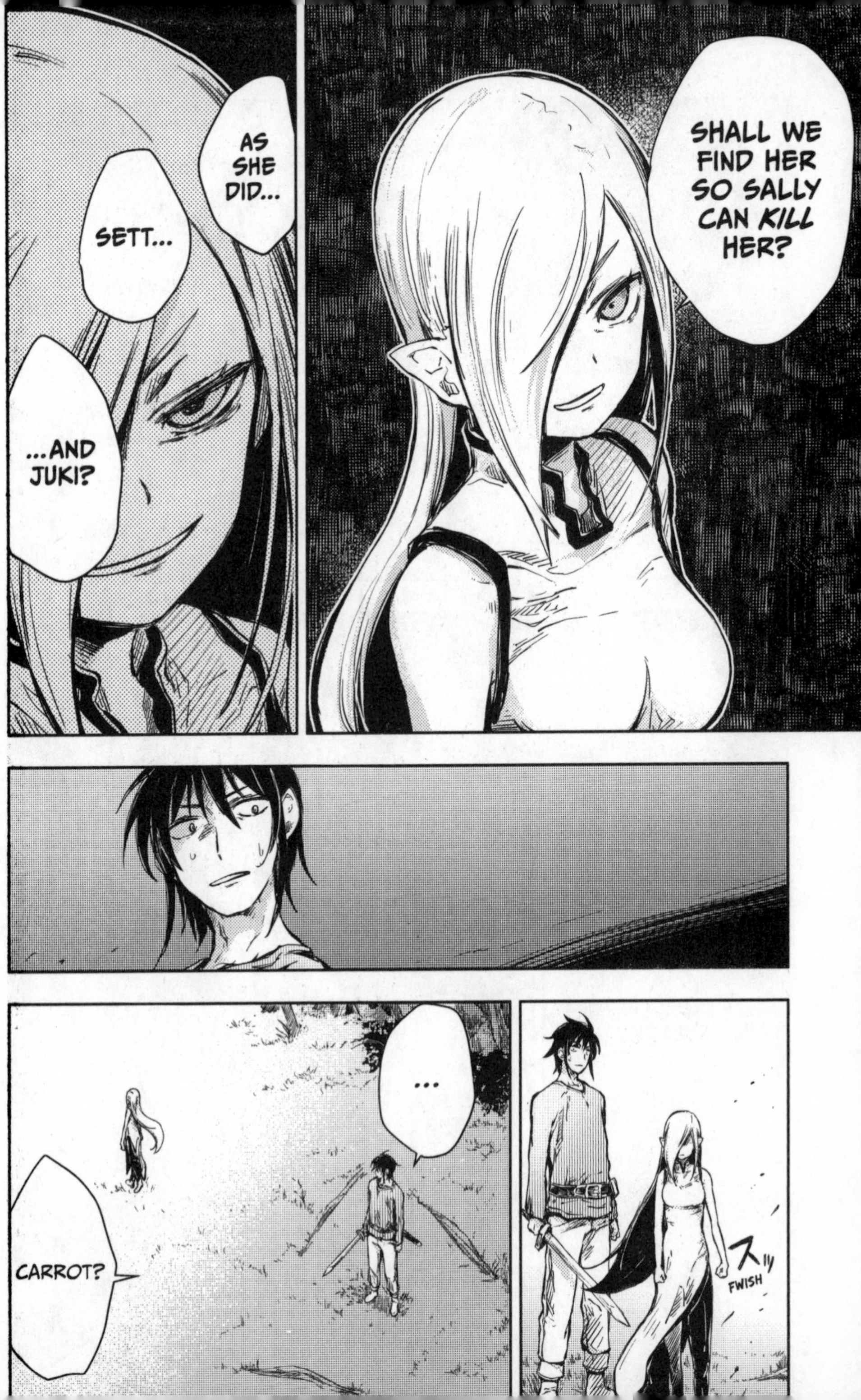
SHALL WE FIND HER SO SALLY CAN *KILL* HER?
AS SHE DID...
SETT...
...AND JUKI?
ス
FWISH
...
CARROT?

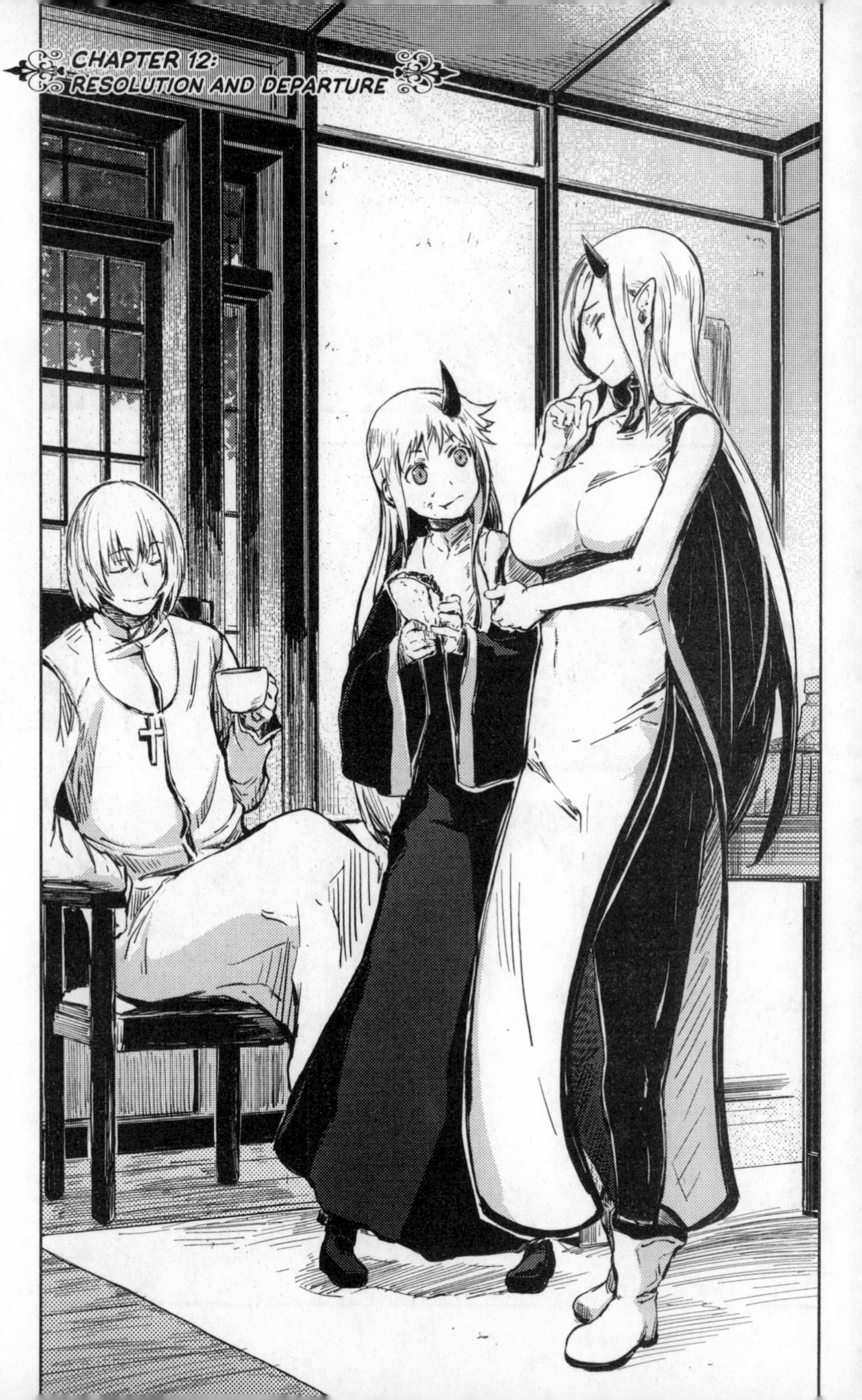
CHAPTER 12:
RESOLUTION AND DEPARTURE

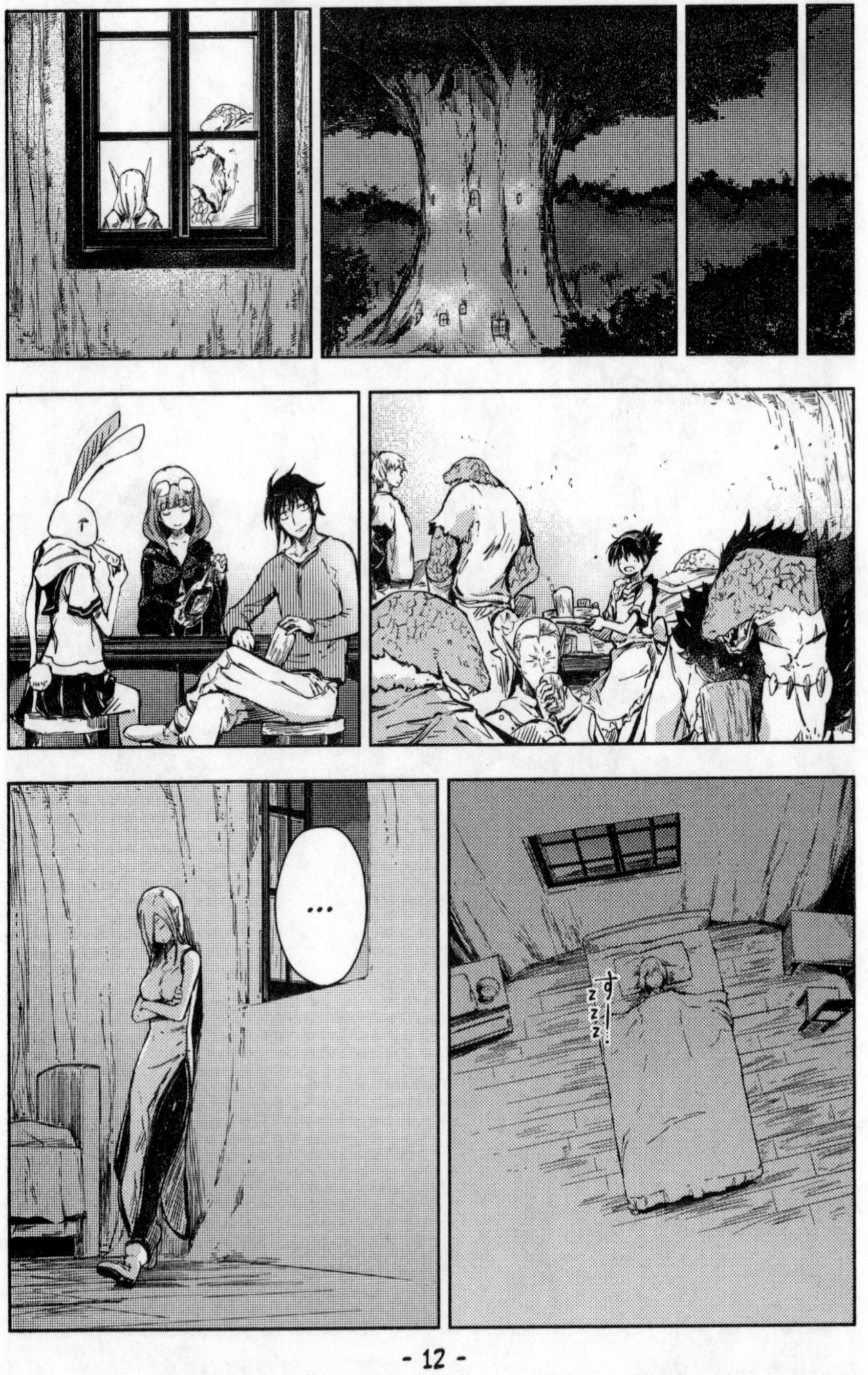
すー…
ZZZ
...

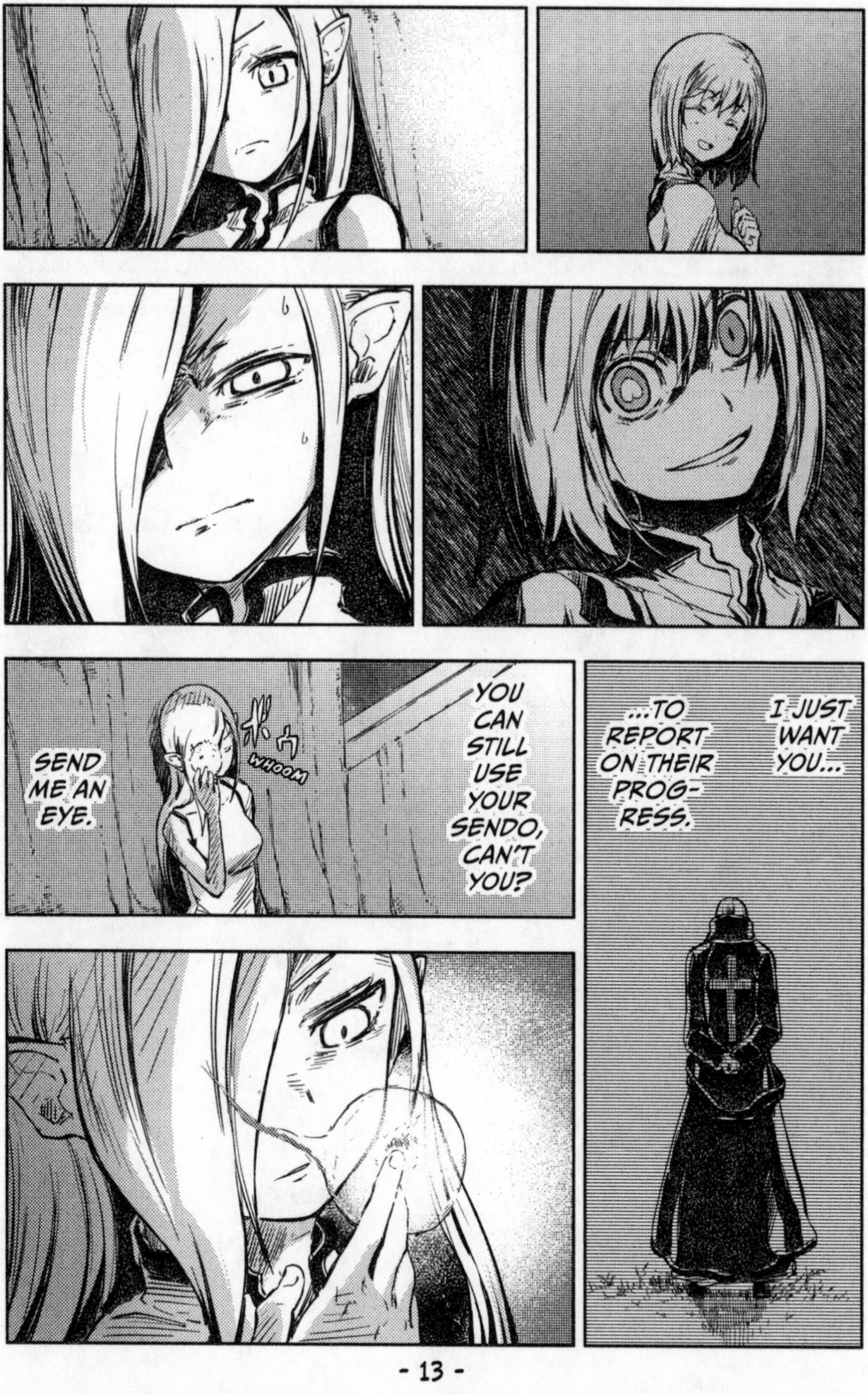
I JUST WANT YOU...
...TO REPORT ON THEIR PROG-RESS.
YOU CAN STILL USE YOUR SENDO, CAN'T YOU?
WHOOM
SEND ME AN EYE.

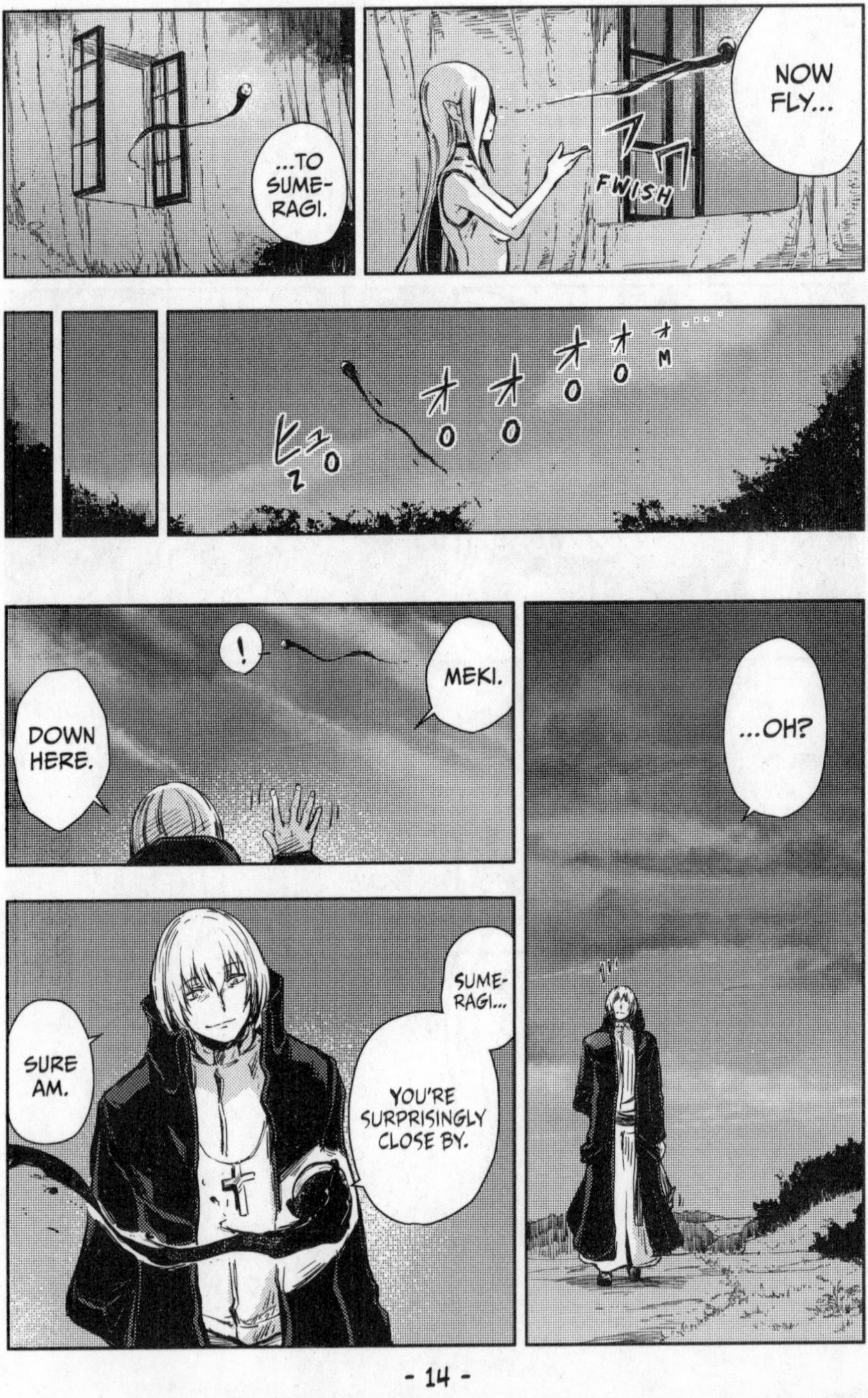

NOW FLY...
FWISH
...TO SUMERAGI.
ZOOOOOM...
...OH?
!
MEKI.
DOWN HERE.
SUMERAGI...
YOU'RE SURPRISINGLY CLOSE BY.
SURE AM.

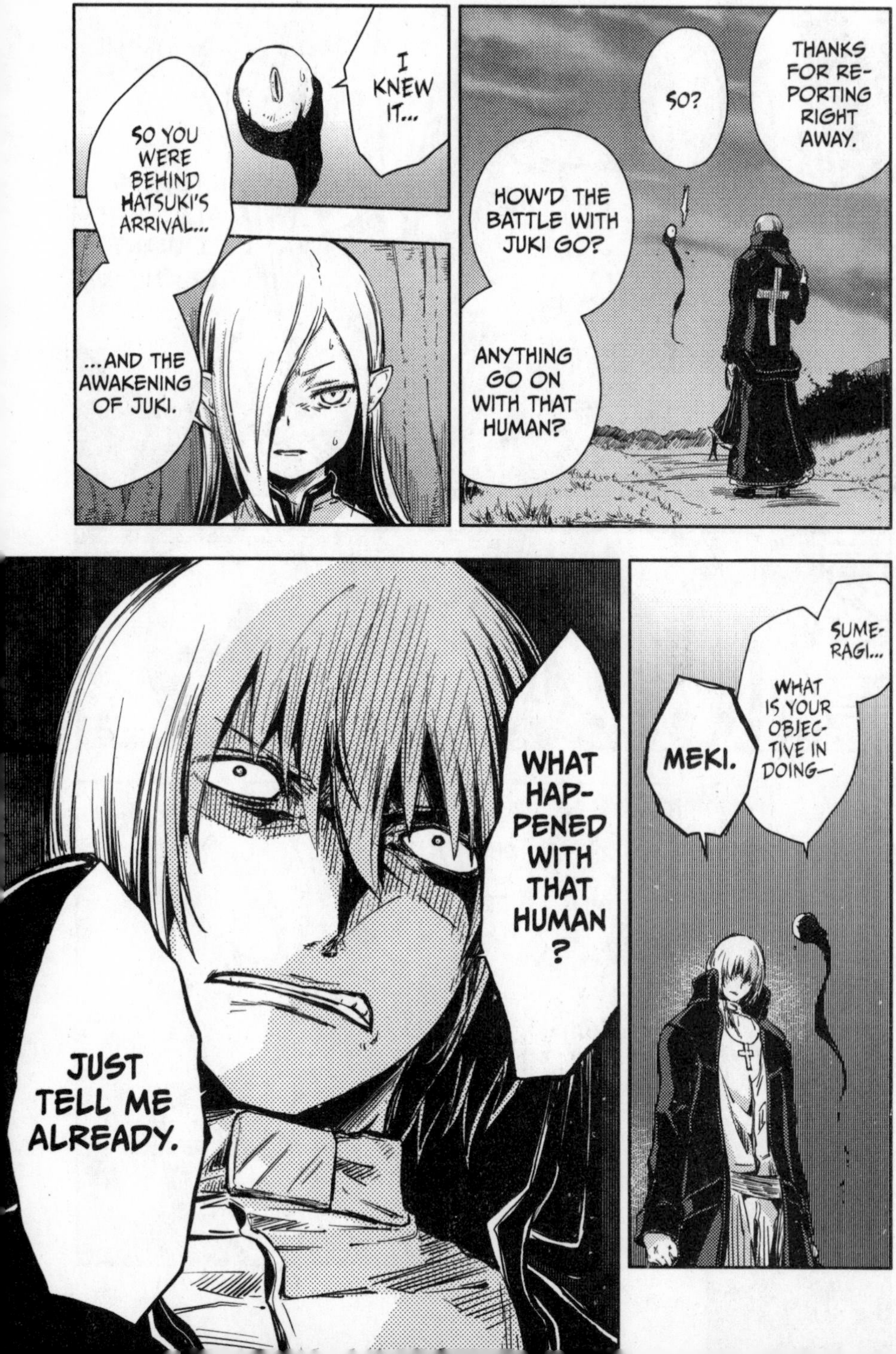
THANKS FOR RE-PORTING RIGHT AWAY.
SO?
HOW'D THE BATTLE WITH JUKI GO?
ANYTHING GO ON WITH THAT HUMAN?
I KNEW IT...
SO YOU WERE BEHIND HATSUKI'S ARRIVAL...
...AND THE AWAKENING OF JUKI.
SUME-RAGI...
WHAT IS YOUR OBJEC-TIVE IN DOING—
MEKI.
WHAT HAP-PENED WITH THAT HUMAN ?
JUST TELL ME ALREADY.

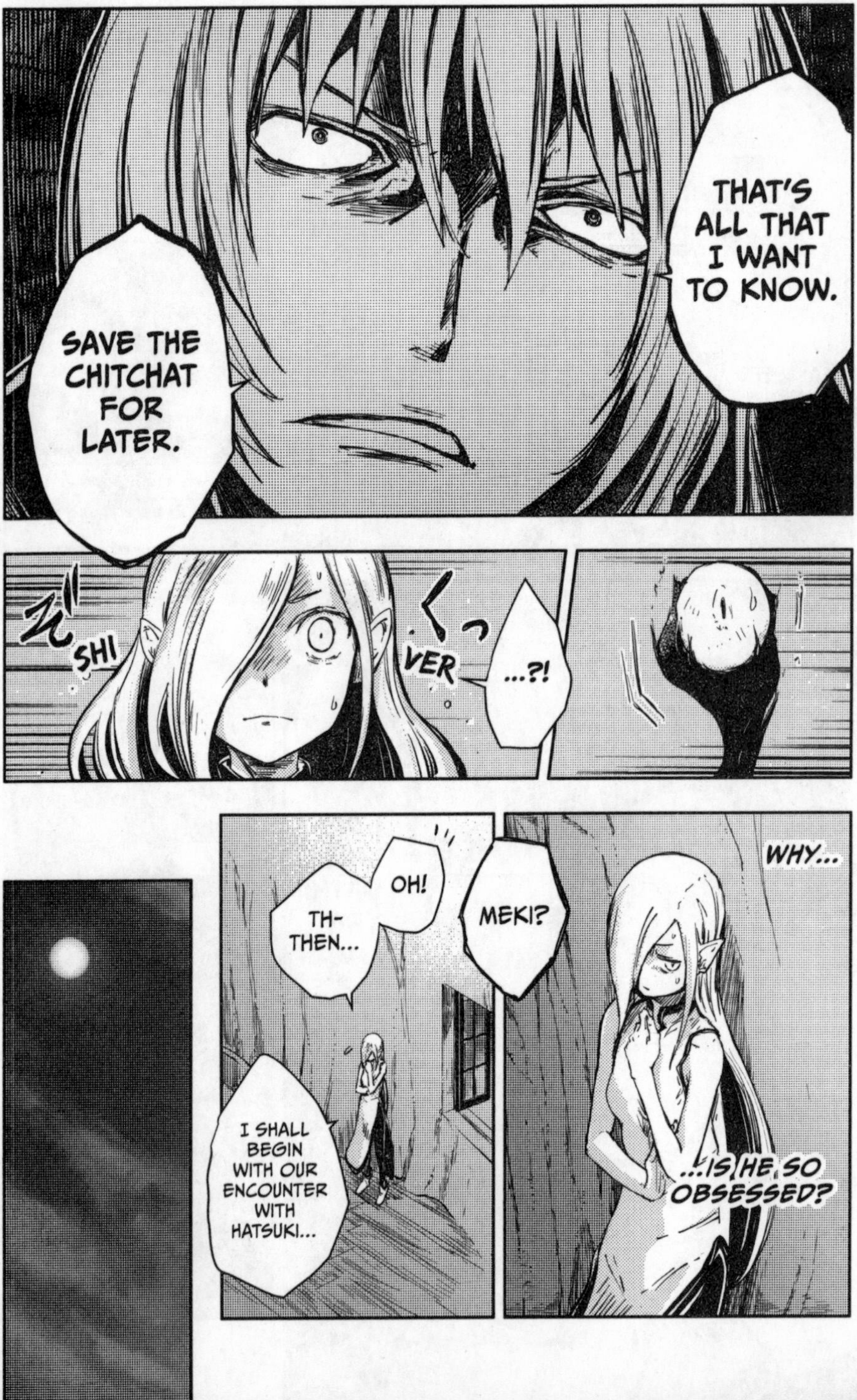
THAT'S ALL THAT I WANT TO KNOW.
SAVE THE CHITCHAT FOR LATER.
SHIVER
...?!
WHY...
...IS HE SO OBSESSED?
MEKI?
OH!
TH- THEN...
I SHALL BEGIN WITH OUR ENCOUNTER WITH HATSUKI...

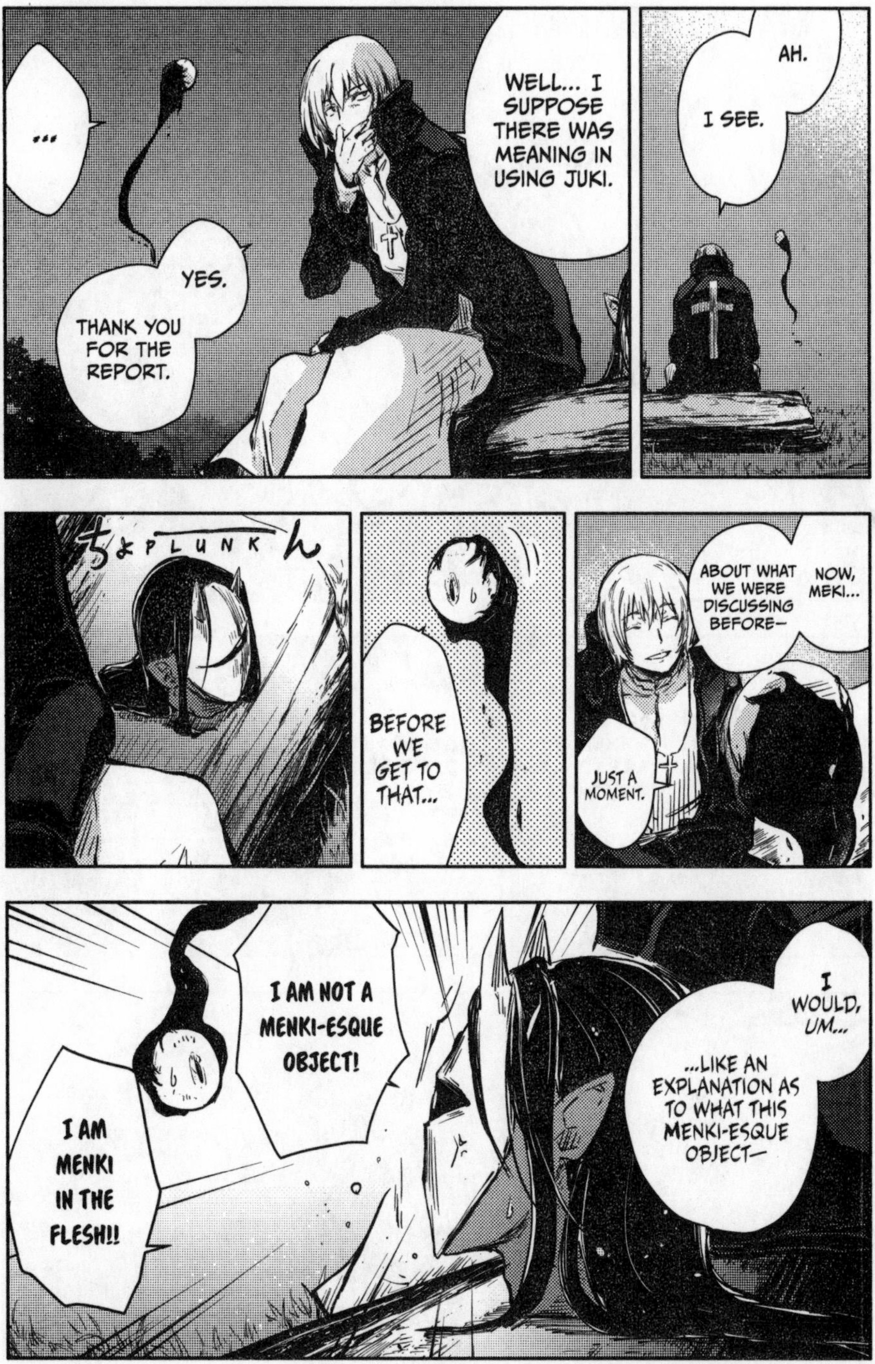
AH.
I SEE.
WELL... I SUPPOSE THERE WAS MEANING IN USING JUKI.
...
YES.
THANK YOU FOR THE REPORT.
NOW, MEKI...
ABOUT WHAT WE WERE DISCUSSING BEFORE—
JUST A MOMENT.
BEFORE WE GET TO THAT...
PLUNK
I WOULD, UM...
...LIKE AN EXPLANATION AS TO WHAT THIS MENKI-ESQUE OBJECT—
I AM NOT A MENKI-ESQUE OBJECT!
I AM MENKI IN THE FLESH!!

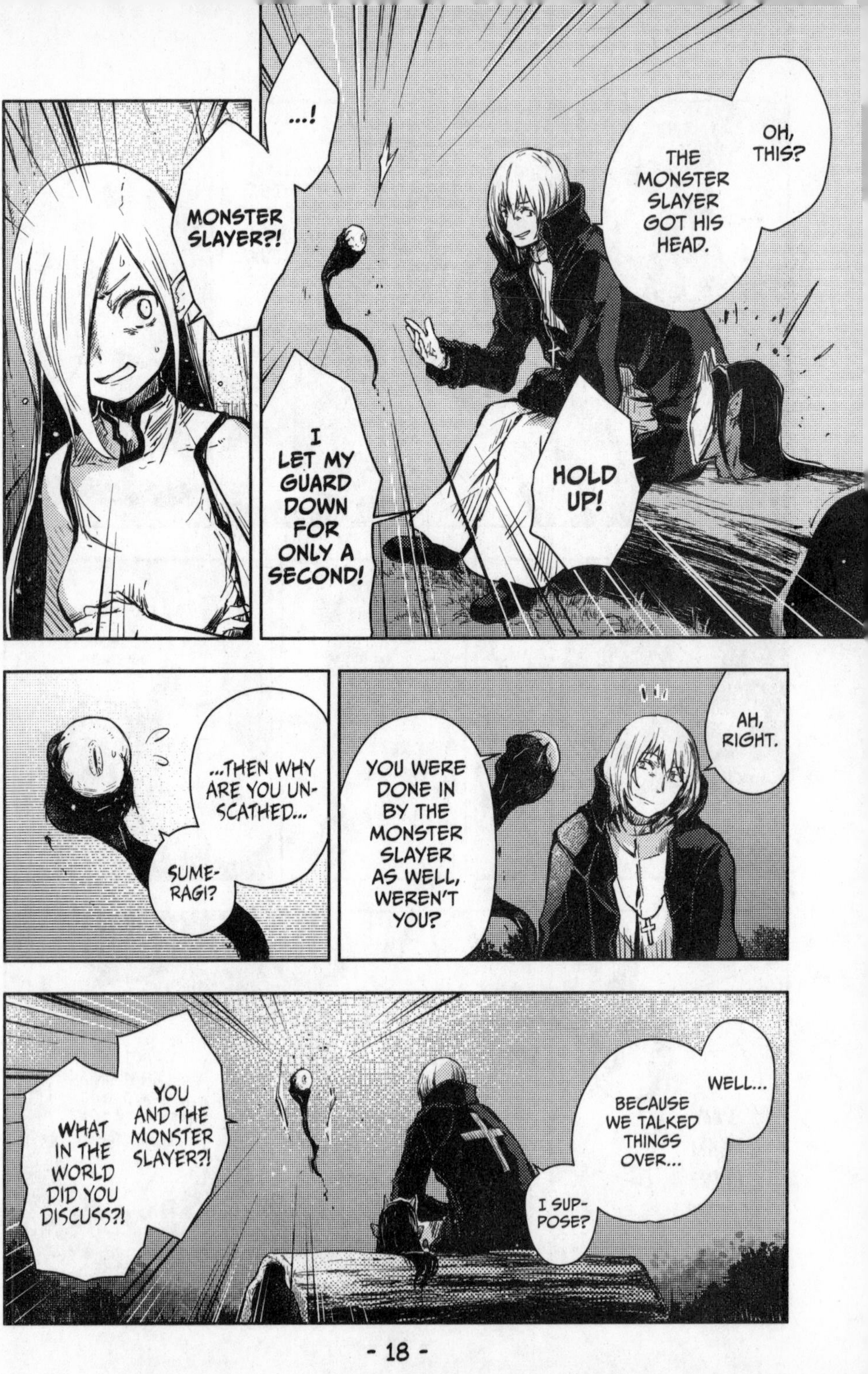
OH, THIS?
THE MONSTER SLAYER GOT HIS HEAD.
...!
MONSTER SLAYER?!
HOLD UP!
I LET MY GUARD DOWN FOR ONLY A SECOND!
AH, RIGHT.
YOU WERE DONE IN BY THE MONSTER SLAYER AS WELL, WEREN'T YOU?
...THEN WHY ARE YOU UN-SCATHED...
SUME-RAGI?
WELL...
BECAUSE WE TALKED THINGS OVER...
I SUP-POSE?
YOU AND THE MONSTER SLAYER?!
WHAT IN THE WORLD DID YOU DISCUSS?!

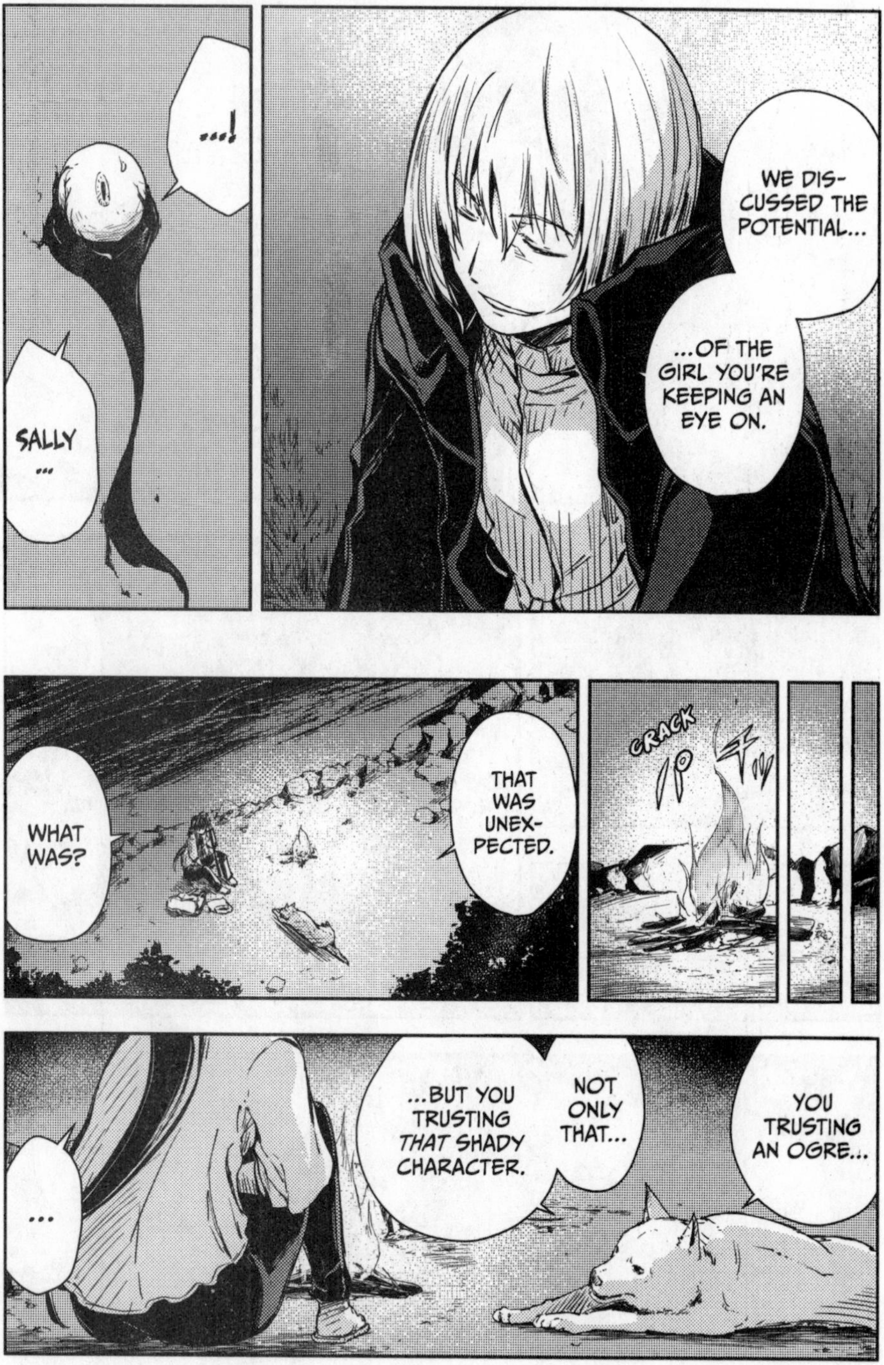
WE DISCUSSED THE POTENTIAL...
...OF THE GIRL YOU'RE KEEPING AN EYE ON.
...!
SALLY...
CRACK
THAT WAS UNEXPECTED.
WHAT WAS?
YOU TRUSTING AN OGRE...
NOT ONLY THAT...
...BUT YOU TRUSTING *THAT* SHADY CHARACTER.
...

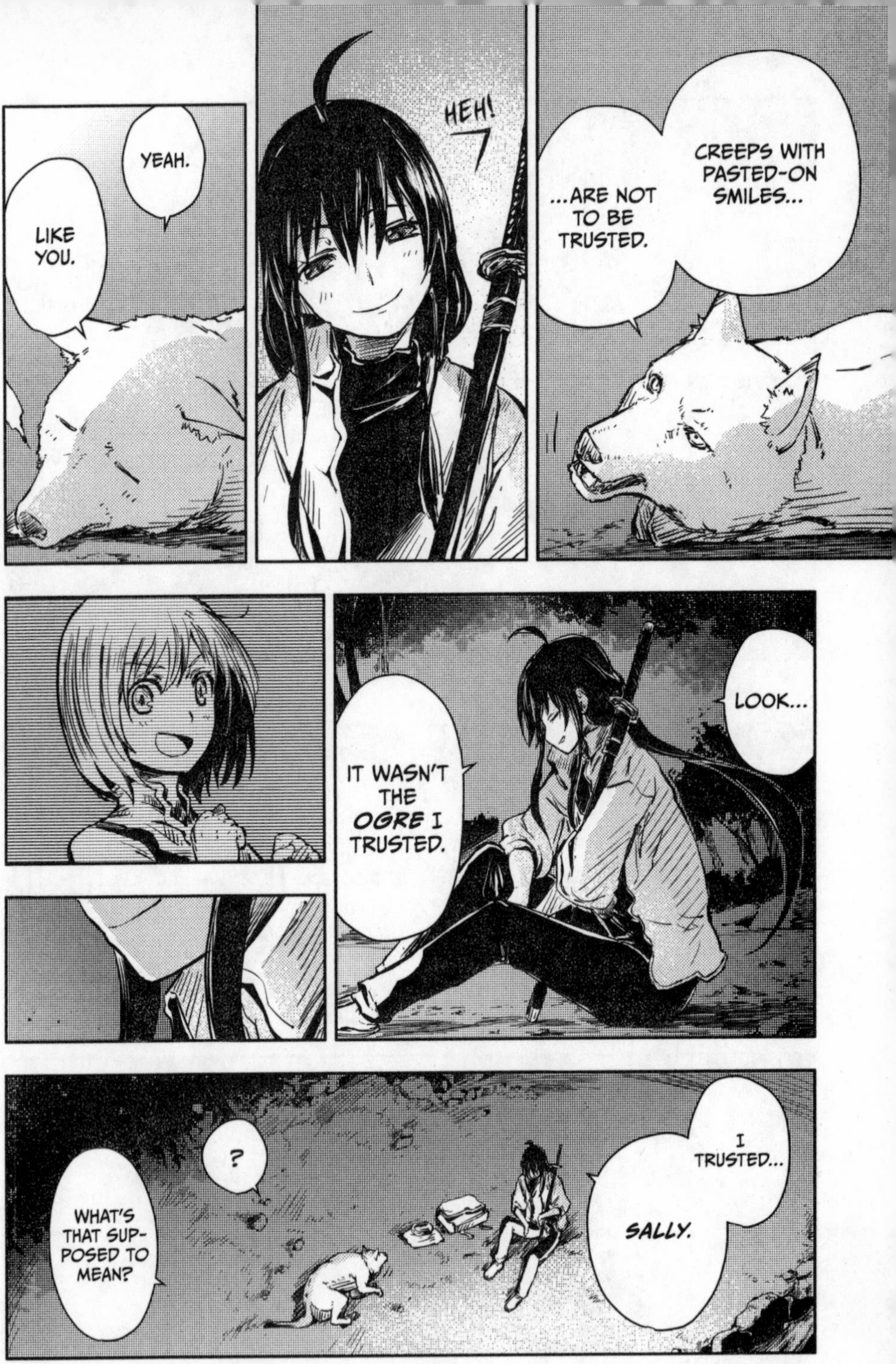
CREEPS WITH PASTED-ON SMILES...
...ARE NOT TO BE TRUSTED.
HEH!
YEAH.
LIKE YOU.
LOOK...
IT WASN'T THE OGRE I TRUSTED.
I TRUSTED...
SALLY.
?
WHAT'S THAT SUP-POSED TO MEAN?

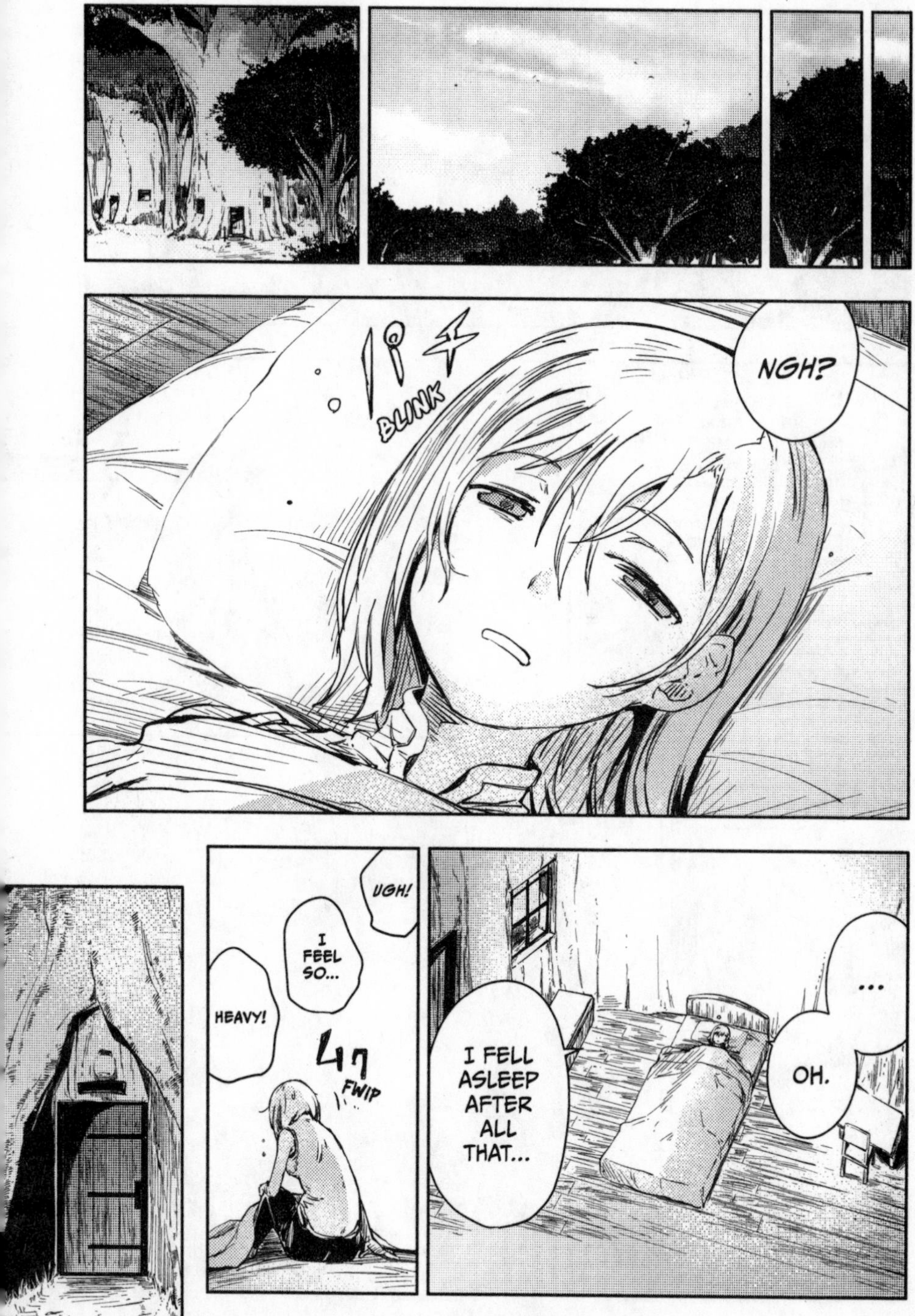
BLINK
NGH?
...
OH.
I FELL ASLEEP AFTER ALL THAT...
UGH!
I FEEL SO...
HEAVY!
FWIP

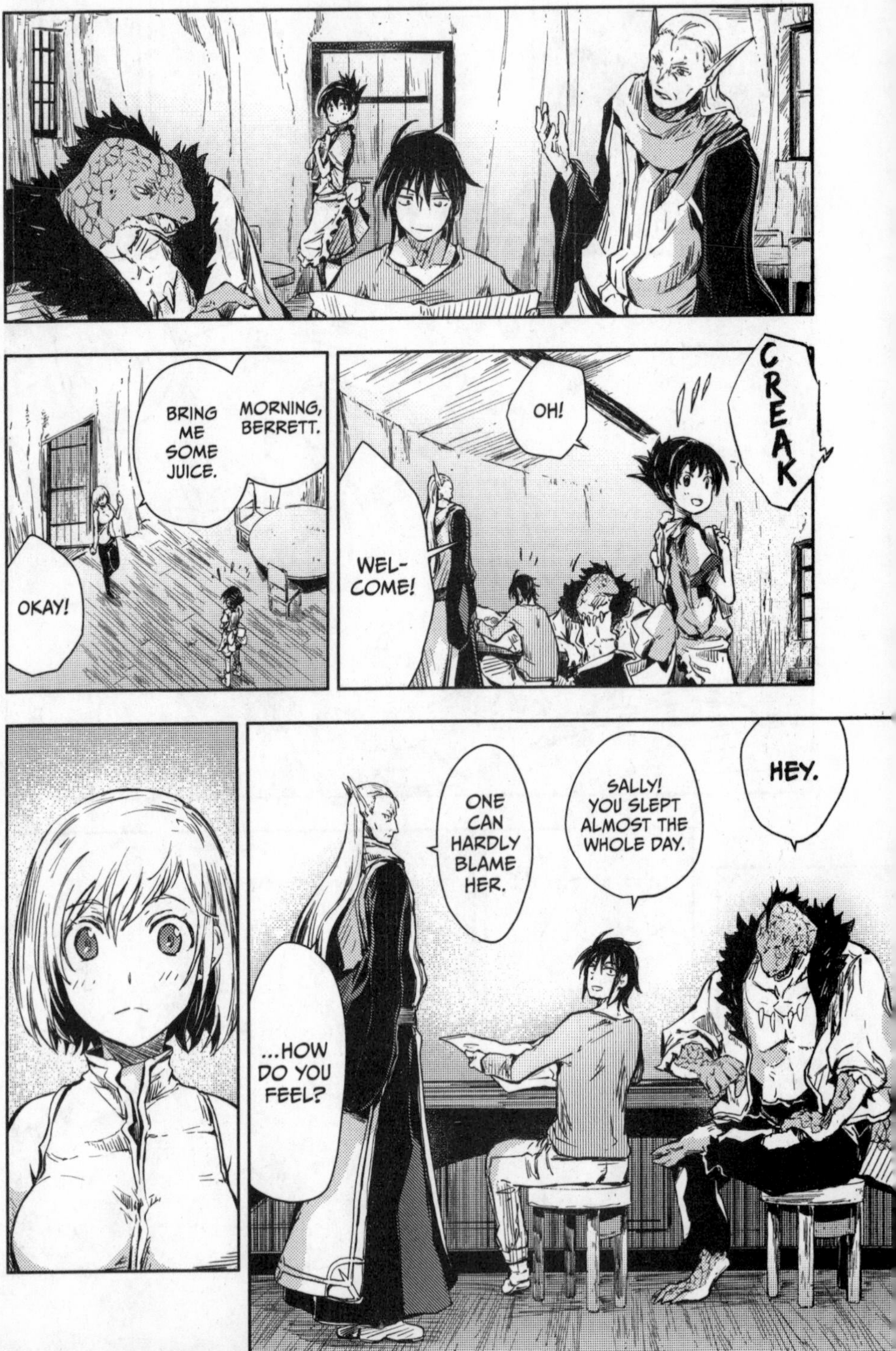
CREAK
OH!
WEL-COME!
MORNING, BERRETT.
BRING ME SOME JUICE.
OKAY!
HEY.
SALLY! YOU SLEPT ALMOST THE WHOLE DAY.
ONE CAN HARDLY BLAME HER.
...HOW DO YOU FEEL?

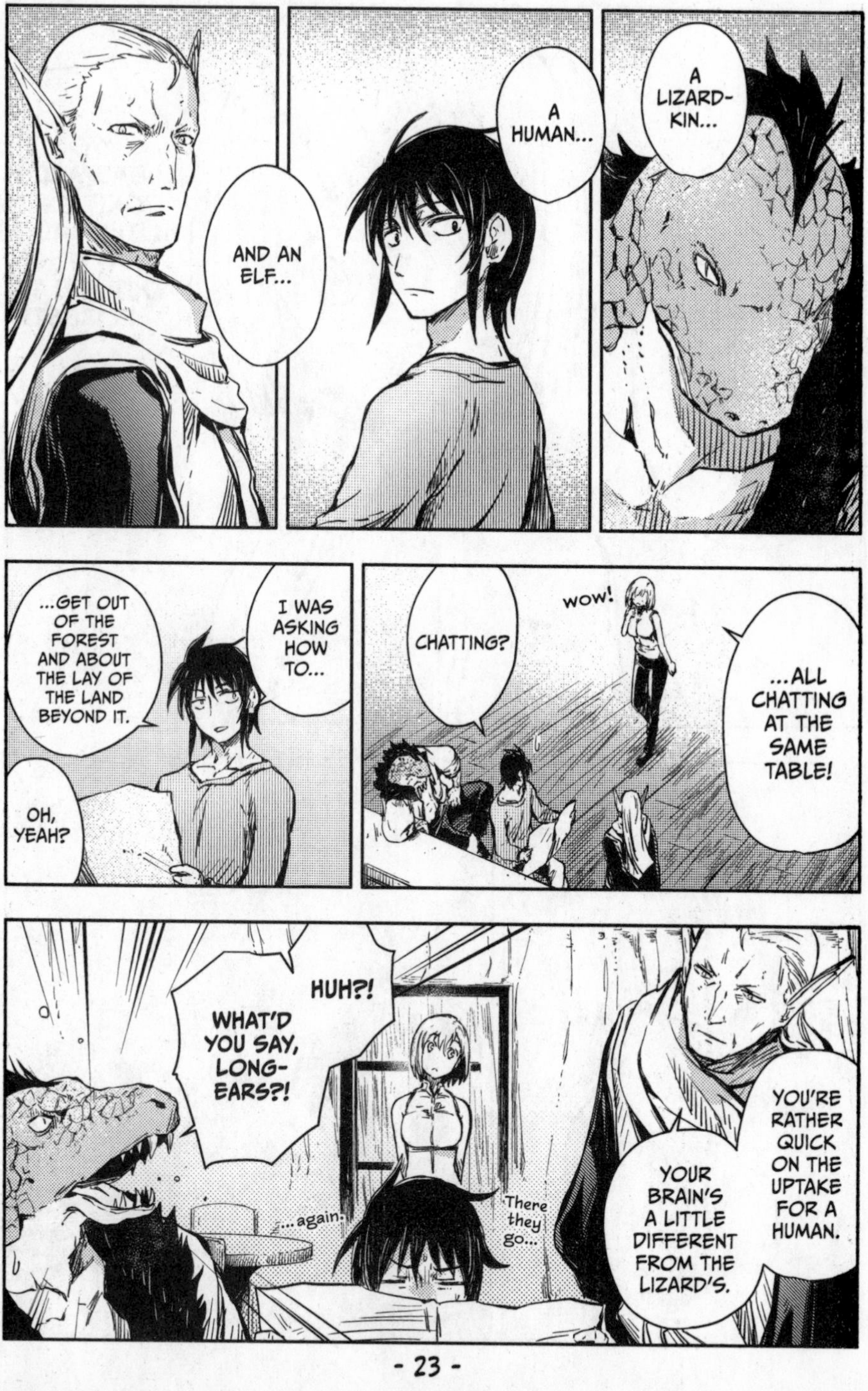
A LIZARD-KIN...
A HUMAN...
AND AN ELF...
...ALL CHATTING AT THE SAME TABLE!
WOW!
CHATTING?
I WAS ASKING HOW TO...
...GET OUT OF THE FOREST AND ABOUT THE LAY OF THE LAND BEYOND IT.
OH, YEAH?
YOU'RE RATHER QUICK ON THE UPTAKE FOR A HUMAN.
YOUR BRAIN'S A LITTLE DIFFERENT FROM THE LIZARD'S.
There they go...
HUH?!
WHAT'D YOU SAY, LONG-EARS?!
...again.

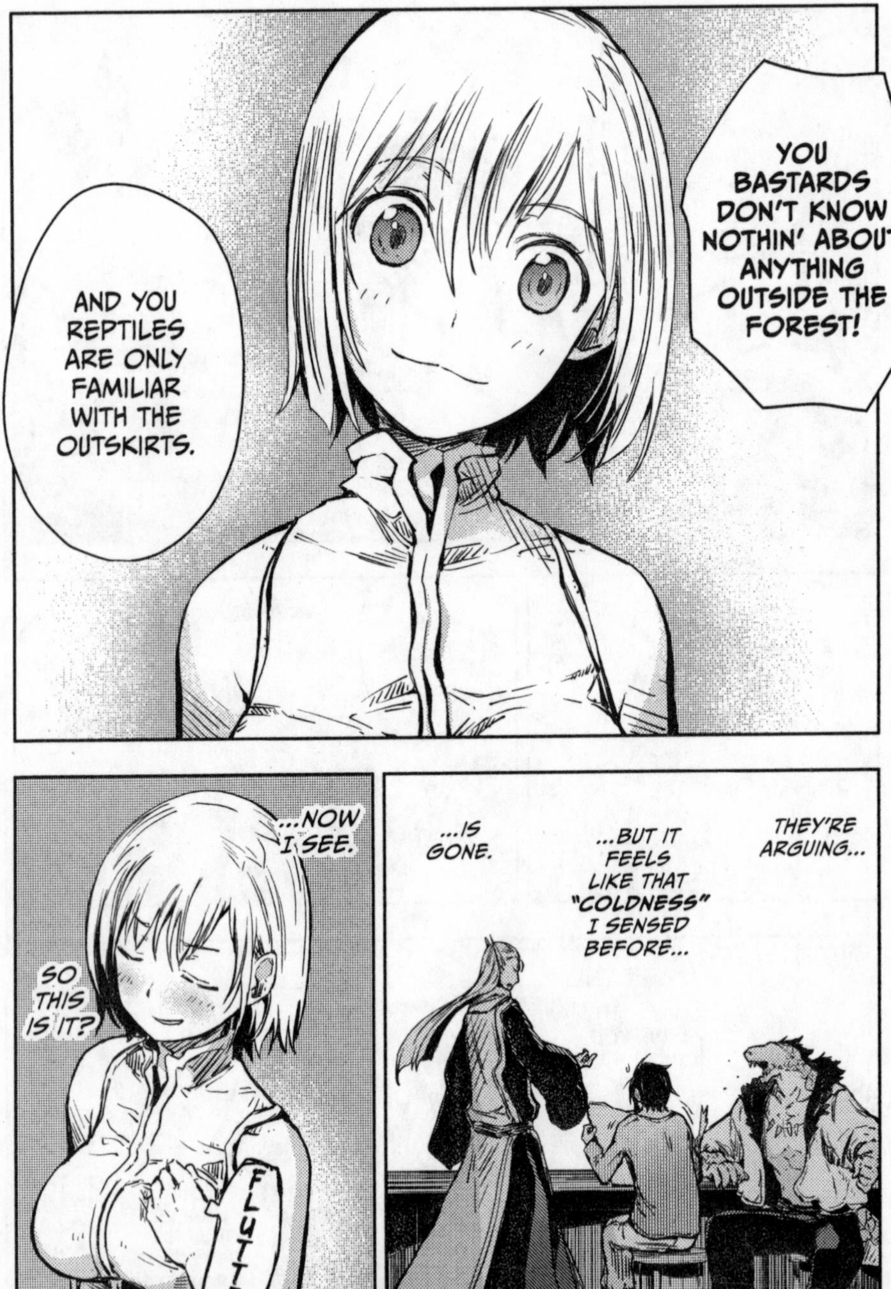
YOU BASTARDS DON'T KNOW NOTHIN' ABOUT ANYTHING OUTSIDE THE FOREST!
AND YOU REPTILES ARE ONLY FAMILIAR WITH THE OUTSKIRTS.
THEY'RE ARGUING...
...BUT IT FEELS LIKE THAT "COLDNESS" I SENSED BEFORE...
...IS GONE.
...NOW I SEE.
SO THIS IS IT?
FLUTTER

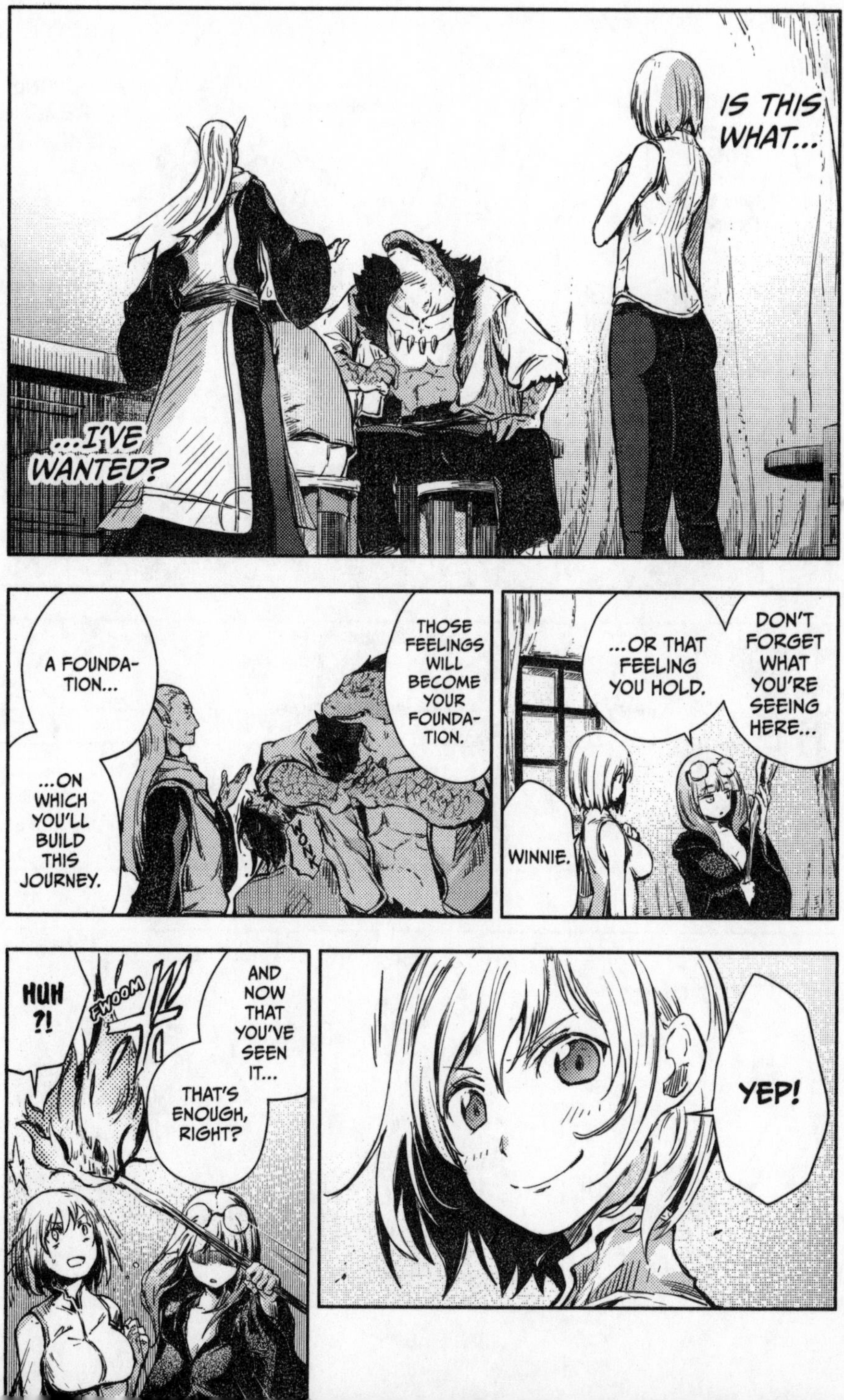
IS THIS WHAT...
...I'VE WANTED?
DON'T FORGET WHAT YOU'RE SEEING HERE...
...OR THAT FEELING YOU HOLD.
WINNIE.
THOSE FEELINGS WILL BECOME YOUR FOUNDATION.
A FOUNDATION...
...ON WHICH YOU'LL BUILD THIS JOURNEY.
WONK
YEP!
AND NOW THAT YOU'VE SEEN IT...
THAT'S ENOUGH, RIGHT?
FWOOM
HUH?!

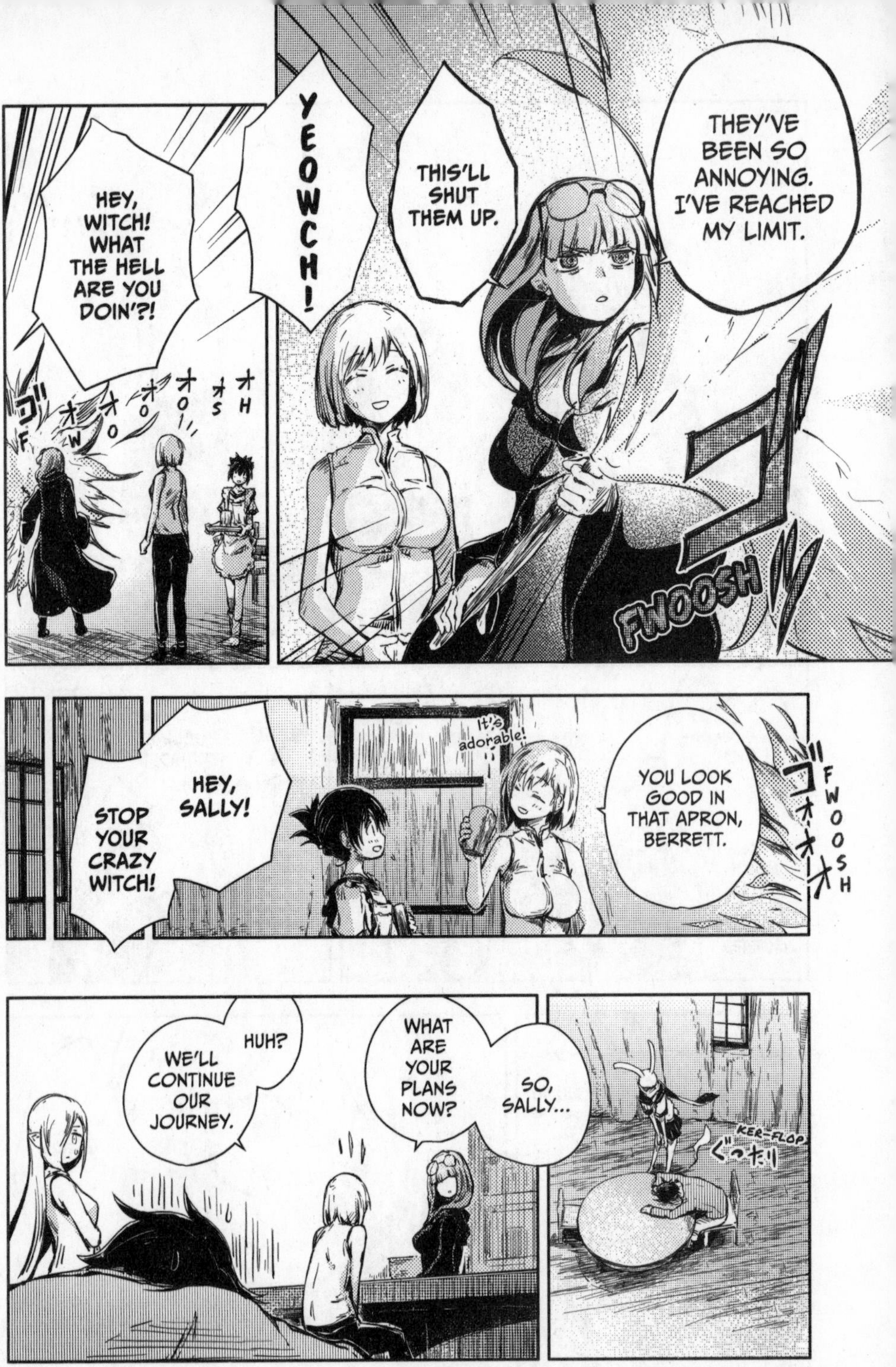

THEY'VE BEEN SO ANNOYING. I'VE REACHED MY LIMIT.
THIS'LL SHUT THEM UP.
YEOWCH!
FWOOSH
HEY, WITCH! WHAT THE HELL ARE YOU DOIN'?!
FWOOSH
FWOOSH
YOU LOOK GOOD IN THAT APRON, BERRETT.
It's adorable!
HEY, SALLY!
STOP YOUR CRAZY WITCH!
KER-FLOP
ぐったり
SO, SALLY...
WHAT ARE YOUR PLANS NOW?
HUH?
WE'LL CONTINUE OUR JOURNEY.

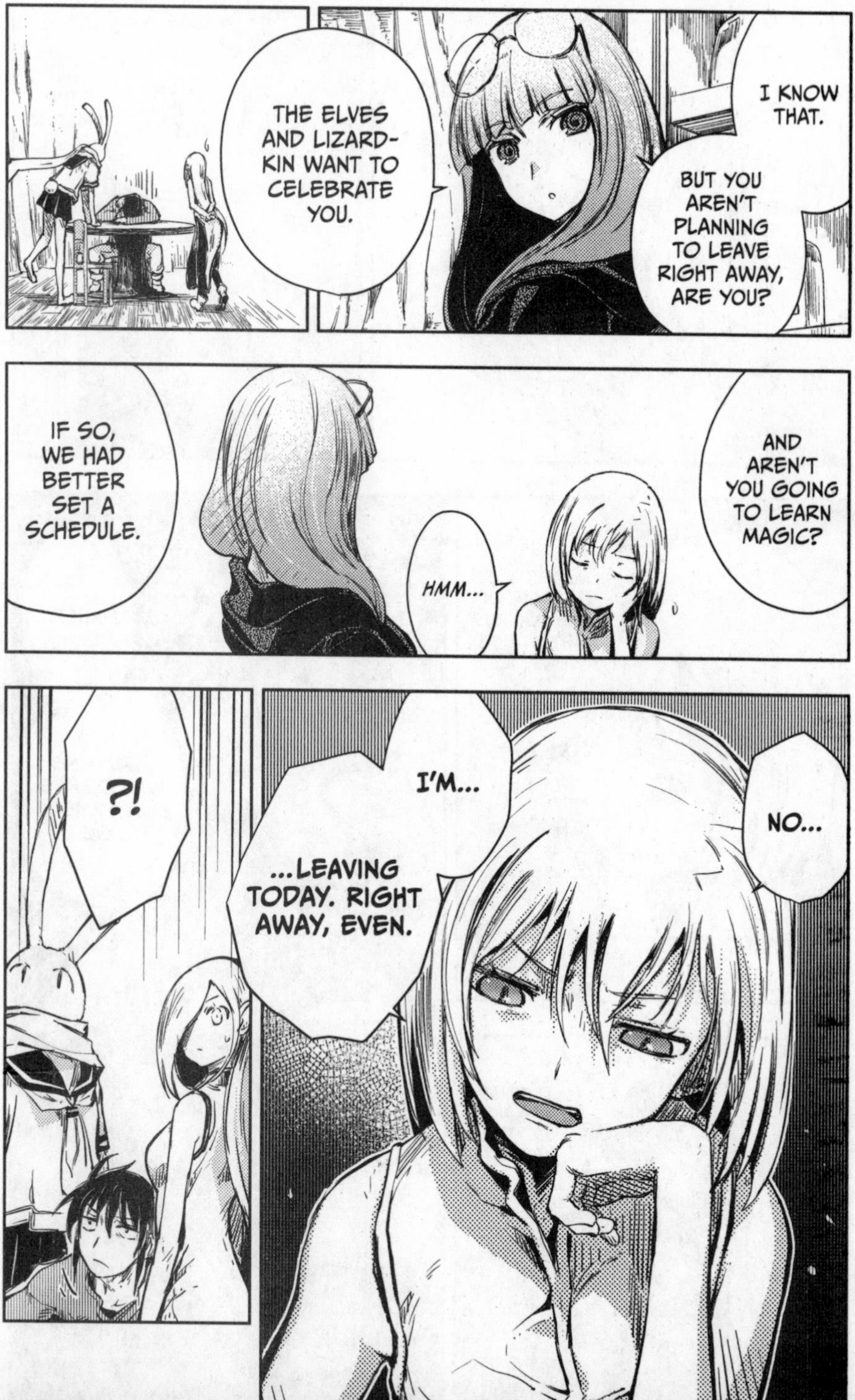
I KNOW THAT.
BUT YOU AREN'T PLANNING TO LEAVE RIGHT AWAY, ARE YOU?
THE ELVES AND LIZARD-KIN WANT TO CELEBRATE YOU.
AND AREN'T YOU GOING TO LEARN MAGIC?
HMM...
IF SO, WE HAD BETTER SET A SCHEDULE.
NO...
I'M...
...LEAVING TODAY. RIGHT AWAY, EVEN.
?!

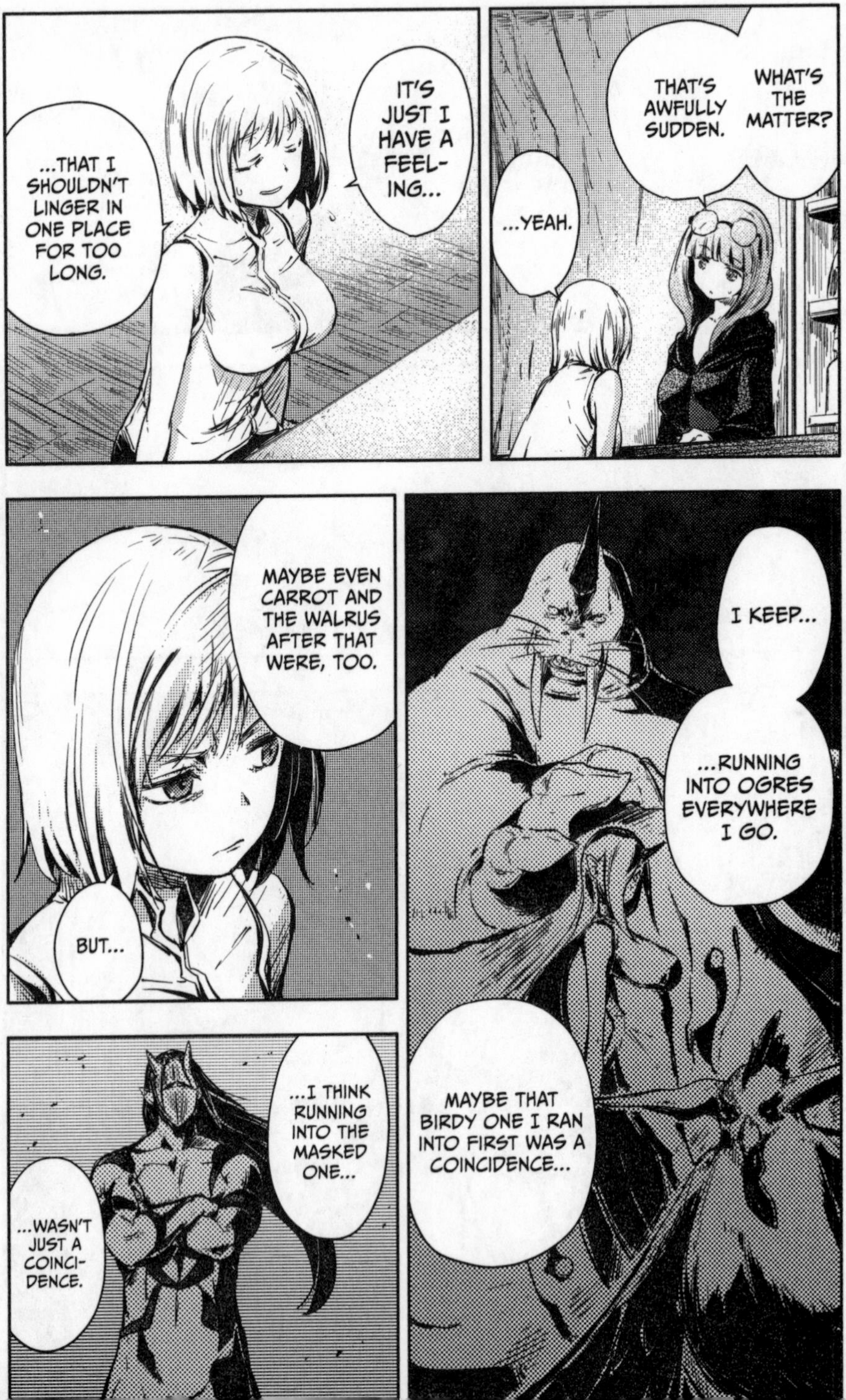
WHAT'S THE MATTER?
THAT'S AWFULLY SUDDEN.
...YEAH.
IT'S JUST I HAVE A FEEL-ING...
...THAT I SHOULDN'T LINGER IN ONE PLACE FOR TOO LONG.
I KEEP...
...RUNNING INTO OGRES EVERYWHERE I GO.
MAYBE THAT BIRDY ONE I RAN INTO FIRST WAS A COINCIDENCE...
MAYBE EVEN CARROT AND THE WALRUS AFTER THAT WERE, TOO.
BUT...
...I THINK RUNNING INTO THE MASKED ONE...
...WASN'T JUST A COINCI-DENCE.

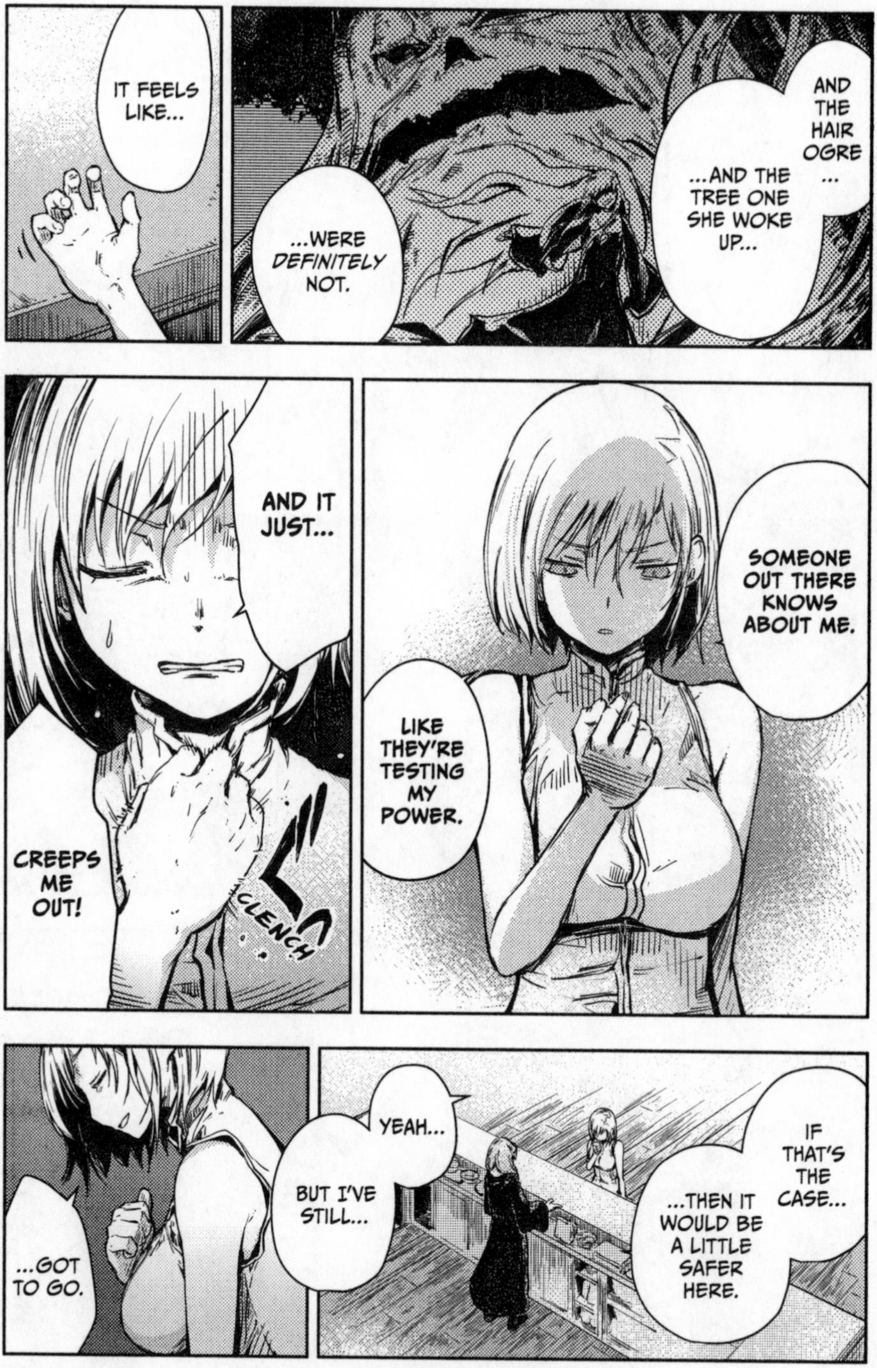
AND THE HAIR OGRE...
...AND THE TREE ONE SHE WOKE UP...
...WERE *DEFINITELY* NOT.
IT FEELS LIKE...
SOMEONE OUT THERE KNOWS ABOUT ME.
LIKE THEY'RE TESTING MY POWER.
AND IT JUST...
CREEPS ME OUT!
CLENCH
IF THAT'S THE CASE...
...THEN IT WOULD BE A LITTLE SAFER HERE.
YEAH...
BUT I'VE STILL...
...GOT TO GO.

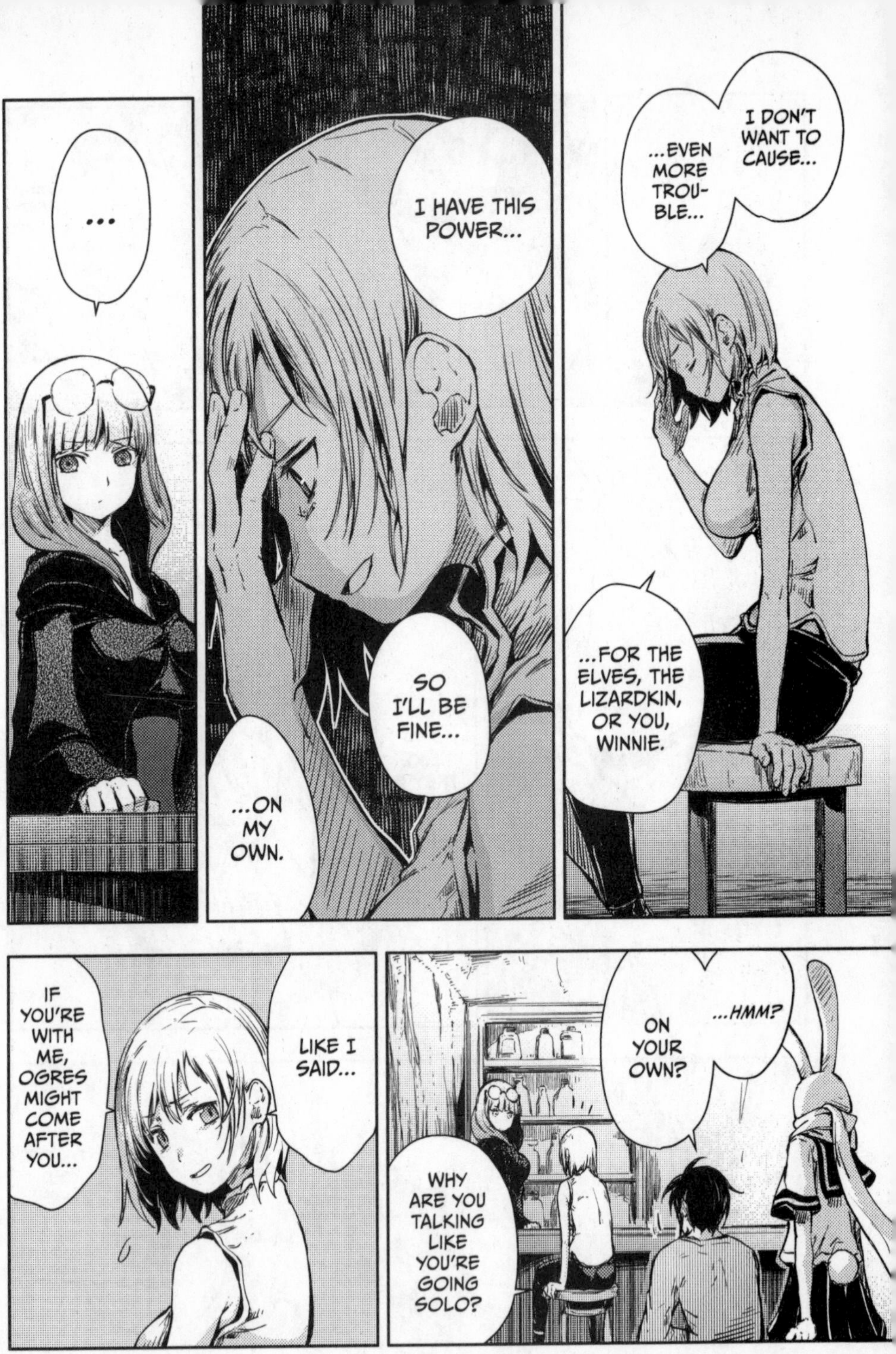
I DON'T WANT TO CAUSE...
...EVEN MORE TROU-BLE...
...FOR THE ELVES, THE LIZARDKIN, OR YOU, WINNIE.
I HAVE THIS POWER...
SO I'LL BE FINE...
...ON MY OWN.
...
...HMM?
ON YOUR OWN?
WHY ARE YOU TALKING LIKE YOU'RE GOING SOLO?
LIKE I SAID...
IF YOU'RE WITH ME, OGRES MIGHT COME AFTER YOU...

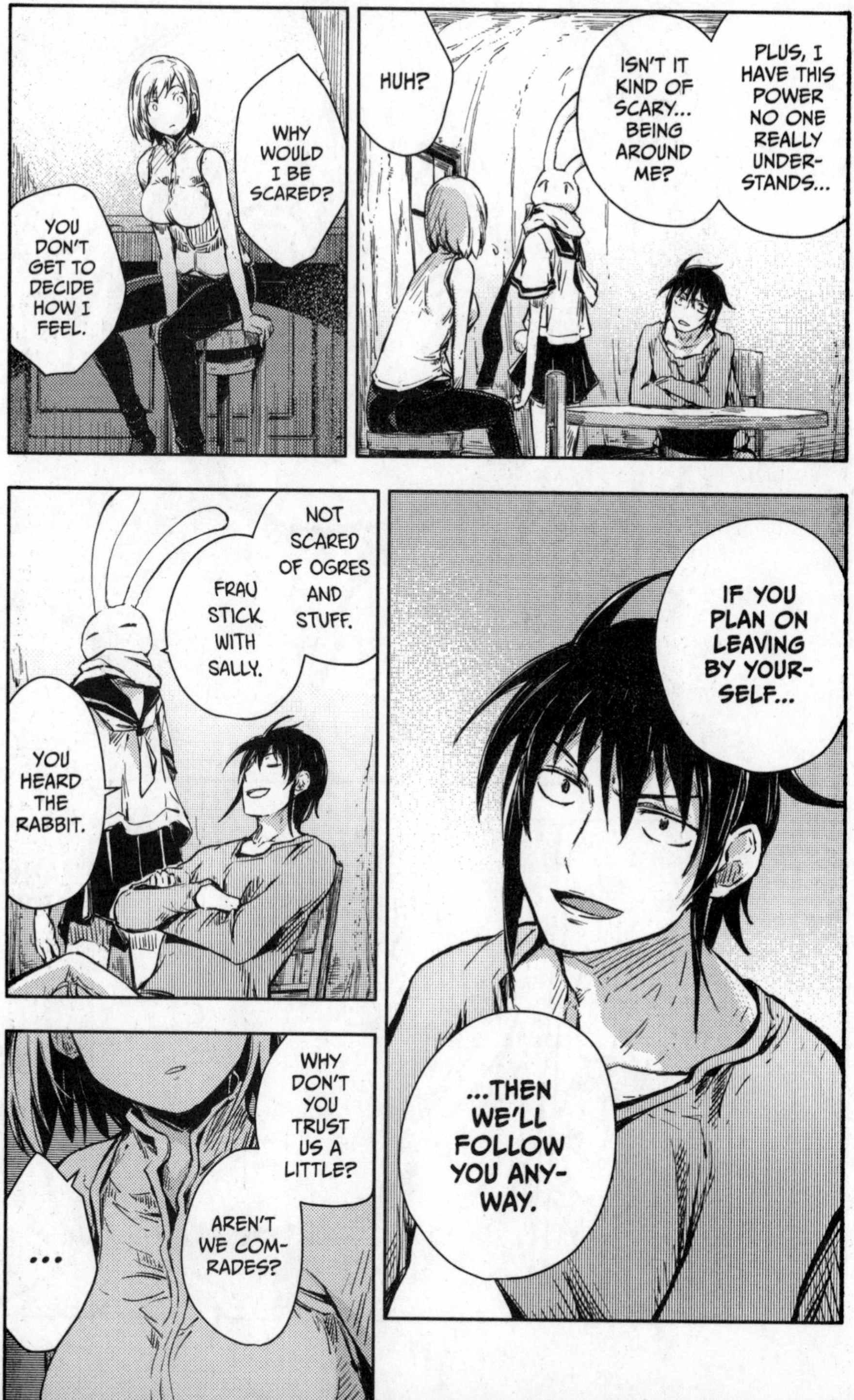
PLUS, I HAVE THIS POWER NO ONE REALLY UNDERSTANDS...
ISN'T IT KIND OF SCARY... BEING AROUND ME?
HUH?
WHY WOULD I BE SCARED?
YOU DON'T GET TO DECIDE HOW I FEEL.
IF YOU PLAN ON LEAVING BY YOURSELF...
...THEN WE'LL FOLLOW YOU ANYWAY.
NOT SCARED OF OGRES AND STUFF.
FRAU STICK WITH SALLY.
YOU HEARD THE RABBIT.
WHY DON'T YOU TRUST US A LITTLE?
AREN'T WE COMRADES?
...

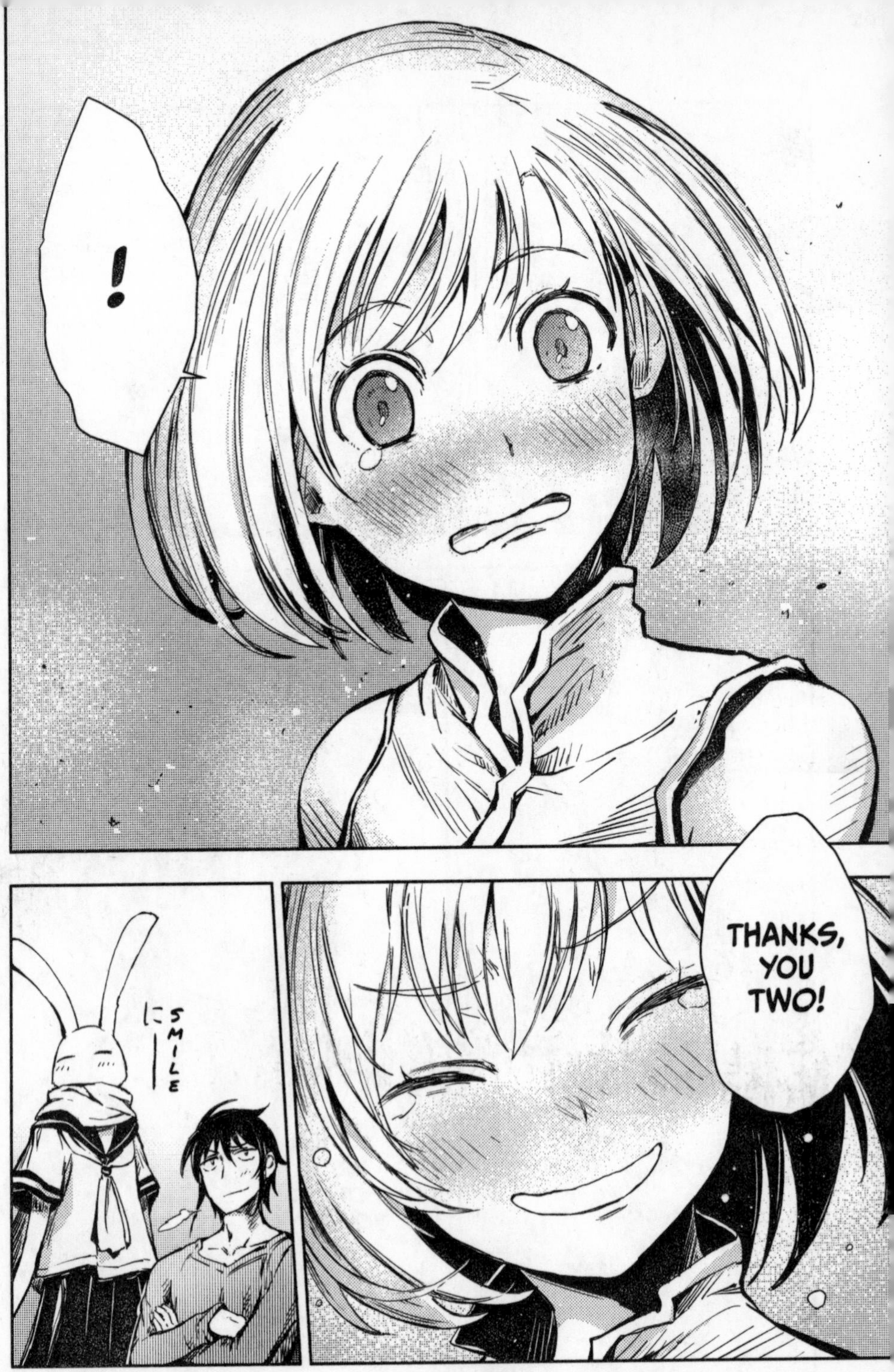
!
THANKS, YOU TWO!
に—
SMILE

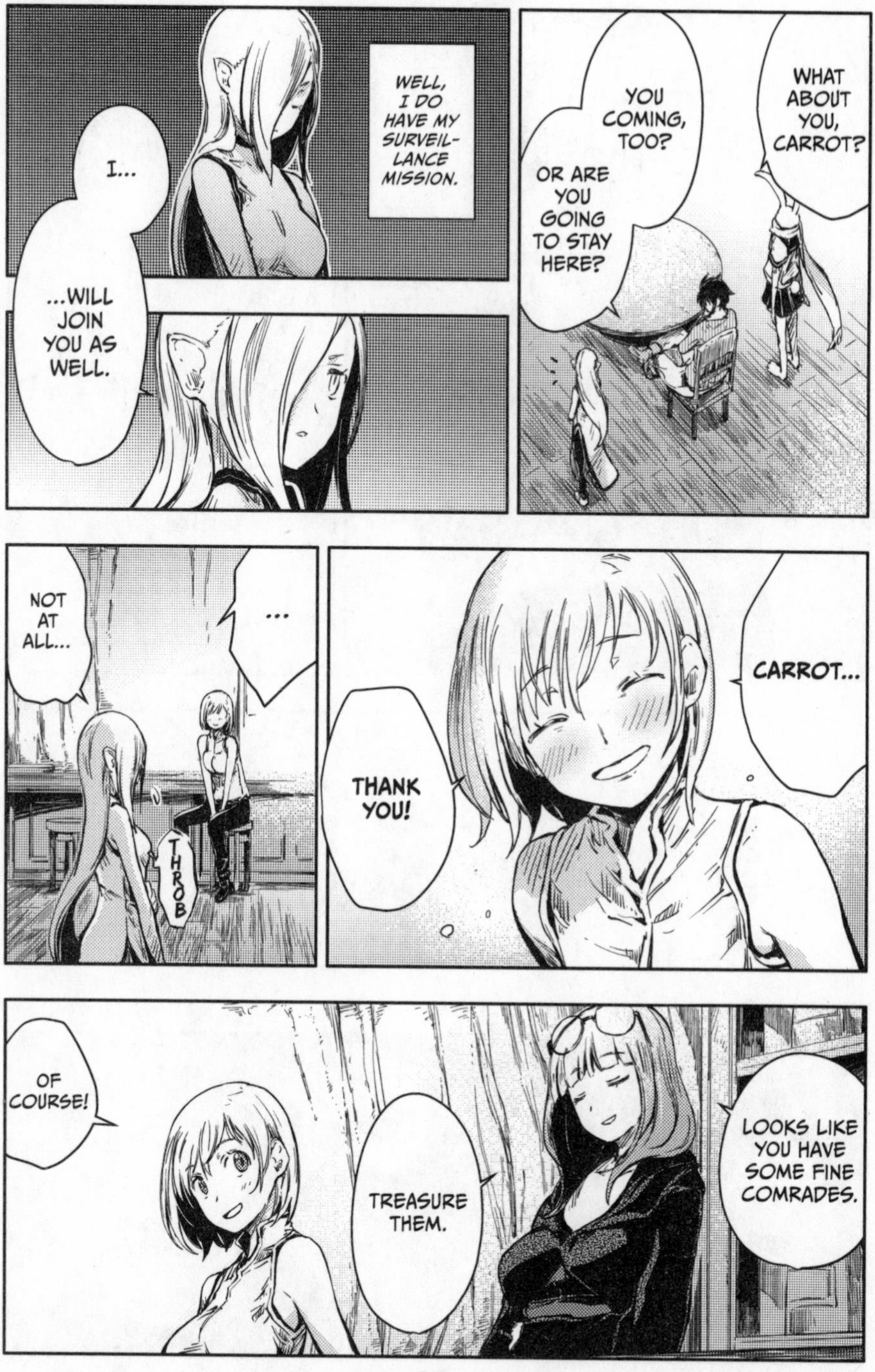
WHAT ABOUT YOU, CARROT?
YOU COMING, TOO?
OR ARE YOU GOING TO STAY HERE?
WELL, I DO HAVE MY SURVEIL-LANCE MISSION.
I...
...WILL JOIN YOU AS WELL.
CARROT...
THANK YOU!
...
NOT AT ALL...
THROB
LOOKS LIKE YOU HAVE SOME FINE COMRADES.
TREASURE THEM.
OF COURSE!

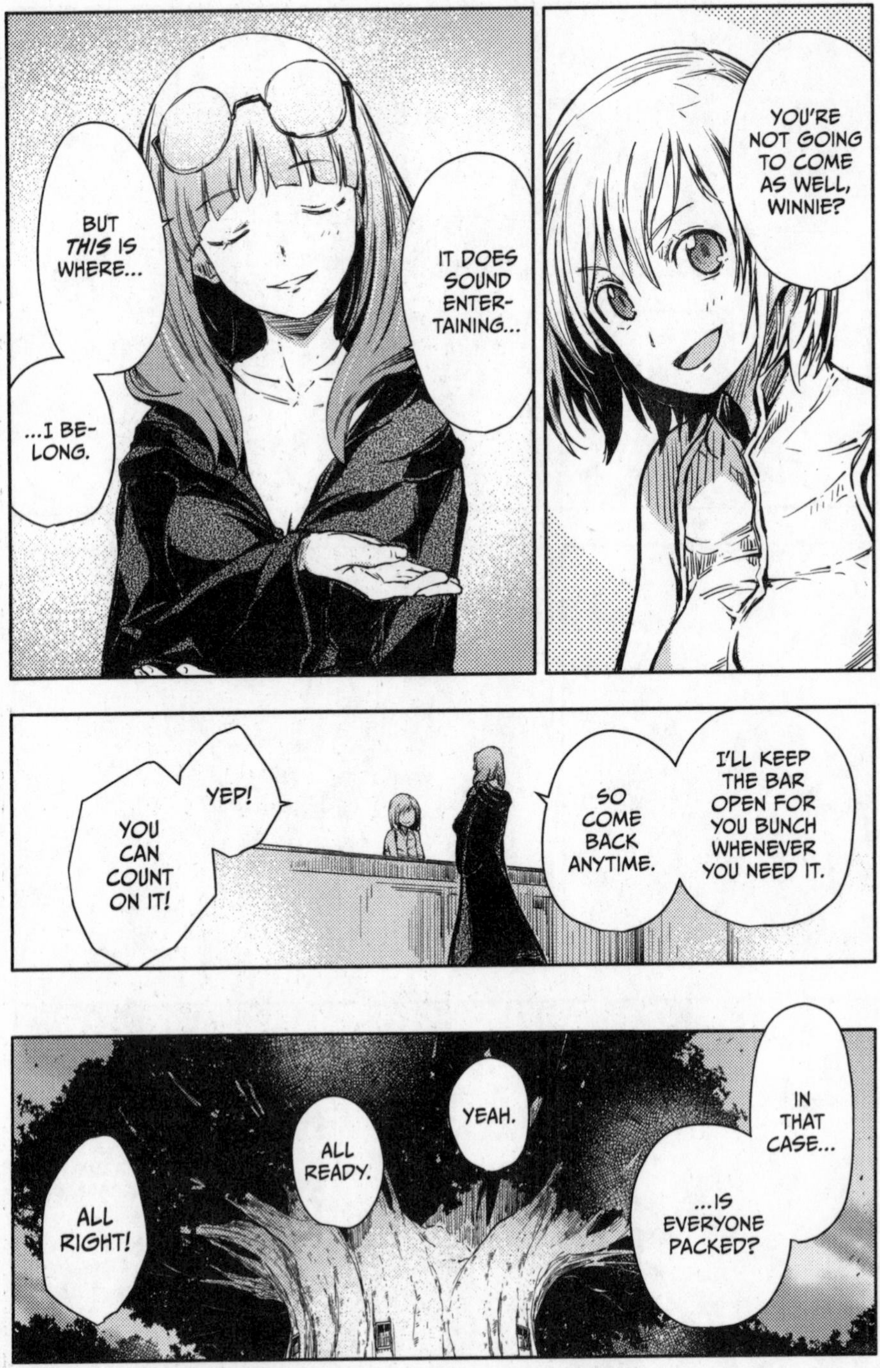
YOU'RE NOT GOING TO COME AS WELL, WINNIE?
IT DOES SOUND ENTERTAINING...
BUT *THIS* IS WHERE...
...I BELONG.
I'LL KEEP THE BAR OPEN FOR YOU BUNCH WHENEVER YOU NEED IT.
SO COME BACK ANYTIME.
YEP!
YOU CAN COUNT ON IT!
IN THAT CASE...
...IS EVERYONE PACKED?
YEAH.
ALL READY.
ALL RIGHT!

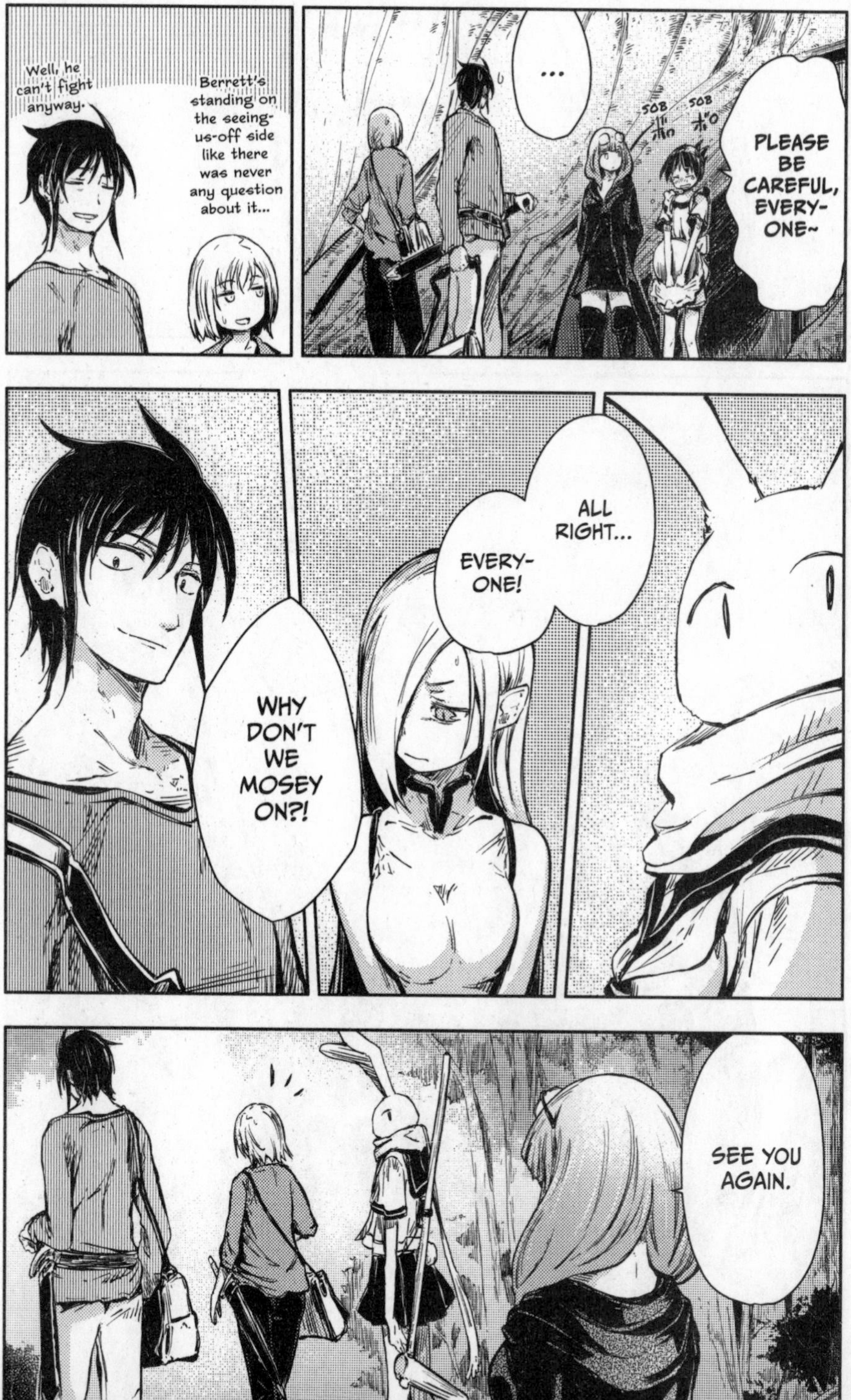
PLEASE BE CAREFUL, EVERY-ONE~
SOB
SOB
...
Berrett's standing on the seeing-us-off side like there was never any question about it...
Well, he can't fight anyway.
ALL RIGHT...
EVERY-ONE!
WHY DON'T WE MOSEY ON?!
SEE YOU AGAIN.

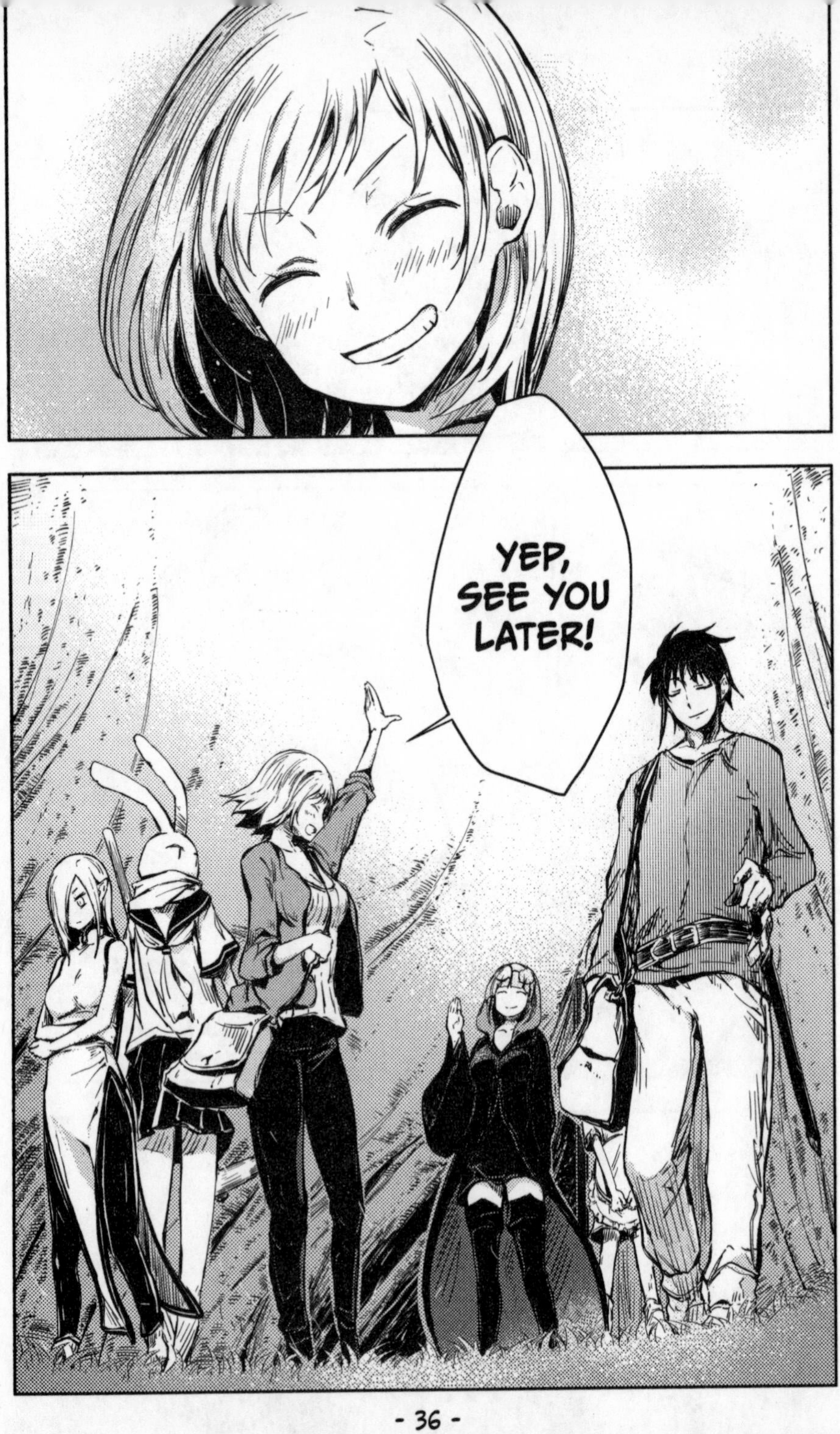
YEP, SEE YOU LATER!

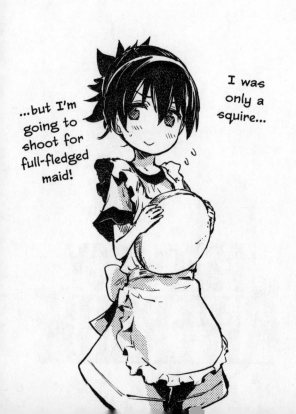

I was only a squire...
...but I'm going to shoot for full-fledged maid!

PEACH BOY
RIVERSIDE

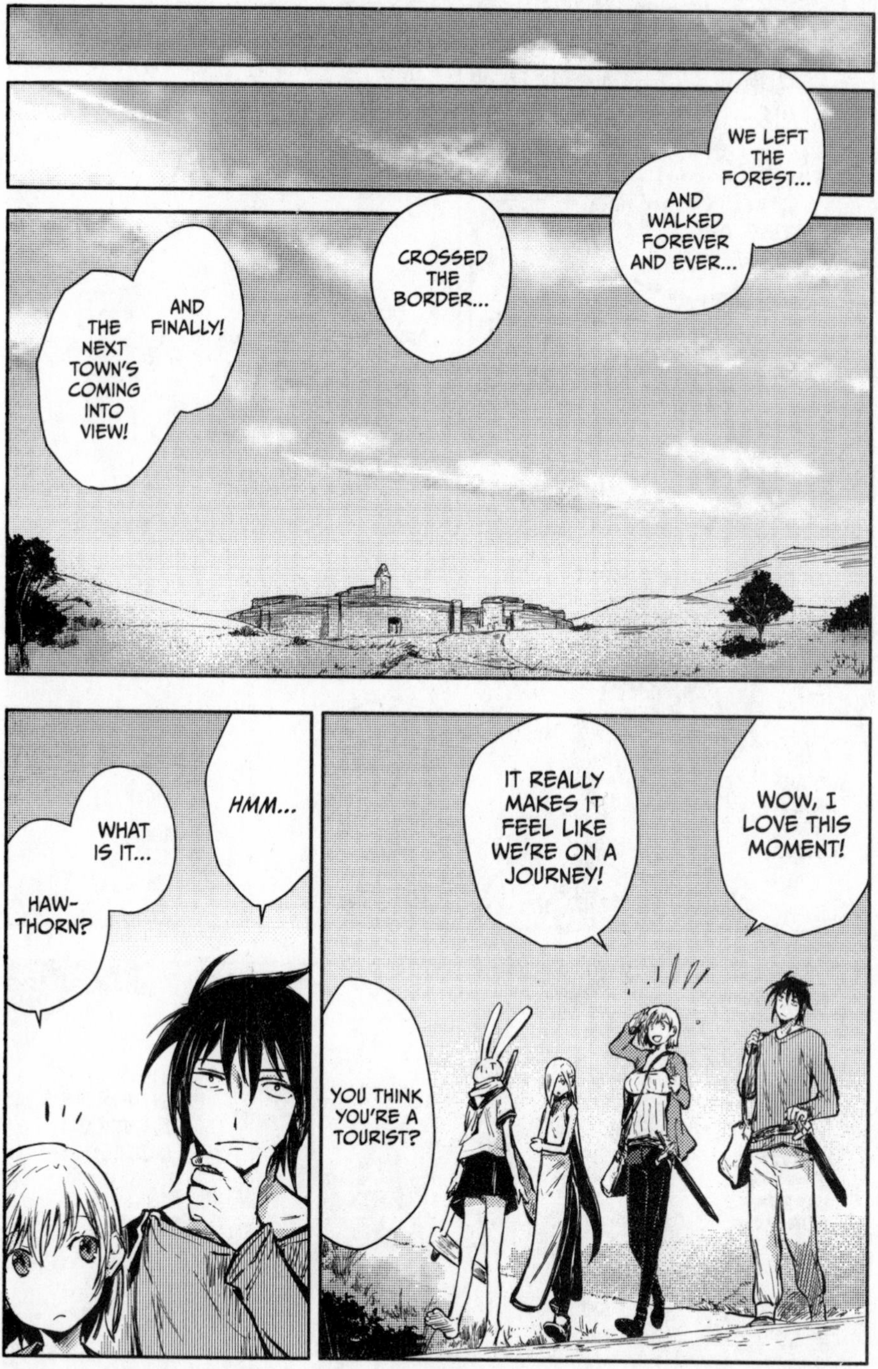
WE LEFT THE FOREST...
AND WALKED FOREVER AND EVER...
CROSSED THE BORDER...
AND FINALLY!
THE NEXT TOWN'S COMING INTO VIEW!
WOW, I LOVE THIS MOMENT!
IT REALLY MAKES IT FEEL LIKE WE'RE ON A JOURNEY!
YOU THINK YOU'RE A TOURIST?
HMM...
WHAT IS IT...
HAW-THORN?

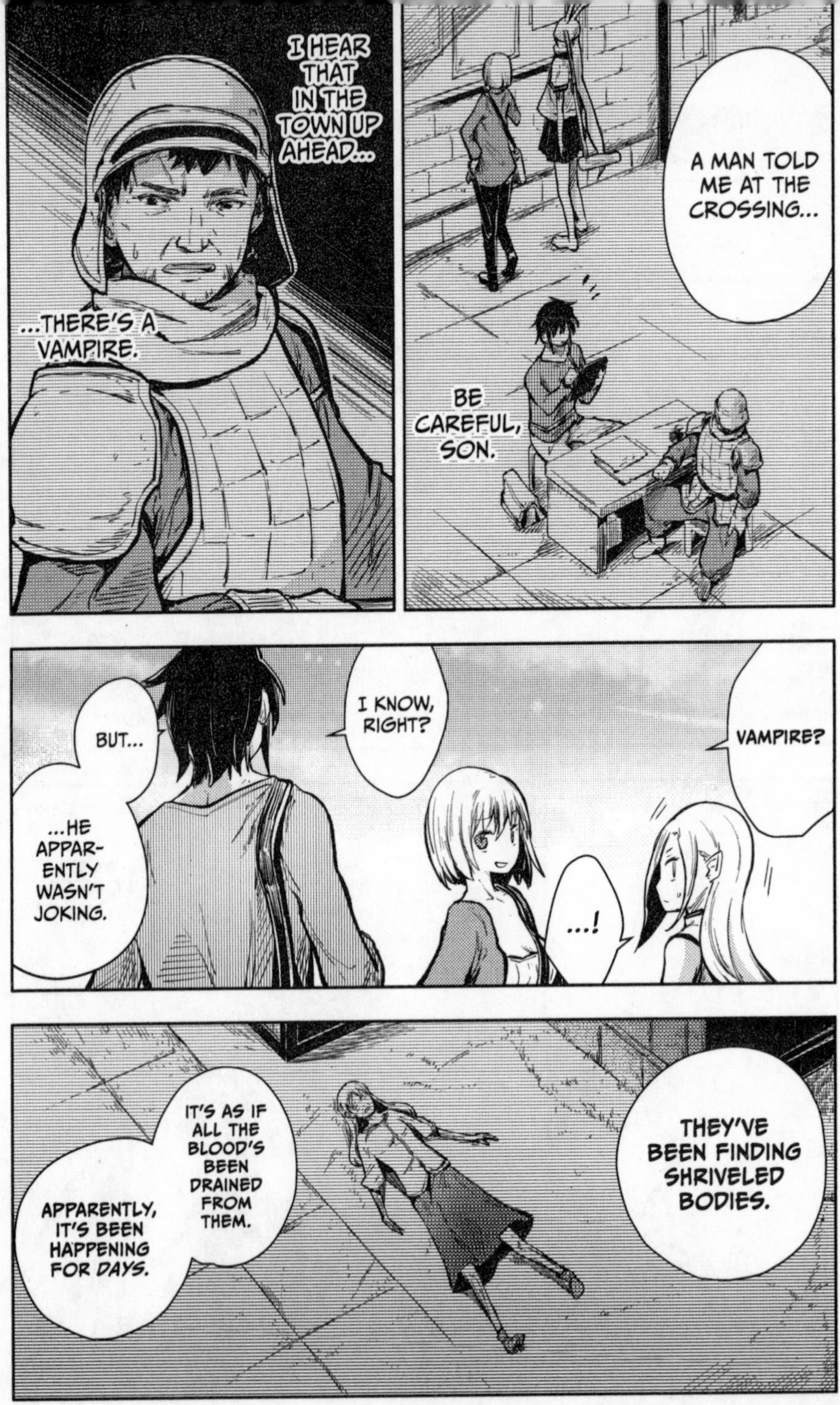
A MAN TOLD ME AT THE CROSSING...
BE CAREFUL, SON.
I HEAR THAT IN THE TOWN UP AHEAD...
...THERE'S A VAMPIRE.
VAMPIRE?
...!
I KNOW, RIGHT?
BUT...
...HE APPARENTLY WASN'T JOKING.
THEY'VE BEEN FINDING SHRIVELED BODIES.
IT'S AS IF ALL THE BLOOD'S BEEN DRAINED FROM THEM.
APPARENTLY, IT'S BEEN HAPPENING FOR *DAYS*.

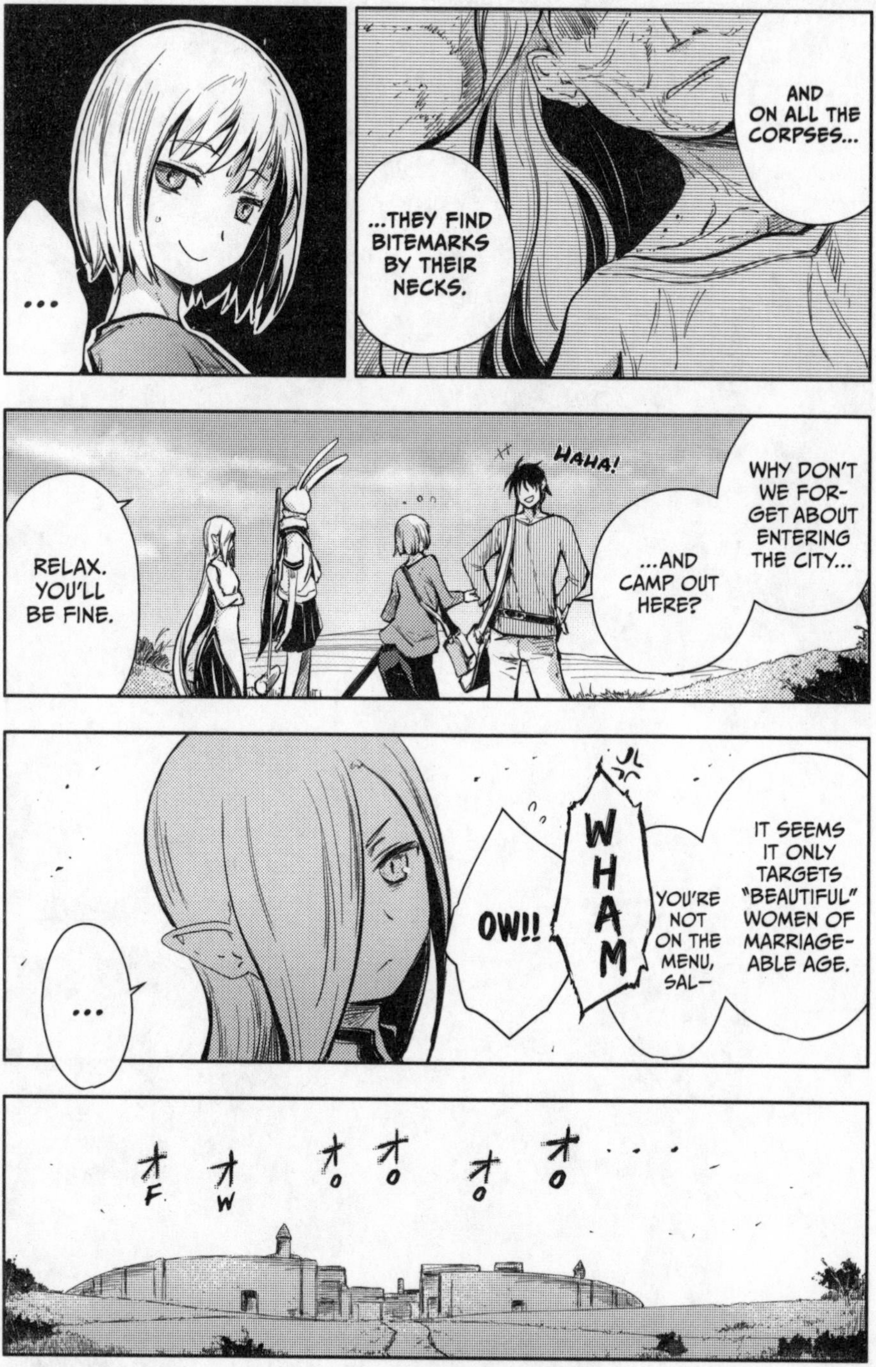
AND ON ALL THE CORPSES...
...THEY FIND BITEMARKS BY THEIR NECKS.
...
WHY DON'T WE FOR-GET ABOUT ENTERING THE CITY...
...AND CAMP OUT HERE?
HAHA!
RELAX. YOU'LL BE FINE.
IT SEEMS IT ONLY TARGETS "BEAUTIFUL" WOMEN OF MARRIAGE-ABLE AGE.
YOU'RE NOT ON THE MENU, SAL—
WHAM
OW!!
...
FWOOOO

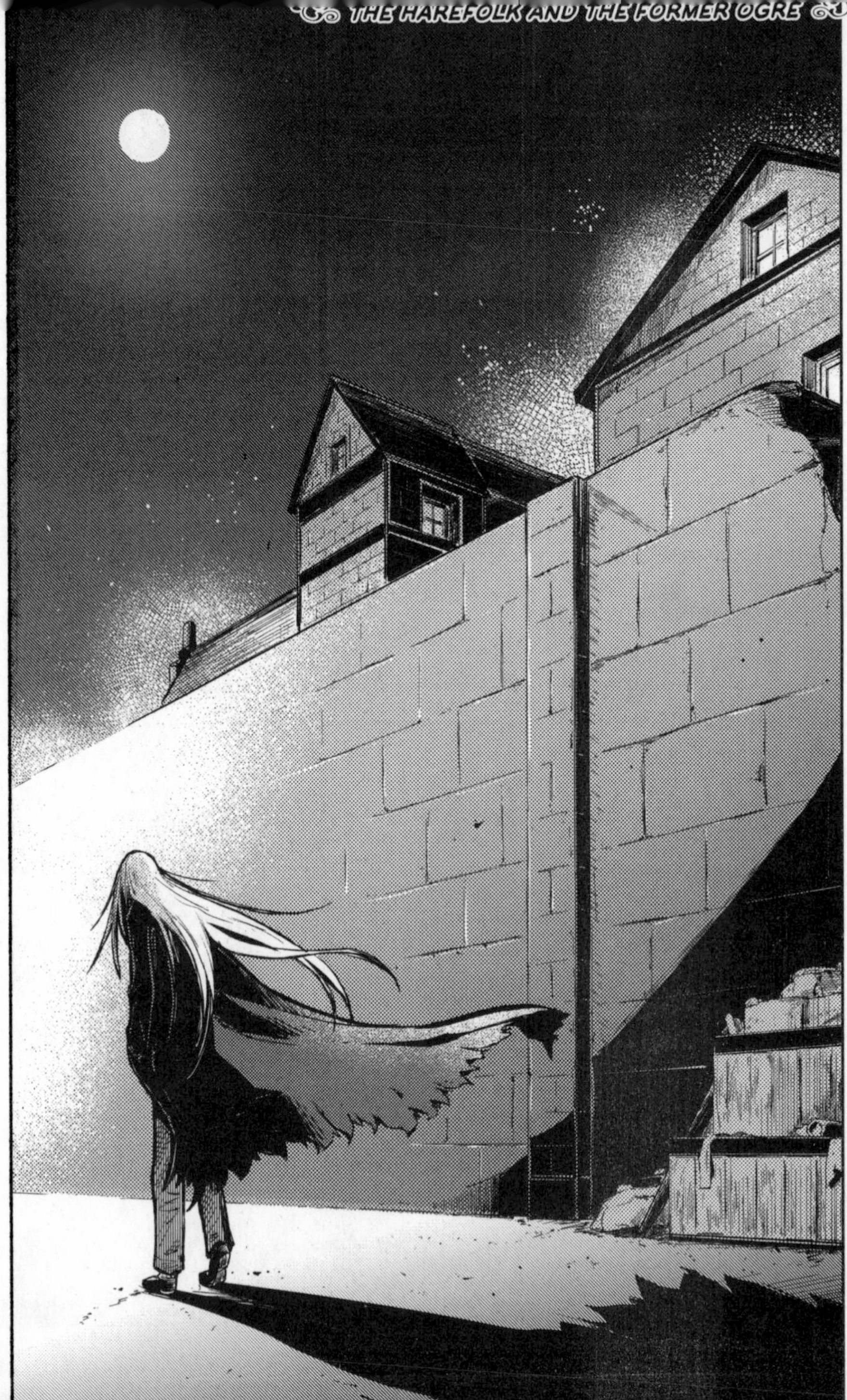

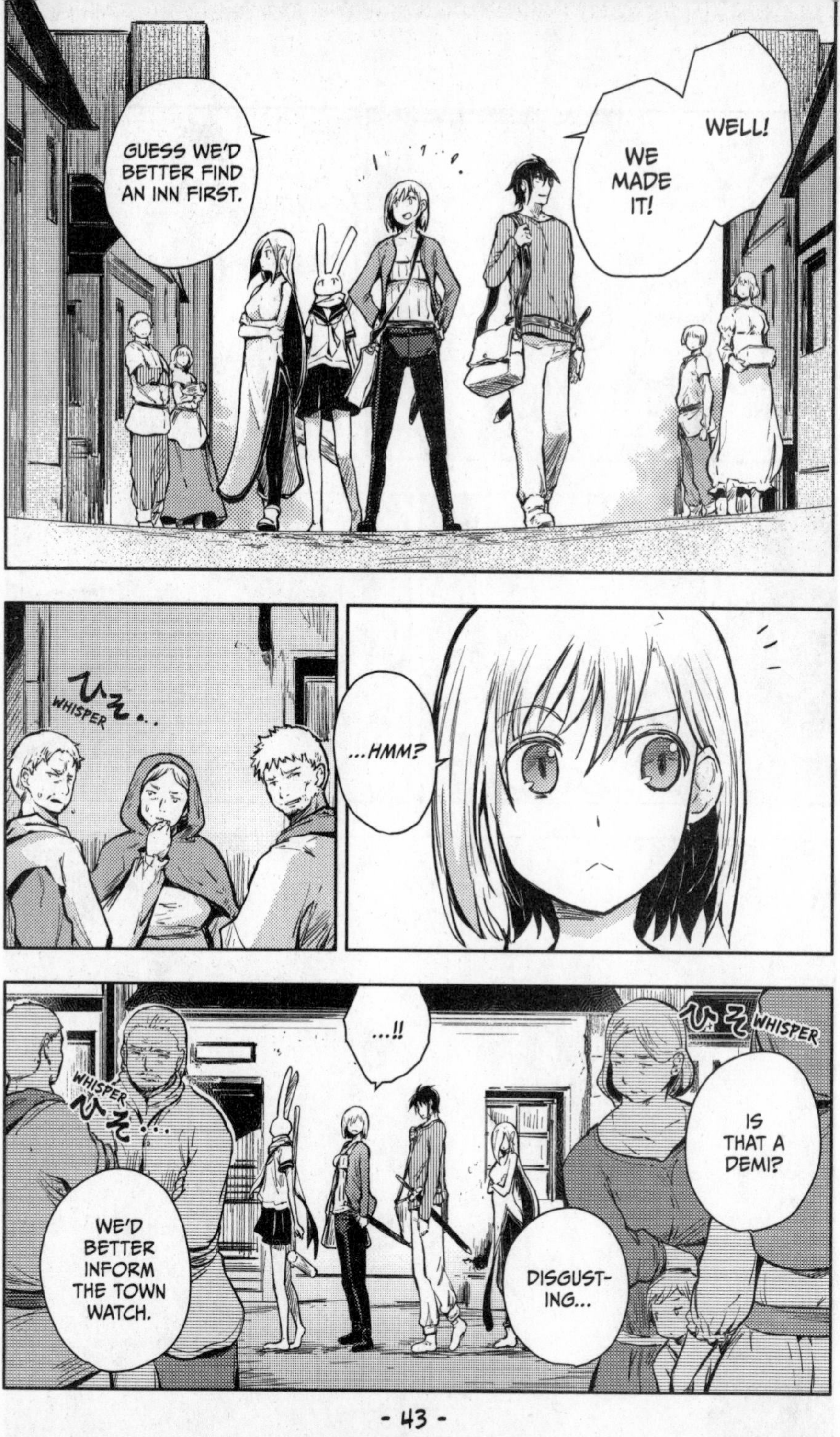
WELL!
WE MADE IT!
GUESS WE'D BETTER FIND AN INN FIRST.
...HMM?
ひそ WHISPER
ひそ WHISPER
IS THAT A DEMI?
...!!
DISGUST-ING...
WHISPER ひそ
WE'D BETTER INFORM THE TOWN WATCH.

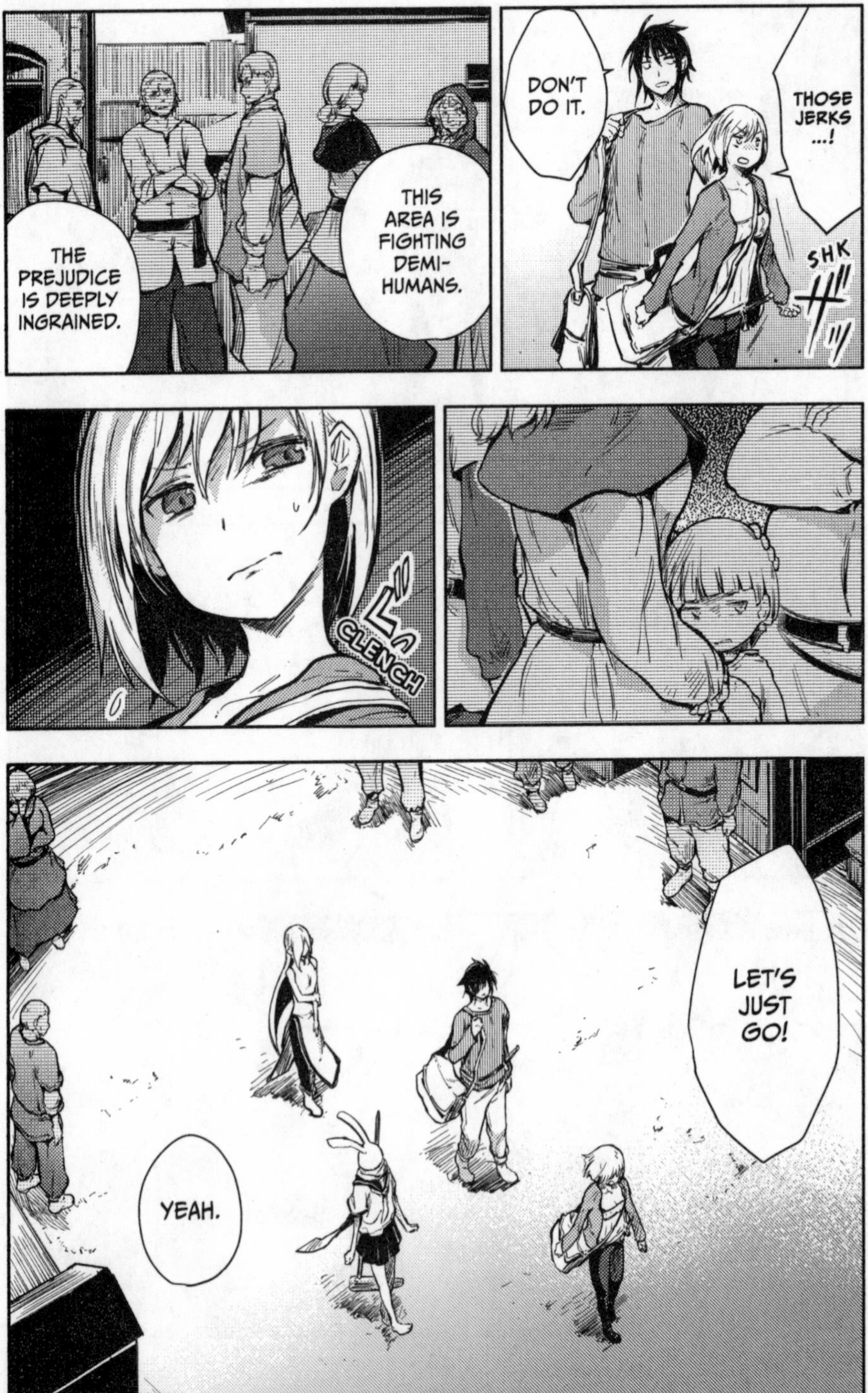
THOSE JERKS ...!
DON'T DO IT.
SHK
THIS AREA IS FIGHTING DEMI-HUMANS.
THE PREJUDICE IS DEEPLY INGRAINED.
CLENCH
LET'S JUST GO!
YEAH.

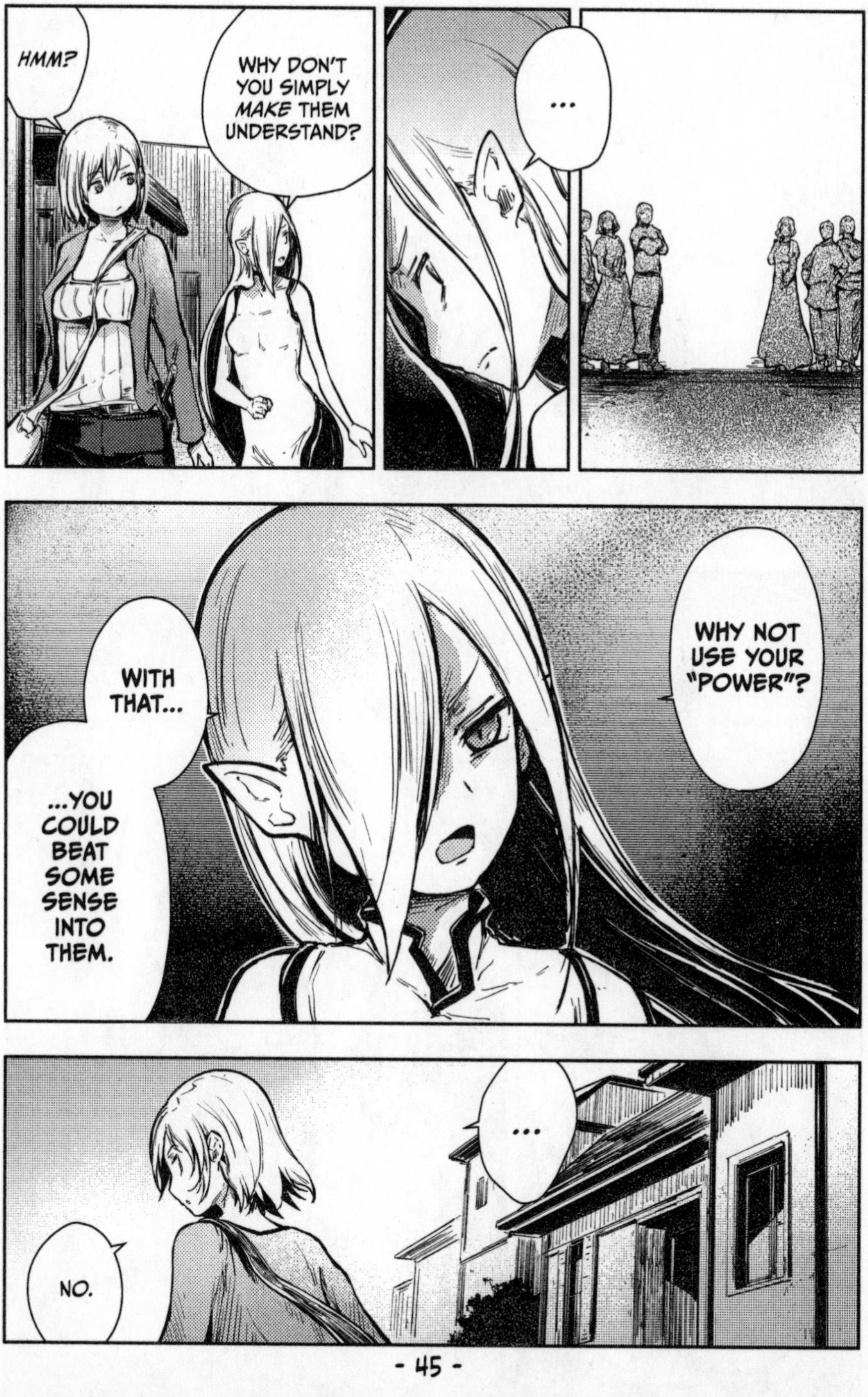
...
WHY DON'T YOU SIMPLY *MAKE* THEM UNDERSTAND?
HMM?
WHY NOT USE YOUR "POWER"?
WITH THAT...
...YOU COULD BEAT SOME SENSE INTO THEM.
...
NO.

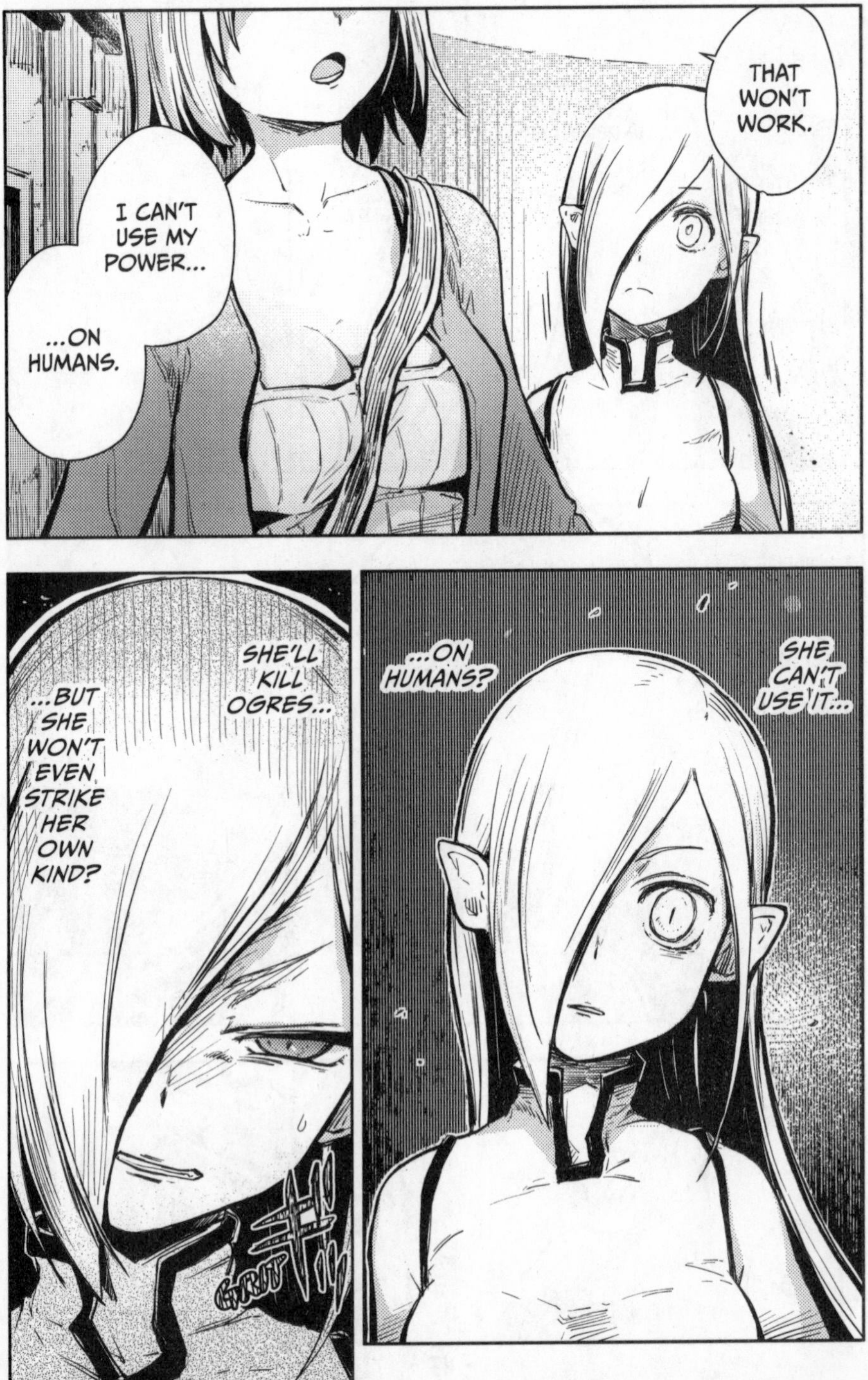
THAT WON'T WORK.
I CAN'T USE MY POWER...
...ON HUMANS.
SHE CAN'T USE IT...
...ON HUMANS?
SHE'LL KILL OGRES...
...BUT SHE WON'T EVEN STRIKE HER OWN KIND?
GRIT

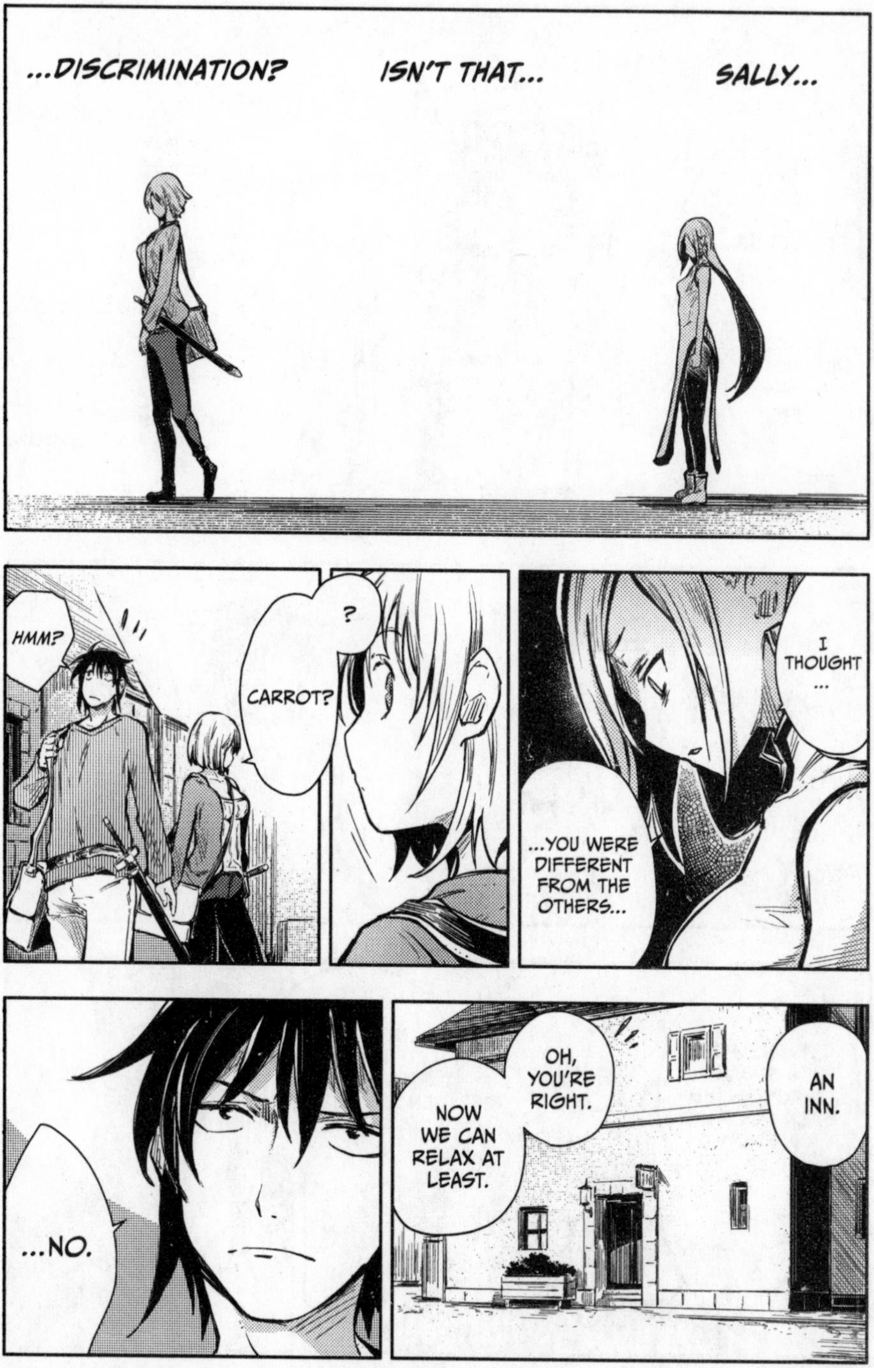
SALLY...
ISN'T THAT...
...DISCRIMINATION?
I THOUGHT ...
...YOU WERE DIFFERENT FROM THE OTHERS...
?
CARROT?
HMM?
AN INN.
OH, YOU'RE RIGHT.
NOW WE CAN RELAX AT LEAST.
...NO.

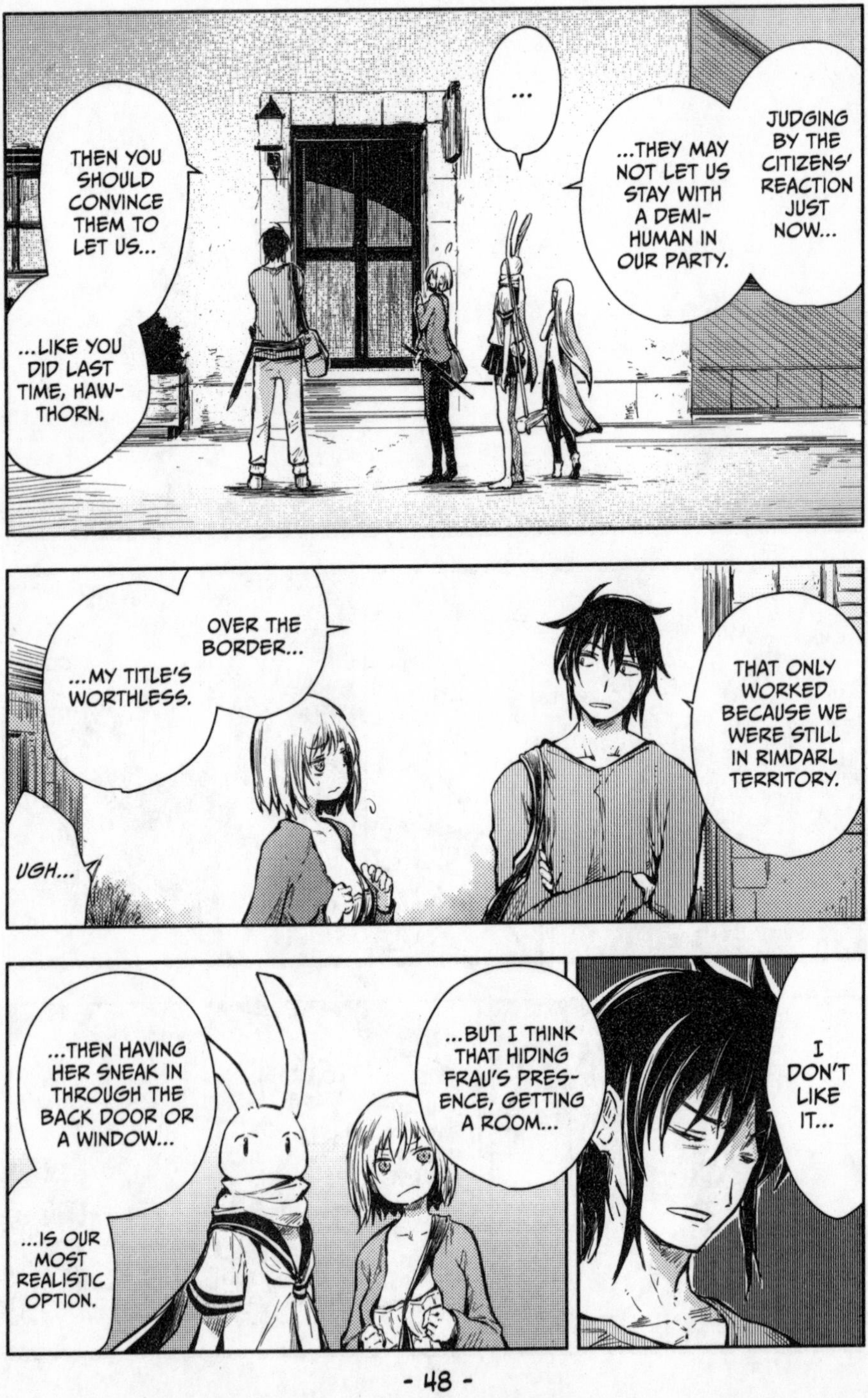
JUDGING BY THE CITIZENS' REACTION JUST NOW...
...THEY MAY NOT LET US STAY WITH A DEMI-HUMAN IN OUR PARTY.
...
THEN YOU SHOULD CONVINCE THEM TO LET US...
...LIKE YOU DID LAST TIME, HAWTHORN.
THAT ONLY WORKED BECAUSE WE WERE STILL IN RIMDARL TERRITORY.
OVER THE BORDER...
...MY TITLE'S WORTHLESS.
UGH...
I DON'T LIKE IT...
...BUT I THINK THAT HIDING FRAU'S PRESENCE, GETTING A ROOM...
...THEN HAVING HER SNEAK IN THROUGH THE BACK DOOR OR A WINDOW...
...IS OUR MOST REALISTIC OPTION.

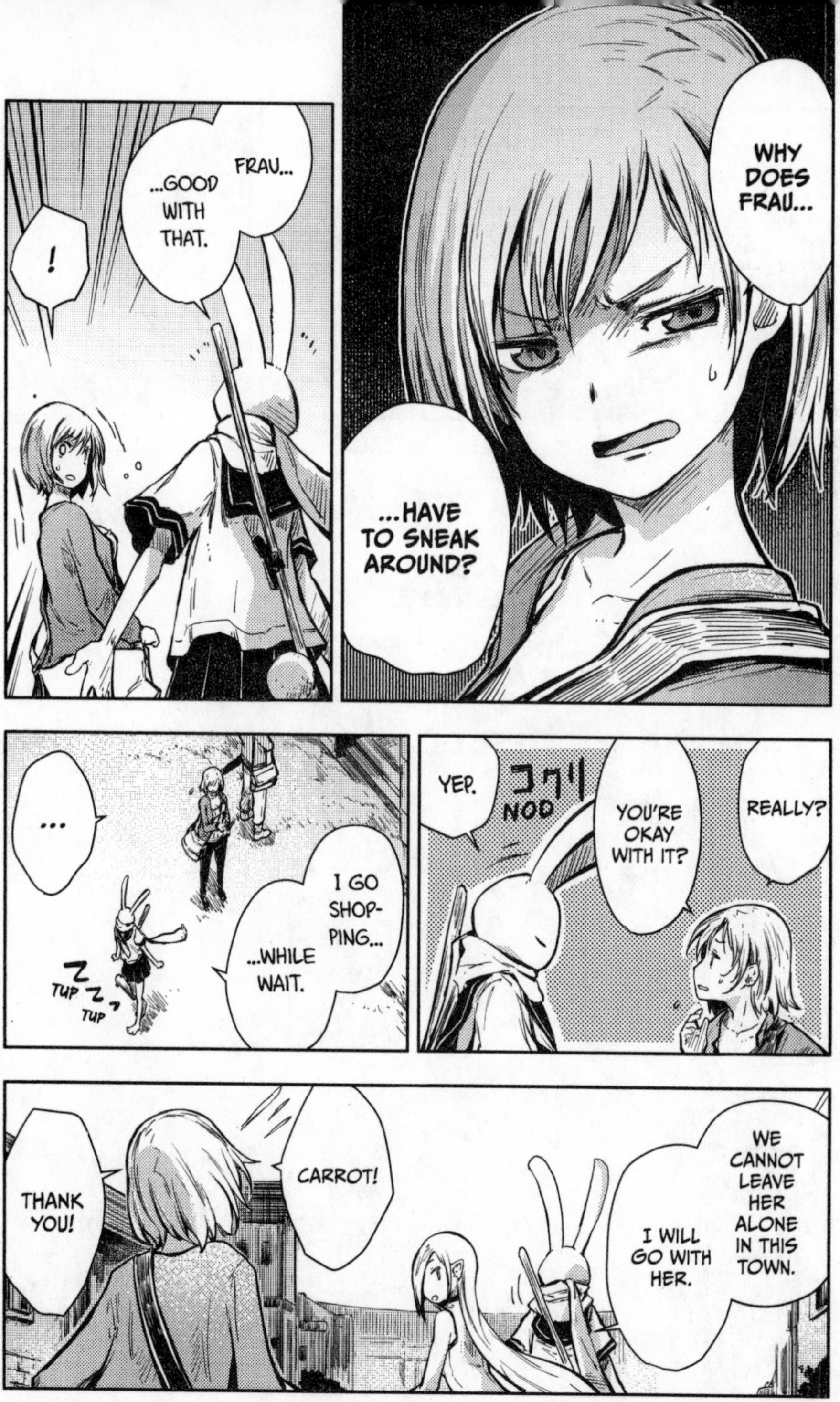
WHY DOES FRAU...
...HAVE TO SNEAK AROUND?
FRAU...
...GOOD WITH THAT.
!
REALLY?
YOU'RE OKAY WITH IT?
コクリ
NOD
YEP.
I GO SHOP-PING...
...WHILE WAIT.
...
TUP TUP
WE CANNOT LEAVE HER ALONE IN THIS TOWN.
I WILL GO WITH HER.
CARROT!
THANK YOU!

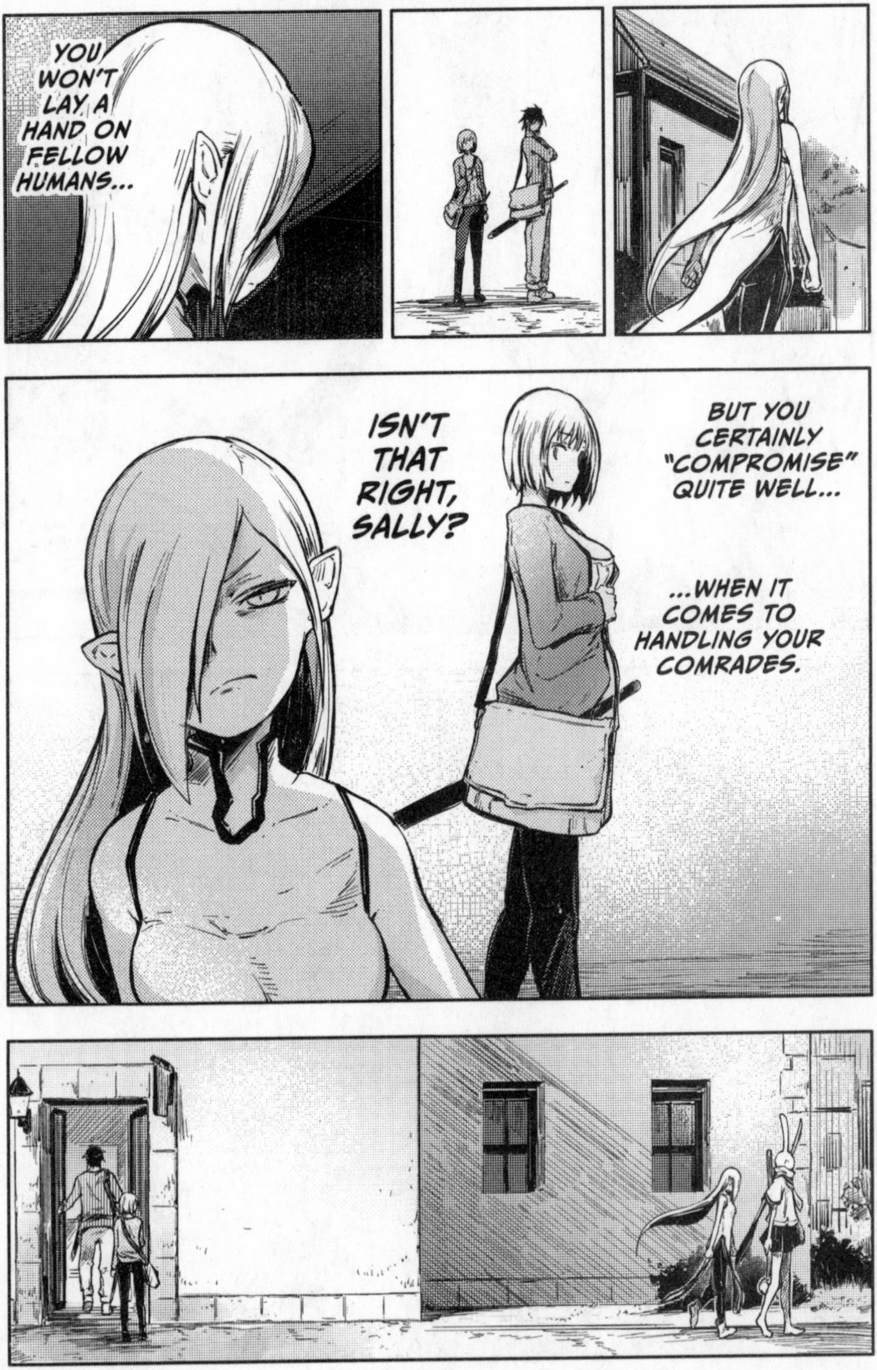
YOU WON'T LAY A HAND ON FELLOW HUMANS...
BUT YOU CERTAINLY "COMPROMISE" QUITE WELL...
...WHEN IT COMES TO HANDLING YOUR COMRADES.
ISN'T THAT RIGHT, SALLY?

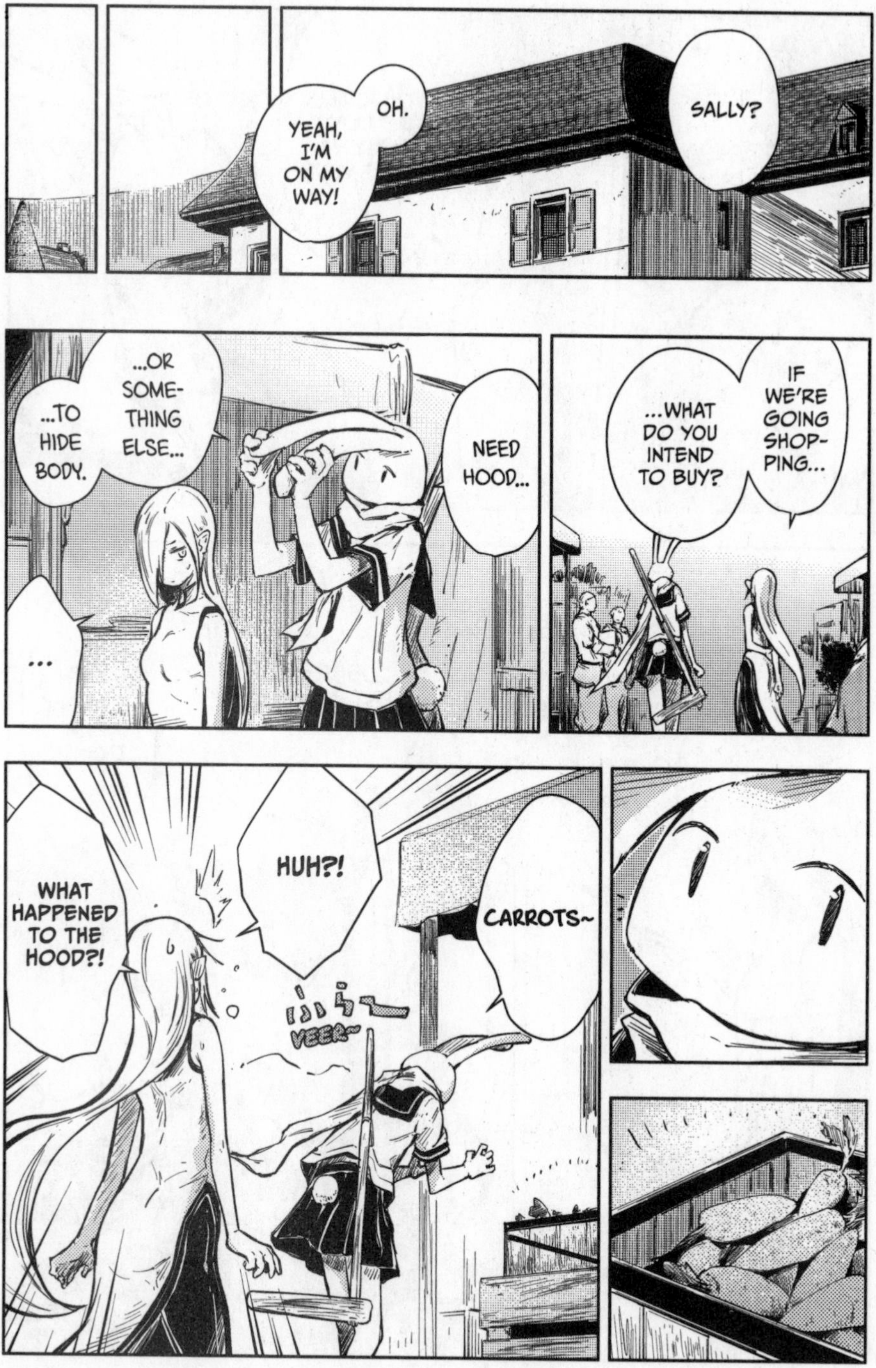
SALLY?
OH.
YEAH, I'M ON MY WAY!
IF WE'RE GOING SHOP-PING...
...WHAT DO YOU INTEND TO BUY?
NEED HOOD...
...OR SOME-THING ELSE...
...TO HIDE BODY.
...
CARROTS~
VEER~
HUH?!
WHAT HAPPENED TO THE HOOD?!

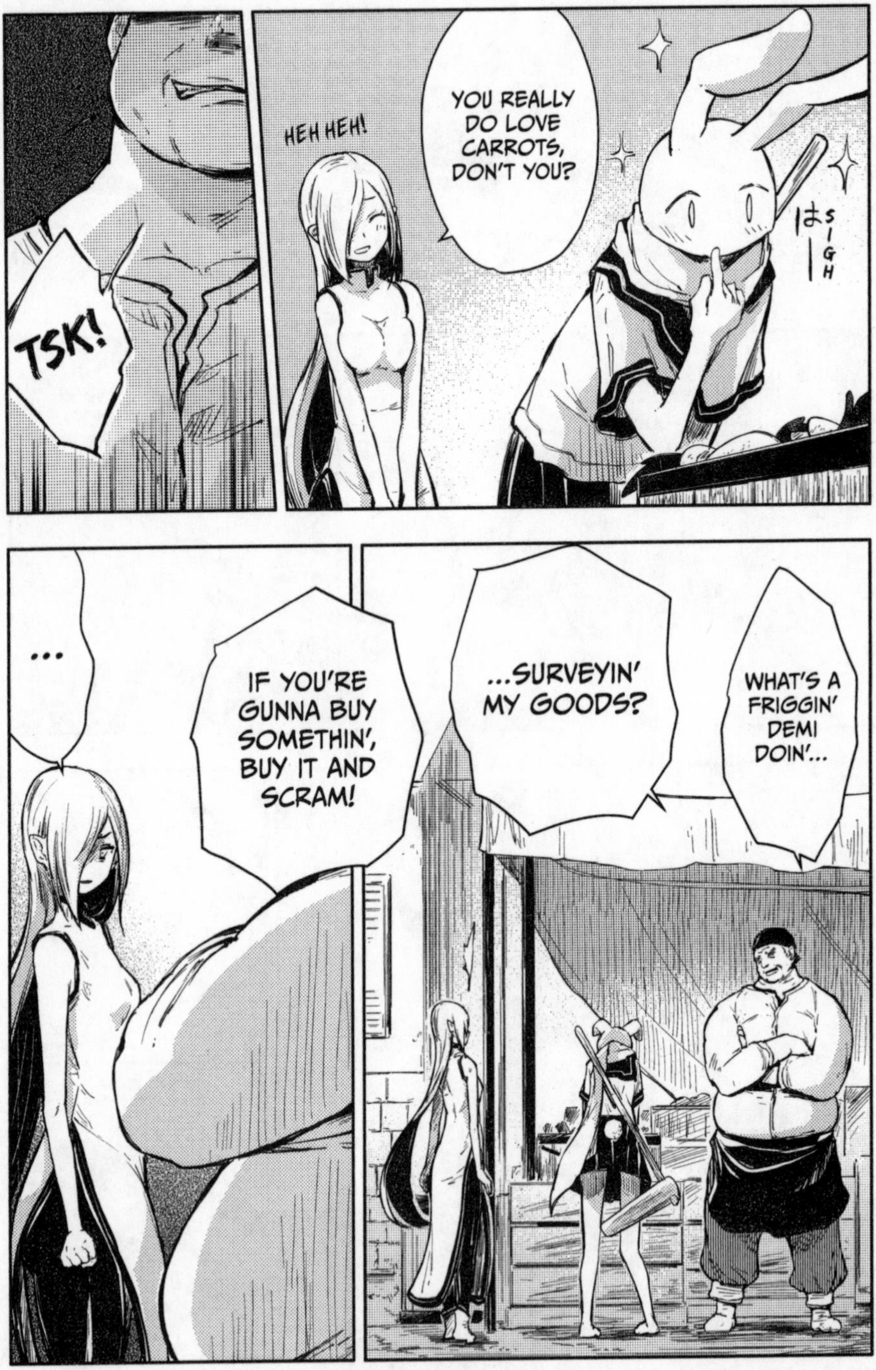
は— SIGH
YOU REALLY DO LOVE CARROTS, DON'T YOU?
HEH HEH!
TSK!
WHAT'S A FRIGGIN' DEMI DOIN'...
...SURVEYIN' MY GOODS?
IF YOU'RE GUNNA BUY SOMETHIN', BUY IT AND SCRAM!
...

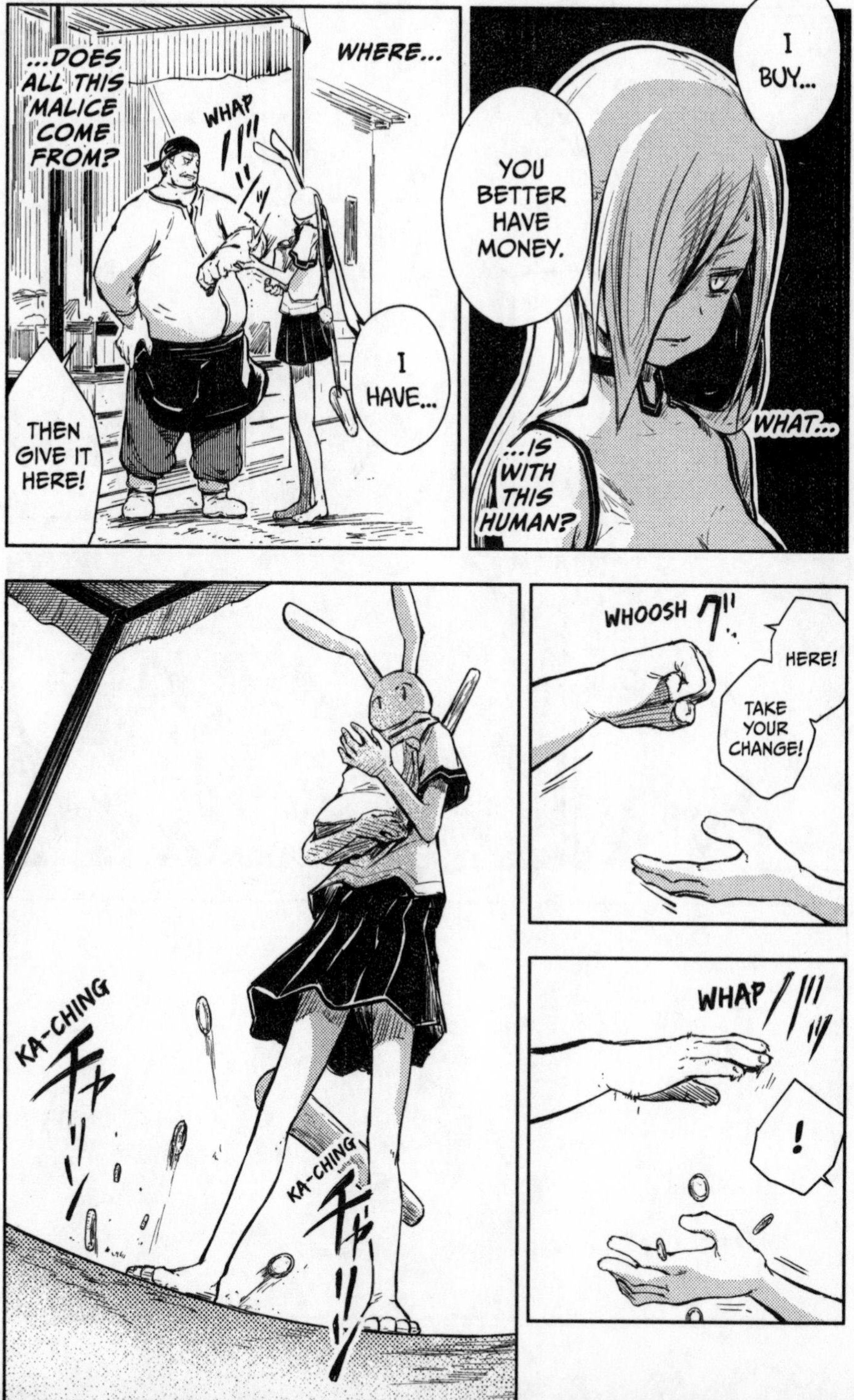
I BUY...
YOU BETTER HAVE MONEY.
WHAT...
...IS WITH THIS HUMAN?
WHERE...
...DOES ALL THIS MALICE COME FROM?
WHAP
I HAVE...
THEN GIVE IT HERE!
WHOOSH
HERE!
TAKE YOUR CHANGE!
WHAP
!
KA-CHING
KA-CHING

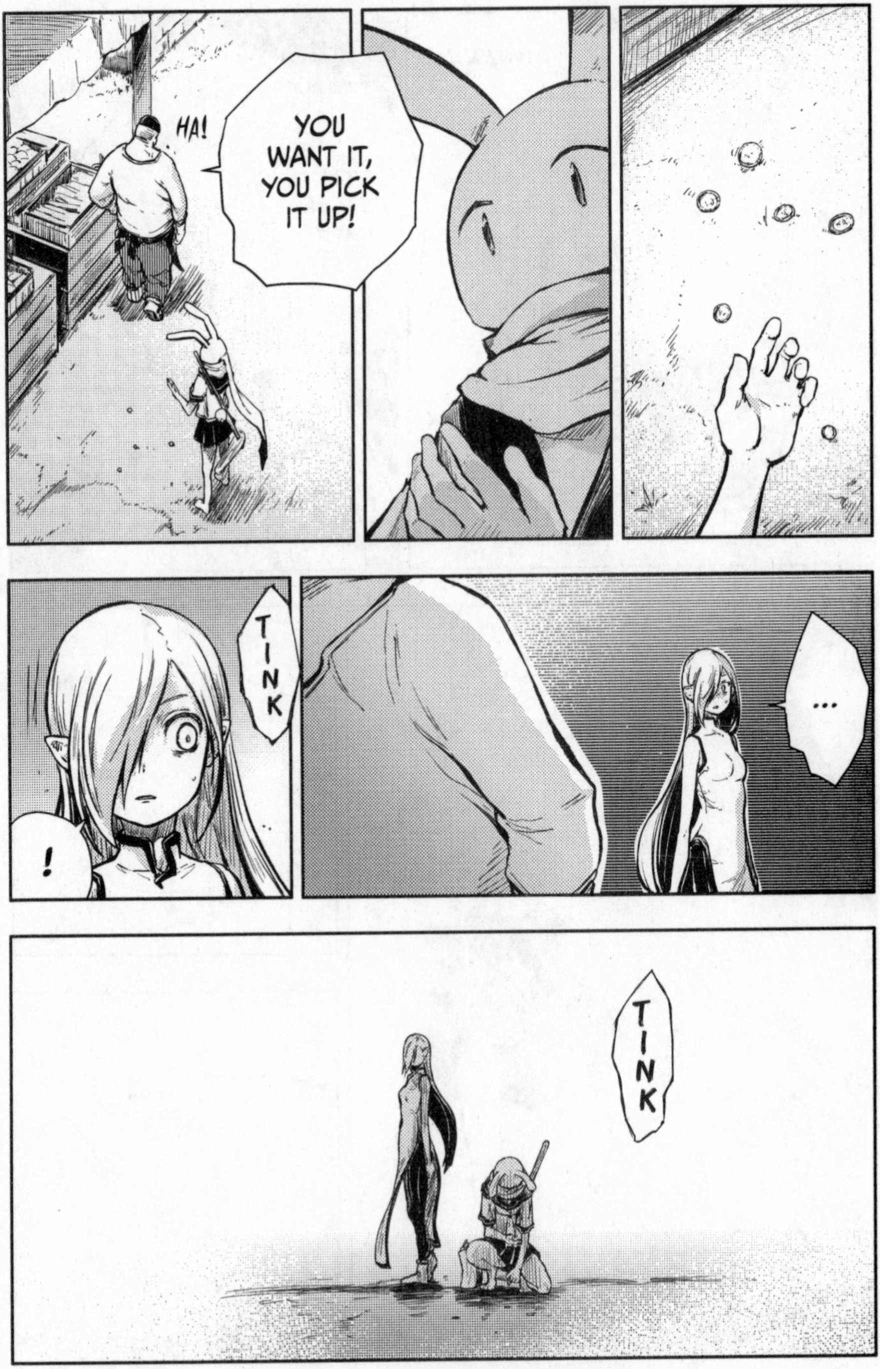
HA!
YOU WANT IT, YOU PICK IT UP!
...
TINK
!
TINK

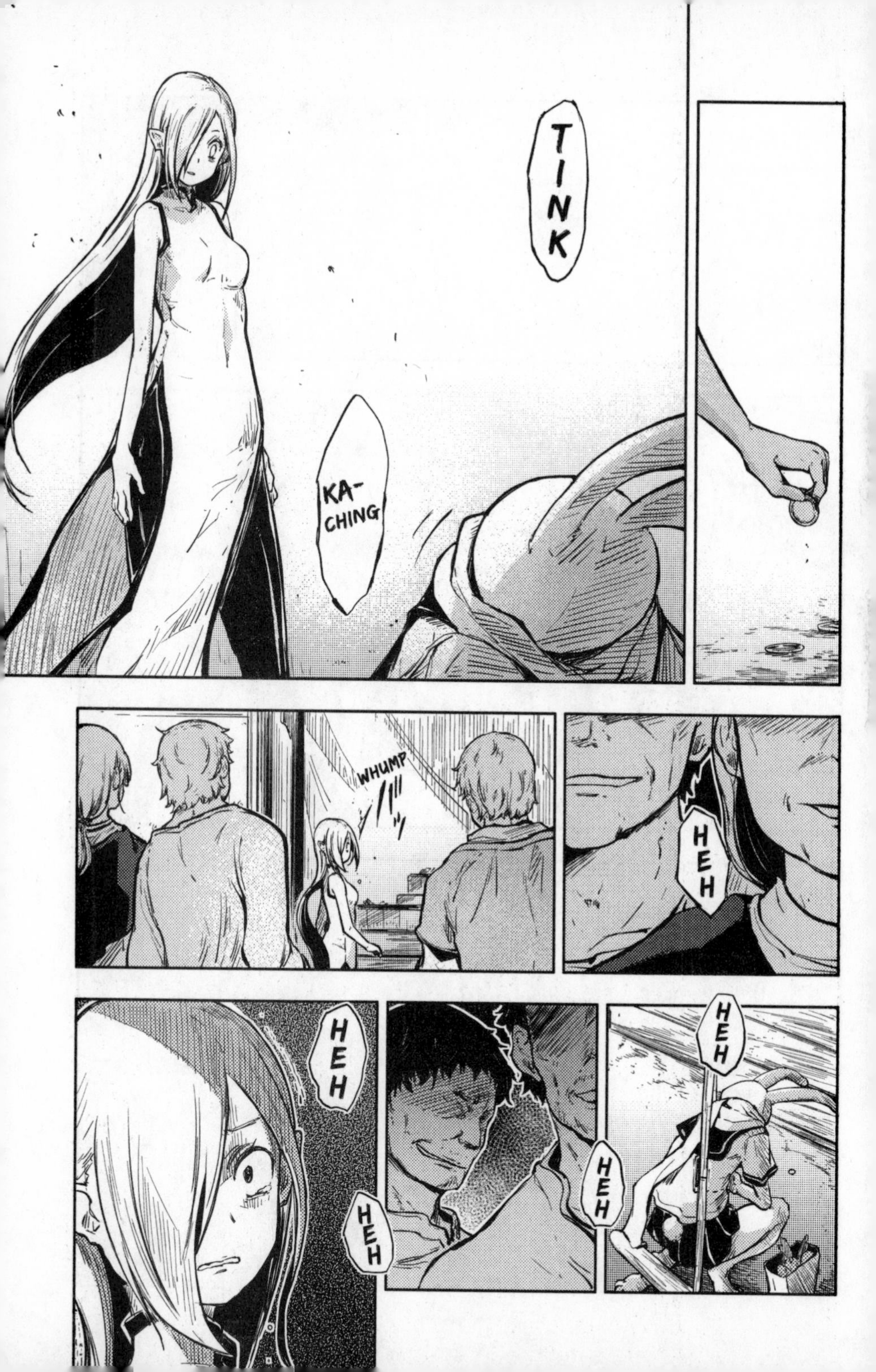
TINK
KA-CHING
HEH HEH
WHUMP
HEH HEH
HEH HEH
HEH HEH
HEH HEH

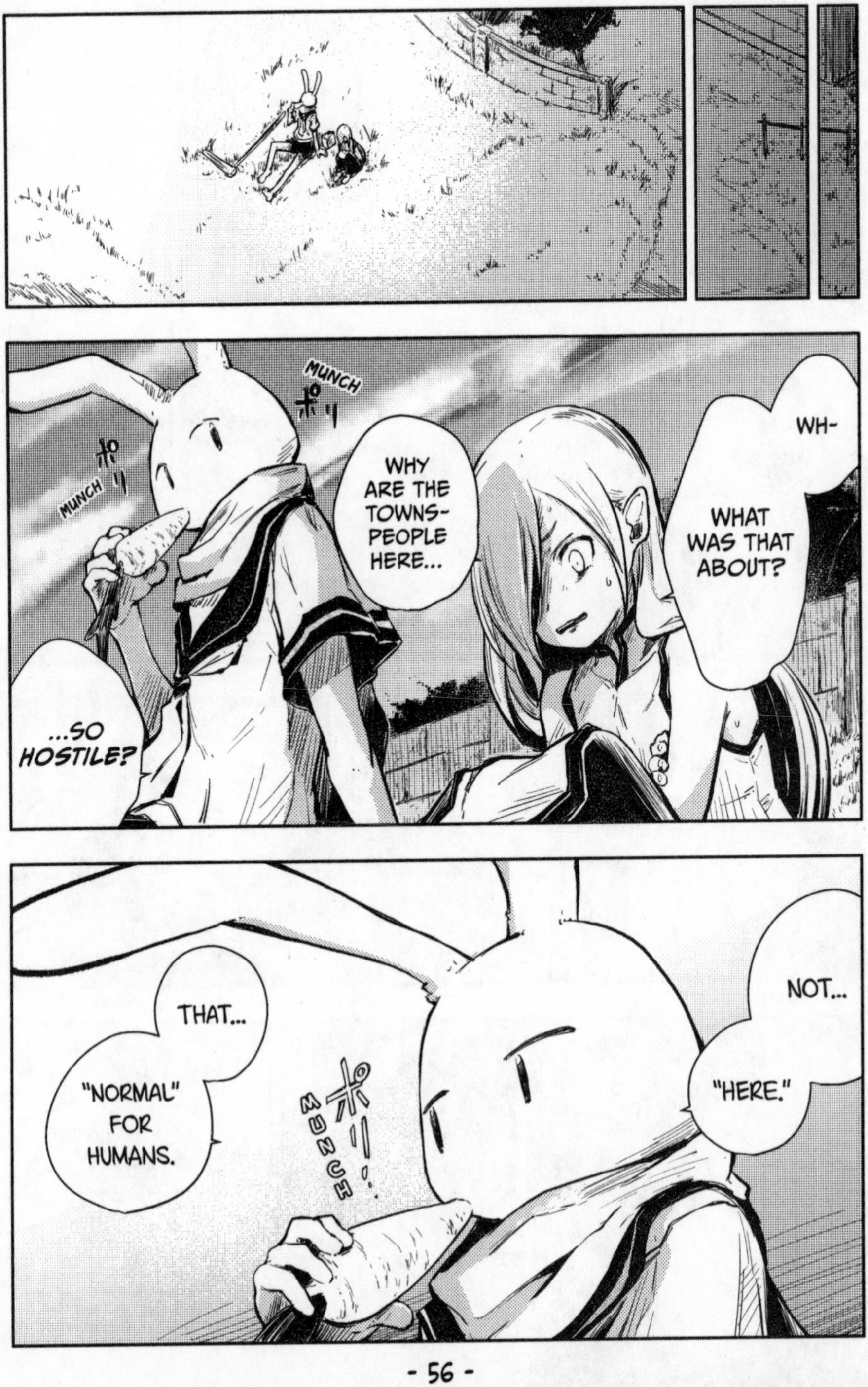
WH-
WHAT WAS THAT ABOUT?
MUNCH
ポリ
WHY ARE THE TOWNS-PEOPLE HERE...
ポリ
MUNCH
...SO HOSTILE?
NOT...
"HERE."
ポリ!
MUNCH
THAT...
"NORMAL" FOR HUMANS.

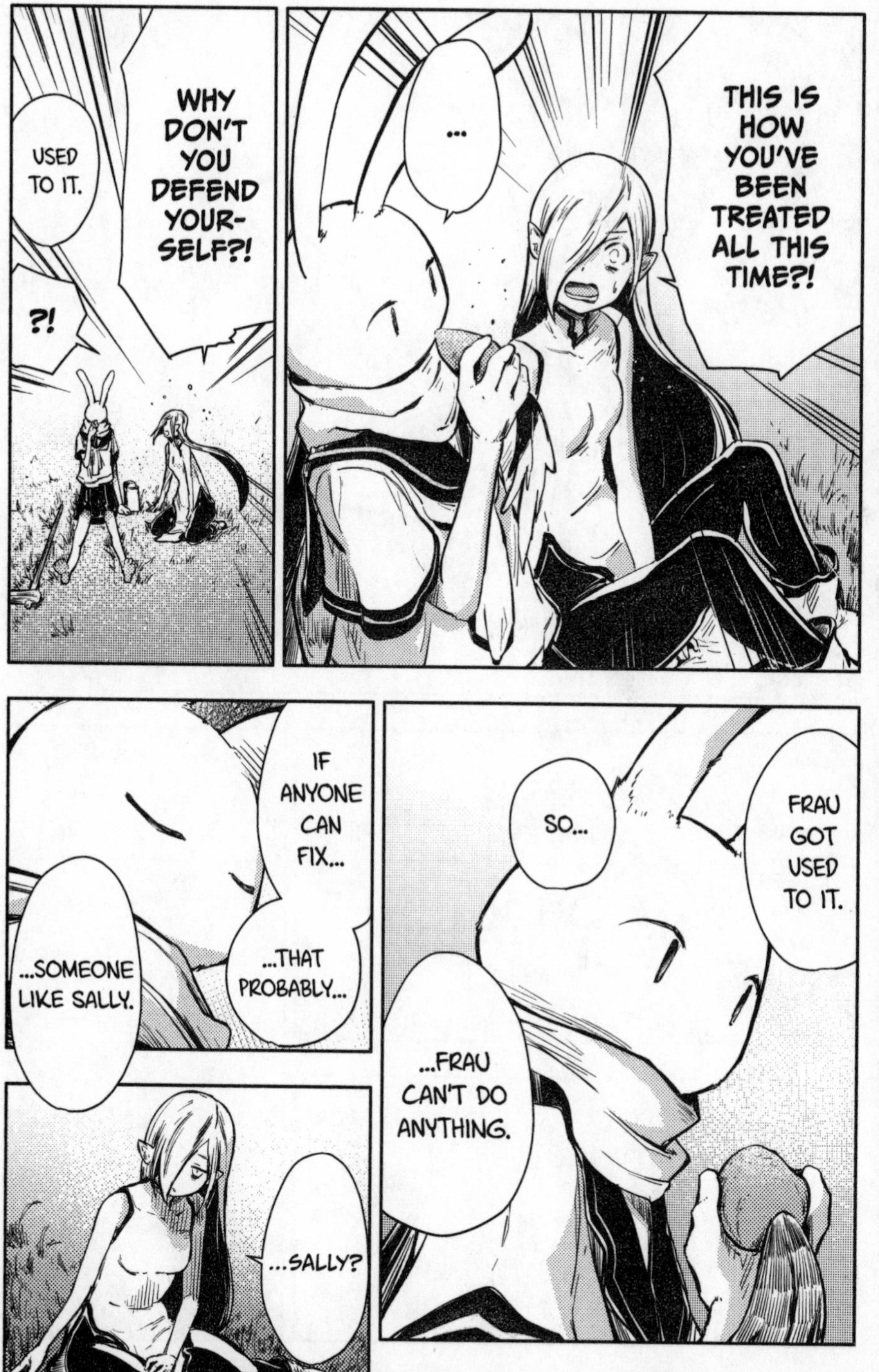
THIS IS HOW YOU'VE BEEN TREATED ALL THIS TIME?!
...
WHY DON'T YOU DEFEND YOUR-SELF?!
USED TO IT.
?!
FRAU GOT USED TO IT.
SO...
...FRAU CAN'T DO ANYTHING.
IF ANYONE CAN FIX...
...THAT PROBABLY...
...SOMEONE LIKE SALLY.
...SALLY?

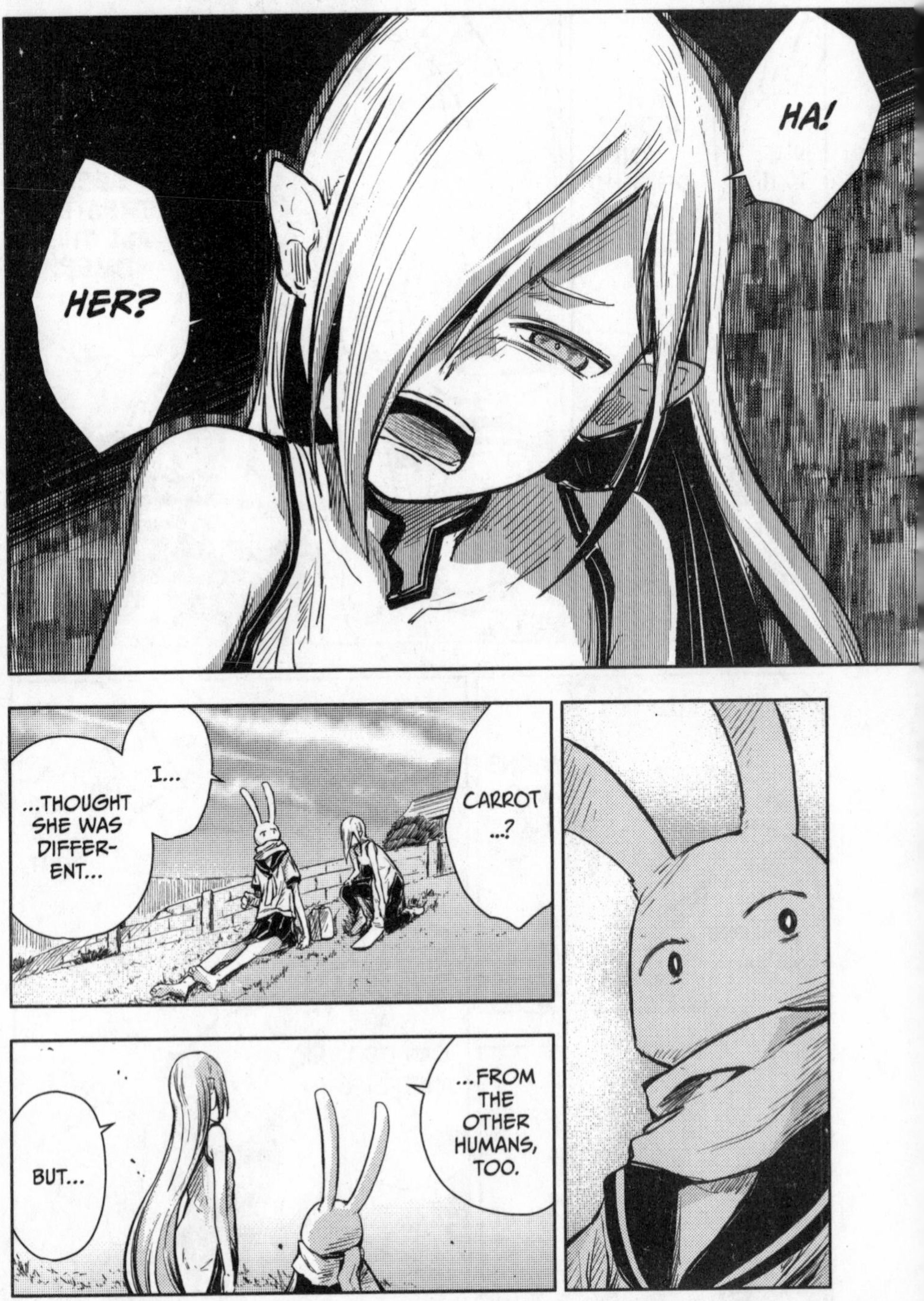
HA!
HER?
CARROT ...?
I...
...THOUGHT SHE WAS DIFFER-ENT...
...FROM THE OTHER HUMANS, TOO.
BUT...

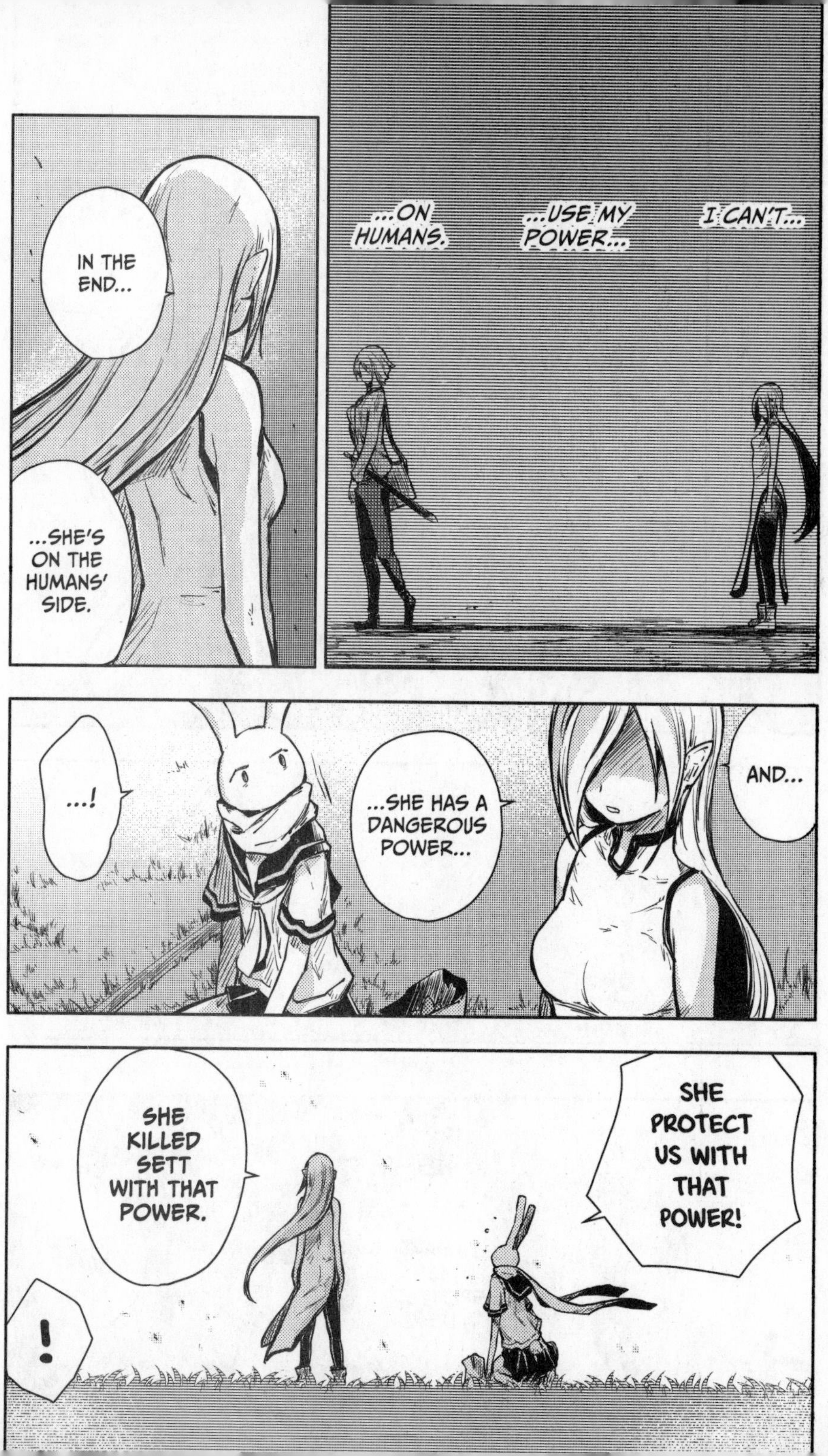
I CAN'T...
...USE MY POWER...
...ON HUMANS.
IN THE END...
...SHE'S ON THE HUMANS' SIDE.
AND...
...SHE HAS A DANGEROUS POWER...
...!
SHE PROTECT US WITH THAT POWER!
SHE KILLED SETT WITH THAT POWER.
!

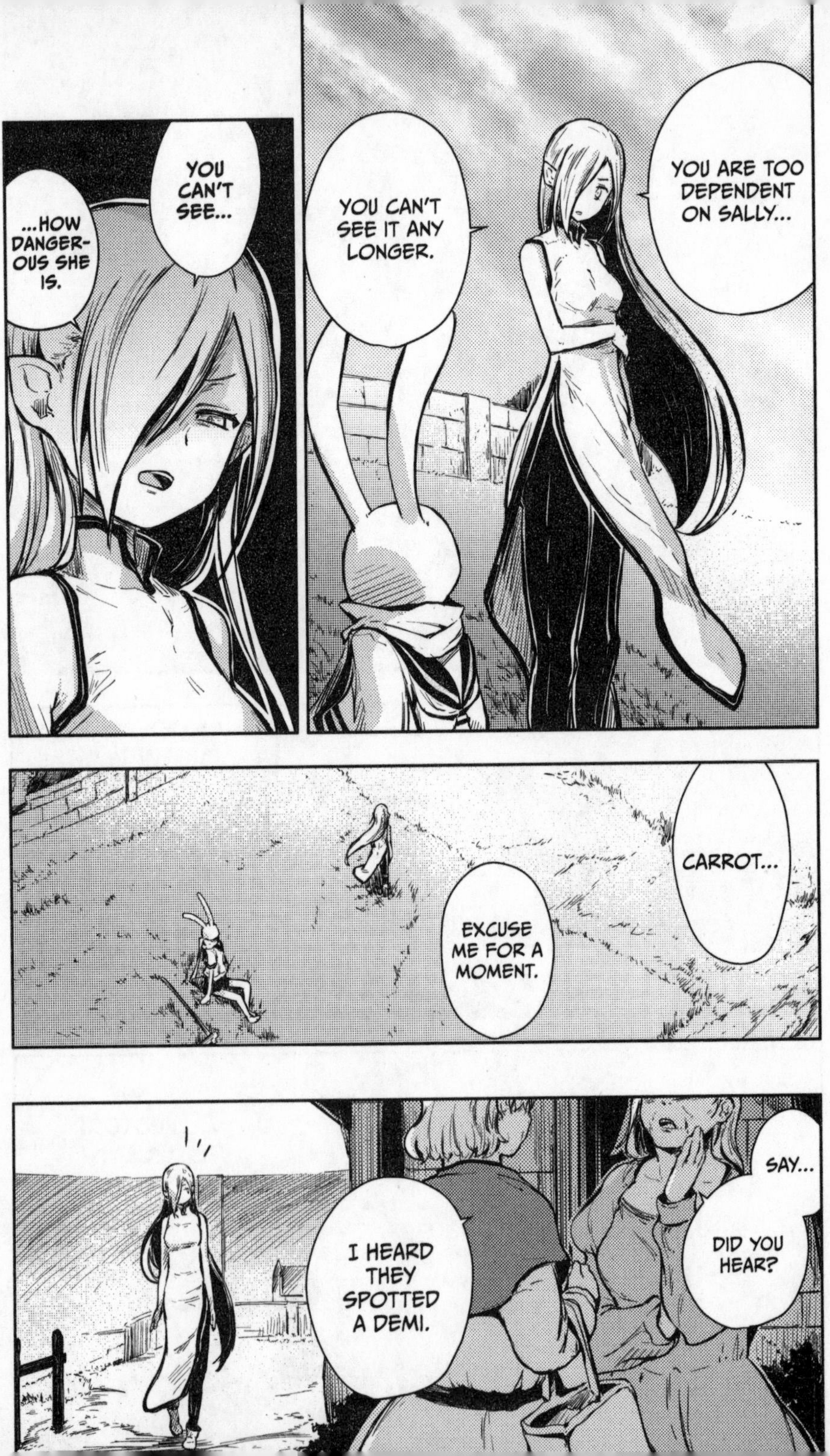
YOU ARE TOO DEPENDENT ON SALLY...
YOU CAN'T SEE IT ANY LONGER.
YOU CAN'T SEE...
...HOW DANGER-OUS SHE IS.
CARROT...
EXCUSE ME FOR A MOMENT.
SAY...
DID YOU HEAR?
I HEARD THEY SPOTTED A DEMI.

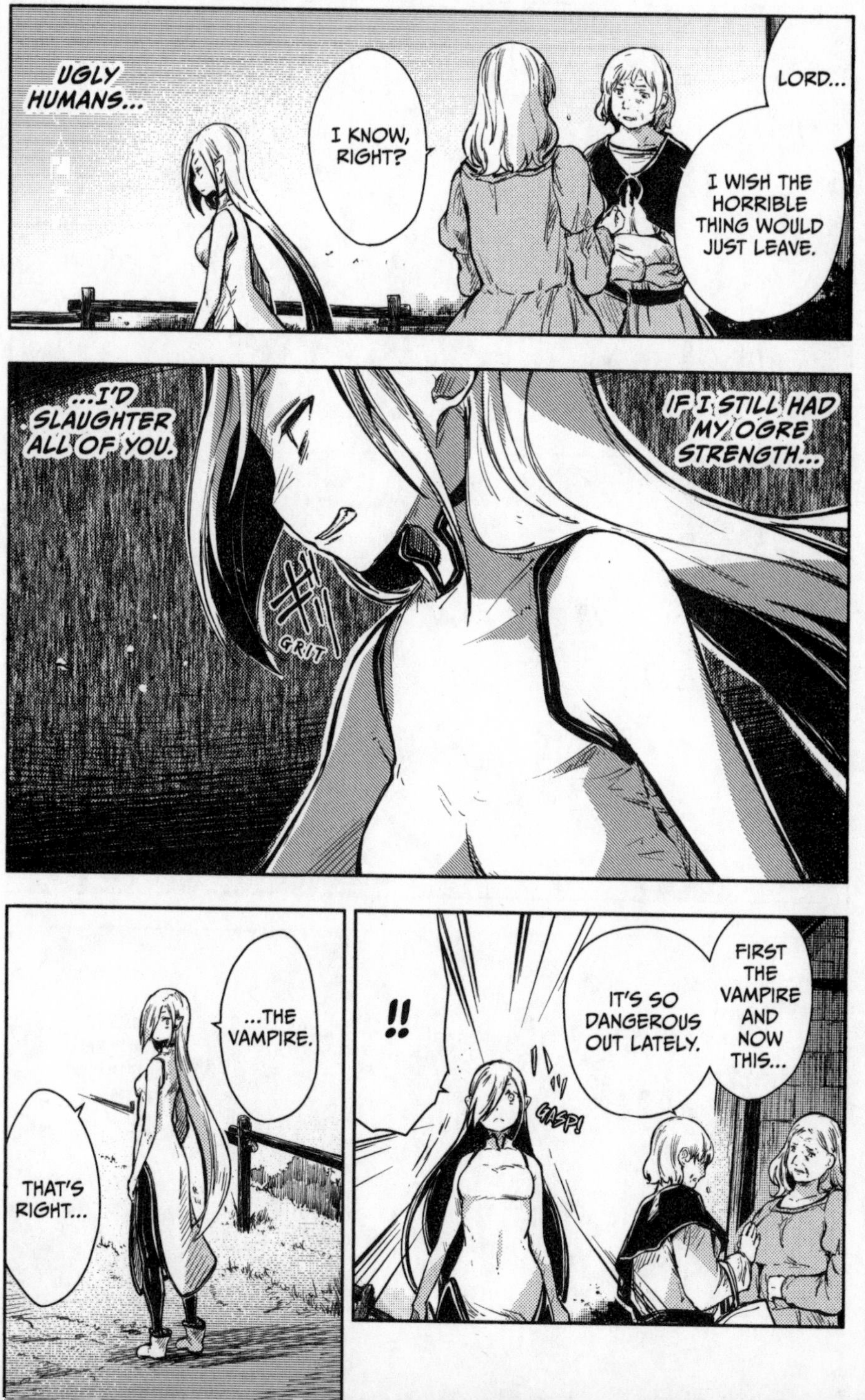
LORD...
I WISH THE HORRIBLE THING WOULD JUST LEAVE.
I KNOW, RIGHT?
UGLY HUMANS...
IF I STILL HAD MY OGRE STRENGTH...
...I'D SLAUGHTER ALL OF YOU.
GRIT
FIRST THE VAMPIRE AND NOW THIS...
IT'S SO DANGEROUS OUT LATELY.
!!
GASP!
...THE VAMPIRE.
THAT'S RIGHT...

!

FWOOOM

FWIP

WOM

...THERE'S NO DOUBT ABOUT IT.

THAT POWER...

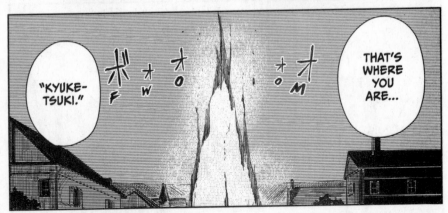

"KYUKE-TSUKI."

FWOOM

THAT'S WHERE YOU ARE...

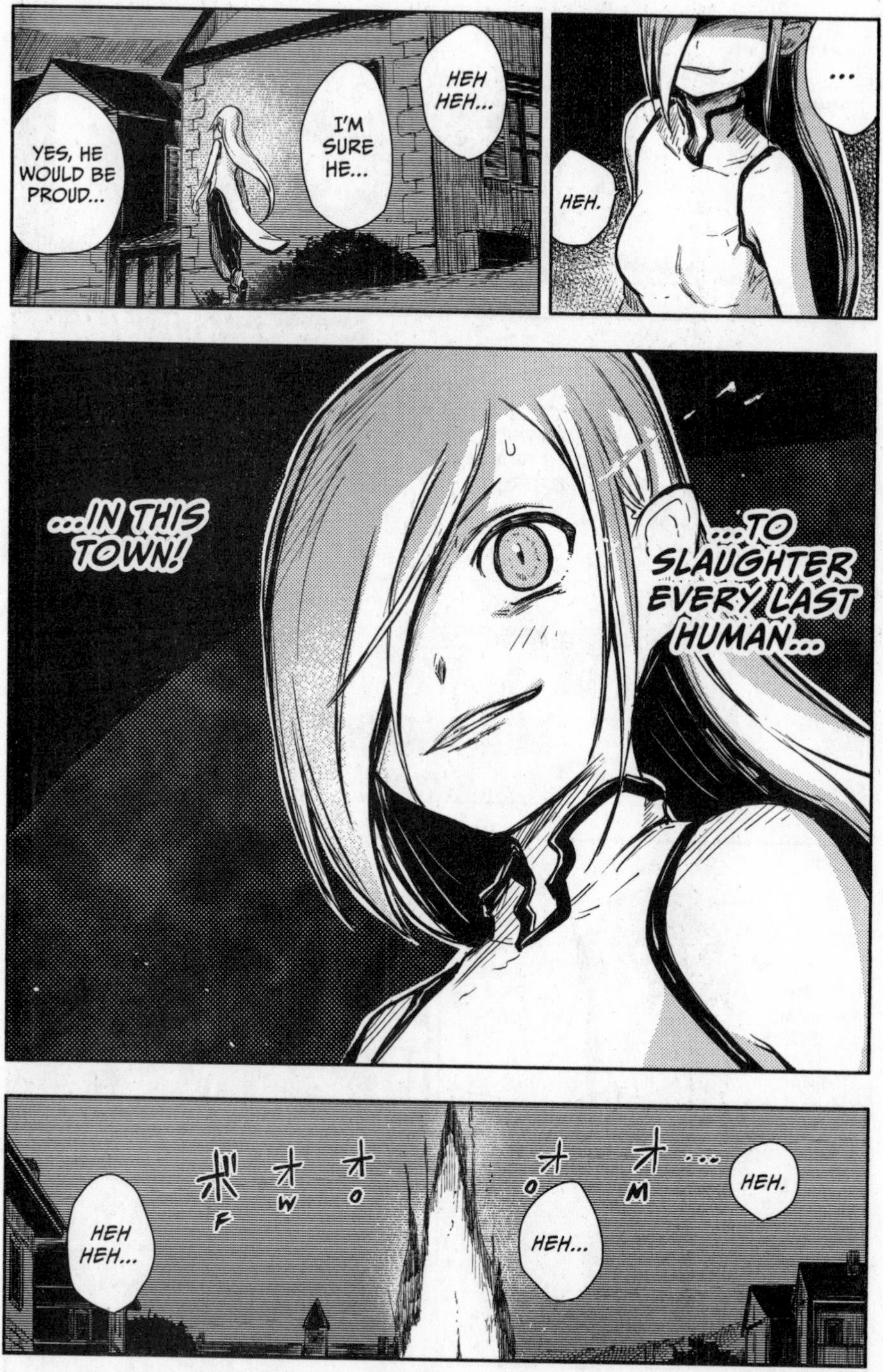
...
HEH.
HEH HEH...
I'M SURE HE...
YES, HE WOULD BE PROUD...
...TO SLAUGHTER EVERY LAST HUMAN...
...IN THIS TOWN!
HEH.
HEH...
ボオオオオ...
FWOOM
HEH HEH...

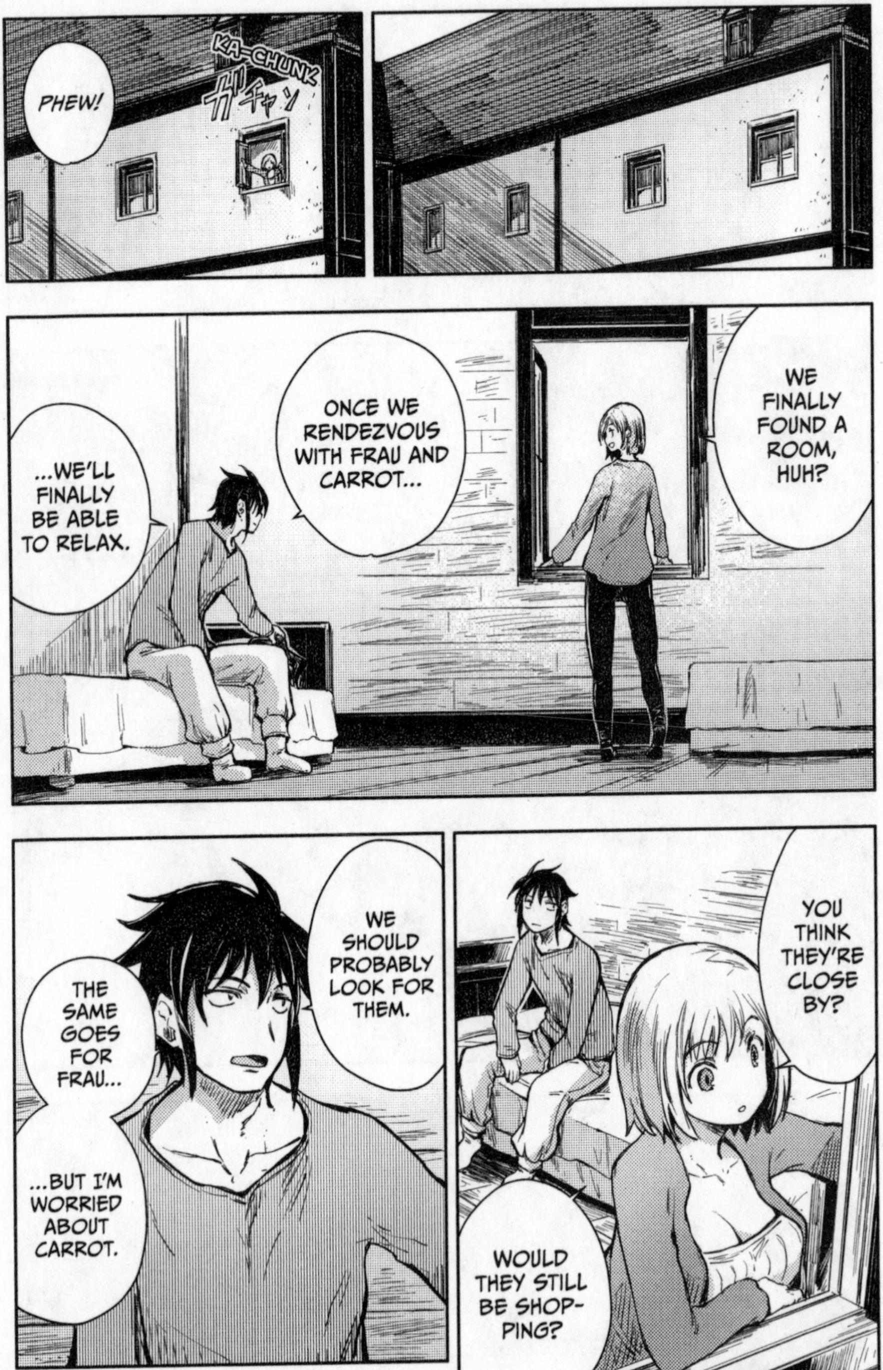
KA-CHUNK
ガチャン
PHEW!
WE FINALLY FOUND A ROOM, HUH?
ONCE WE RENDEZVOUS WITH FRAU AND CARROT...
...WE'LL FINALLY BE ABLE TO RELAX.
YOU THINK THEY'RE CLOSE BY?
WOULD THEY STILL BE SHOP-PING?
WE SHOULD PROBABLY LOOK FOR THEM.
THE SAME GOES FOR FRAU...
...BUT I'M WORRIED ABOUT CARROT.

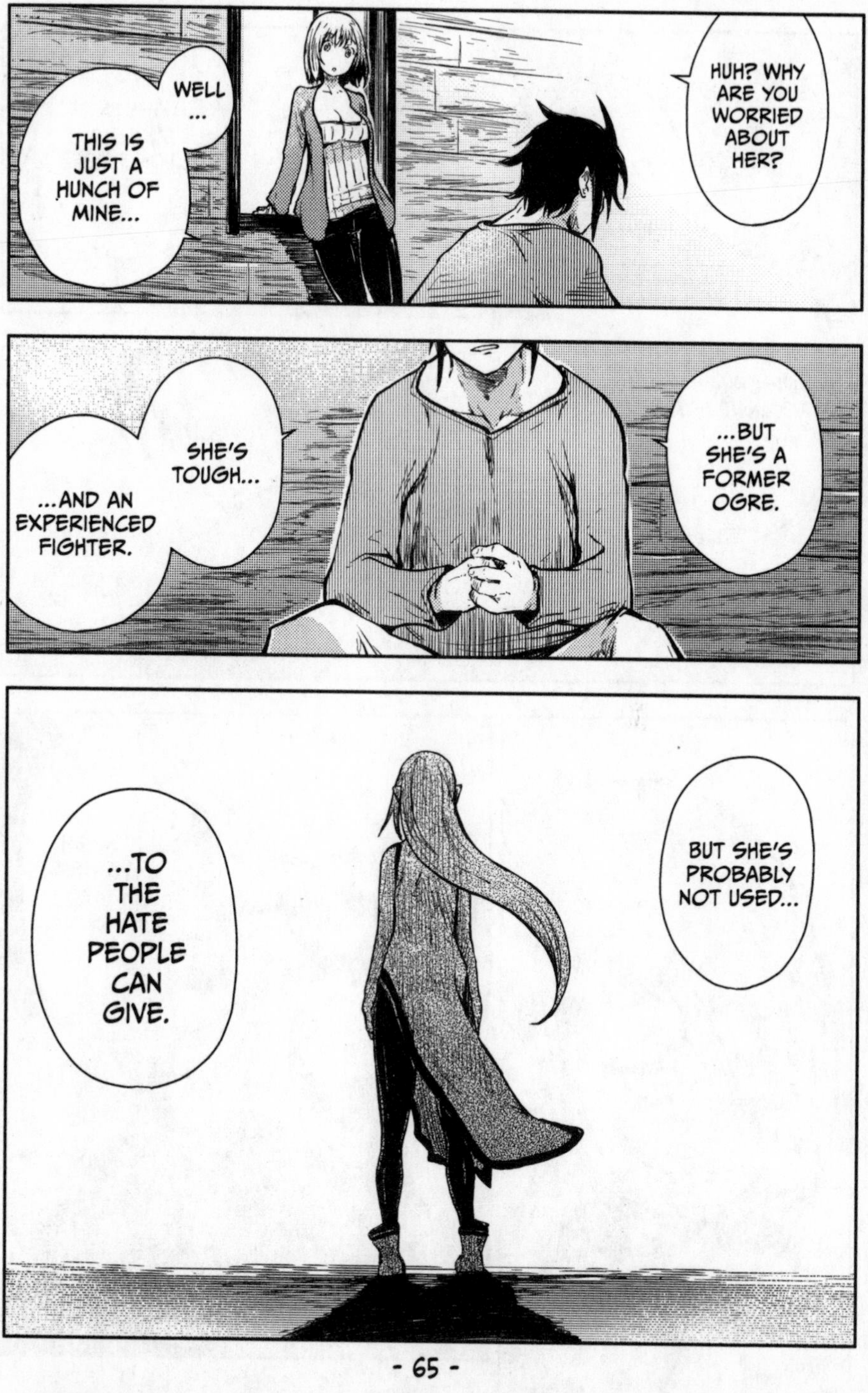
HUH? WHY ARE YOU WORRIED ABOUT HER?
WELL ...
THIS IS JUST A HUNCH OF MINE...
...BUT SHE'S A FORMER OGRE.
SHE'S TOUGH...
...AND AN EXPERIENCED FIGHTER.
BUT SHE'S PROBABLY NOT USED...
...TO THE HATE PEOPLE CAN GIVE.

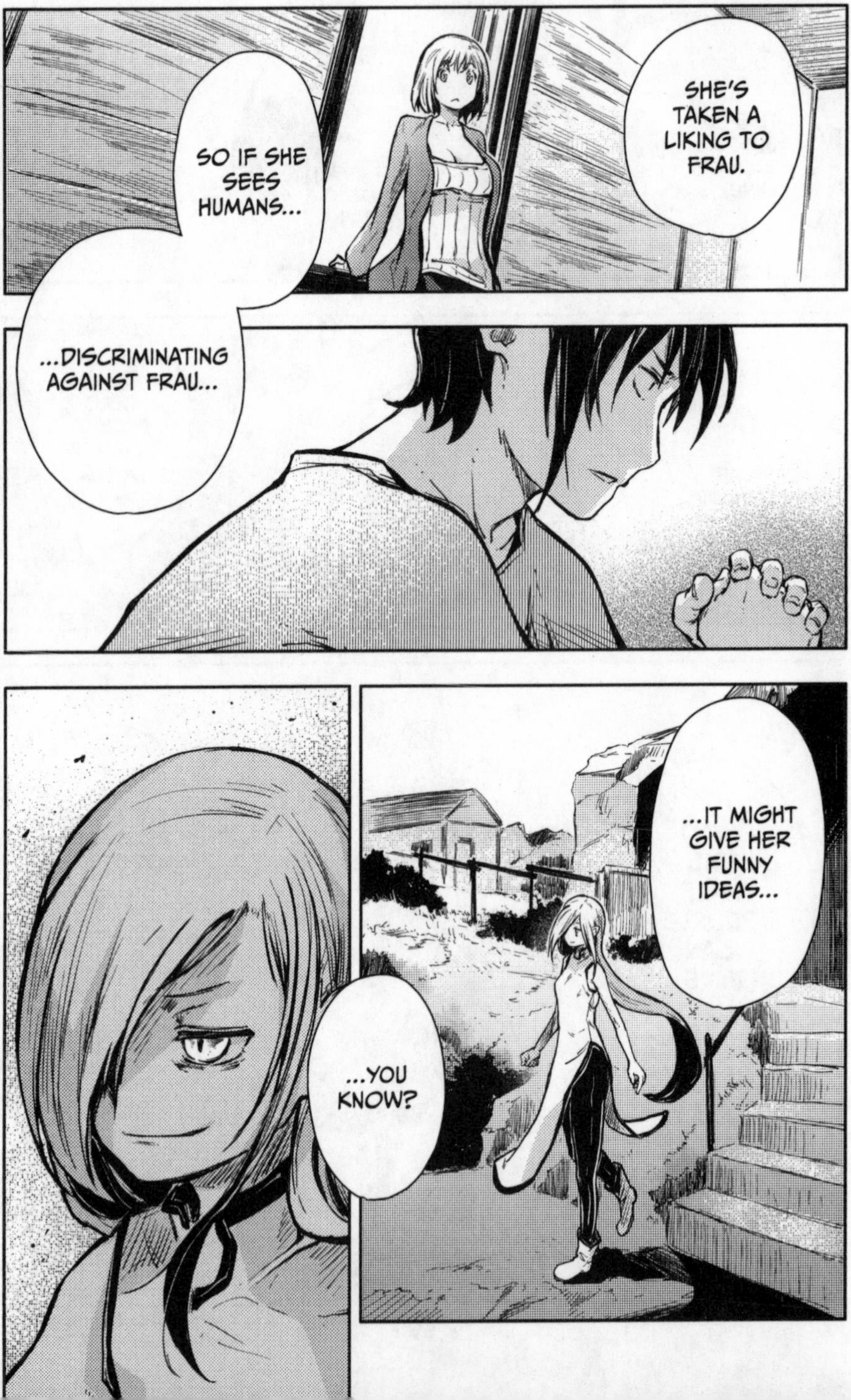
SHE'S TAKEN A LIKING TO FRAU.
SO IF SHE SEES HUMANS...
...DISCRIMINATING AGAINST FRAU...
...IT MIGHT GIVE HER FUNNY IDEAS...
...YOU KNOW?

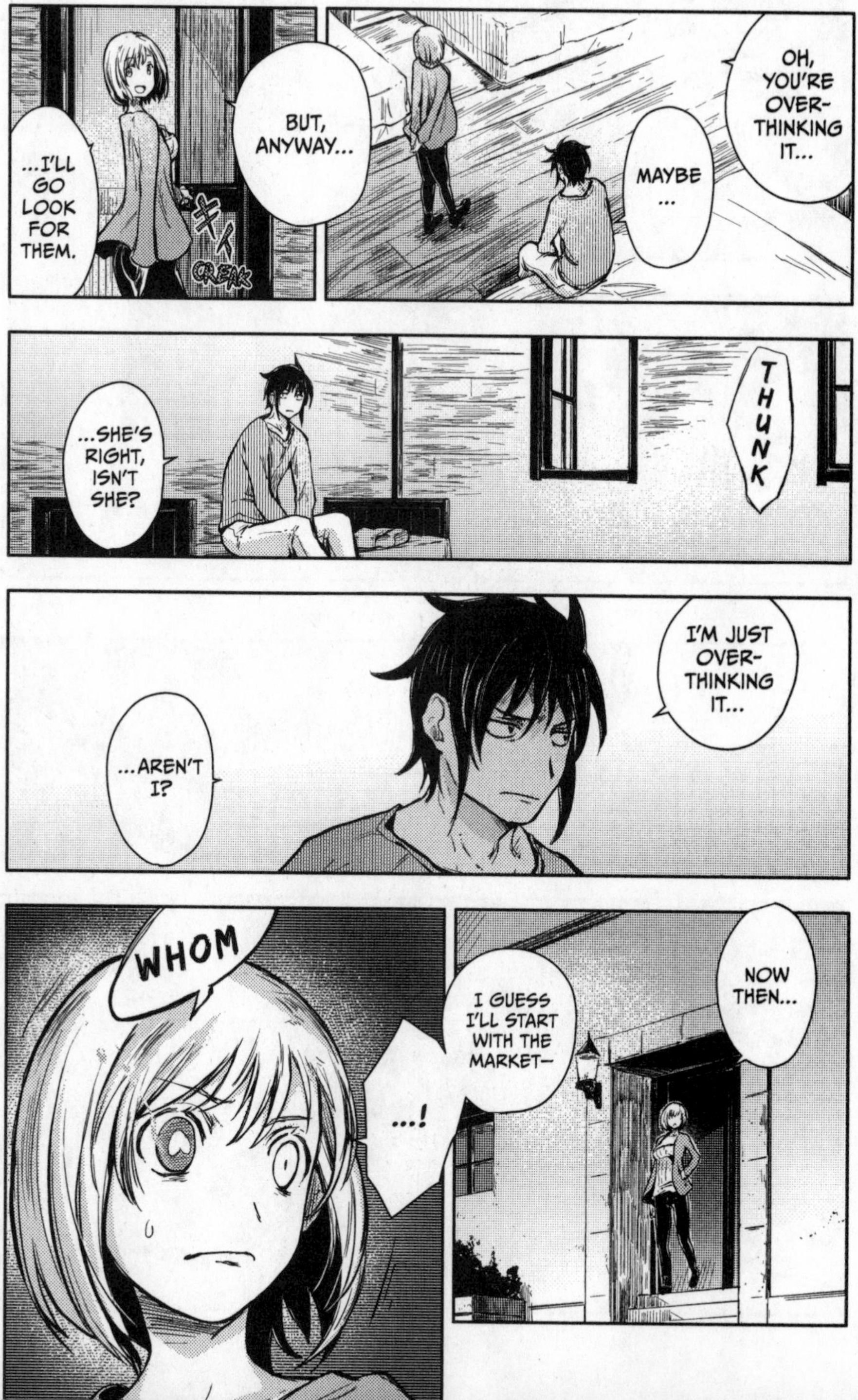
OH, YOU'RE OVER-THINKING IT...
MAYBE ...
BUT, ANYWAY...
...I'LL GO LOOK FOR THEM.
キィ
CREAK
THUNK
...SHE'S RIGHT, ISN'T SHE?
I'M JUST OVER-THINKING IT...
...AREN'T I?
NOW THEN...
I GUESS I'LL START WITH THE MARKET—
WHOM
...!

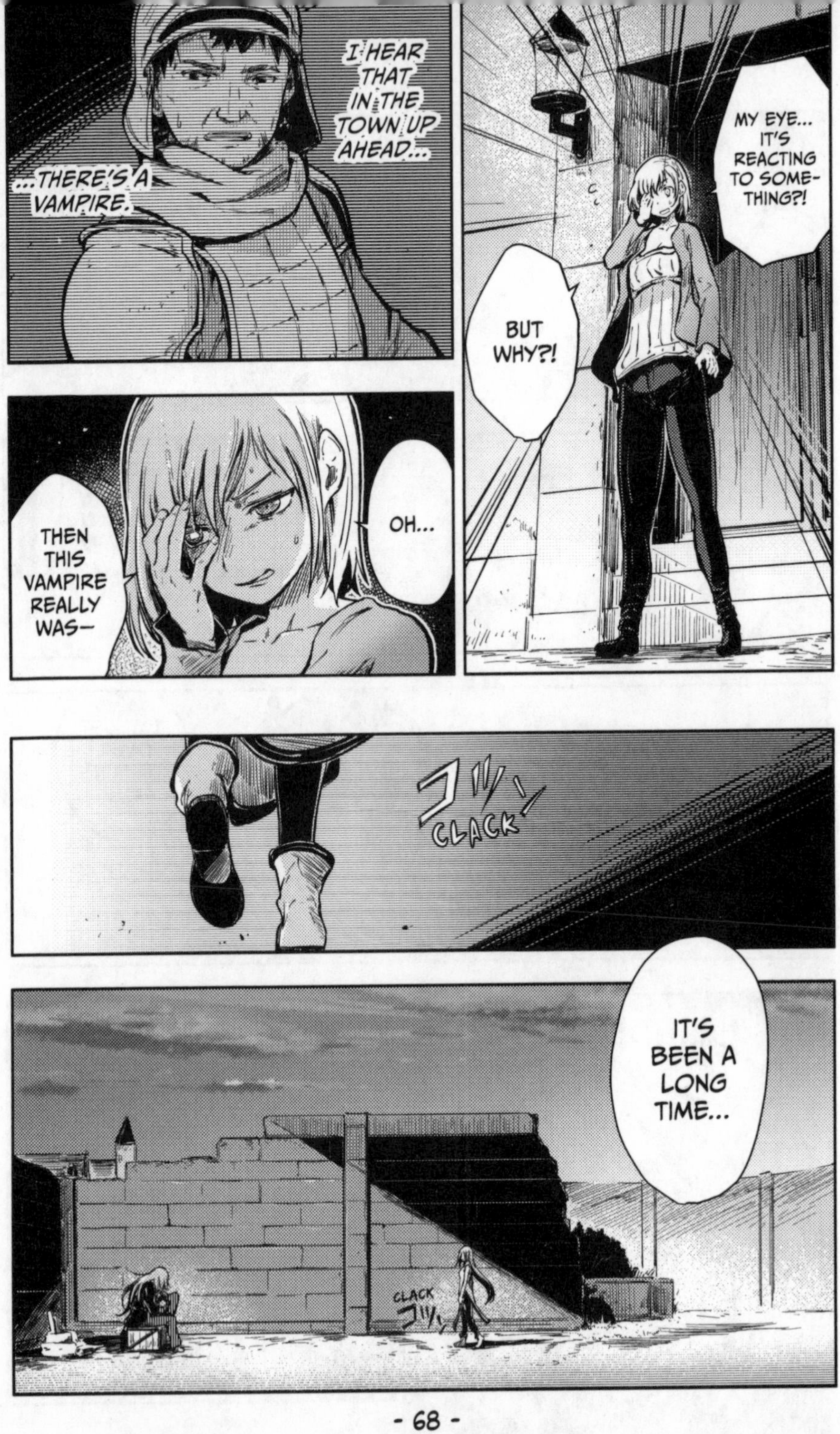
MY EYE... IT'S REACTING TO SOME-THING?!
BUT WHY?!
I HEAR THAT IN THE TOWN UP AHEAD...
...THERE'S A VAMPIRE.
OH...
THEN THIS VAMPIRE REALLY WAS—
CLACK
IT'S BEEN A LONG TIME...
CLACK

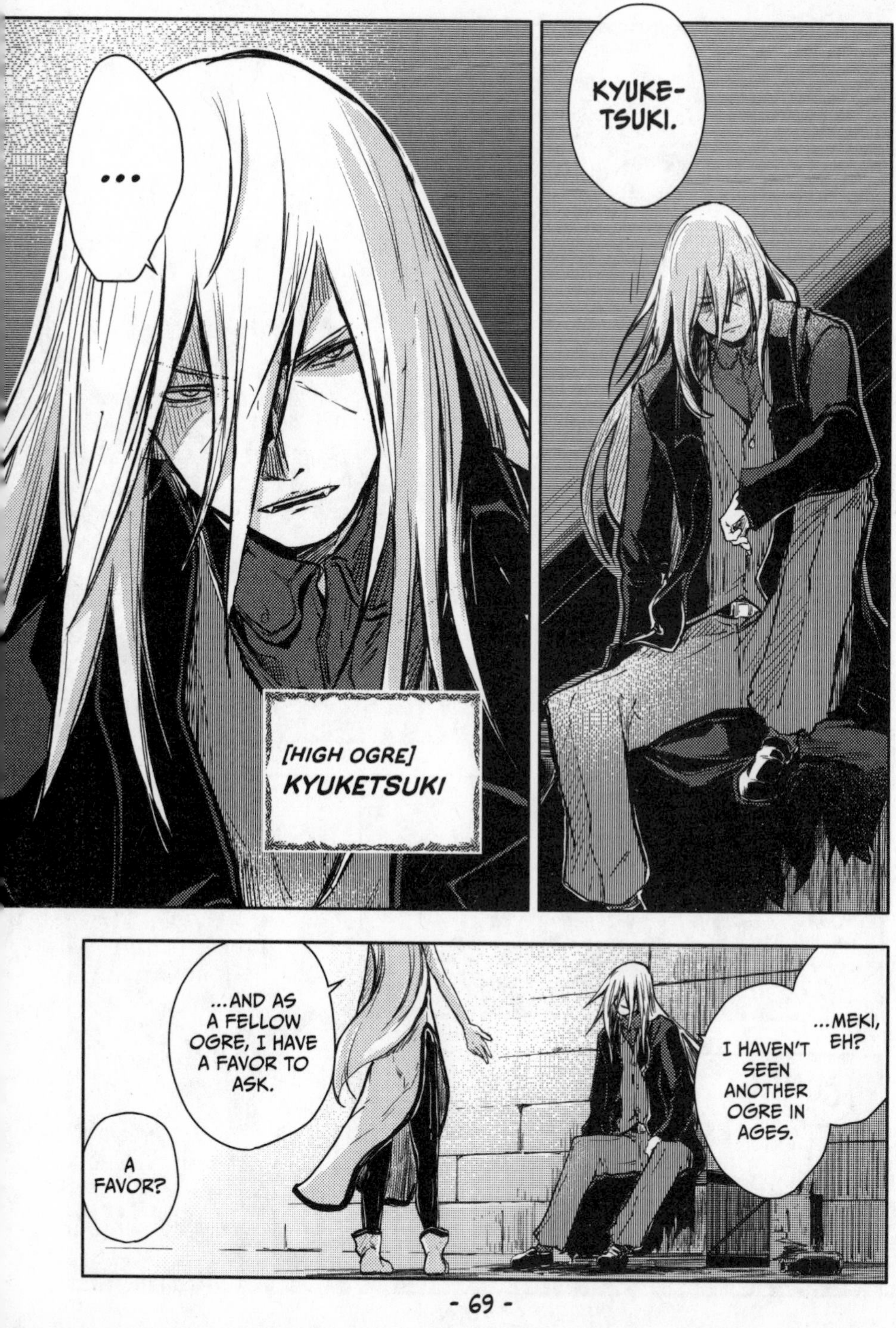
KYUKE-TSUKI.
...
[HIGH OGRE] KYUKETSUKI
...MEKI, EH?
I HAVEN'T SEEN ANOTHER OGRE IN AGES.
...AND AS A FELLOW OGRE, I HAVE A FAVOR TO ASK.
A FAVOR?

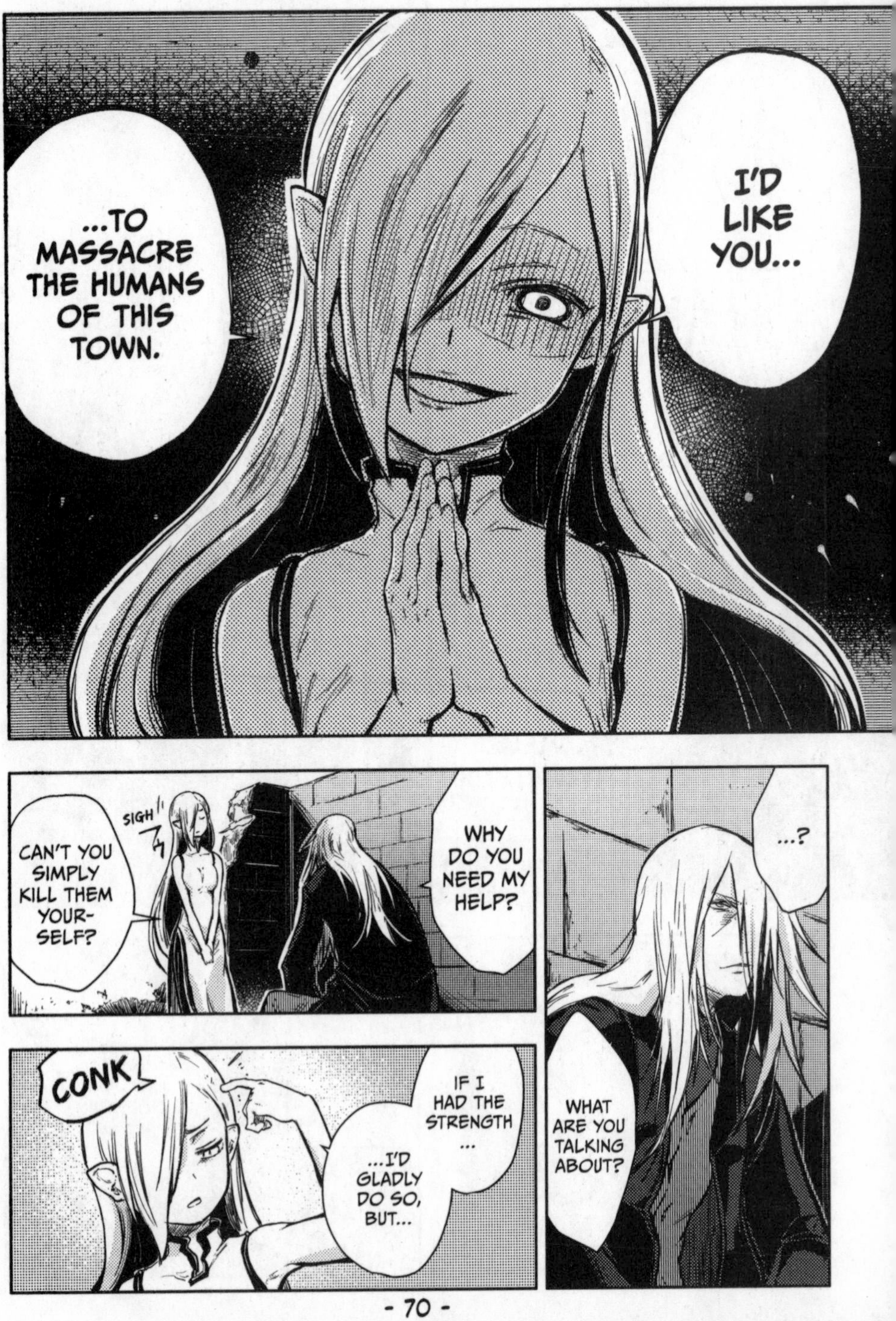
I'D LIKE YOU...
...TO MASSACRE THE HUMANS OF THIS TOWN.
...?
WHAT ARE YOU TALKING ABOUT?
WHY DO YOU NEED MY HELP?
SIGH
CAN'T YOU SIMPLY KILL THEM YOUR-SELF?
IF I HAD THE STRENGTH...
...I'D GLADLY DO SO, BUT...
CONK

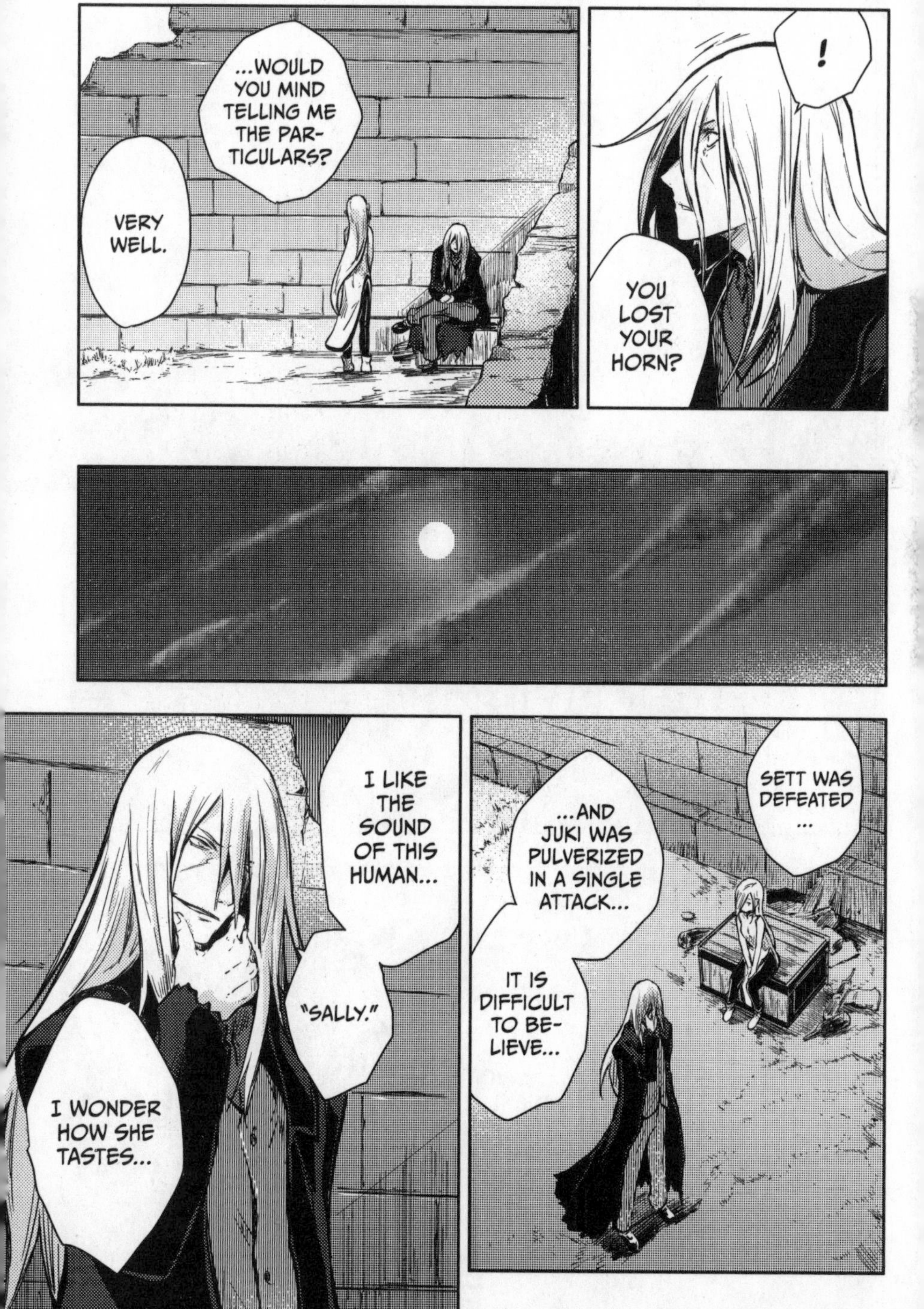
!
YOU LOST YOUR HORN?
...WOULD YOU MIND TELLING ME THE PAR-TICULARS?
VERY WELL.
SETT WAS DEFEATED ...
...AND JUKI WAS PULVERIZED IN A SINGLE ATTACK...
IT IS DIFFICULT TO BE-LIEVE...
I LIKE THE SOUND OF THIS HUMAN...
"SALLY."
I WONDER HOW SHE TASTES...

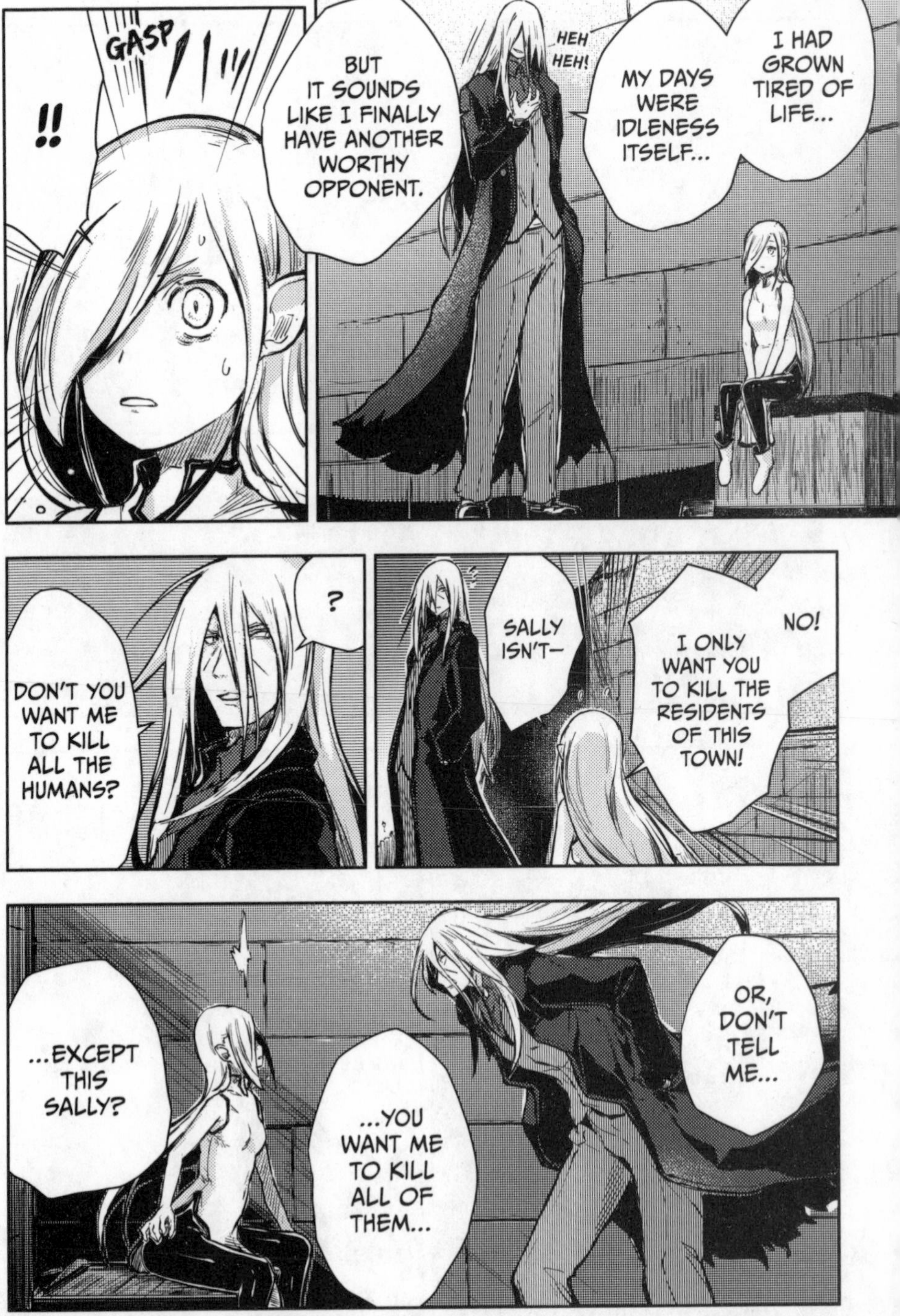
I HAD GROWN TIRED OF LIFE...
MY DAYS WERE IDLENESS ITSELF...
HEH HEH!
BUT IT SOUNDS LIKE I FINALLY HAVE ANOTHER WORTHY OPPONENT.
GASP
!!
NO!
I ONLY WANT YOU TO KILL THE RESIDENTS OF THIS TOWN!
SALLY ISN'T—
?
DON'T YOU WANT ME TO KILL ALL THE HUMANS?
OR, DON'T TELL ME...
...YOU WANT ME TO KILL ALL OF THEM...
...EXCEPT THIS SALLY?

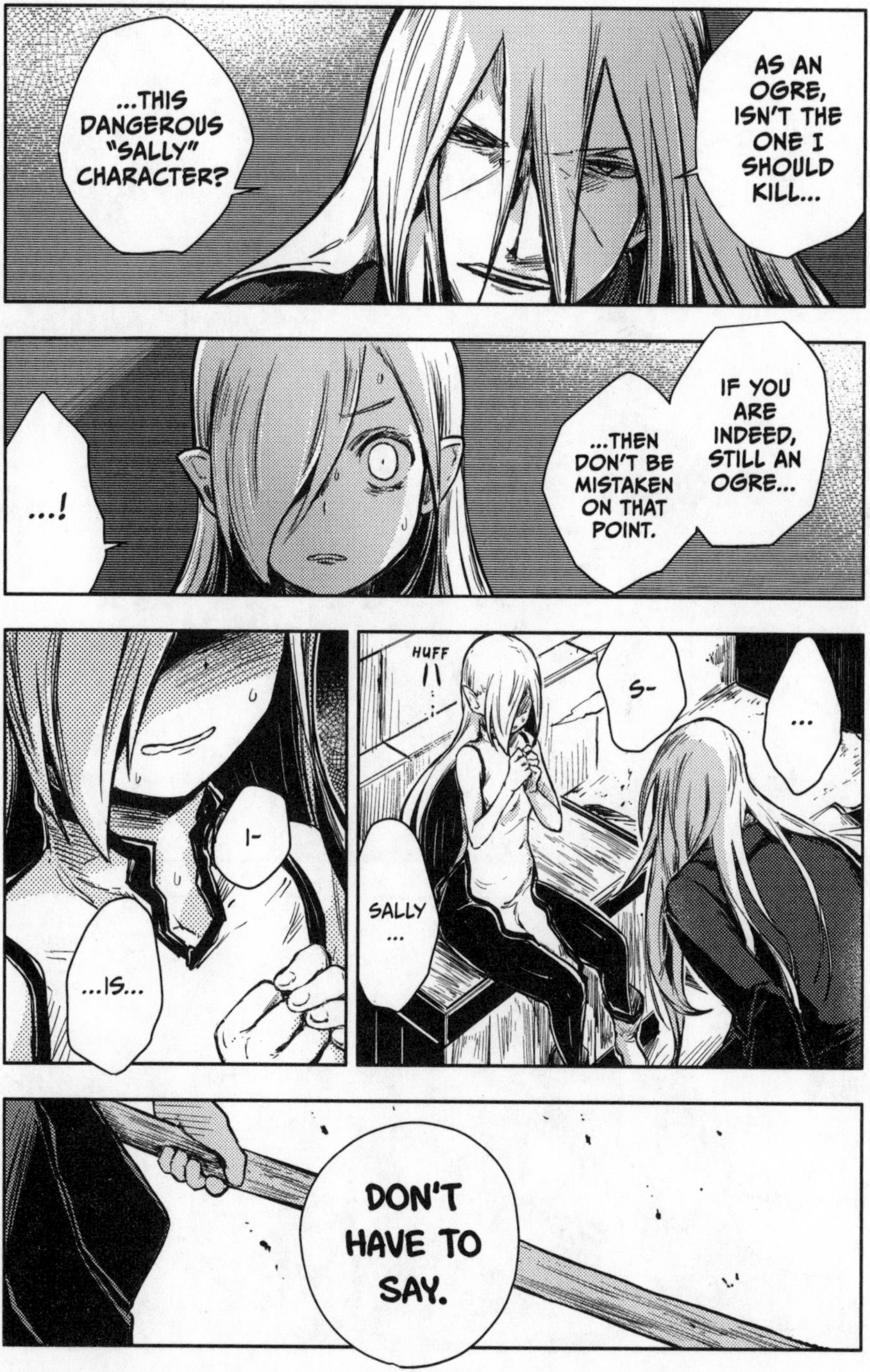
AS AN OGRE, ISN'T THE ONE I SHOULD KILL...
...THIS DANGEROUS "SALLY" CHARACTER?
IF YOU ARE INDEED, STILL AN OGRE...
...THEN DON'T BE MISTAKEN ON THAT POINT.
...!
...
S-
HUFF
SALLY ...
I-
...IS...
DON'T HAVE TO SAY.

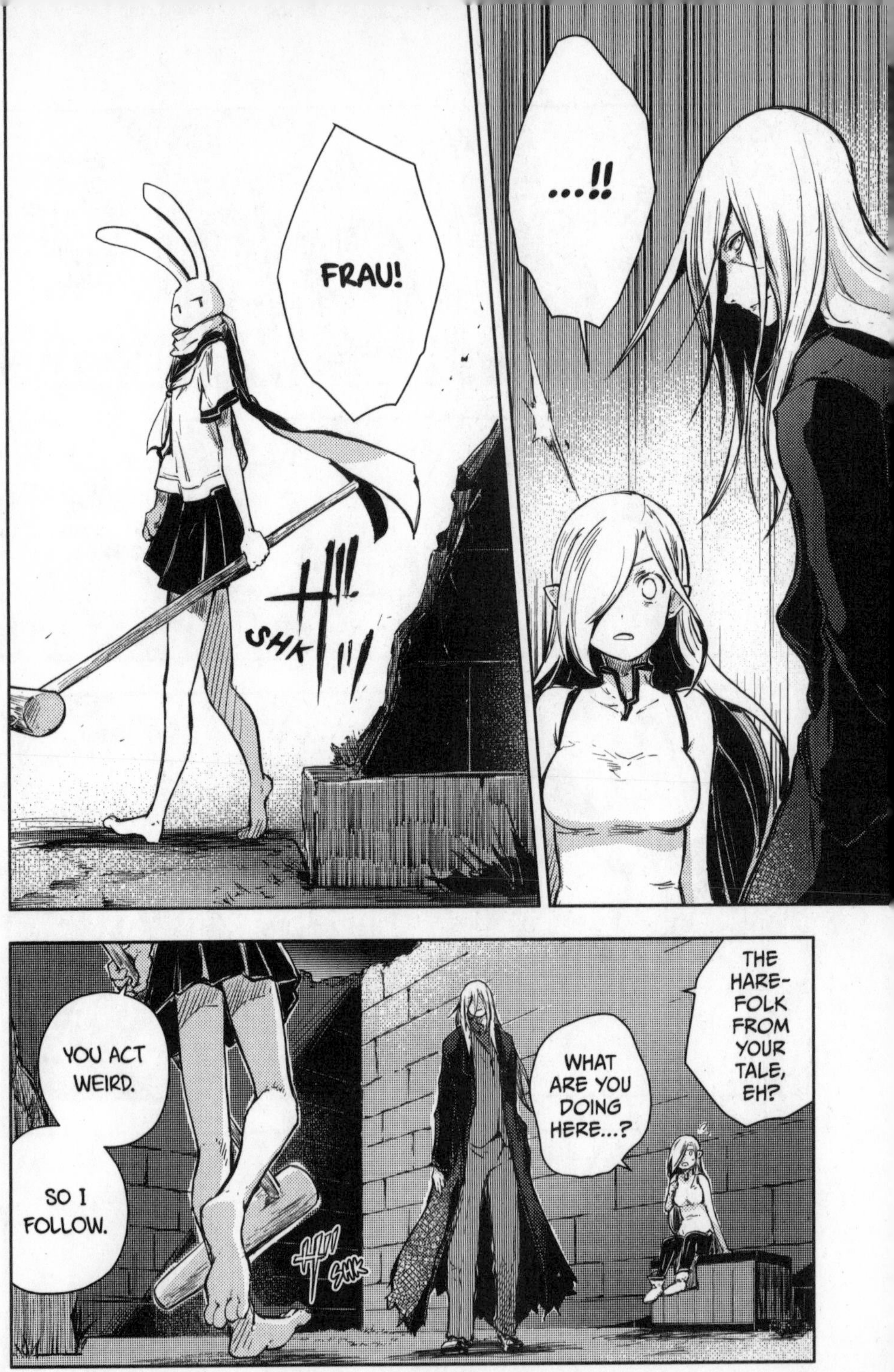
...!!
FRAU!
SHK
THE HARE-FOLK FROM YOUR TALE, EH?
WHAT ARE YOU DOING HERE...?
SHK
YOU ACT WEIRD.
SO I FOLLOW.

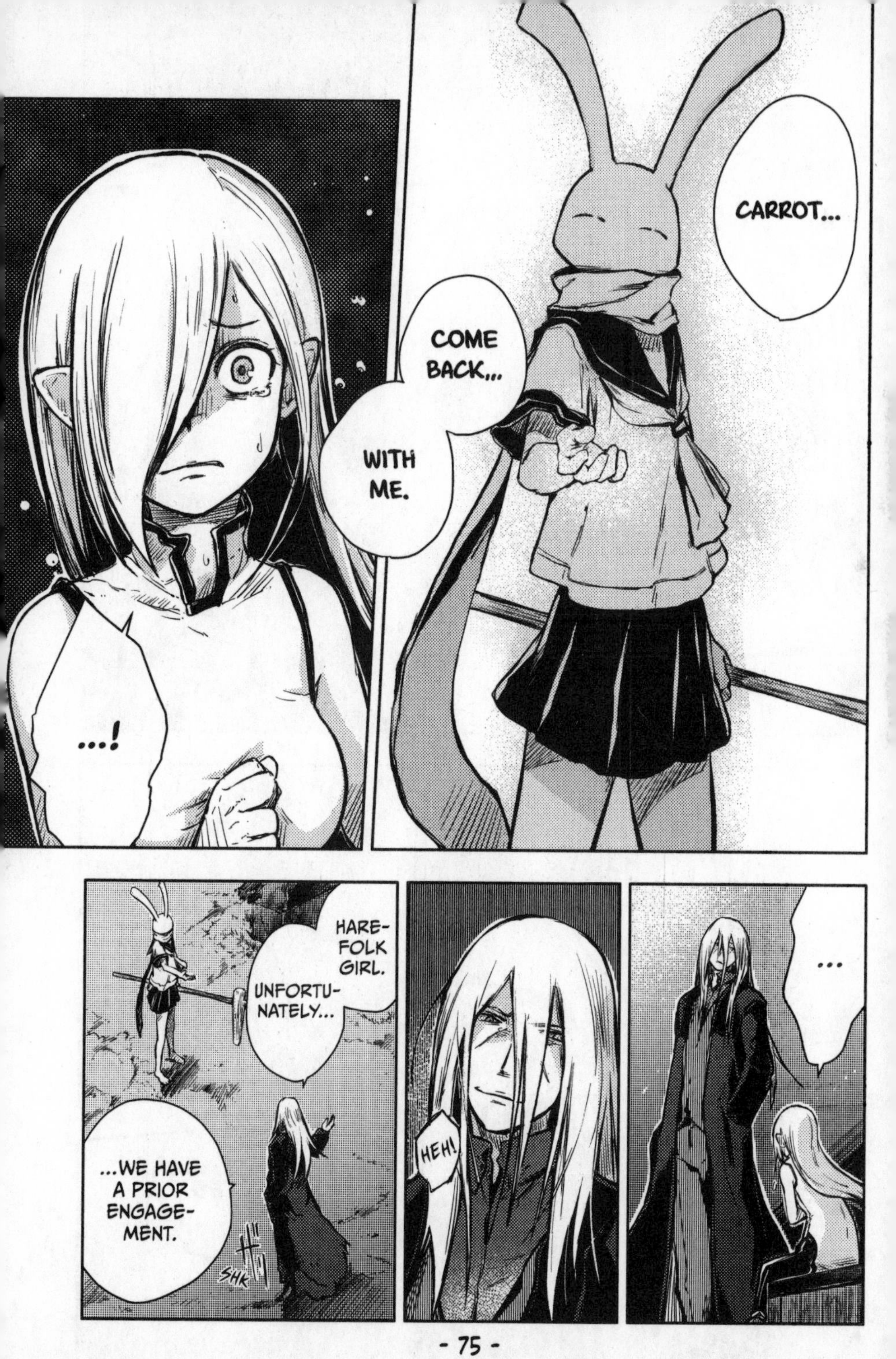
CARROT...
COME BACK...
WITH ME.
...!
...
HEH!
HARE-FOLK GIRL.
UNFORTUNATELY...
...WE HAVE A PRIOR ENGAGEMENT.
SHK

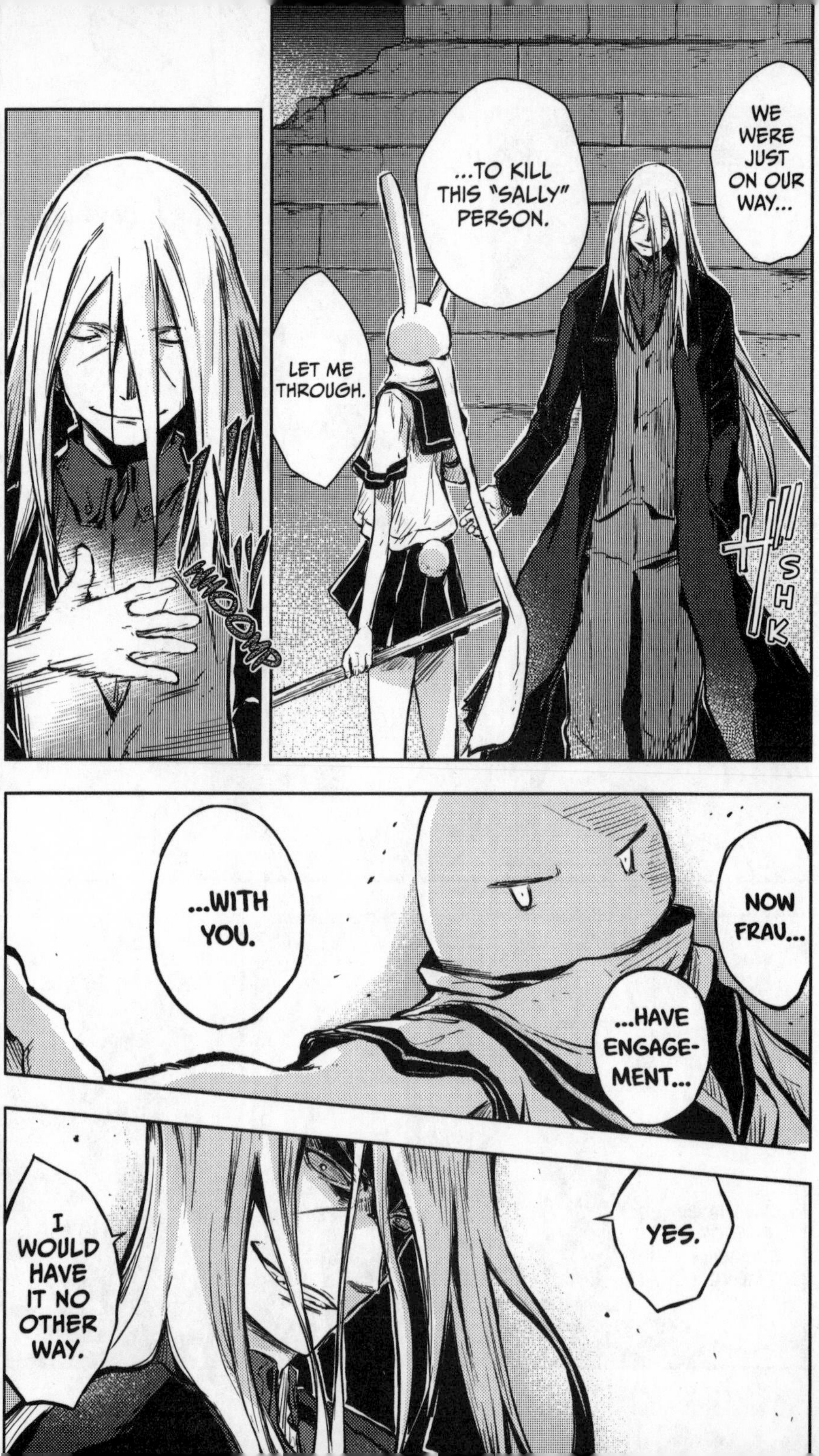
WE WERE JUST ON OUR WAY...
...TO KILL THIS "SALLY" PERSON.
LET ME THROUGH.
SHK
WHOOMP
NOW FRAU...
...HAVE ENGAGEMENT...
...WITH YOU.
YES.
I WOULD HAVE IT NO OTHER WAY.

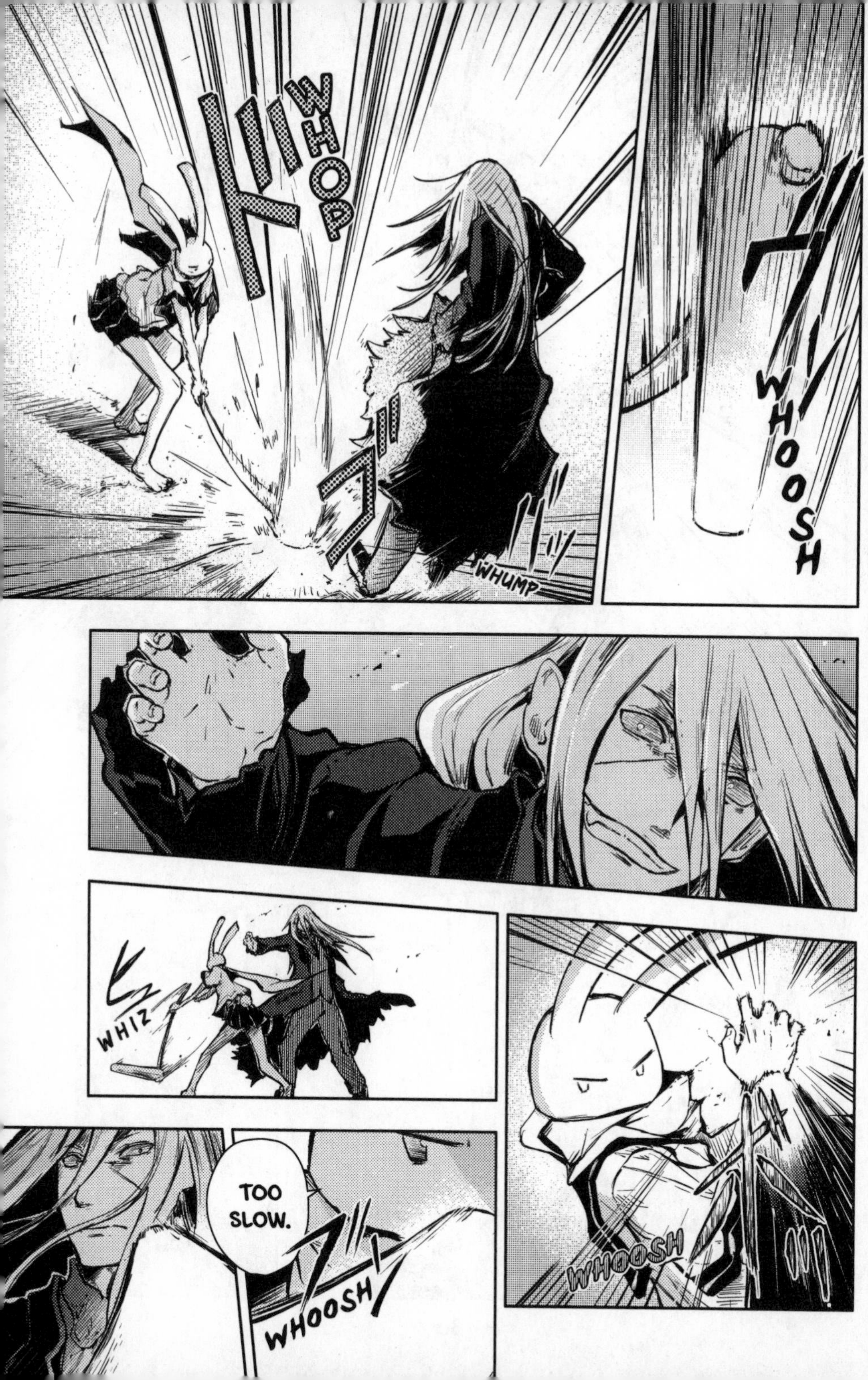
WHOOSH
WHOP
WHUMP
WHOOSH
WHIZ
TOO SLOW.
WHOOSH

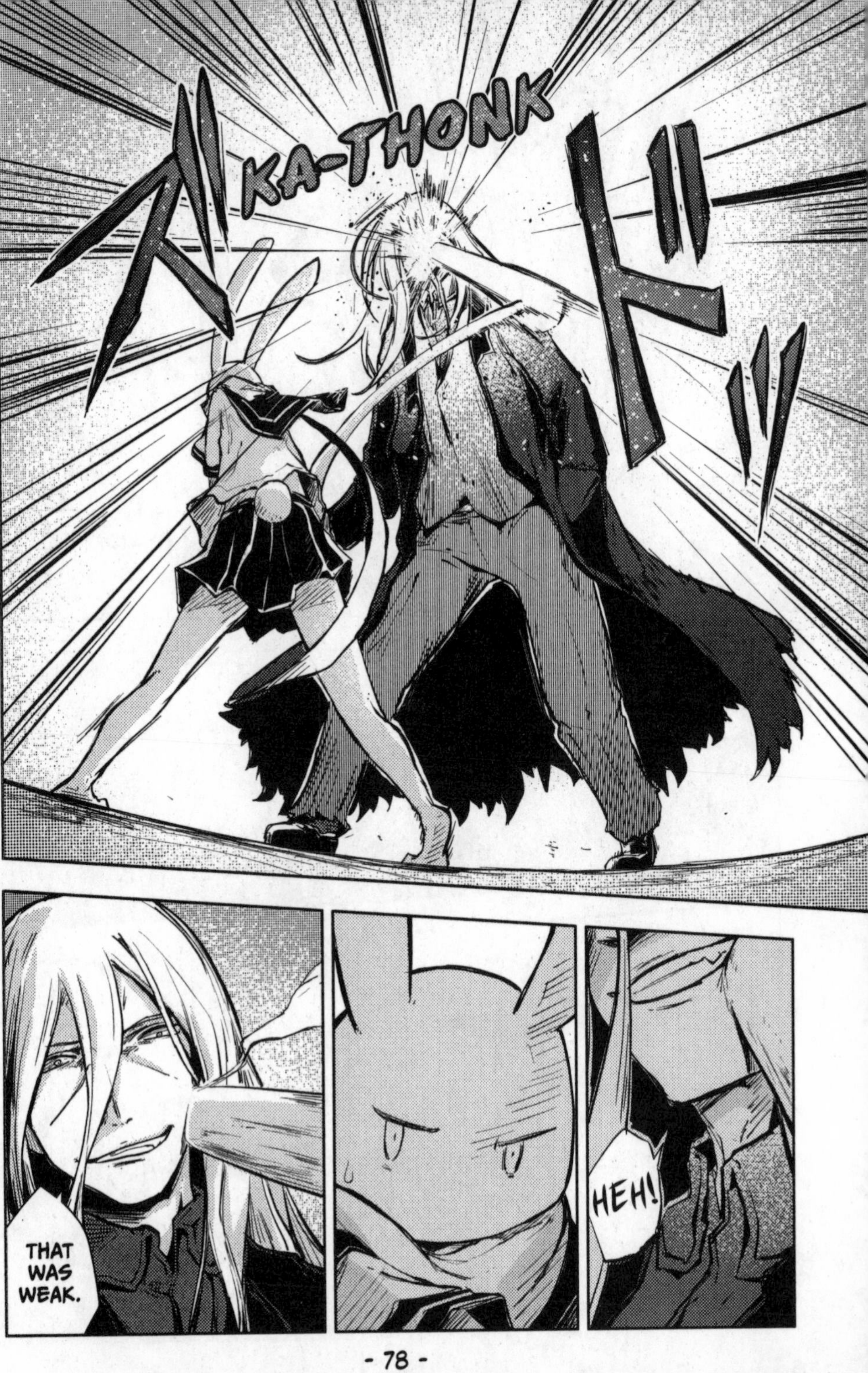
KA-THONK
ズドッ
HEH!
THAT WAS WEAK.

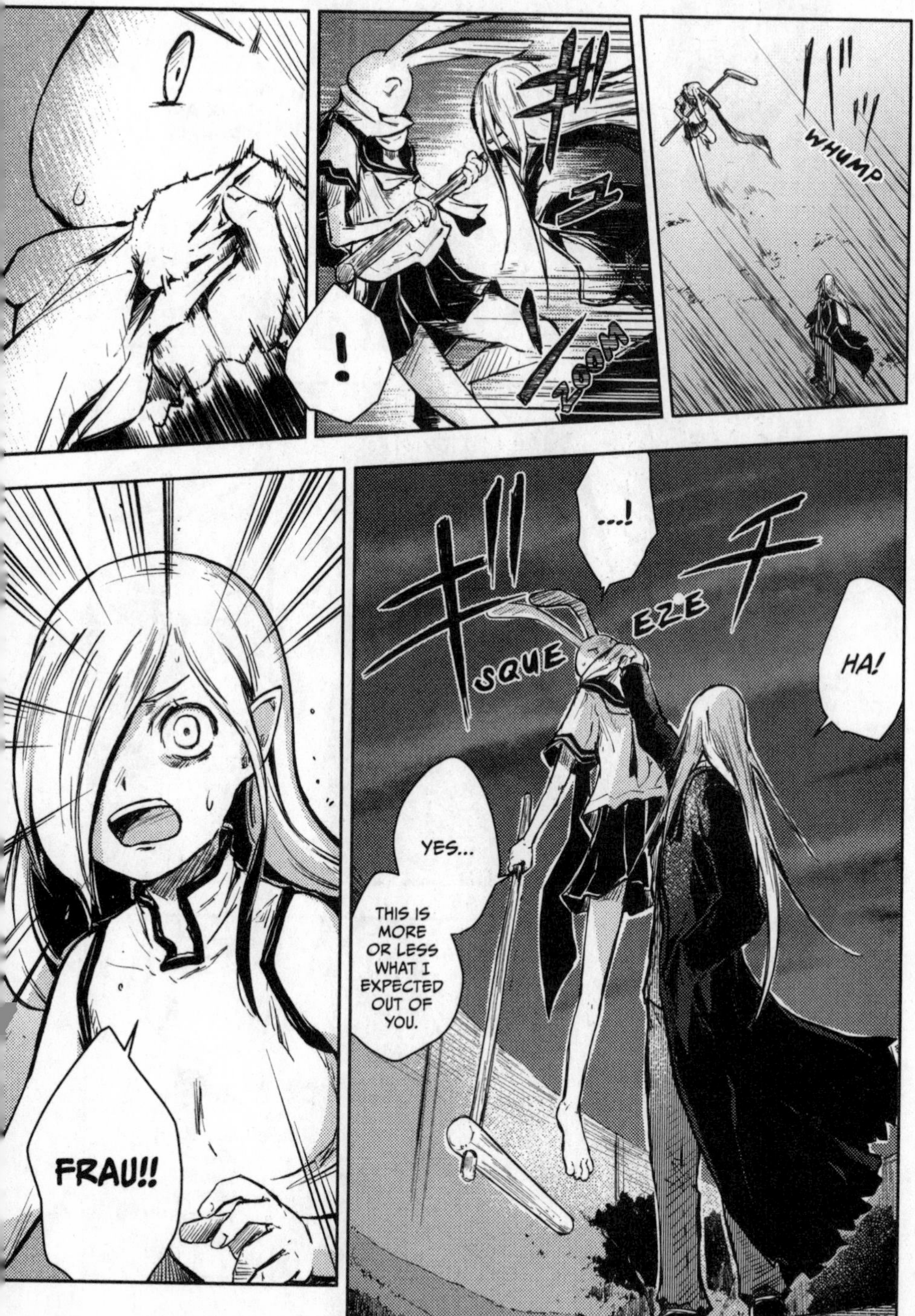
WHUMP
ZOOM
!
...!
SQUEEZE
HA!
YES...
THIS IS MORE OR LESS WHAT I EXPECTED OUT OF YOU.
FRAU!!

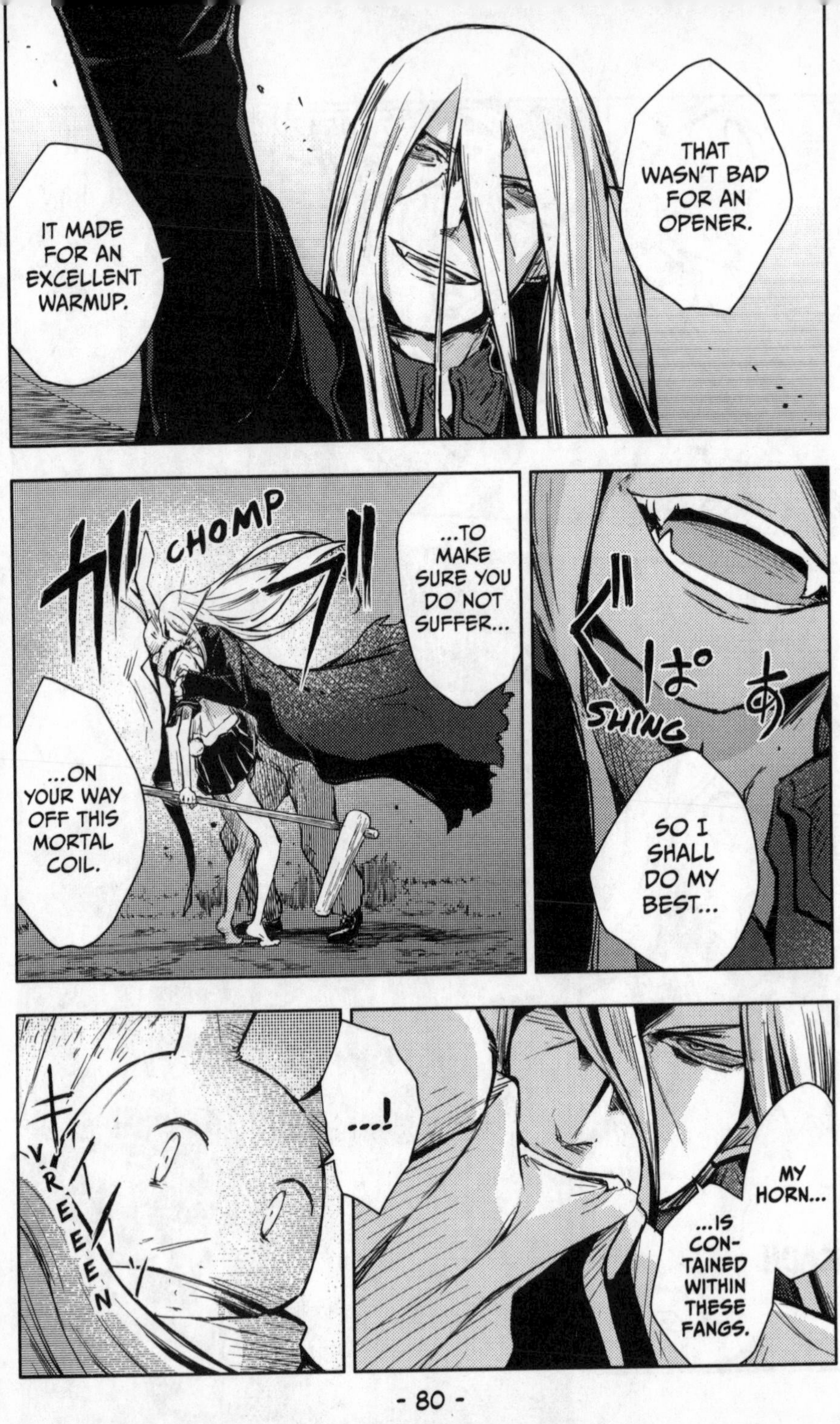
THAT WASN'T BAD FOR AN OPENER.
IT MADE FOR AN EXCELLENT WARMUP.
ぐぱあ
SHING
SO I SHALL DO MY BEST...
CHOMP
...TO MAKE SURE YOU DO NOT SUFFER...
...ON YOUR WAY OFF THIS MORTAL COIL.
MY HORN...
...IS CONTAINED WITHIN THESE FANGS.
...!
VREEEEN

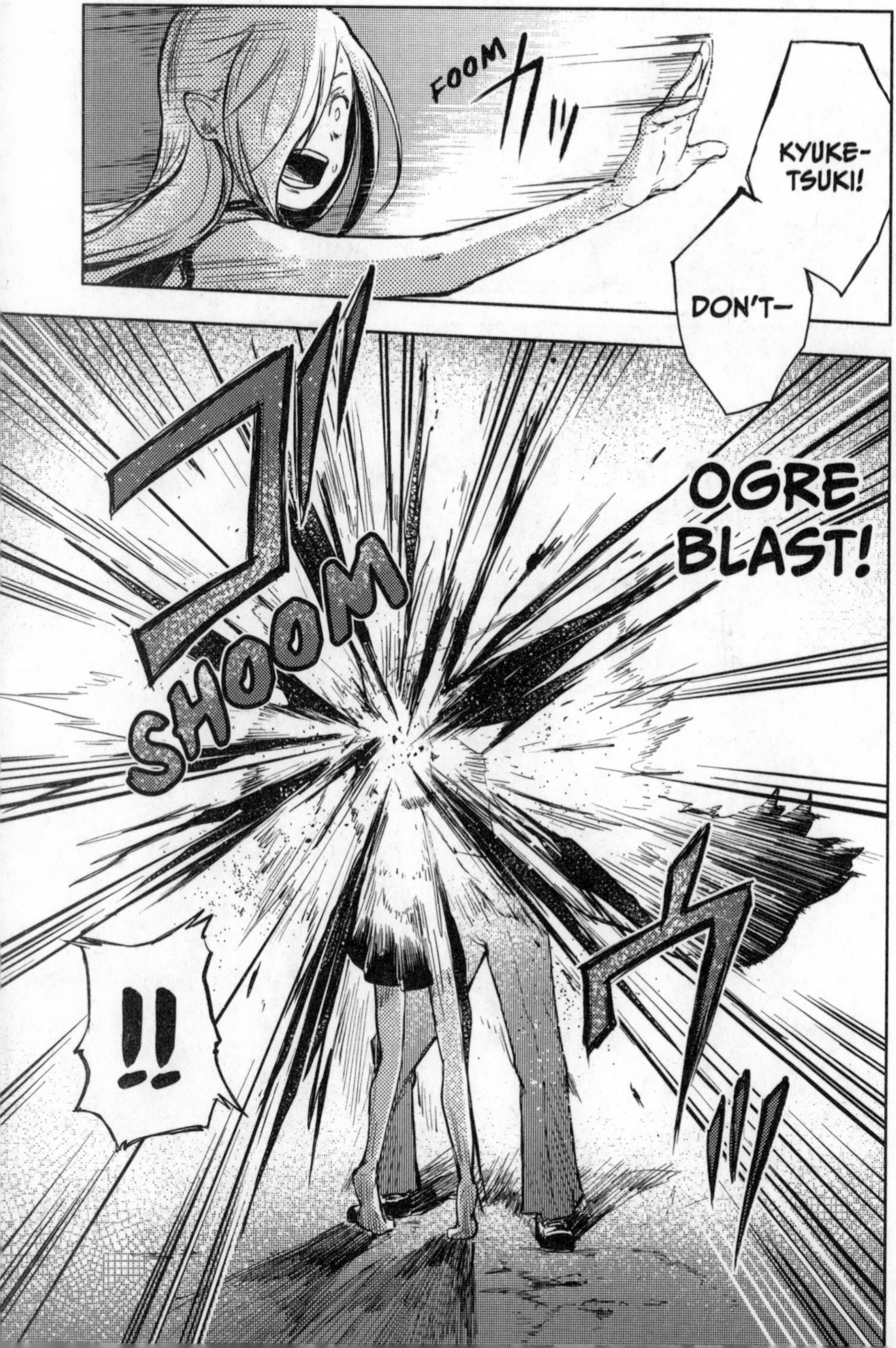
KYUKE-TSUKI!
DON'T–
FOOM
OGRE BLAST!
SHOOM
!!

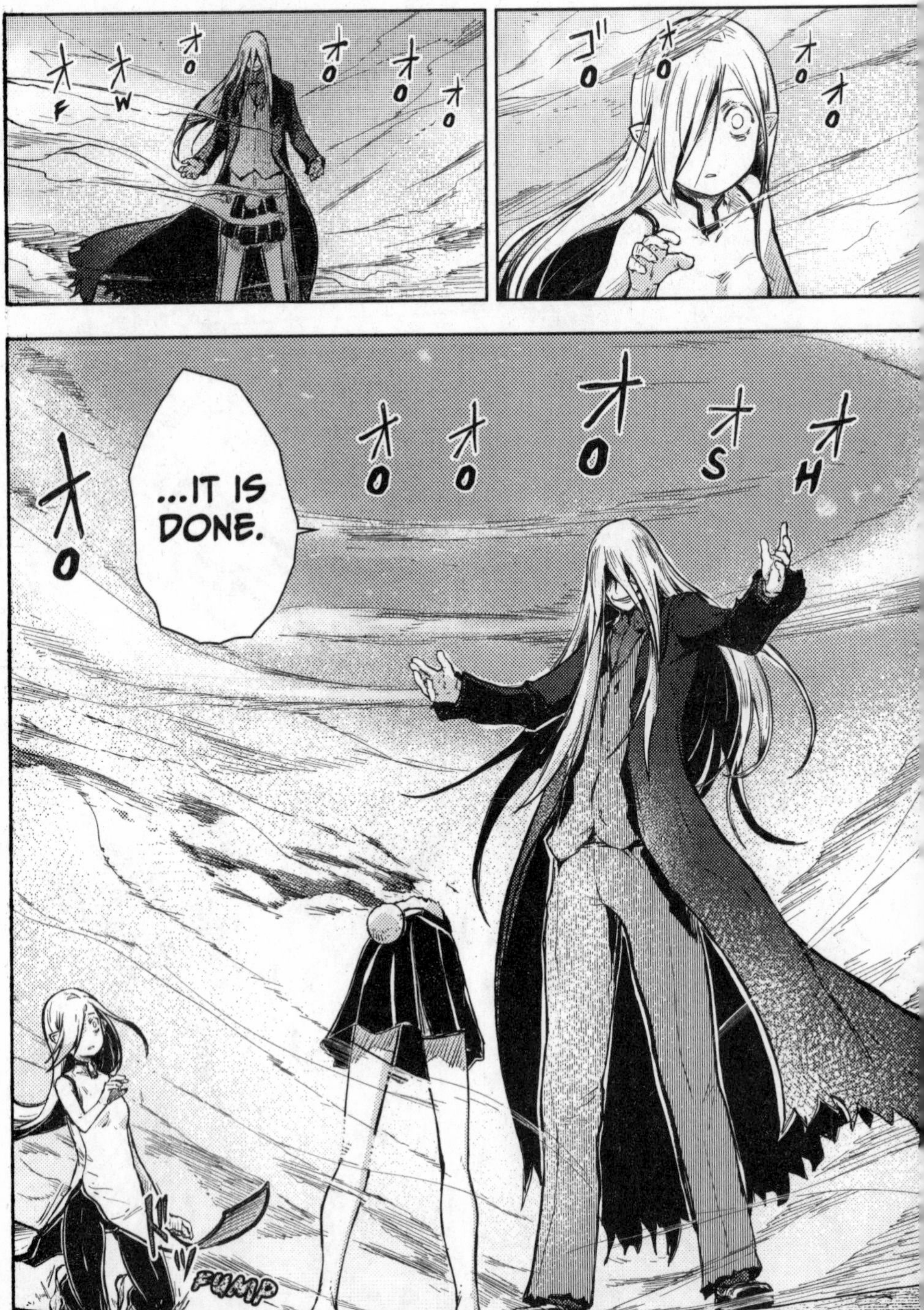

ゴオオオオ
OOOO
オオオオオオ
FWOOOO
オオオオオオ
OOOOSH
...IT IS DONE.
FUMP

PEACH BOY
RIVERSIDE

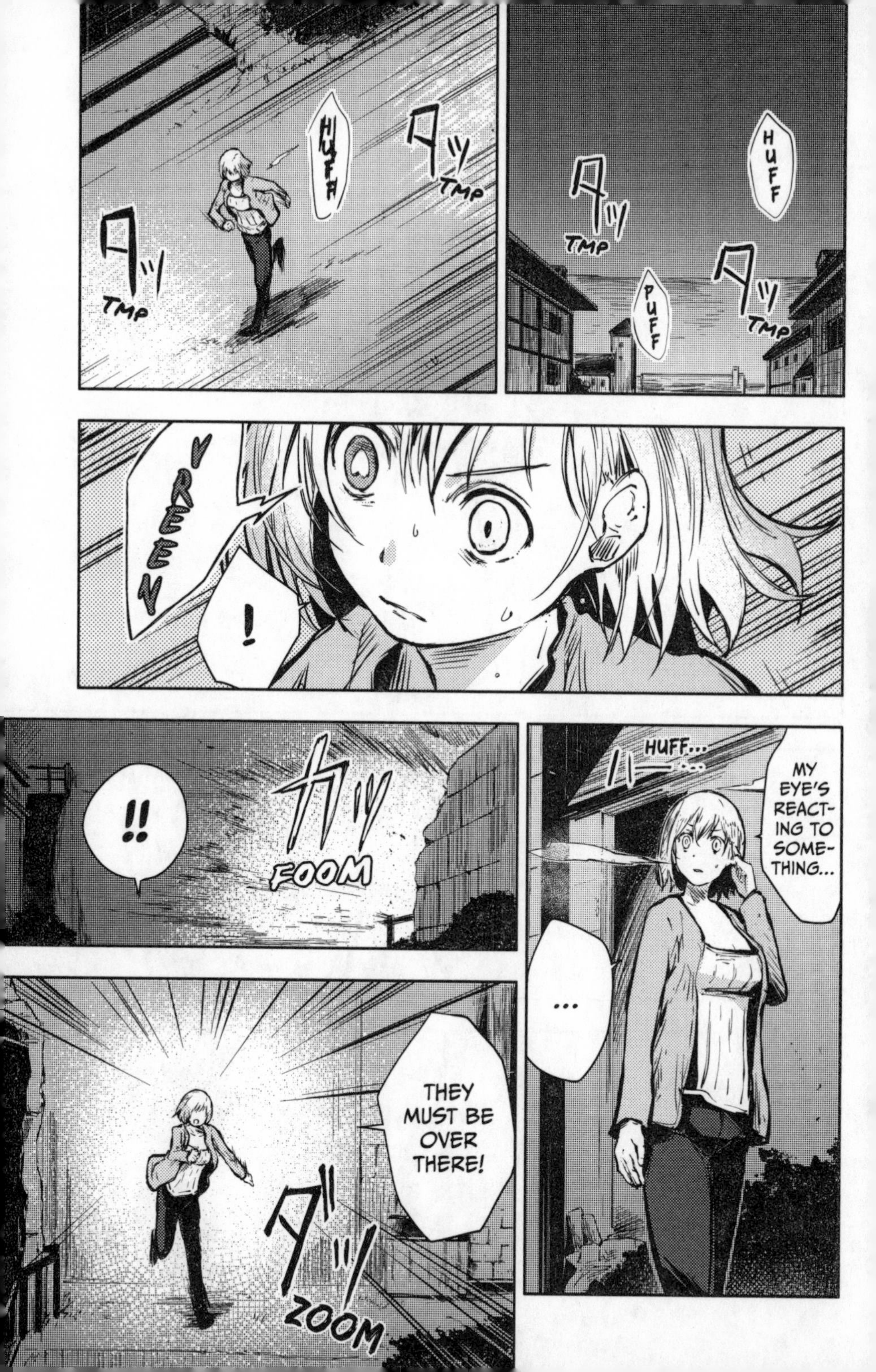
HUFF
TMP
PUFF
TMP
HUFF
TMP
TMP
VREEN
!
HUFF...
MY EYE'S REACTING TO SOMETHING...
...
!!
FOOM
THEY MUST BE OVER THERE!
ZOOM

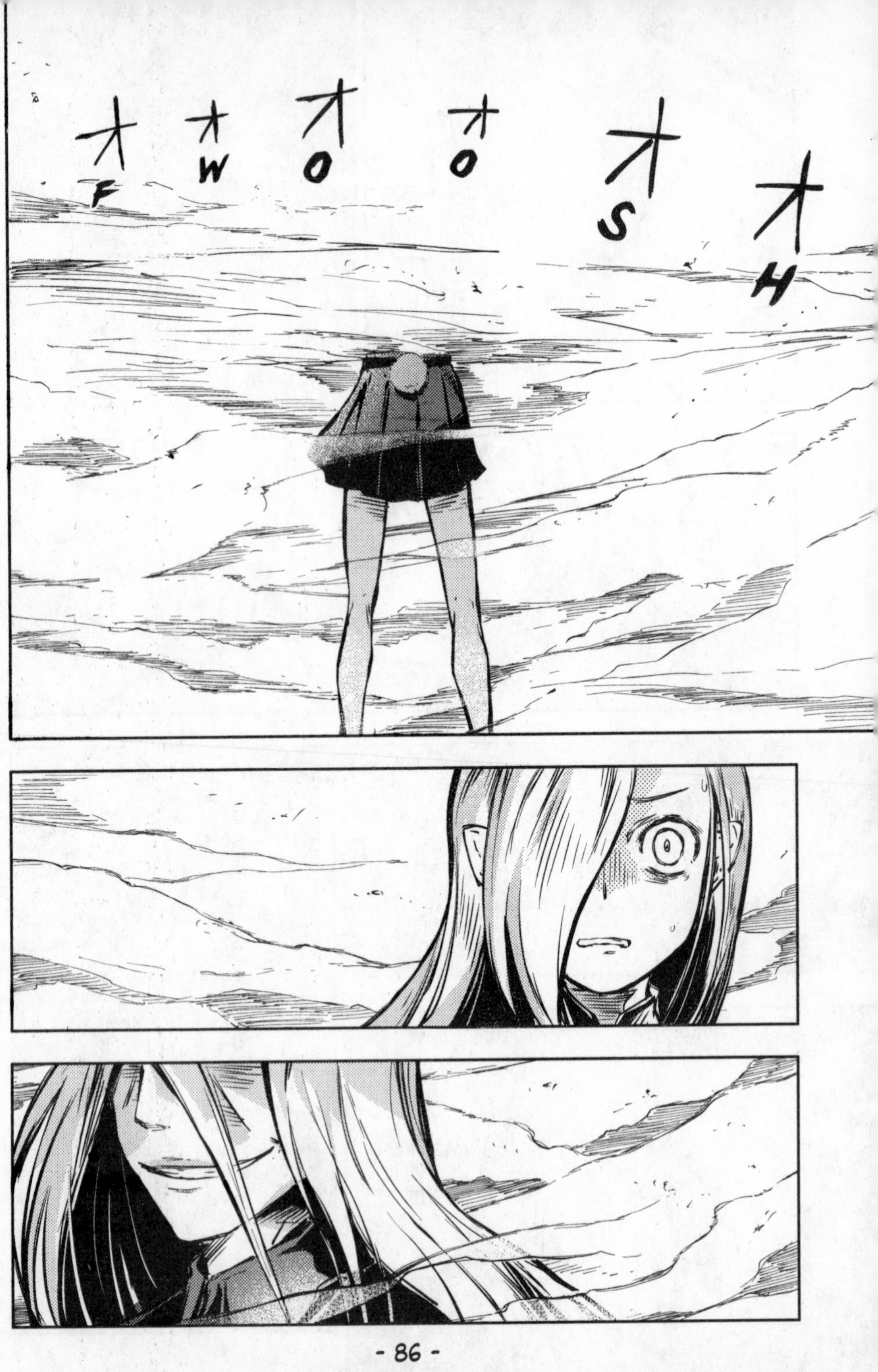
FWOOSH

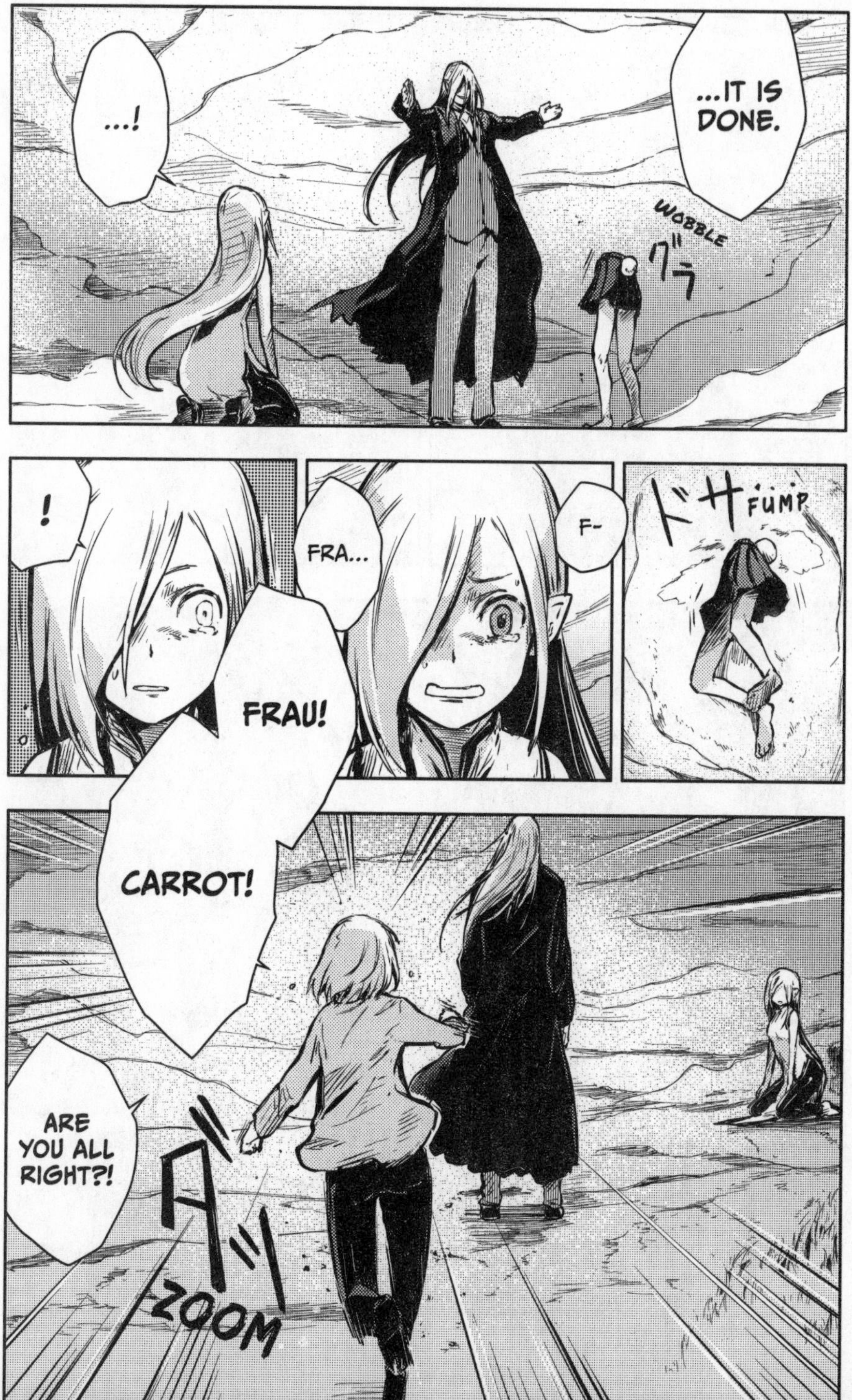
...IT IS DONE.
WOBBLE
グラ
...!
ドサ FUMP
F-
FRA...
!
FRAU!
CARROT!
ARE YOU ALL RIGHT?!
ZOOM

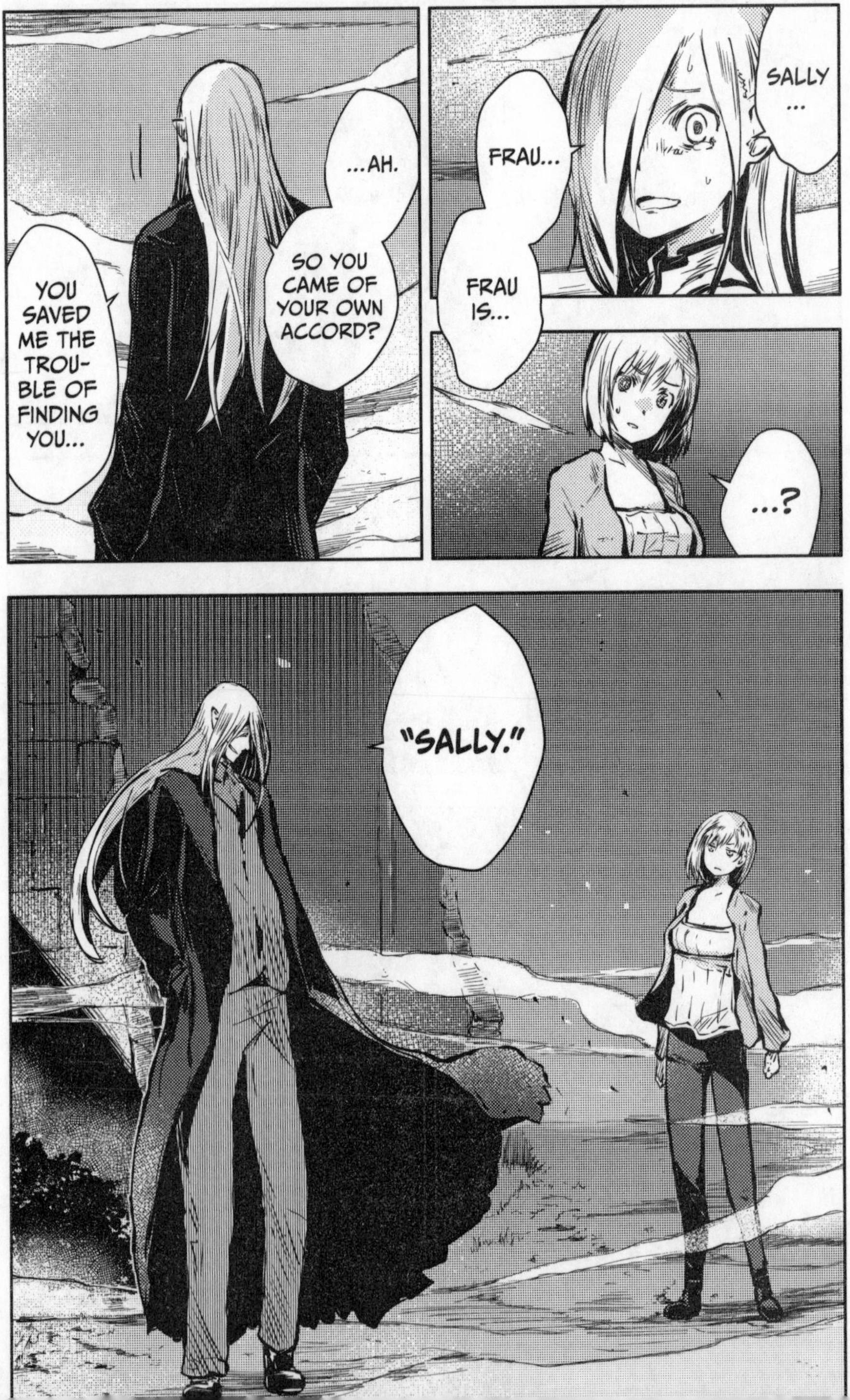
SALLY ...
FRAU...
FRAU IS...
...?
...AH.
SO YOU CAME OF YOUR OWN ACCORD?
YOU SAVED ME THE TROUBLE OF FINDING YOU...
"SALLY."

CHAPTER 14: HEAVEN AND TRUE IDENTITY

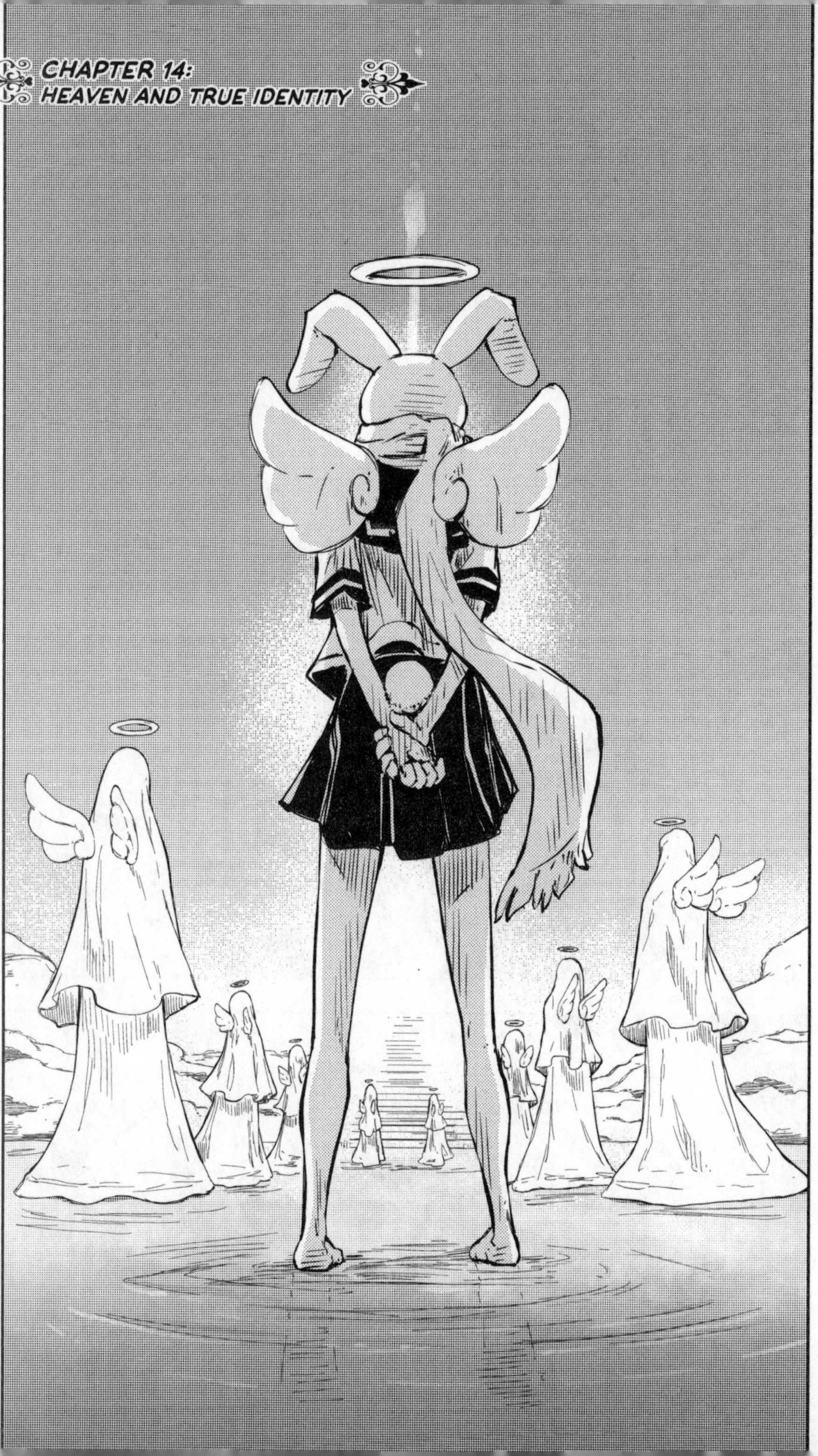

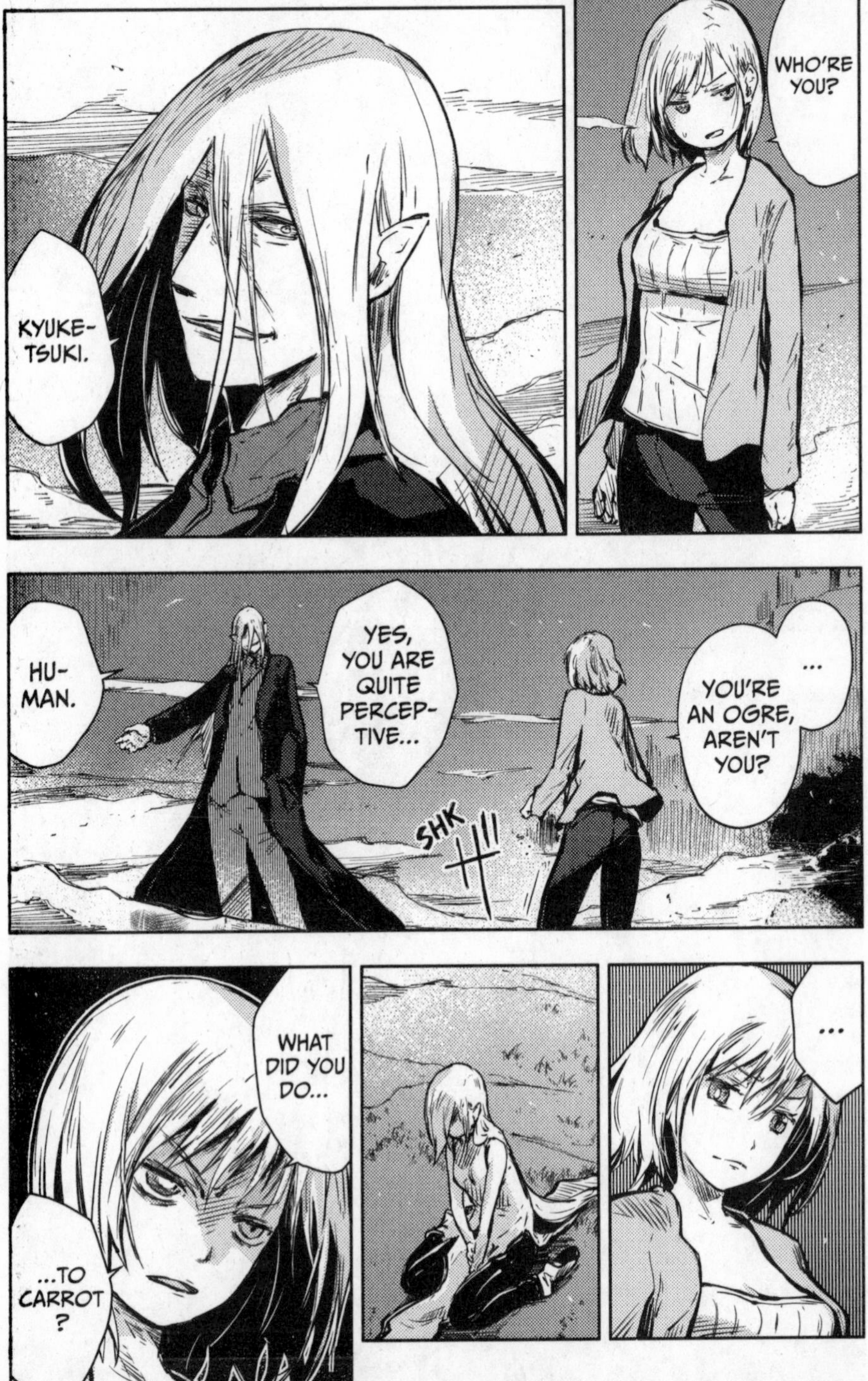
WHO'RE YOU?
KYUKE-TSUKI.
...
YOU'RE AN OGRE, AREN'T YOU?
YES, YOU ARE QUITE PERCEP-TIVE...
HU-MAN.
SHK
...
WHAT DID YOU DO...
...TO CARROT?

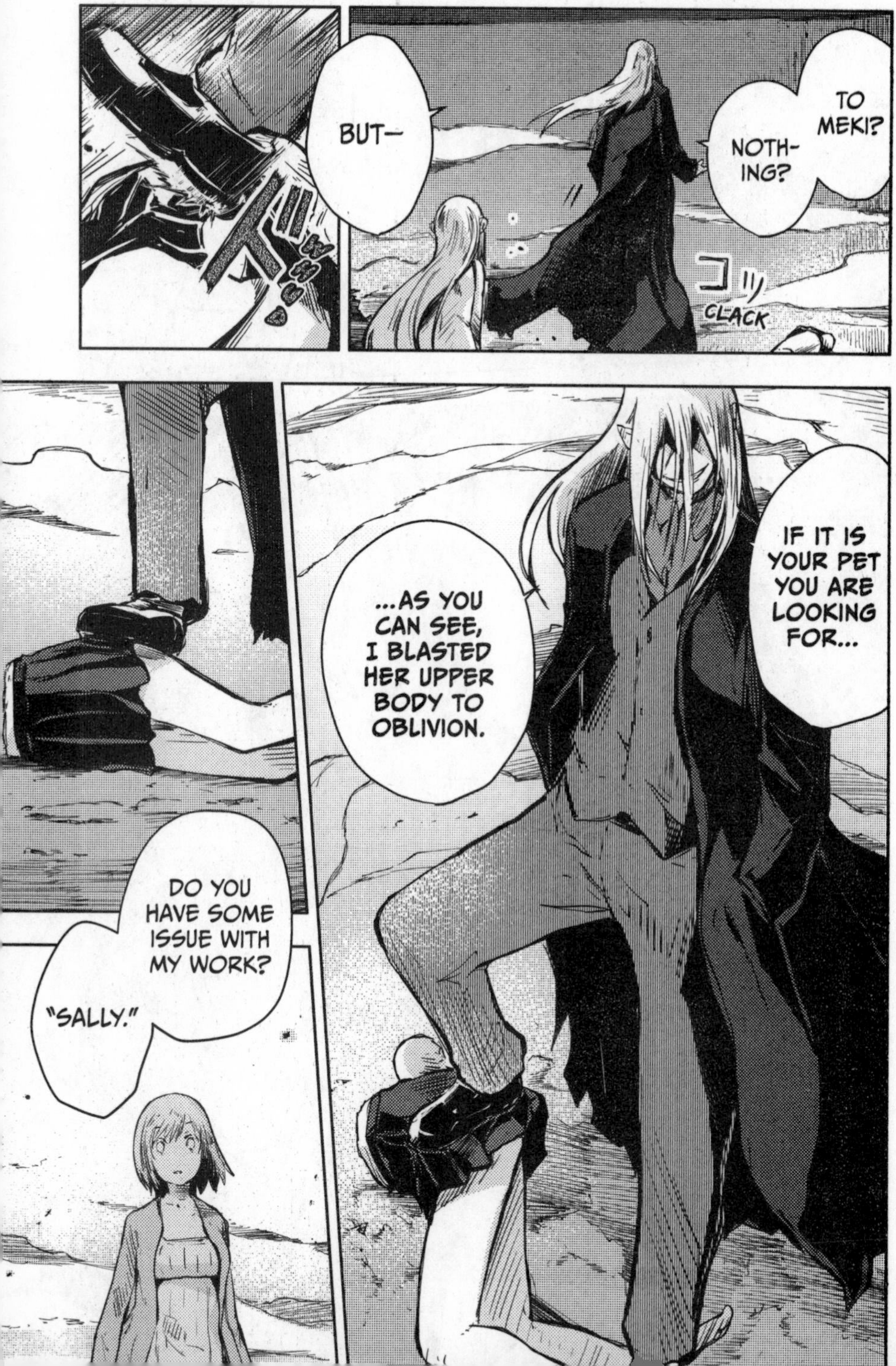
TO MEKI?
NOTHING?
コッ
CLACK
BUT—
IF IT IS YOUR PET YOU ARE LOOKING FOR...
...AS YOU CAN SEE, I BLASTED HER UPPER BODY TO OBLIVION.
DO YOU HAVE SOME ISSUE WITH MY WORK?
"SALLY."

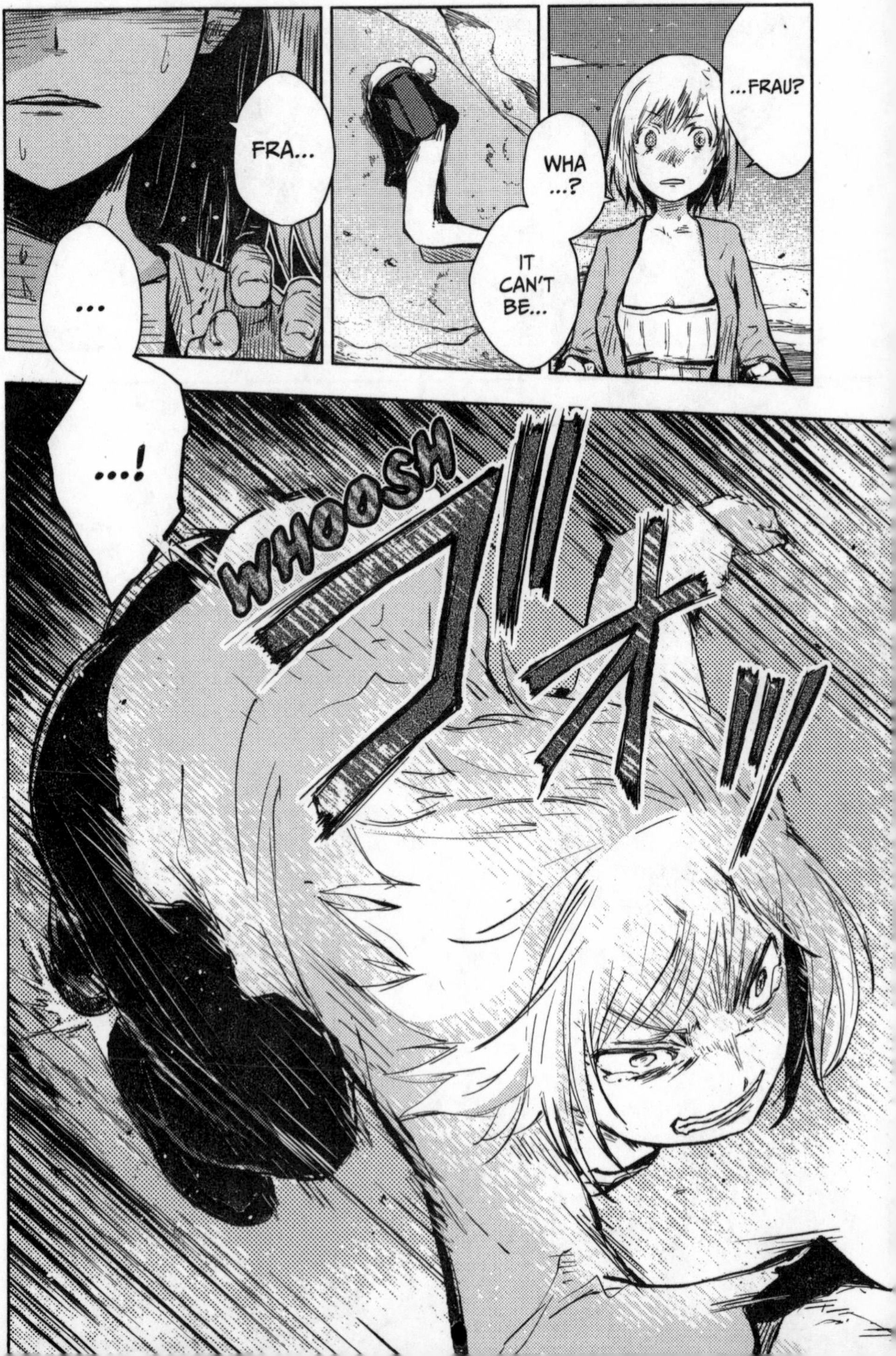
...FRAU?
WHA ...?
IT CAN'T BE...
FRA...
...
...!
WHOOSH

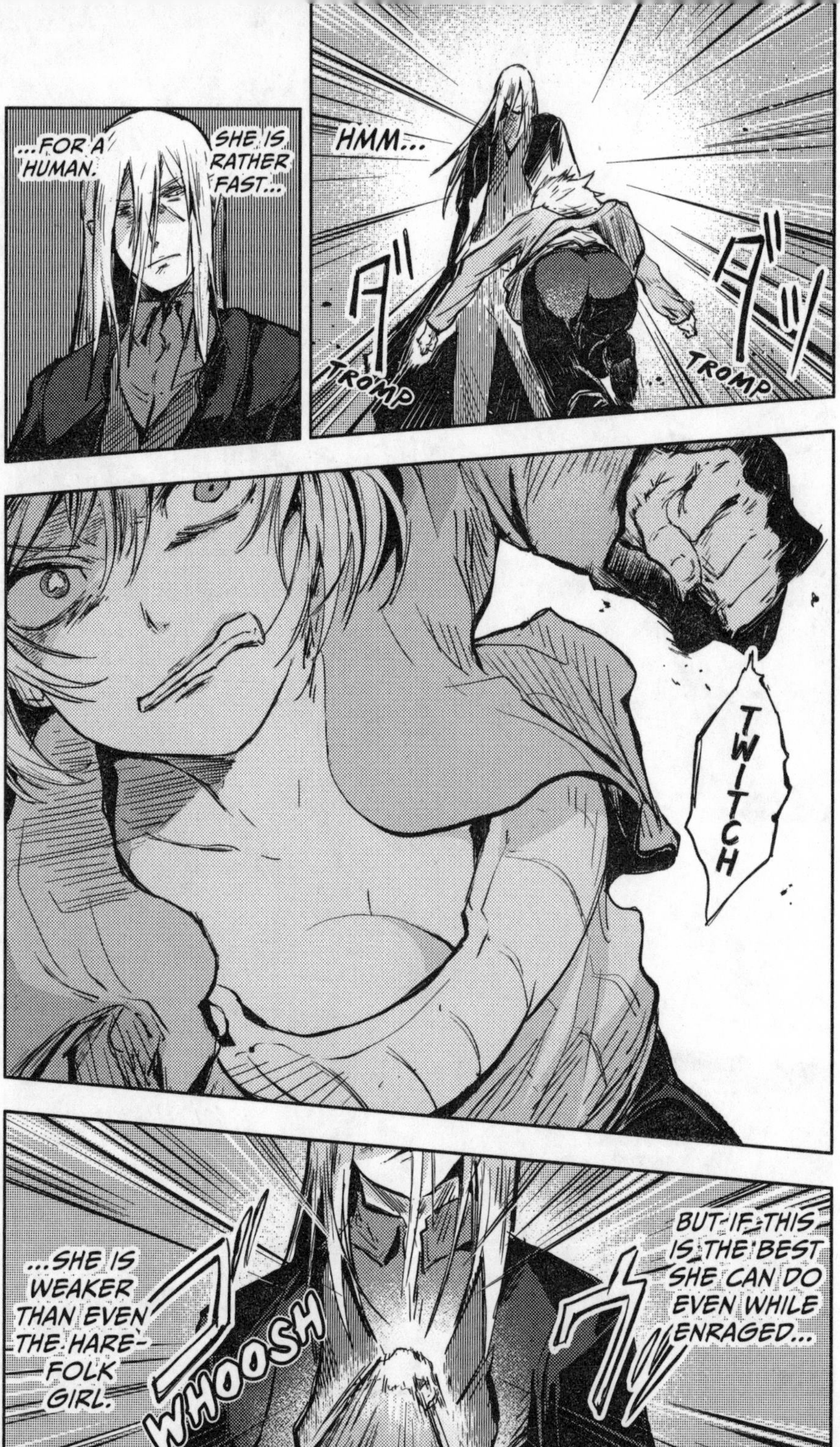
HMM...
ダッ
TROMP
TROMP
SHE IS RATHER FAST...
...FOR A HUMAN.
TWITCH
BUT IF THIS IS THE BEST SHE CAN DO EVEN WHILE ENRAGED...
WHOOSH
...SHE IS WEAKER THAN EVEN THE HARE-FOLK GIRL.

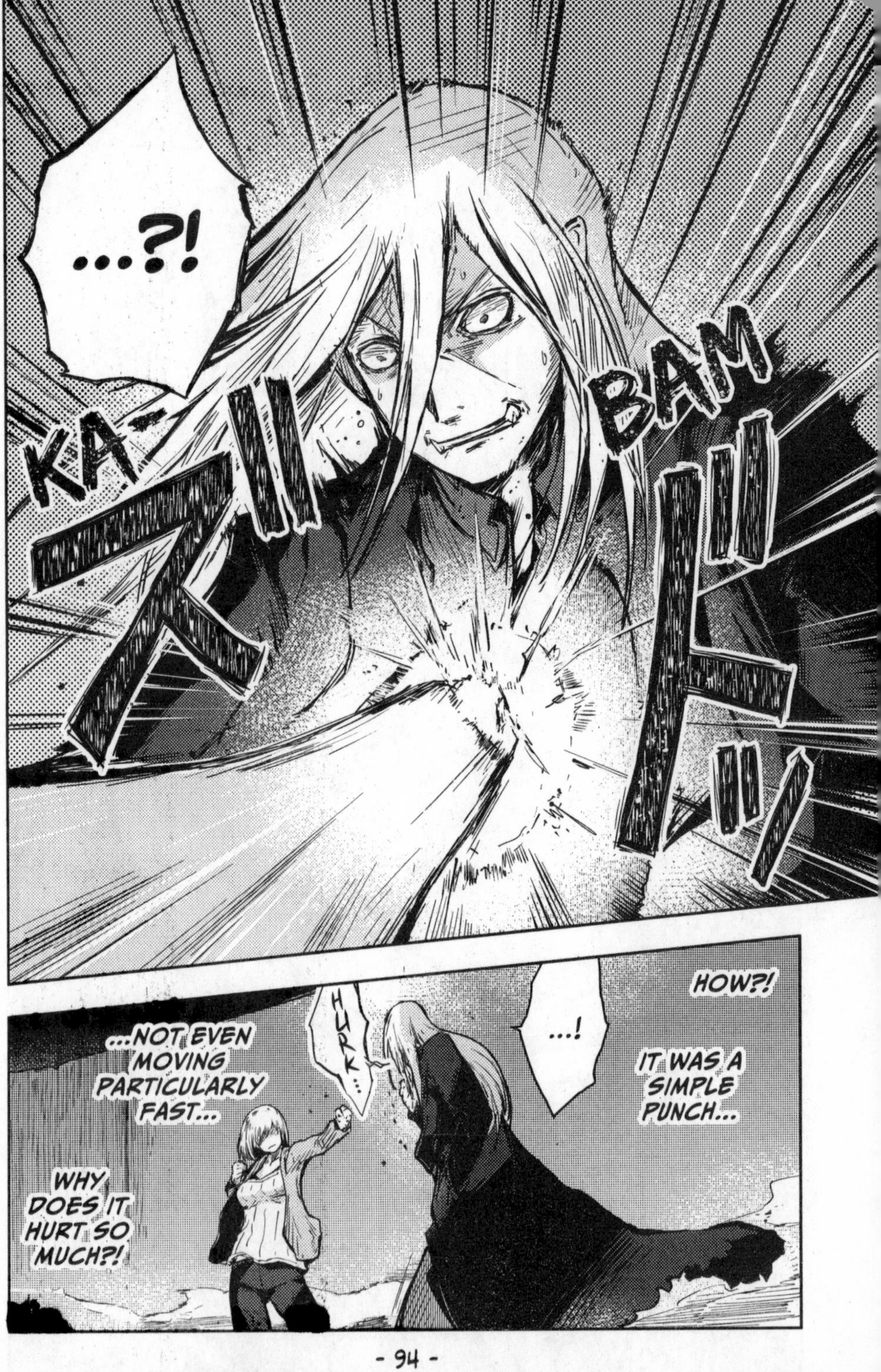
...?!
BAM
KA-
HOW?!
IT WAS A SIMPLE PUNCH...
...!
HURK...
...NOT EVEN MOVING PARTICULARLY FAST...
WHY DOES IT HURT SO MUCH?!

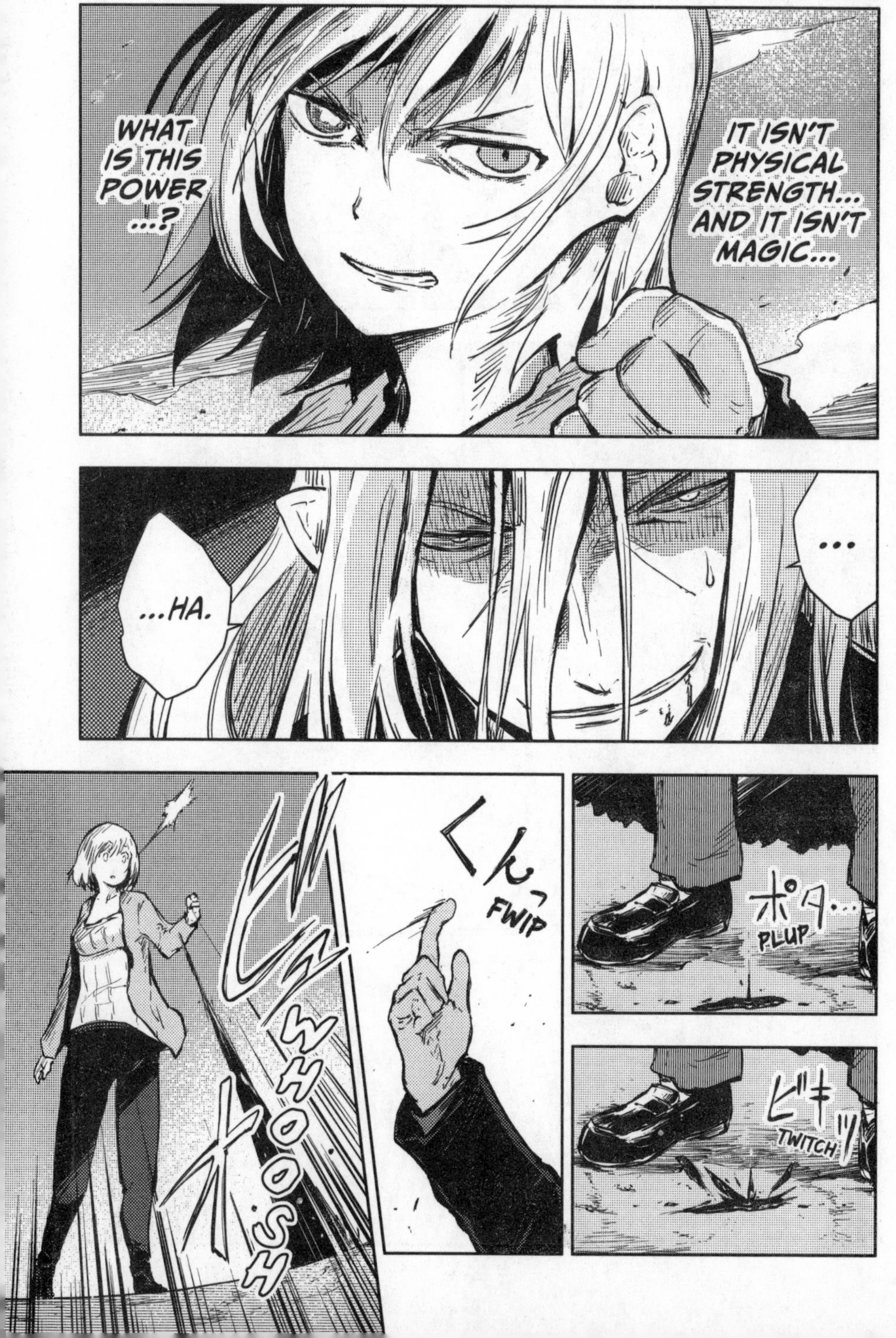
IT ISN'T PHYSICAL STRENGTH... AND IT ISN'T MAGIC...
WHAT IS THIS POWER ...?
...
...HA.
ポタ...
PLUP
ビキッ
TWITCH
くんっ
FWIP
WHOOSH

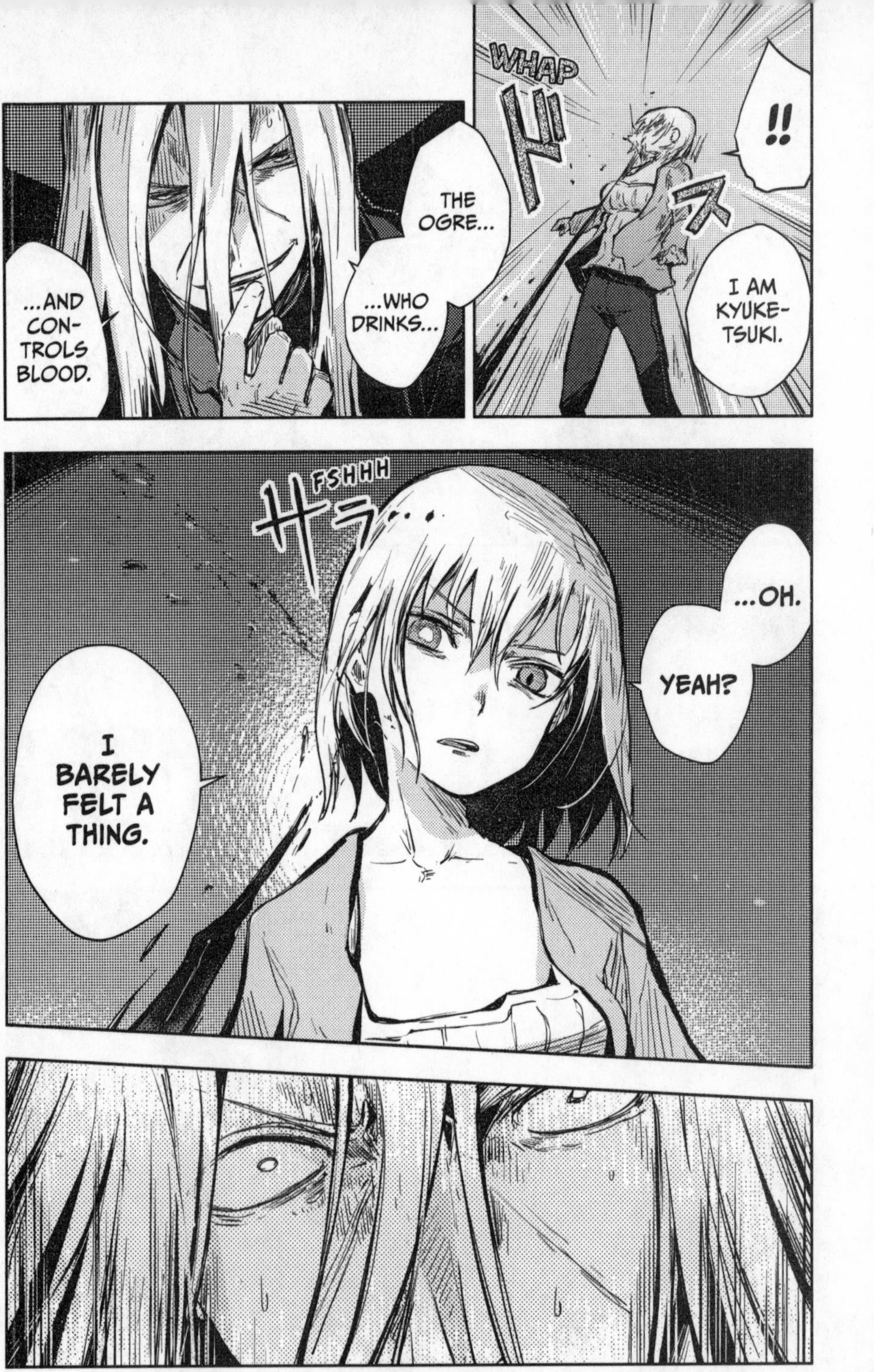
WHAP
!!
I AM KYUKE-TSUKI.
THE OGRE...
...WHO DRINKS...
...AND CON-TROLS BLOOD.
FSHHH
...OH.
YEAH?
I BARELY FELT A THING.

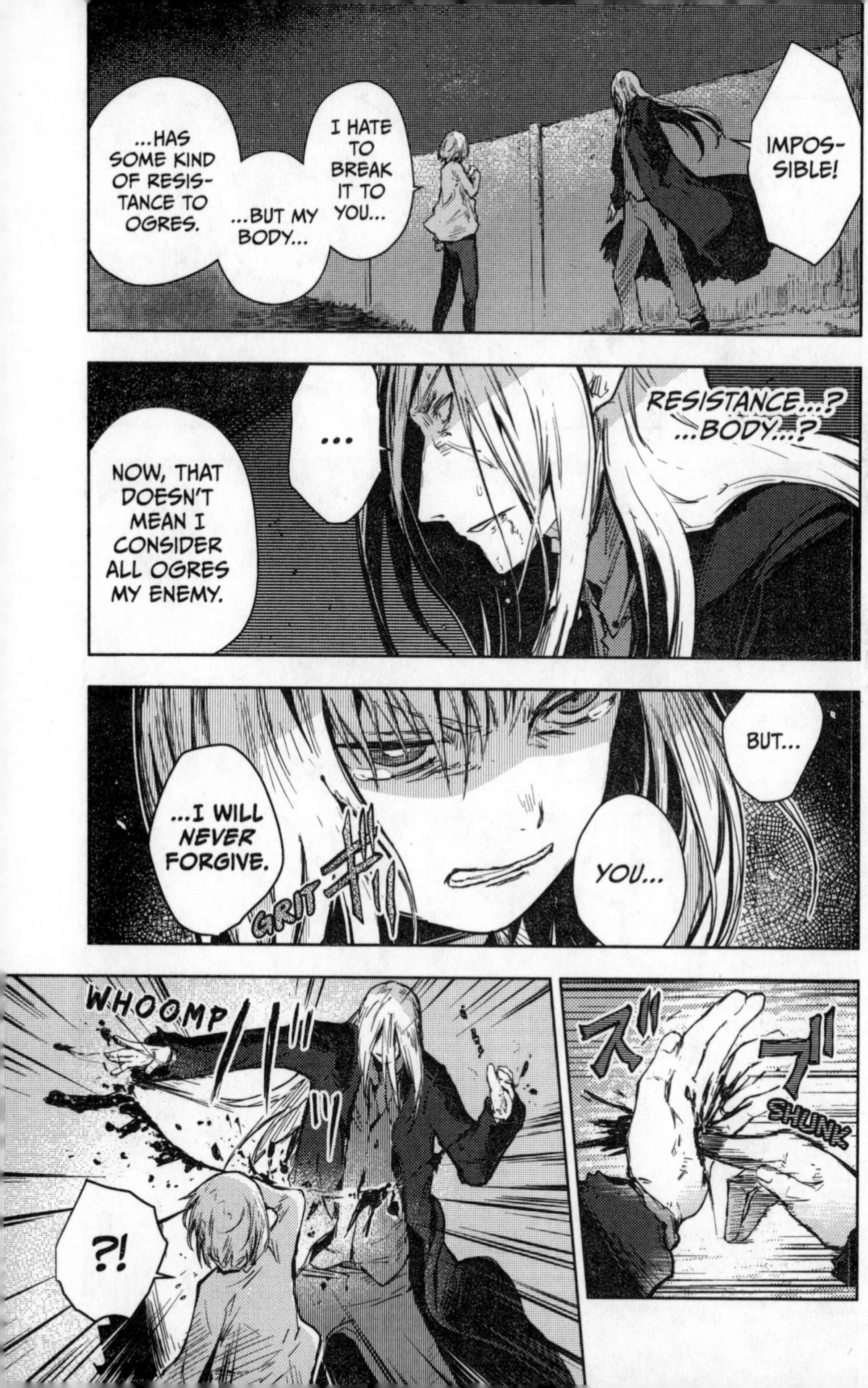
IMPOSSIBLE!
I HATE TO BREAK IT TO YOU...
...BUT MY BODY...
...HAS SOME KIND OF RESISTANCE TO OGRES.
RESISTANCE...? ...BODY...?
...
NOW, THAT DOESN'T MEAN I CONSIDER ALL OGRES MY ENEMY.
BUT...
YOU...
...I WILL NEVER FORGIVE.
GRIT
ズブ
SHUNK
WHOOMP
?!

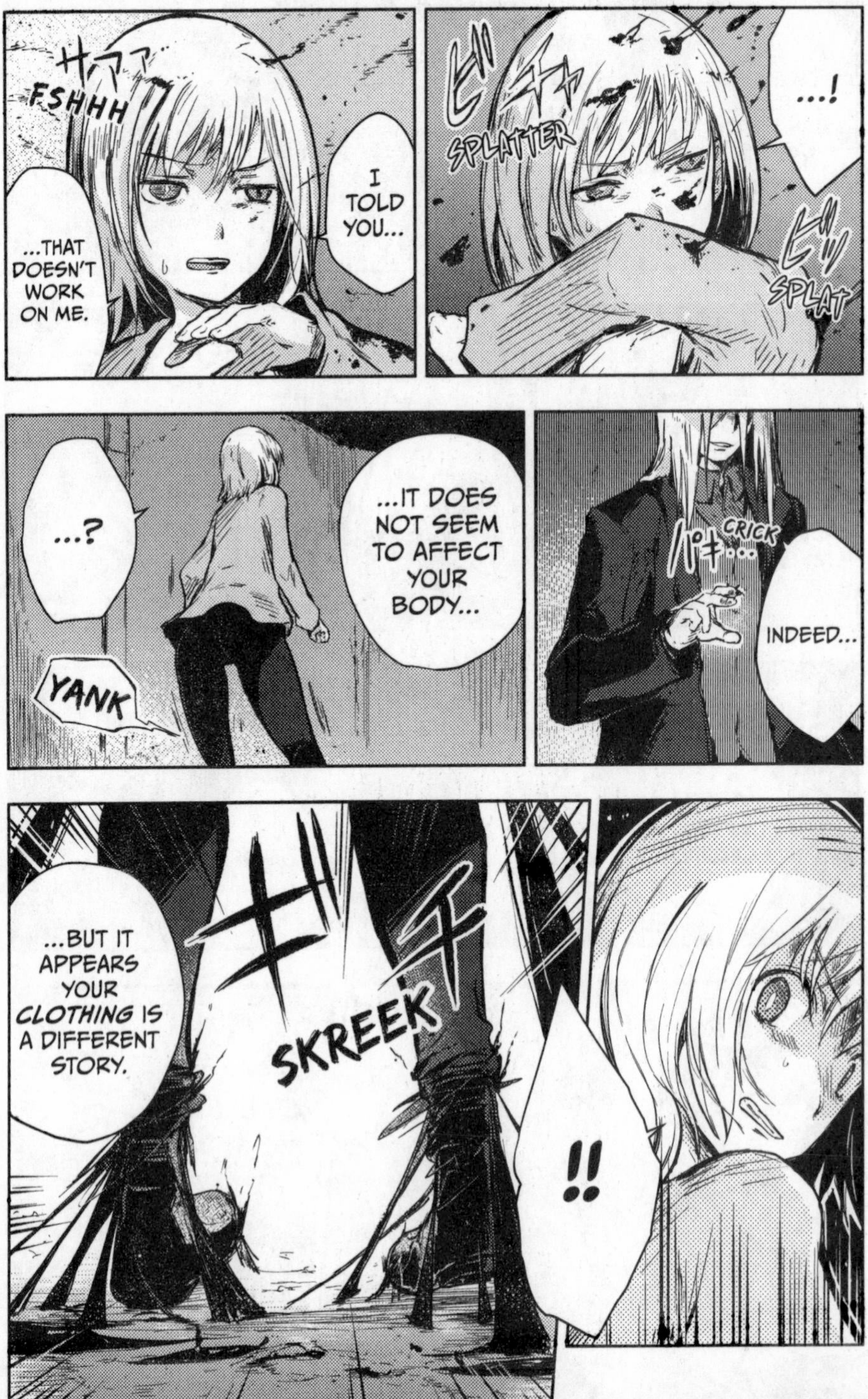
ビチャ
SPLATTER
...!
ビッ
SPLAT
サァァ...
FSHHH
I TOLD YOU...
...THAT DOESN'T WORK ON ME.
パキ...
CRICK
INDEED...
...IT DOES NOT SEEM TO AFFECT YOUR BODY...
...?
YANK
!!
...BUT IT APPEARS YOUR *CLOTHING* IS A DIFFERENT STORY.
ギチ
SKREEK

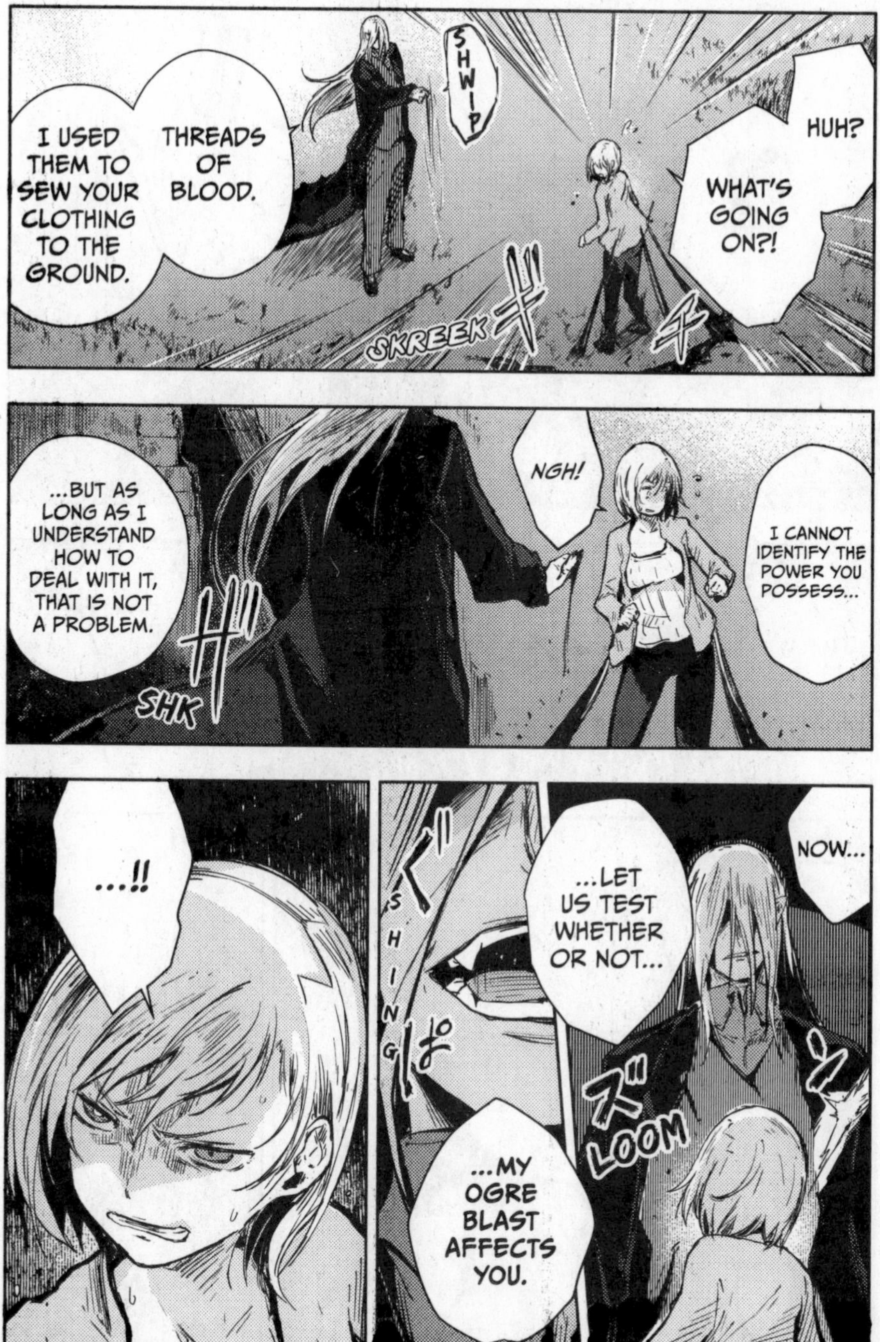
HUH?
WHAT'S GOING ON?!
SHWIP
THREADS OF BLOOD.
I USED THEM TO SEW YOUR CLOTHING TO THE GROUND.
SKREEK
I CANNOT IDENTIFY THE POWER YOU POSSESS...
NGH!
...BUT AS LONG AS I UNDERSTAND HOW TO DEAL WITH IT, THAT IS NOT A PROBLEM.
SHK
NOW...
...LET US TEST WHETHER OR NOT...
SHING
...MY OGRE BLAST AFFECTS YOU.
LOOM
...!!

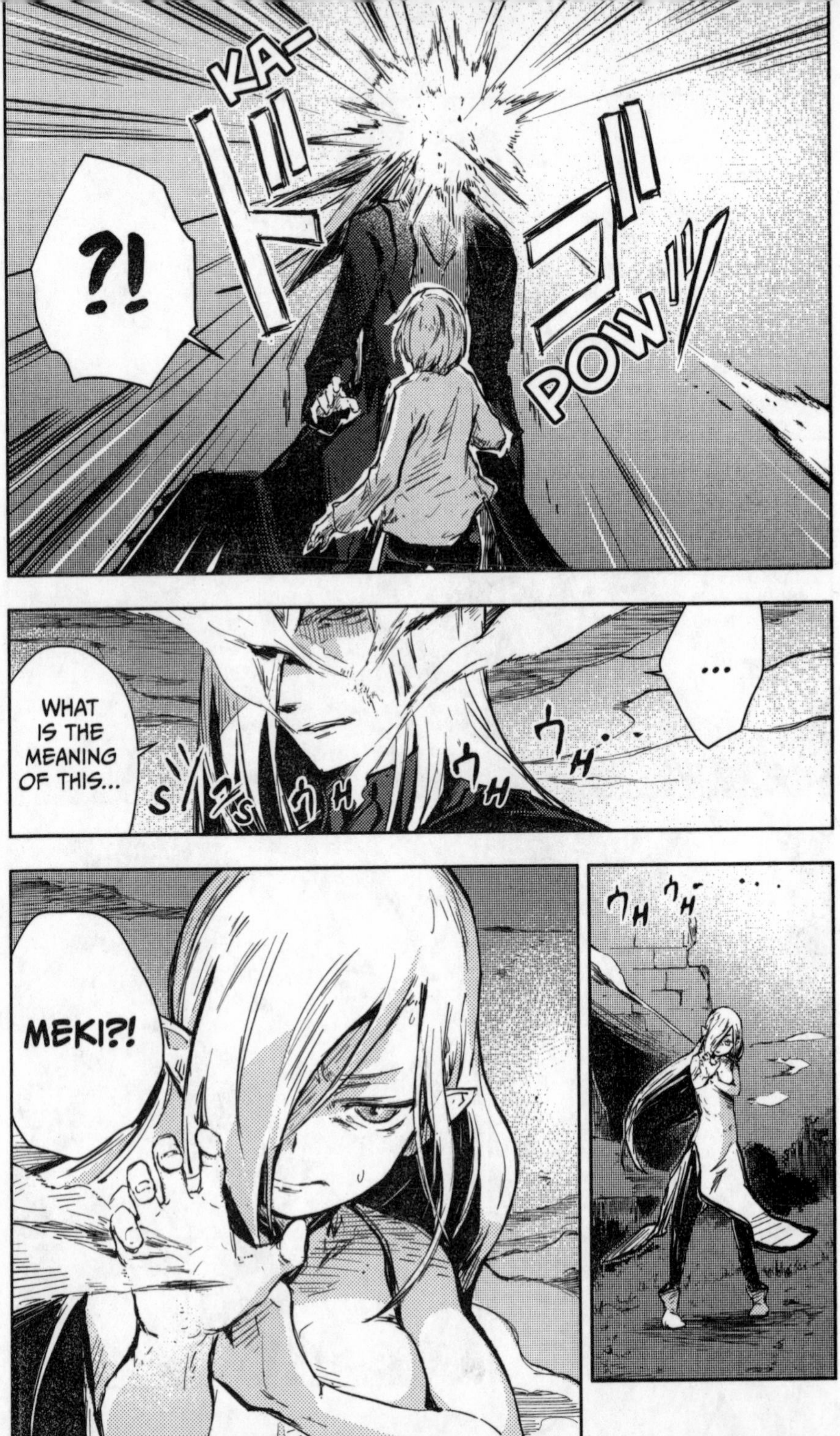
KA-
POW
?!
...
WHAT IS THE MEANING OF THIS...
MEKI?!

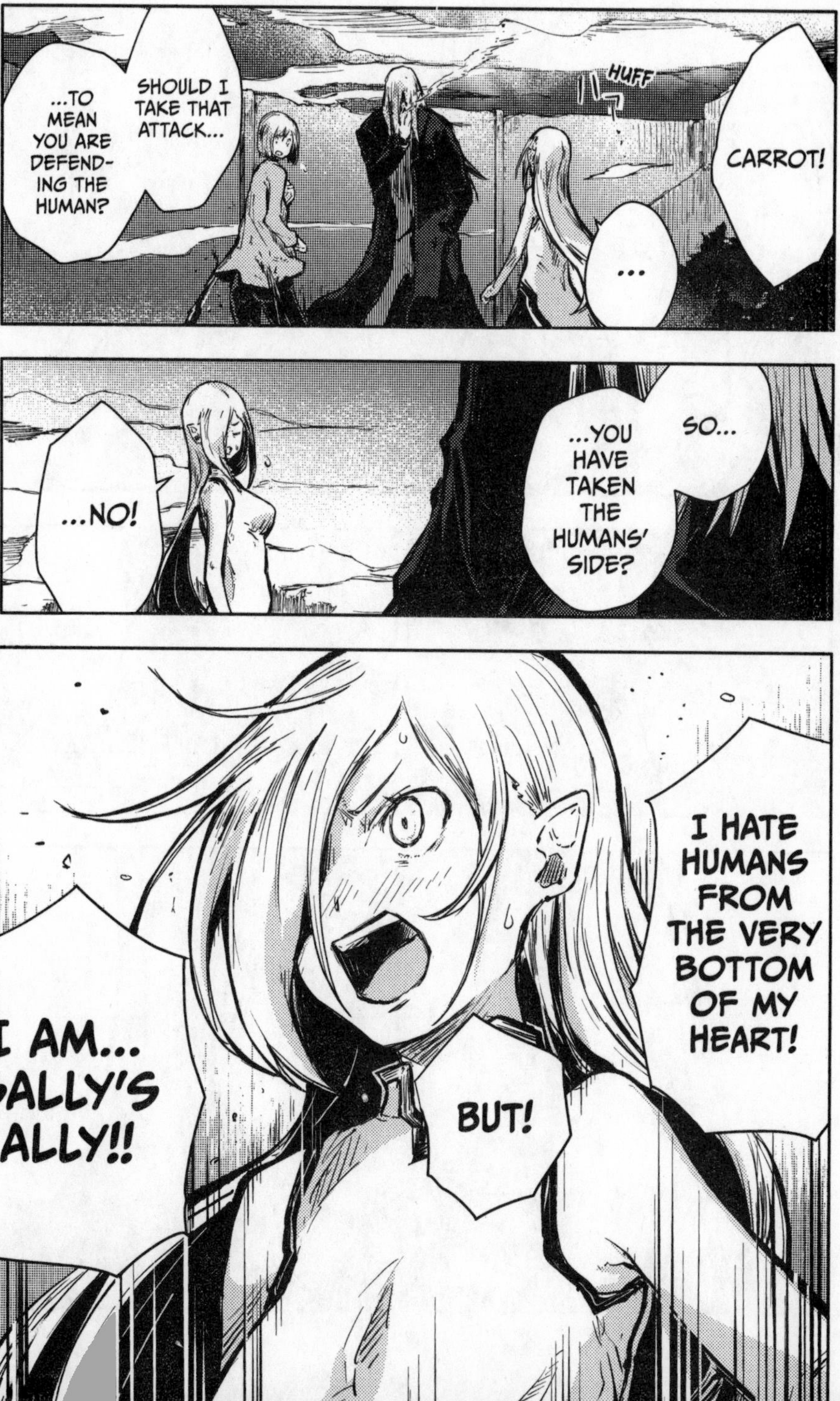
CARROT!
HUFF
...
SHOULD I TAKE THAT ATTACK...
...TO MEAN YOU ARE DEFEND-ING THE HUMAN?
SO...
...YOU HAVE TAKEN THE HUMANS' SIDE?
...NO!
I HATE HUMANS FROM THE VERY BOTTOM OF MY HEART!
BUT!
I AM... SALLY'S ALLY!!

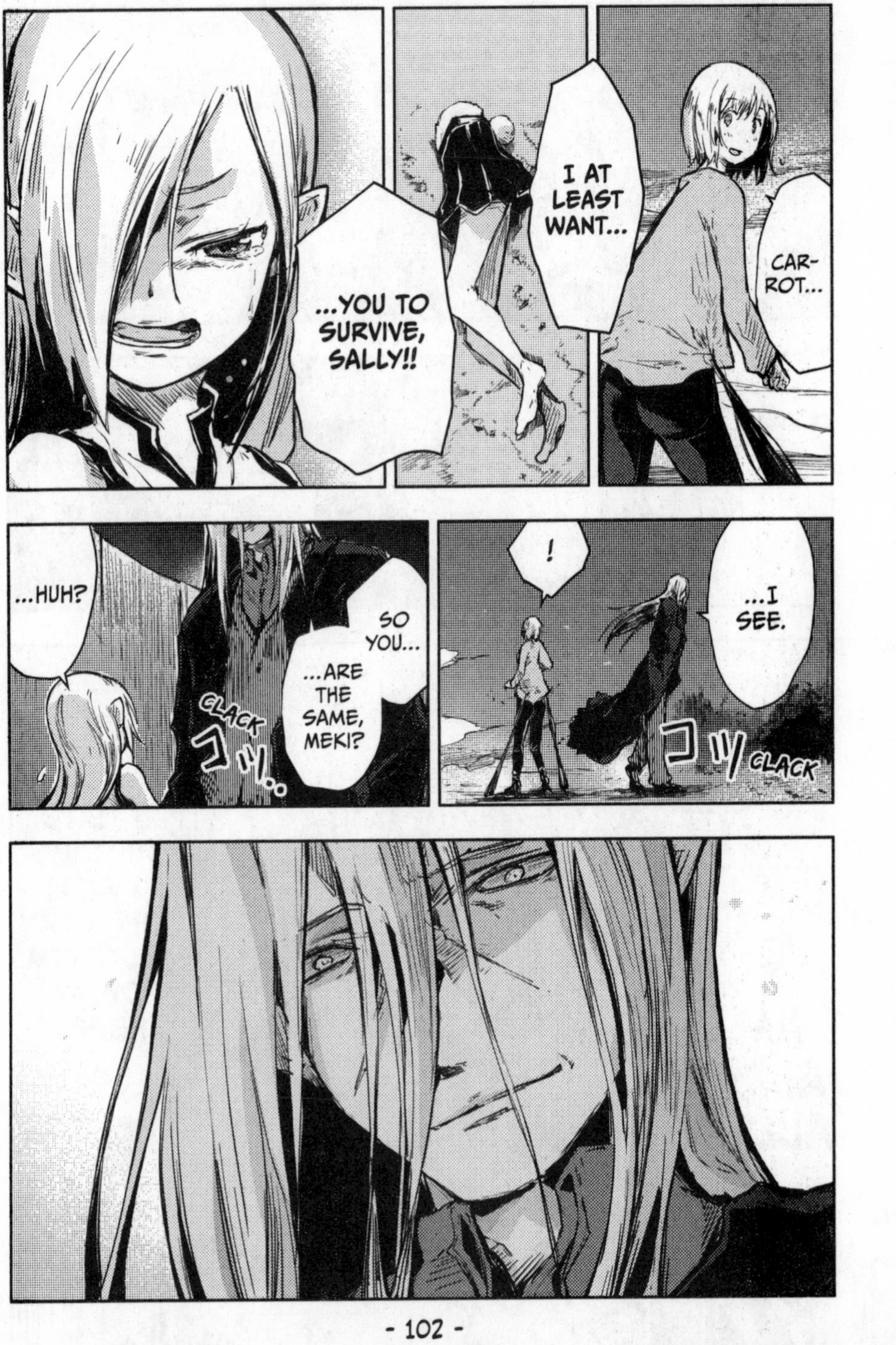
CAR-ROT...
I AT LEAST WANT...
...YOU TO SURVIVE, SALLY!!
...I SEE.
!
コツ CLACK
SO YOU...
...ARE THE SAME, MEKI?
...HUH?
CLACK コツ..

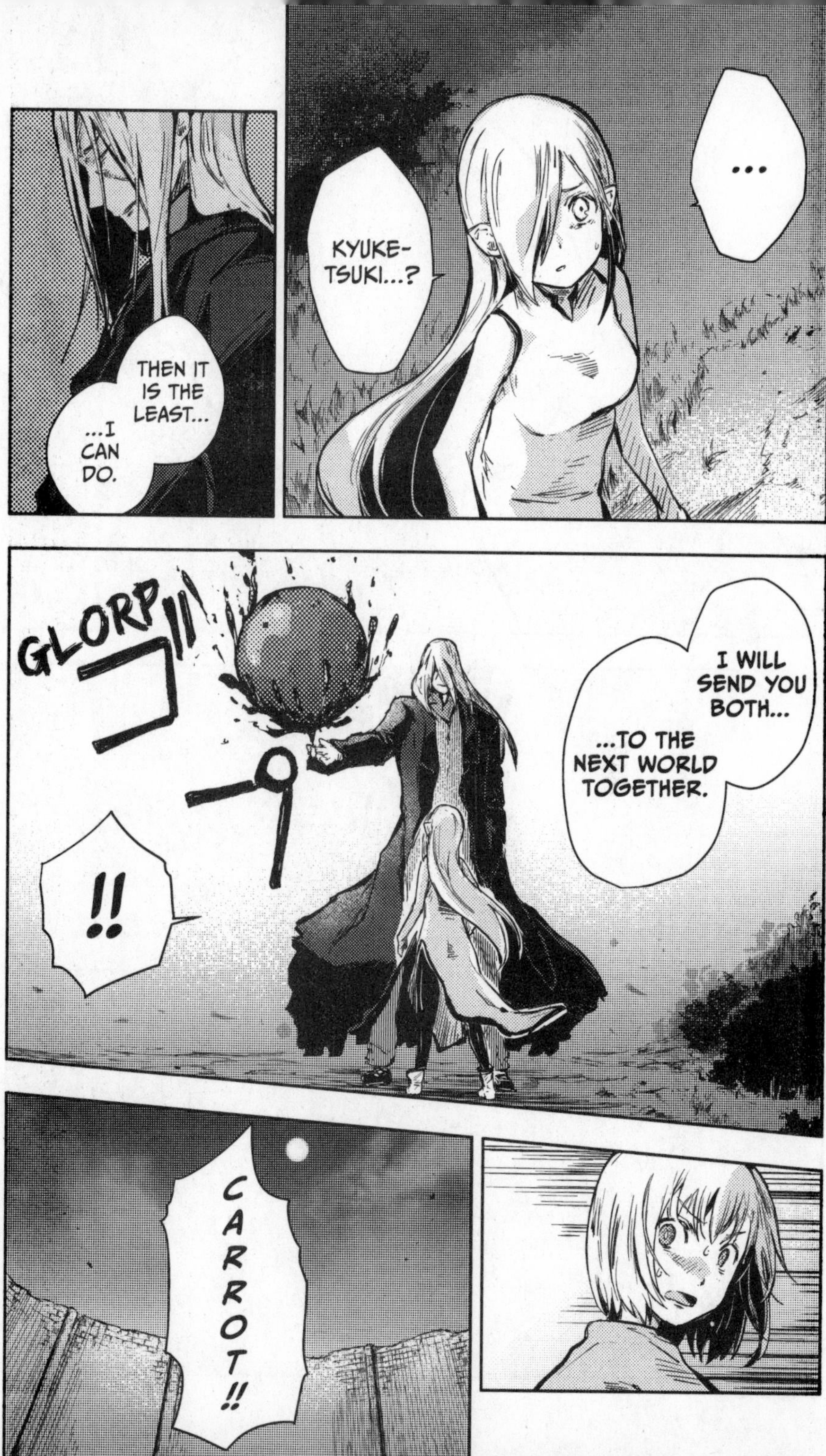
...
KYUKE-TSUKI...?
THEN IT IS THE LEAST...
...I CAN DO.
I WILL SEND YOU BOTH...
...TO THE NEXT WORLD TOGETHER.
GLORP
!!
CARROT!!

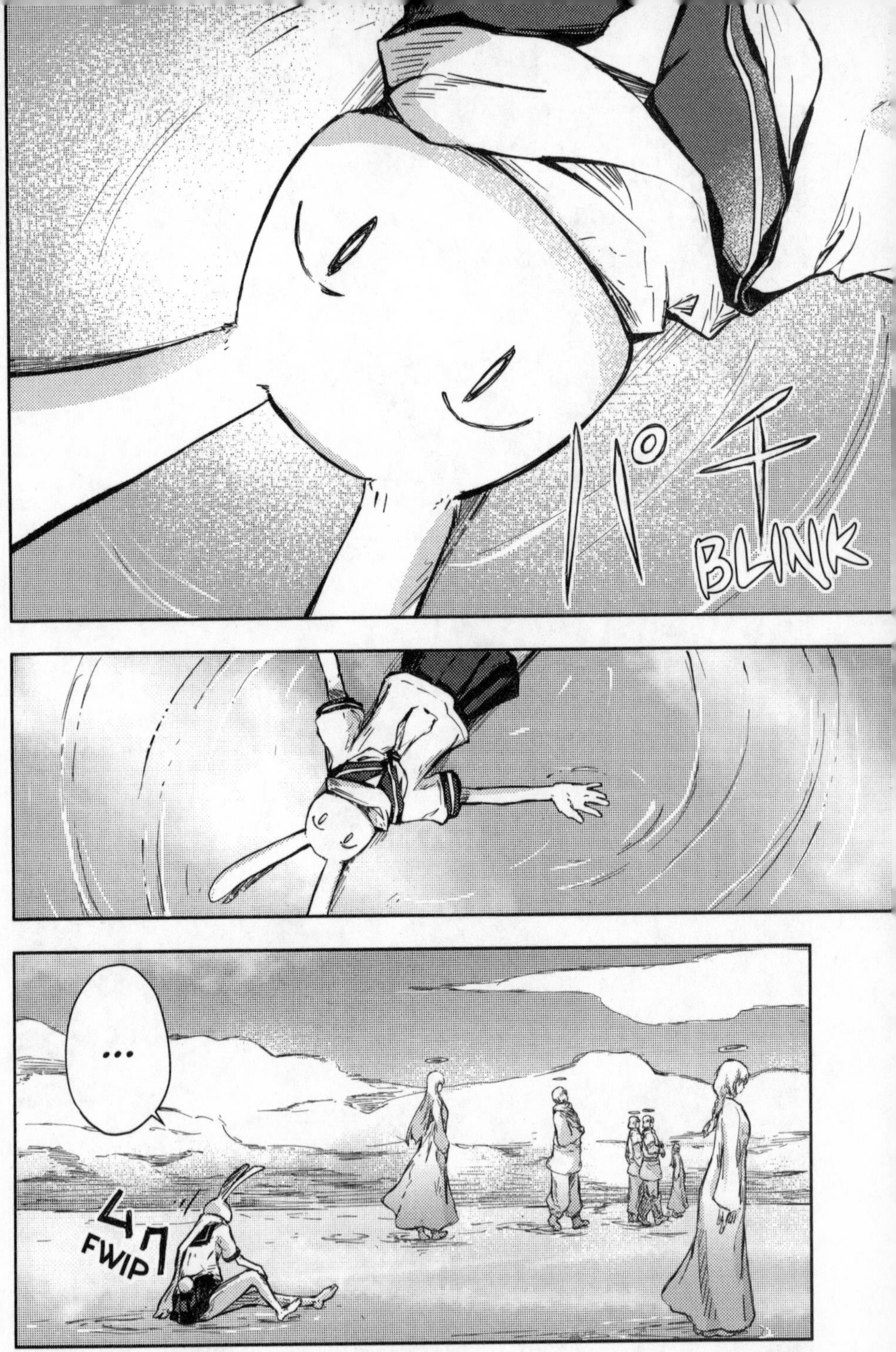
パチ
BLINK
...
FWIP

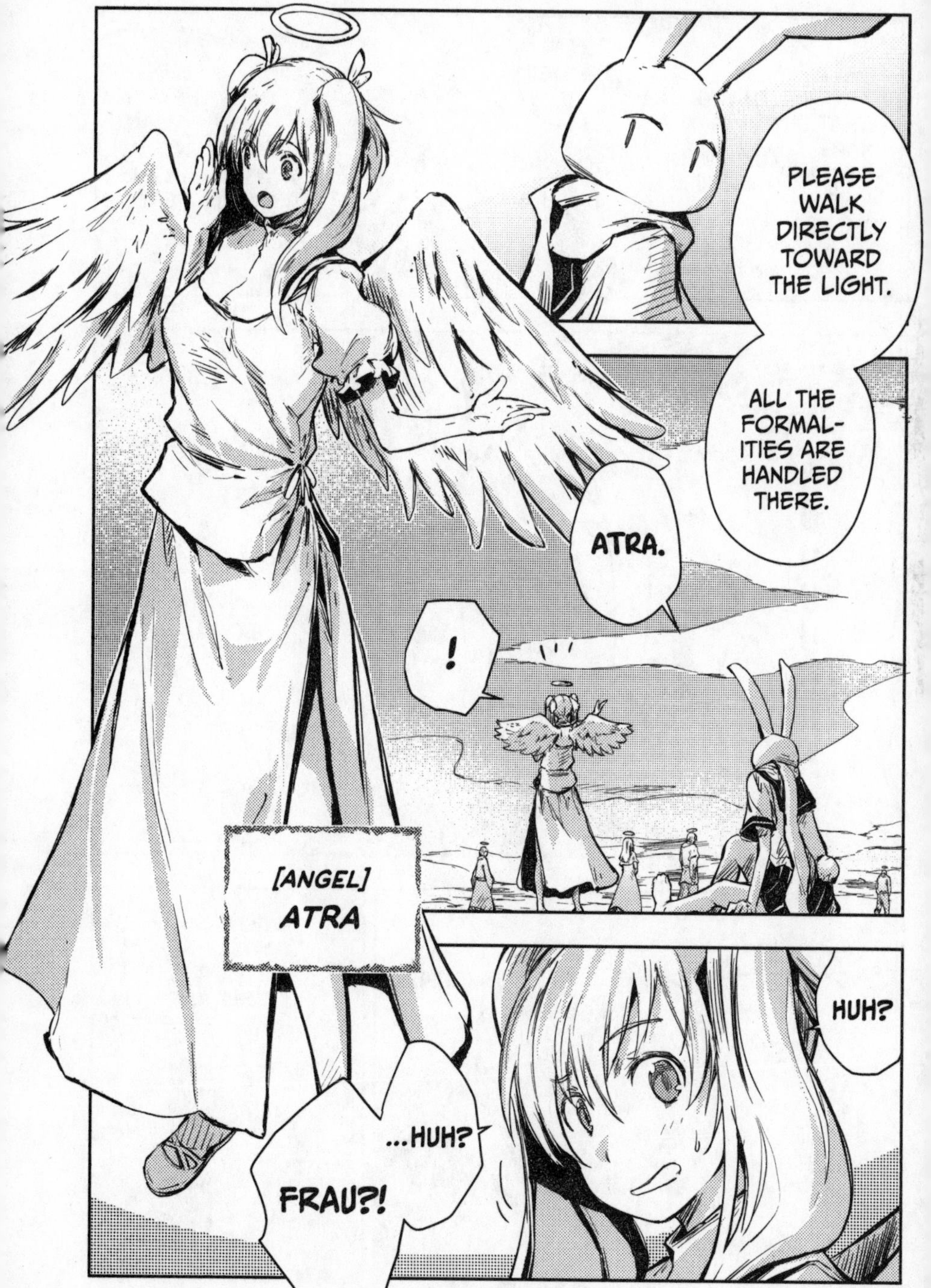
PLEASE WALK DIRECTLY TOWARD THE LIGHT.
ALL THE FORMAL-ITIES ARE HANDLED THERE.
ATRA.
!
[ANGEL] ATRA
HUH?
...HUH?
FRAU?!

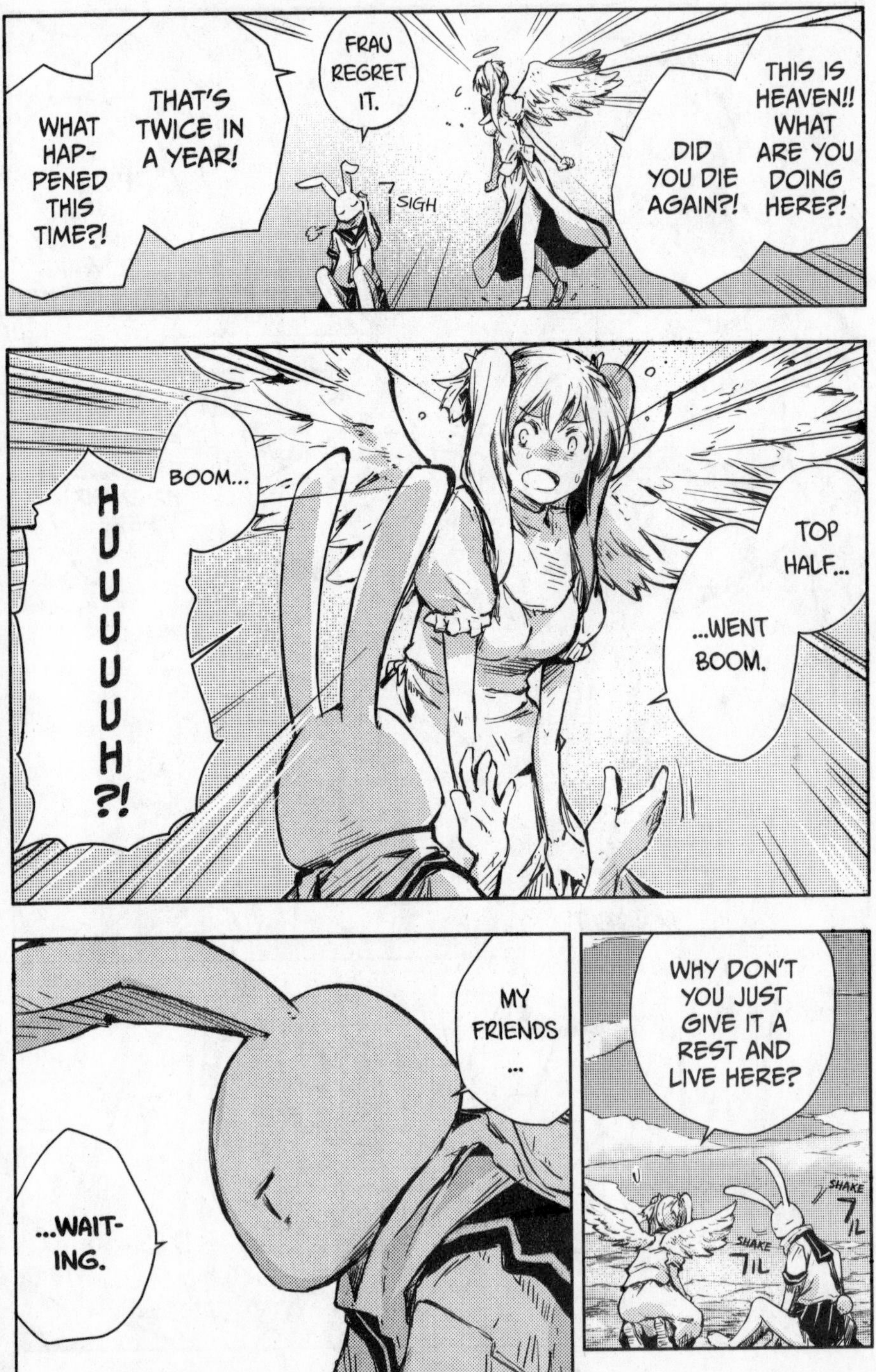
THIS IS HEAVEN!! WHAT ARE YOU DOING HERE?!
DID YOU DIE AGAIN?!
FRAU REGRET IT.
SIGH
THAT'S TWICE IN A YEAR!
WHAT HAP-PENED THIS TIME?!
TOP HALF...
...WENT BOOM.
BOOM...
HUUUUUUH?!
WHY DON'T YOU JUST GIVE IT A REST AND LIVE HERE?
SHAKE
SHAKE
MY FRIENDS ...
...WAIT-ING.

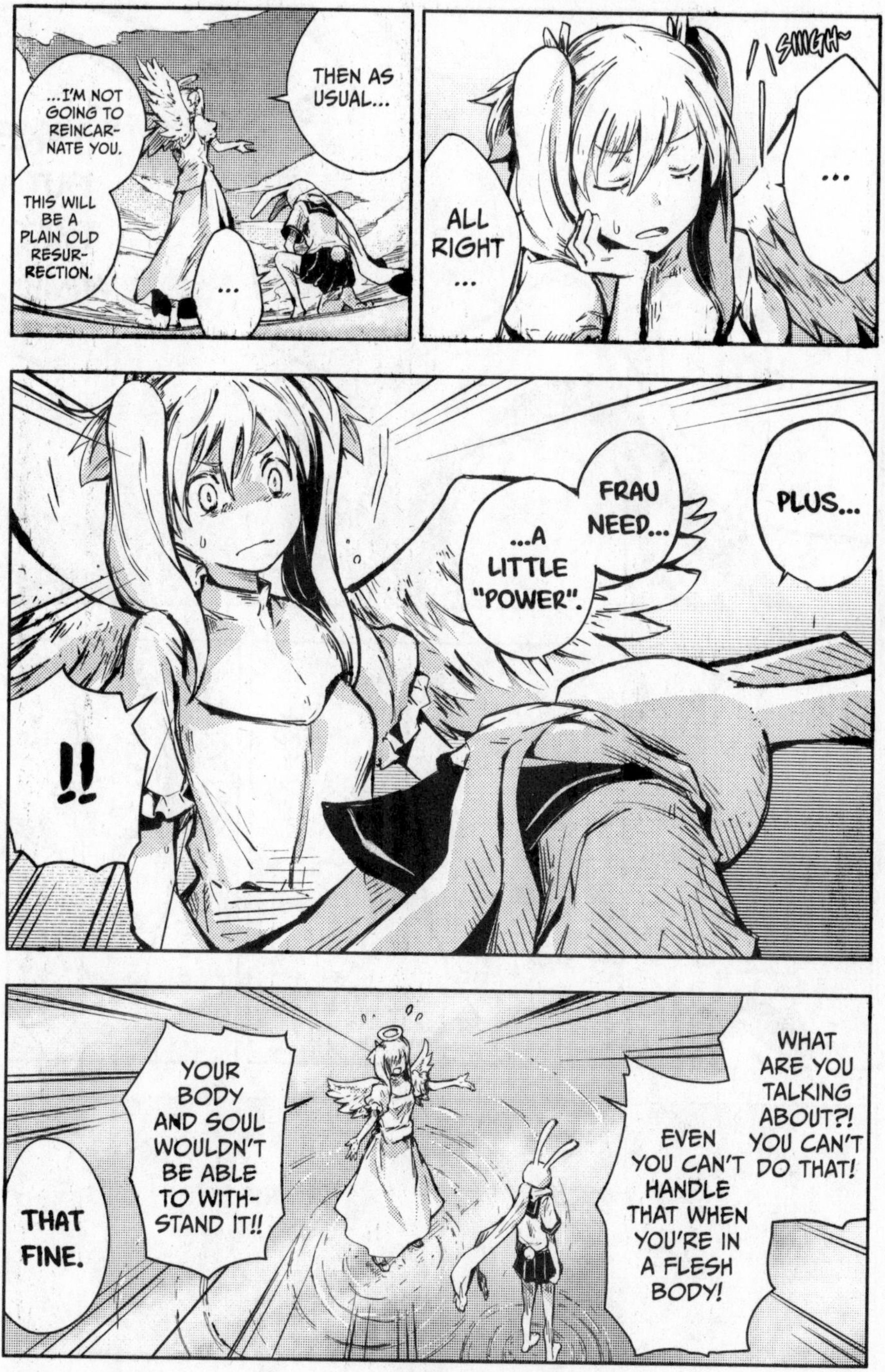
SHIGH~
...
ALL RIGHT ...
THEN AS USUAL...
...I'M NOT GOING TO REINCARNATE YOU.
THIS WILL BE A PLAIN OLD RESURRECTION.
...
PLUS...
FRAU NEED...
...A LITTLE "POWER".
!!
WHAT ARE YOU TALKING ABOUT?! YOU CAN'T DO THAT!
EVEN YOU CAN'T HANDLE THAT WHEN YOU'RE IN A FLESH BODY!
YOUR BODY AND SOUL WOULDN'T BE ABLE TO WITHSTAND IT!!
THAT FINE.

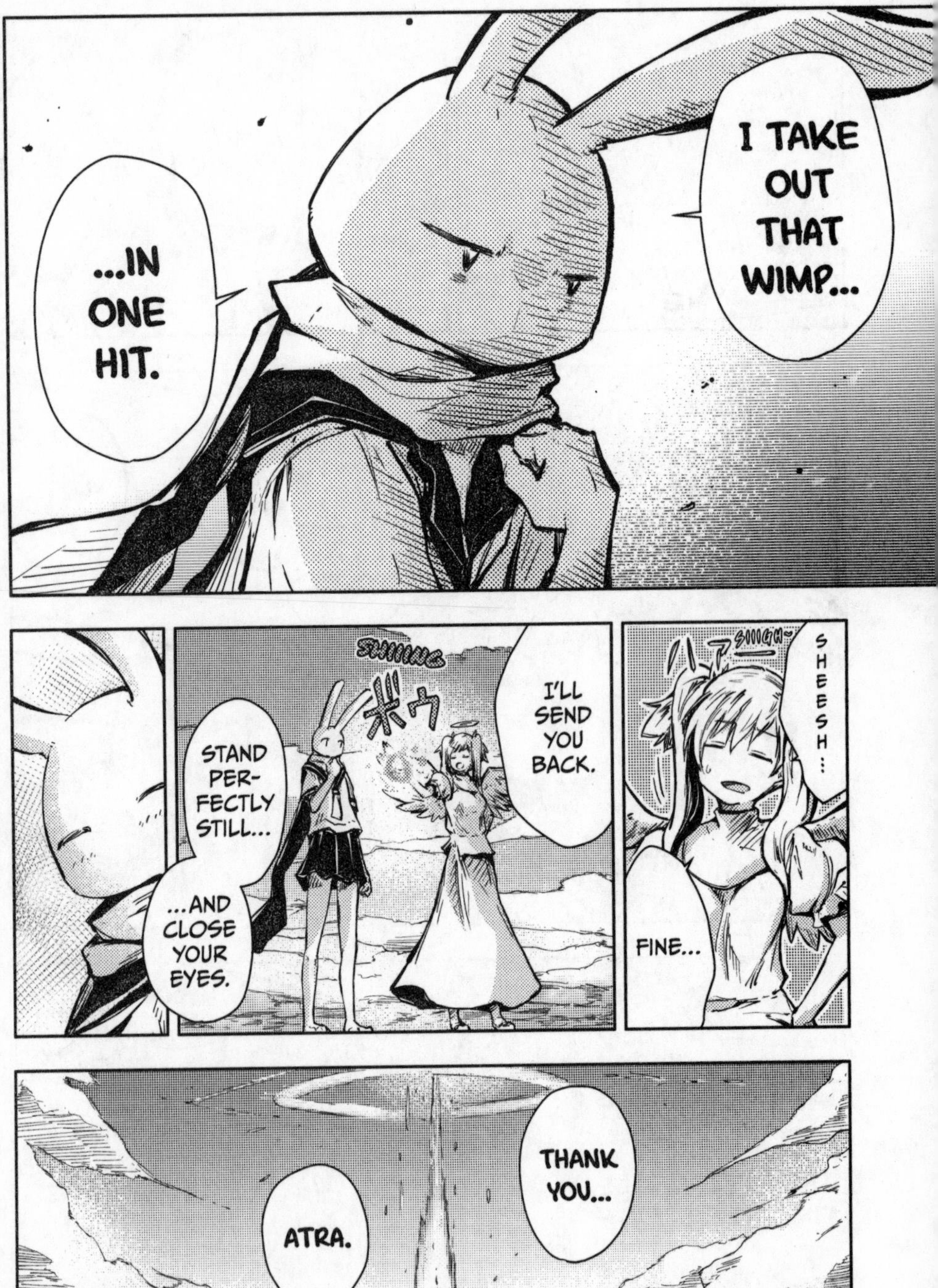
I TAKE OUT THAT WIMP...
...IN ONE HIT.
ハァー
SIIIGH~
SHEESH...
FINE...
I'LL SEND YOU BACK.
SHIIIING
ボウ
STAND PER-FECTLY STILL...
...AND CLOSE YOUR EYES.
THANK YOU...
ATRA.

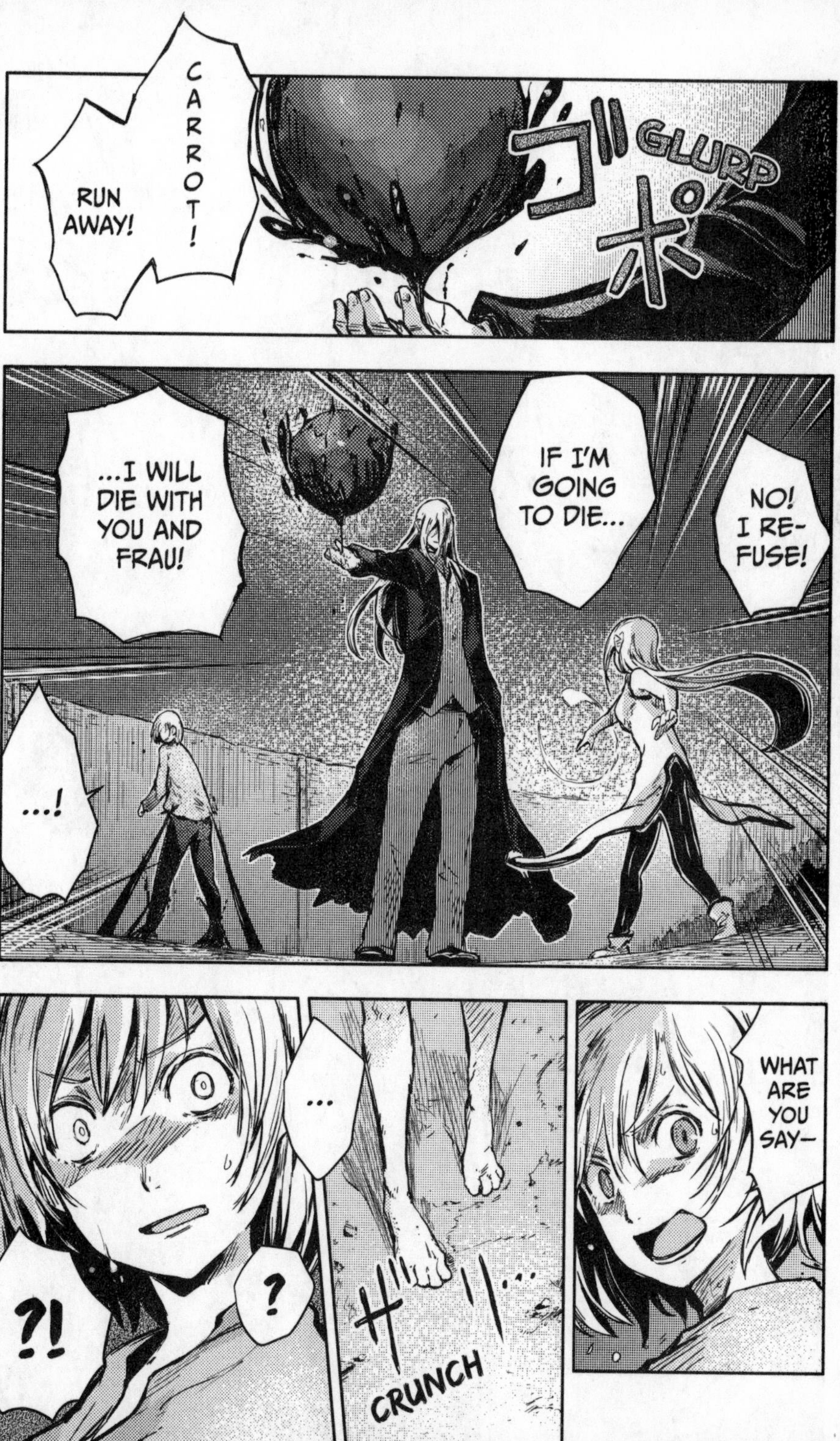
GLURP
CARROT!
RUN AWAY!
NO! I RE-FUSE!
IF I'M GOING TO DIE...
...I WILL DIE WITH YOU AND FRAU!
...!
WHAT ARE YOU SAY—
...
CRUNCH
?
?!

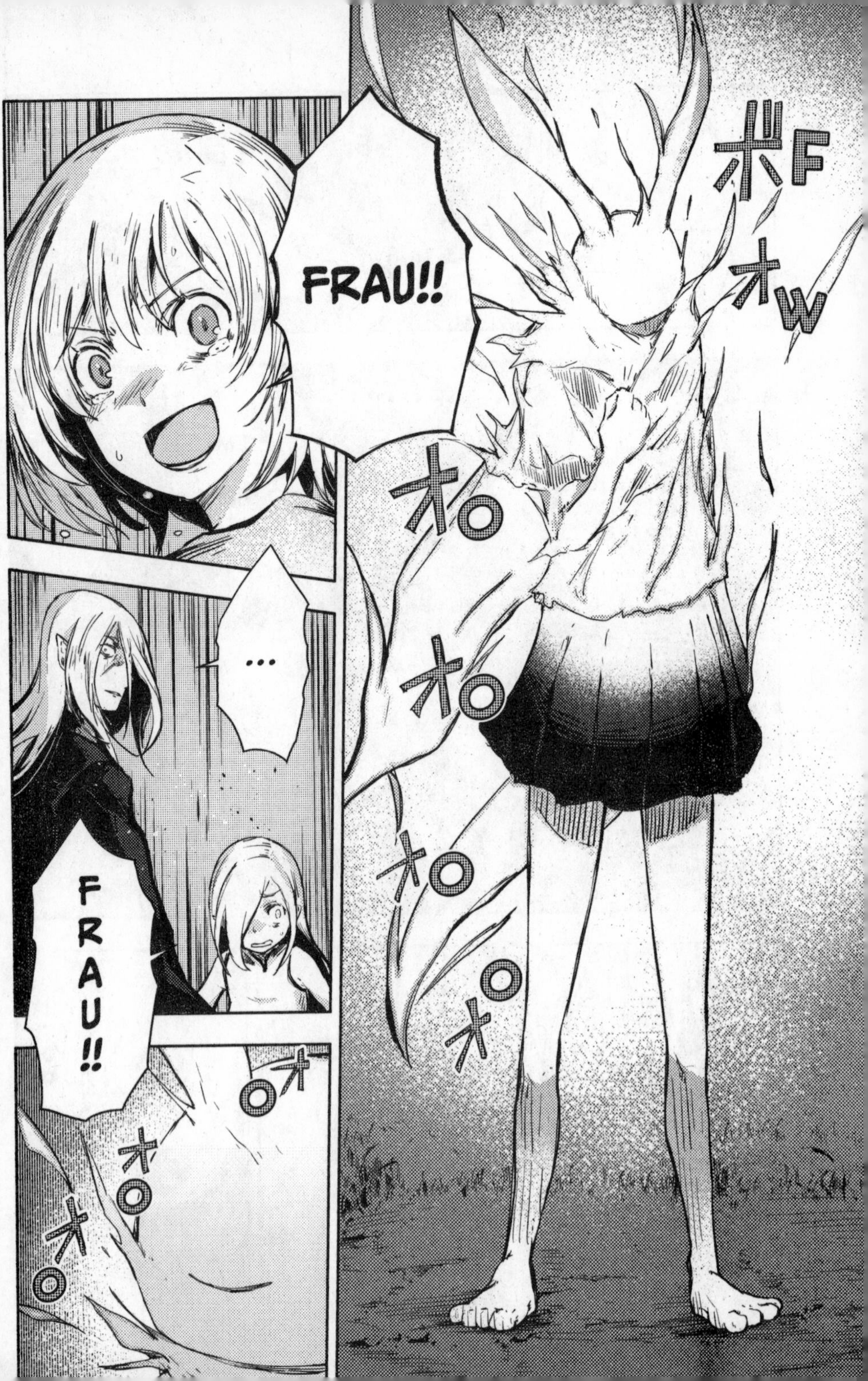
ボF
オW
オO
オO
オO
オO
FRAU!!
...
FRAU!!
オO
オO
オO

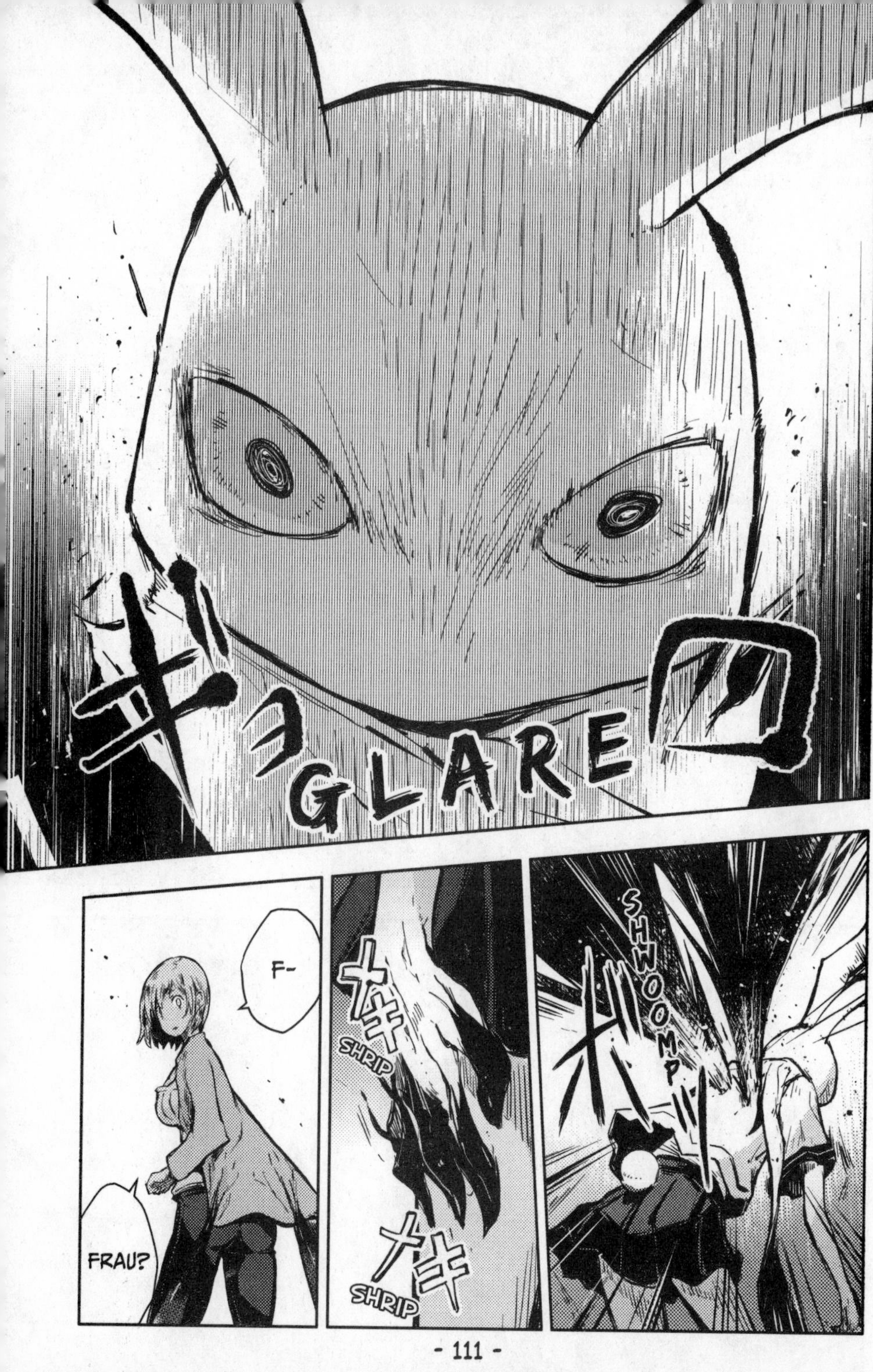
GLARE
SHWOOMP!!
SHRIP
SHRIP
F-
FRAU?

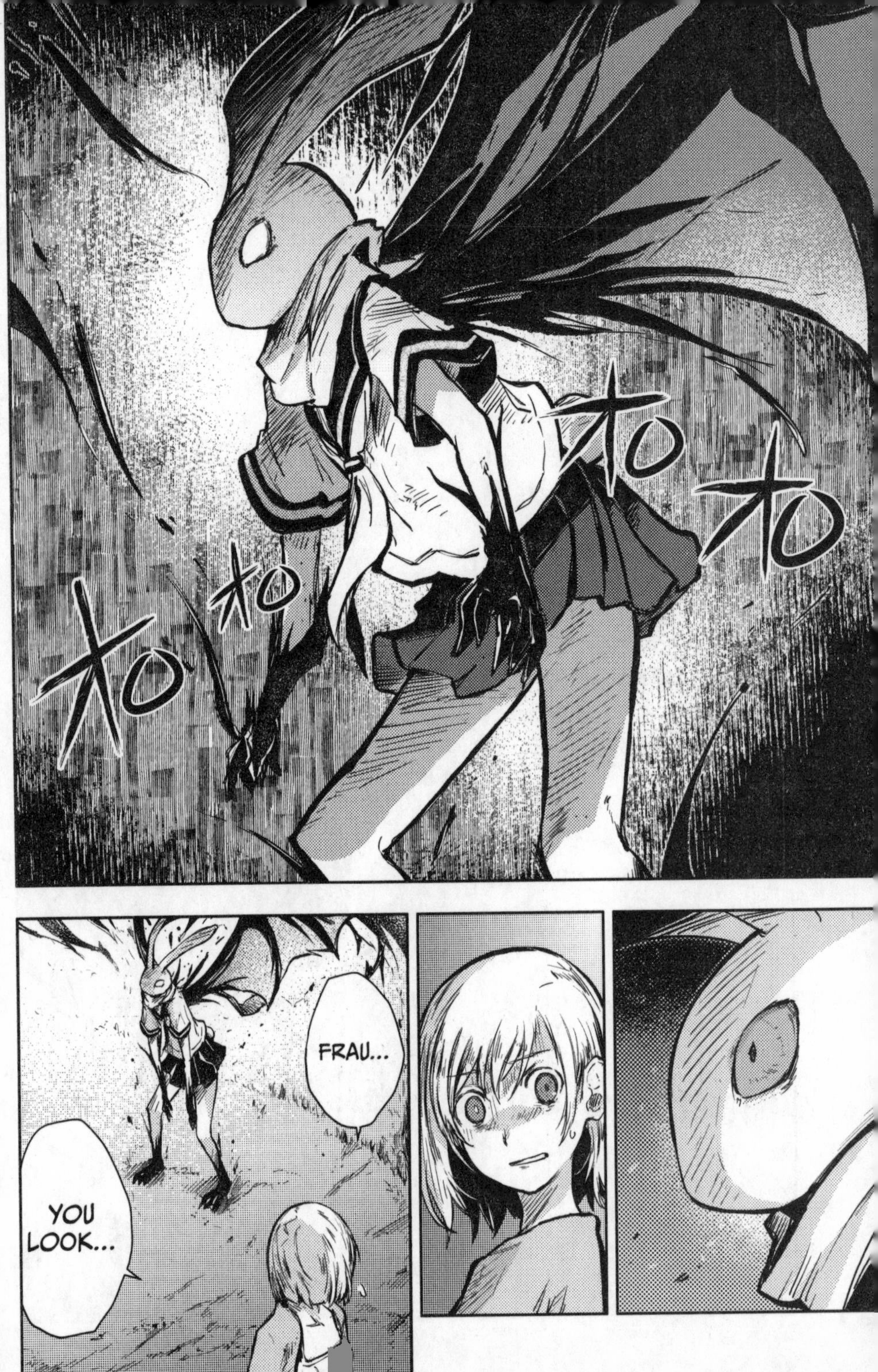
FRAU...
YOU LOOK...

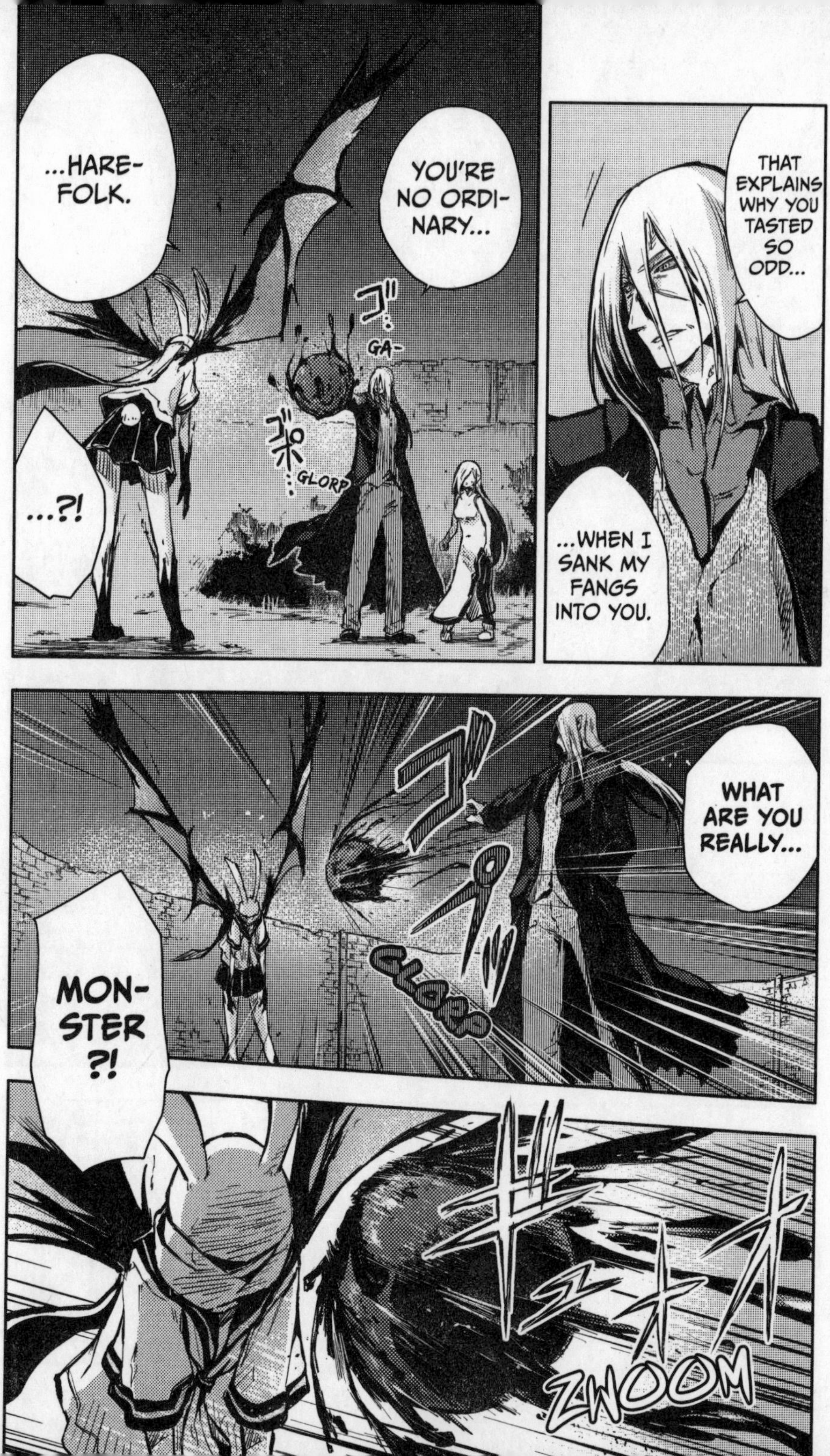
THAT EXPLAINS WHY YOU TASTED SO ODD...
...WHEN I SANK MY FANGS INTO YOU.
YOU'RE NO ORDINARY...
...HARE-FOLK.
ゴ
GA-
ゴポ
GLORP
...?!
WHAT ARE YOU REALLY...
GLORP
MON-STER ?!
ZWOOM

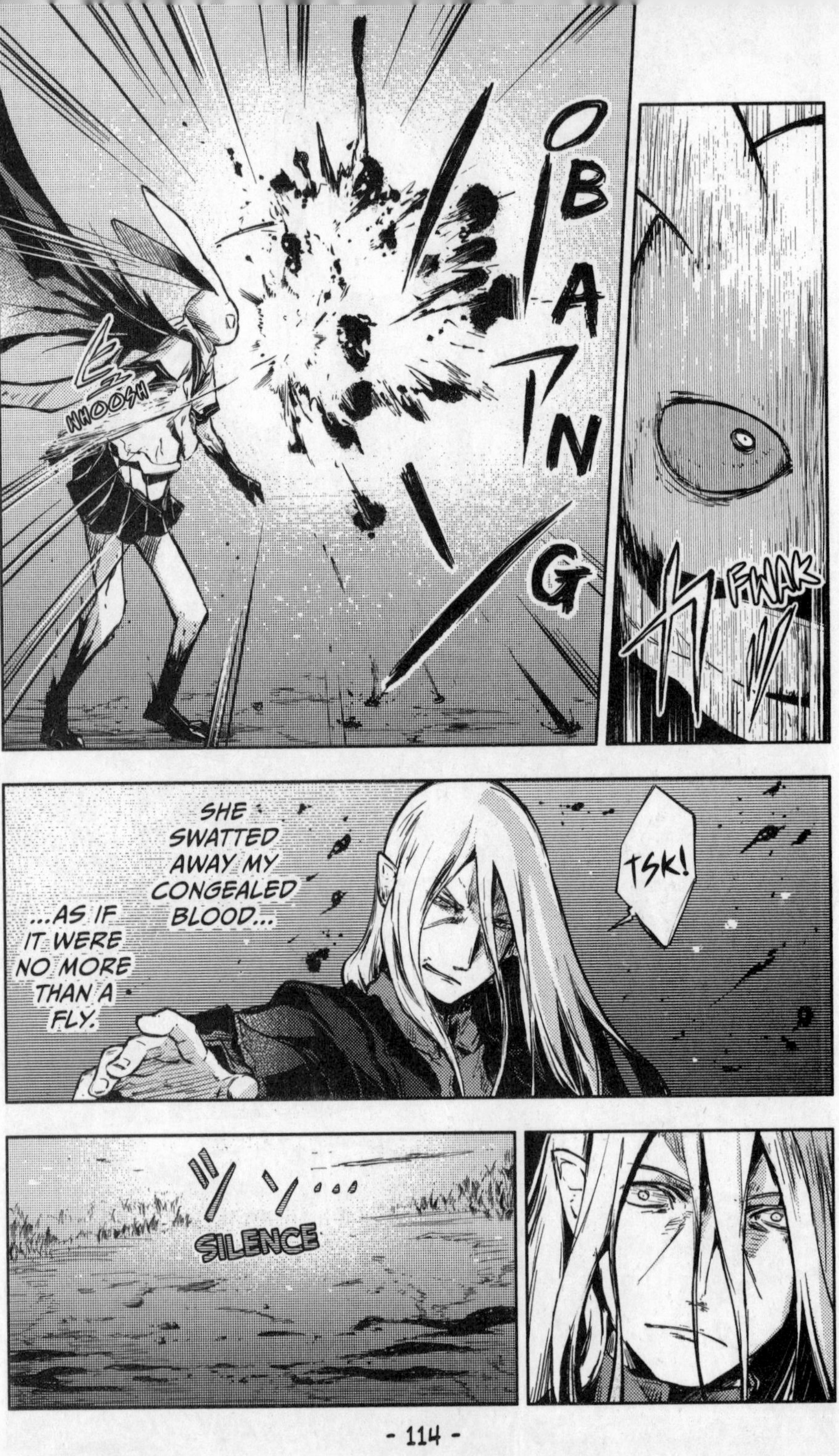
FWAK
BANG
WHOOSH
TSK!
SHE SWATTED AWAY MY CONGEALED BLOOD...
...AS IF IT WERE NO MORE THAN A FLY.
SILENCE

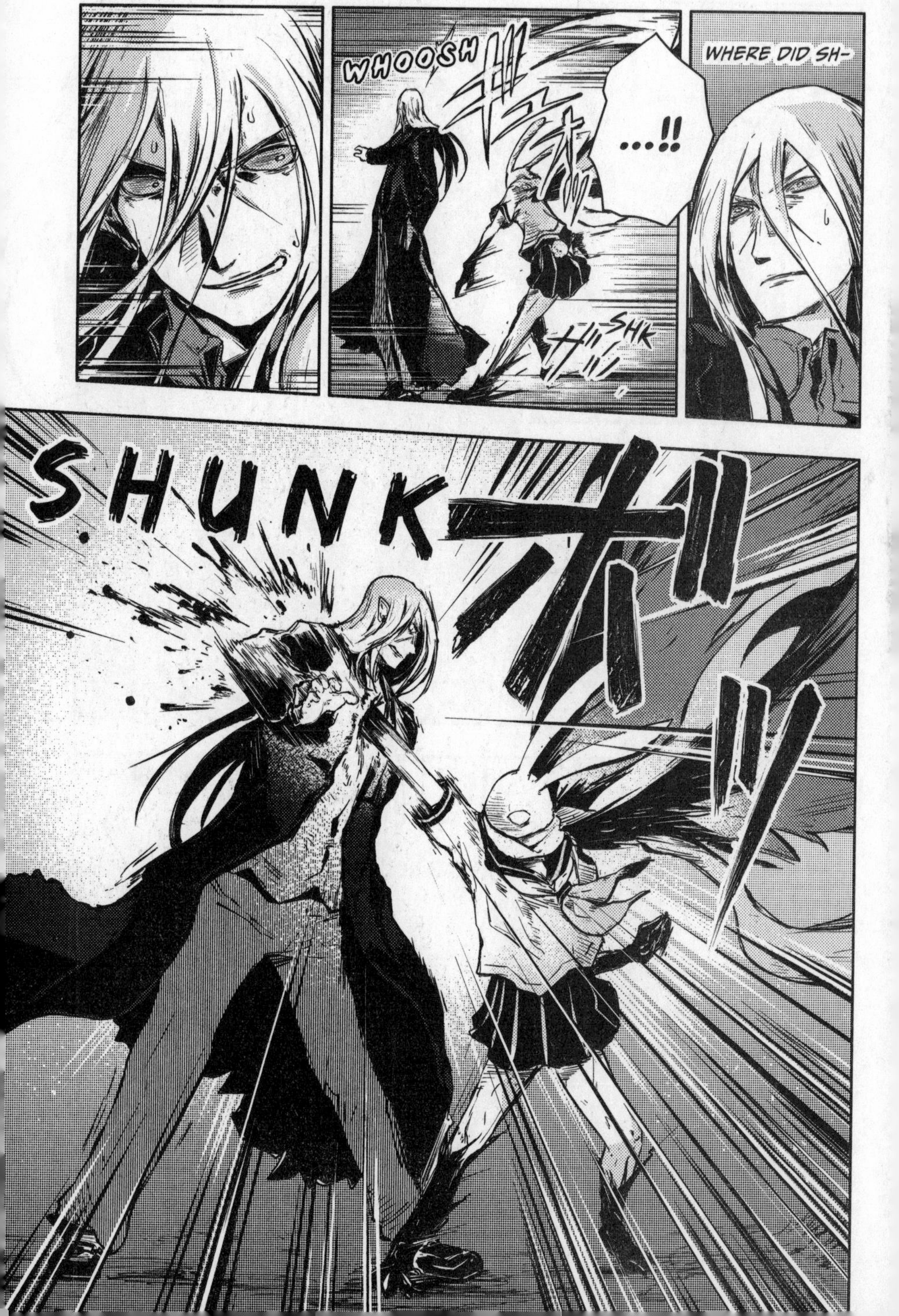
WHERE DID SH-
...!!
WHOOSH
SHK
SHUNK

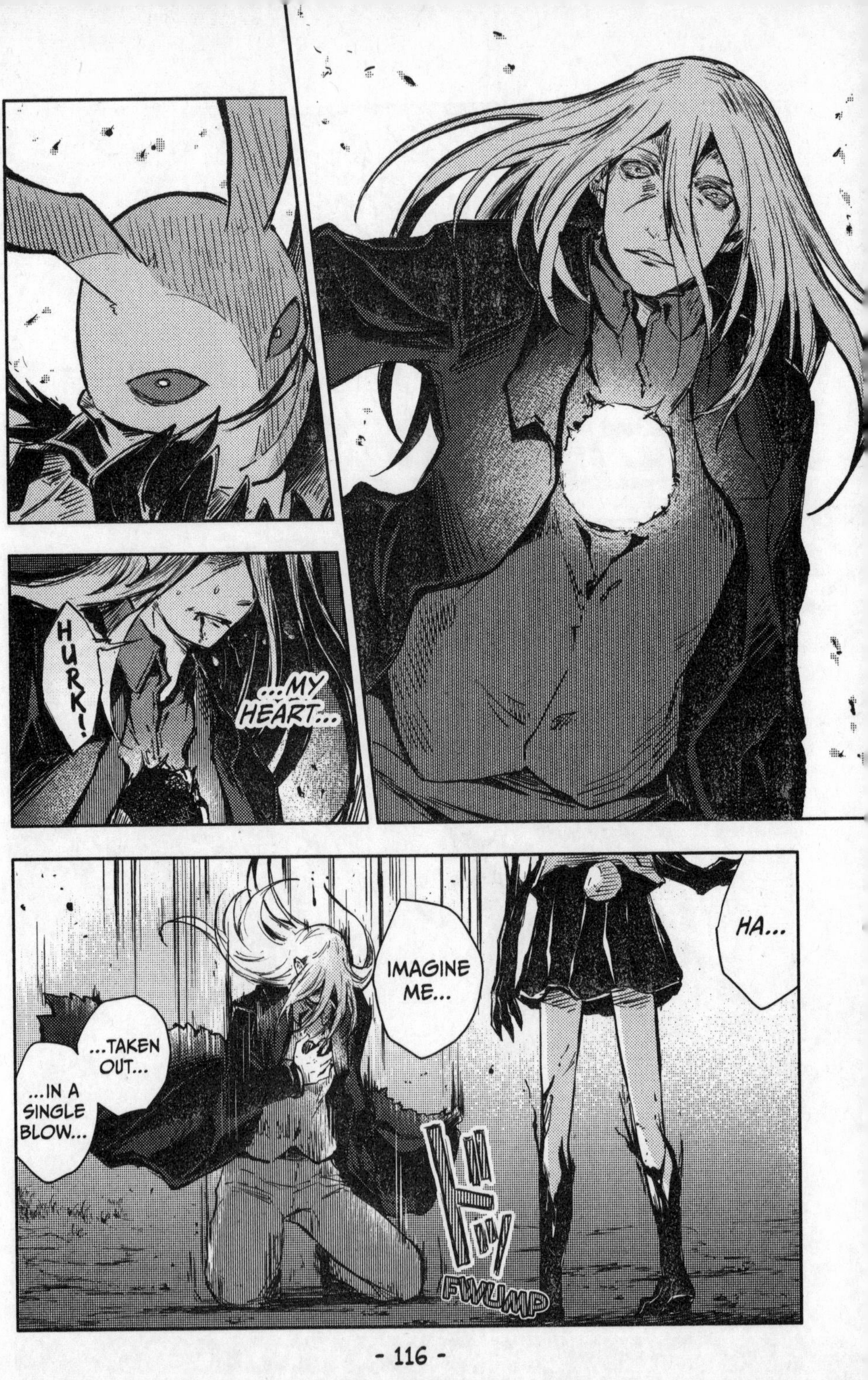
...MY HEART...
HURK!
HA...
IMAGINE ME...
...TAKEN OUT...
...IN A SINGLE BLOW...
FWUMP

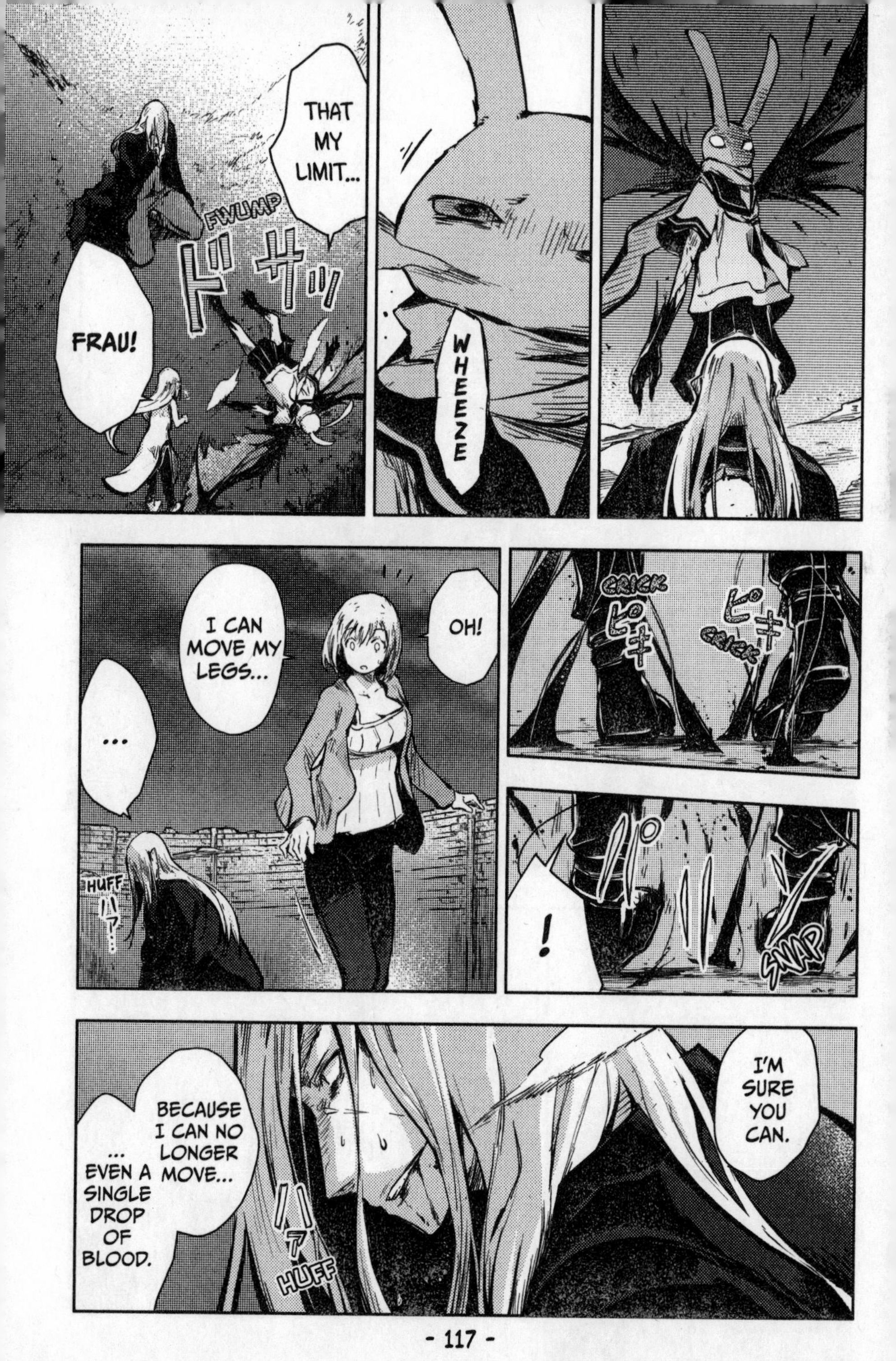
WHEEZE
THAT MY LIMIT...
FWUMP
ドサッ
FRAU!
CRICK
ピキ
ピキ
CRICK
パ
SNAP
!
OH!
I CAN MOVE MY LEGS...
...
HUFF
ハァ...
I'M SURE YOU CAN.
BECAUSE I CAN NO LONGER MOVE...
... EVEN A SINGLE DROP OF BLOOD.
ハァ
HUFF

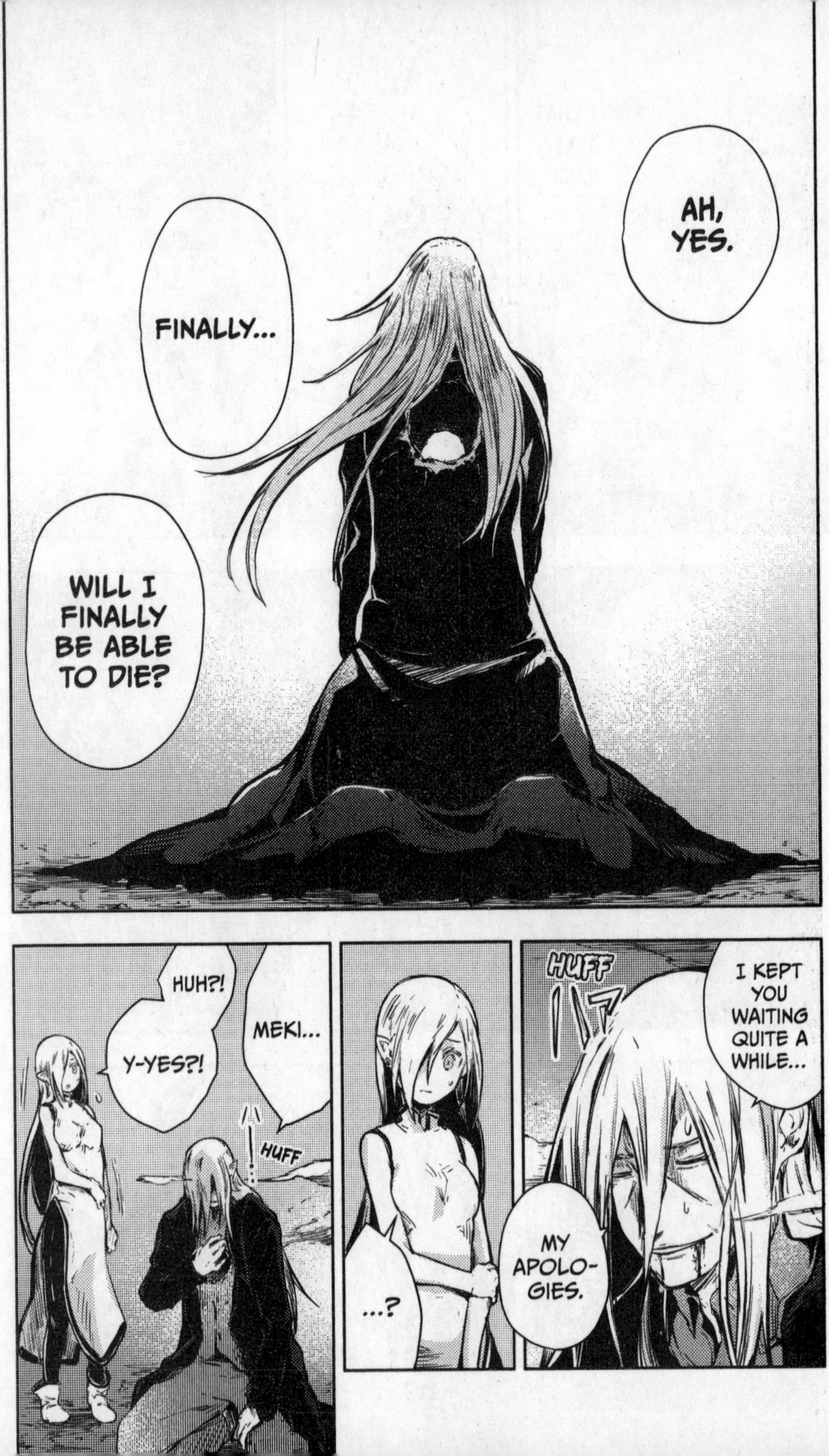
AH, YES.
FINALLY...
WILL I FINALLY BE ABLE TO DIE?
HUFF
I KEPT YOU WAITING QUITE A WHILE...
MY APOLOGIES.
...?
MEKI...
HUH?!
Y-YES?!
HUFF

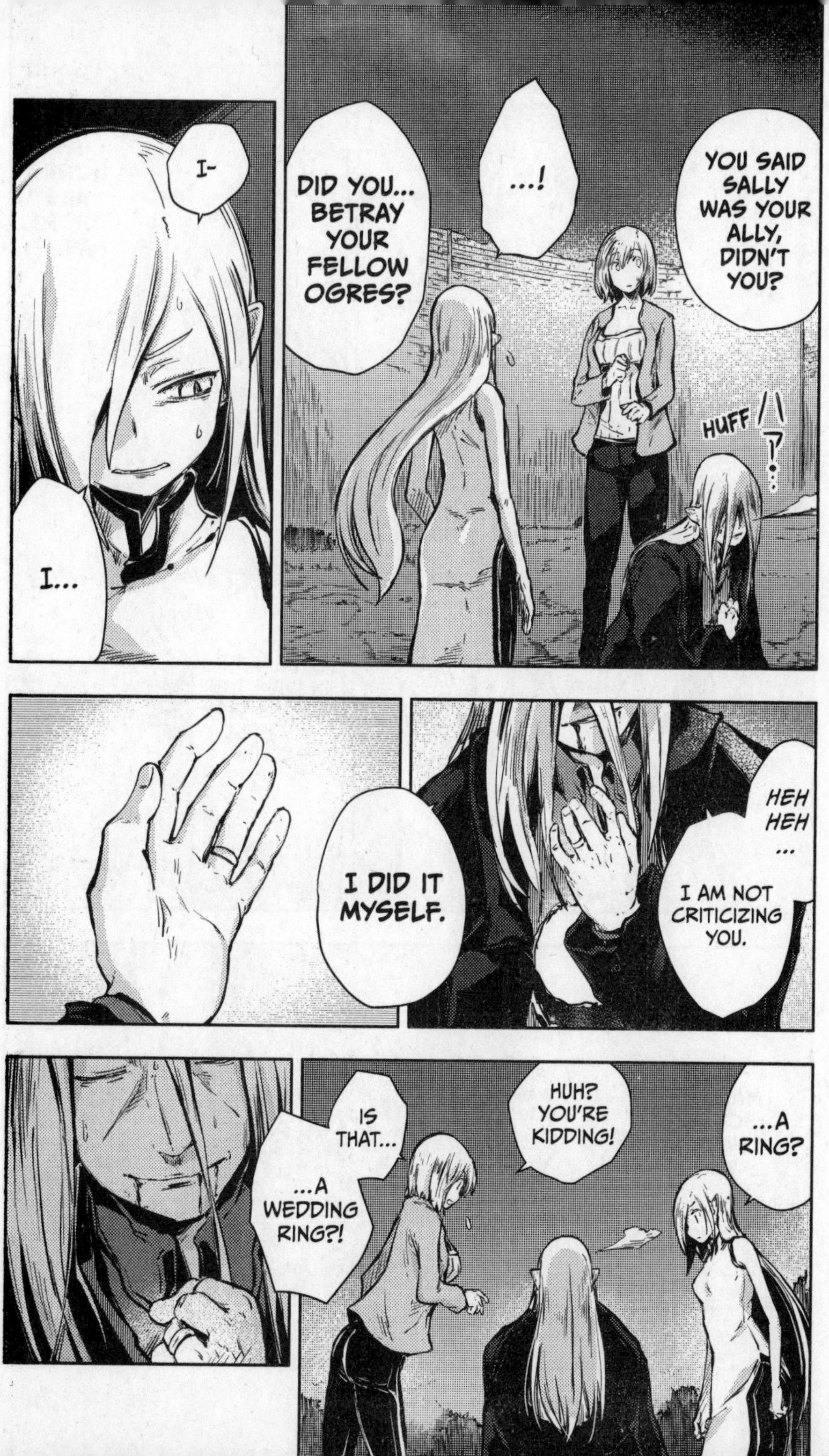
YOU SAID SALLY WAS YOUR ALLY, DIDN'T YOU?
...!
DID YOU... BETRAY YOUR FELLOW OGRES?
HUFF
ハァ…
I-
I...
HEH HEH ...
I AM NOT CRITICIZING YOU.
I DID IT MYSELF.
...A RING?
HUH? YOU'RE KIDDING!
IS THAT...
...A WEDDING RING?!

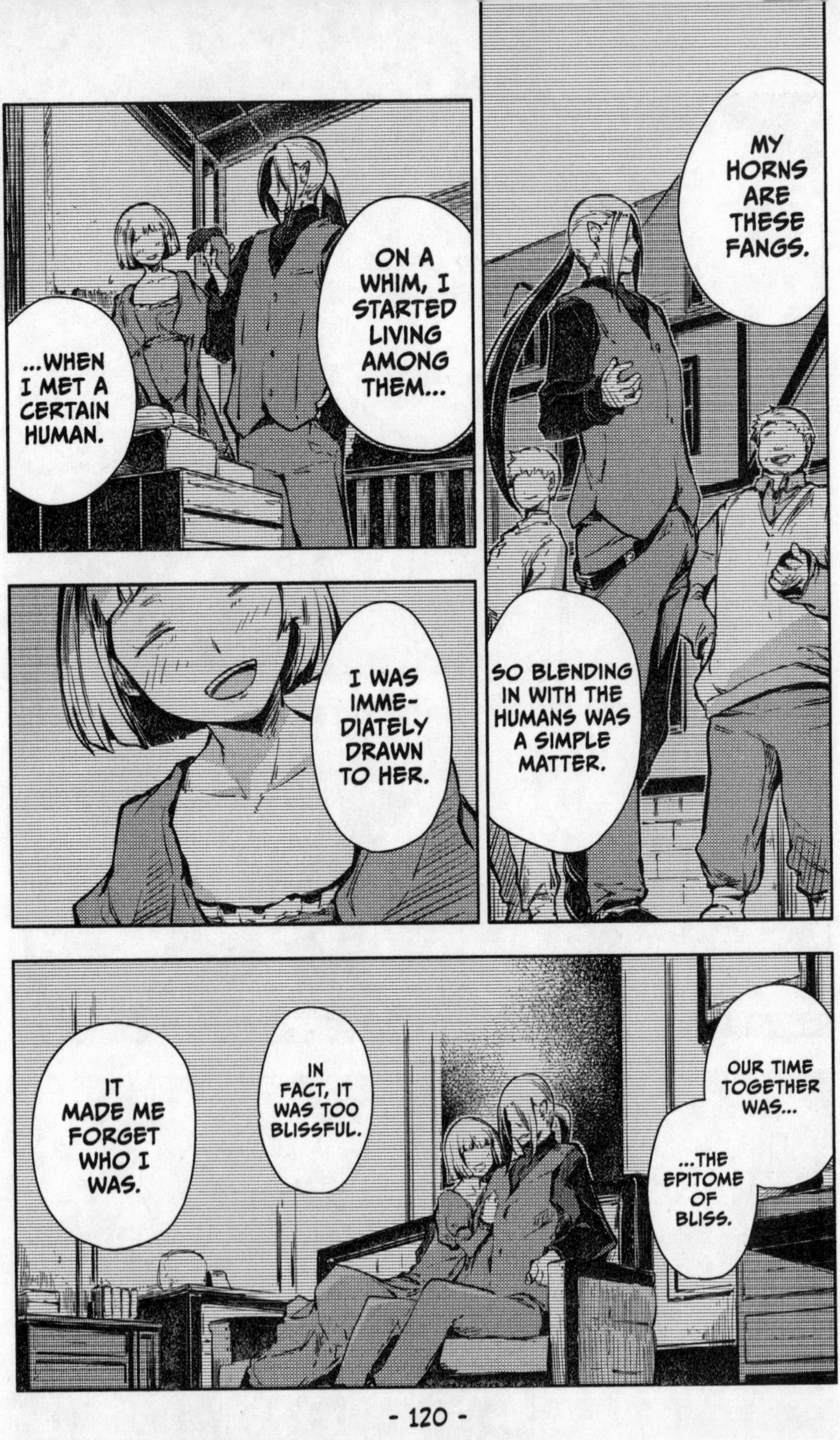
MY HORNS ARE THESE FANGS.
SO BLENDING IN WITH THE HUMANS WAS A SIMPLE MATTER.
ON A WHIM, I STARTED LIVING AMONG THEM...
...WHEN I MET A CERTAIN HUMAN.
I WAS IMME-DIATELY DRAWN TO HER.
OUR TIME TOGETHER WAS...
...THE EPITOME OF BLISS.
IN FACT, IT WAS TOO BLISSFUL.
IT MADE ME FORGET WHO I WAS.

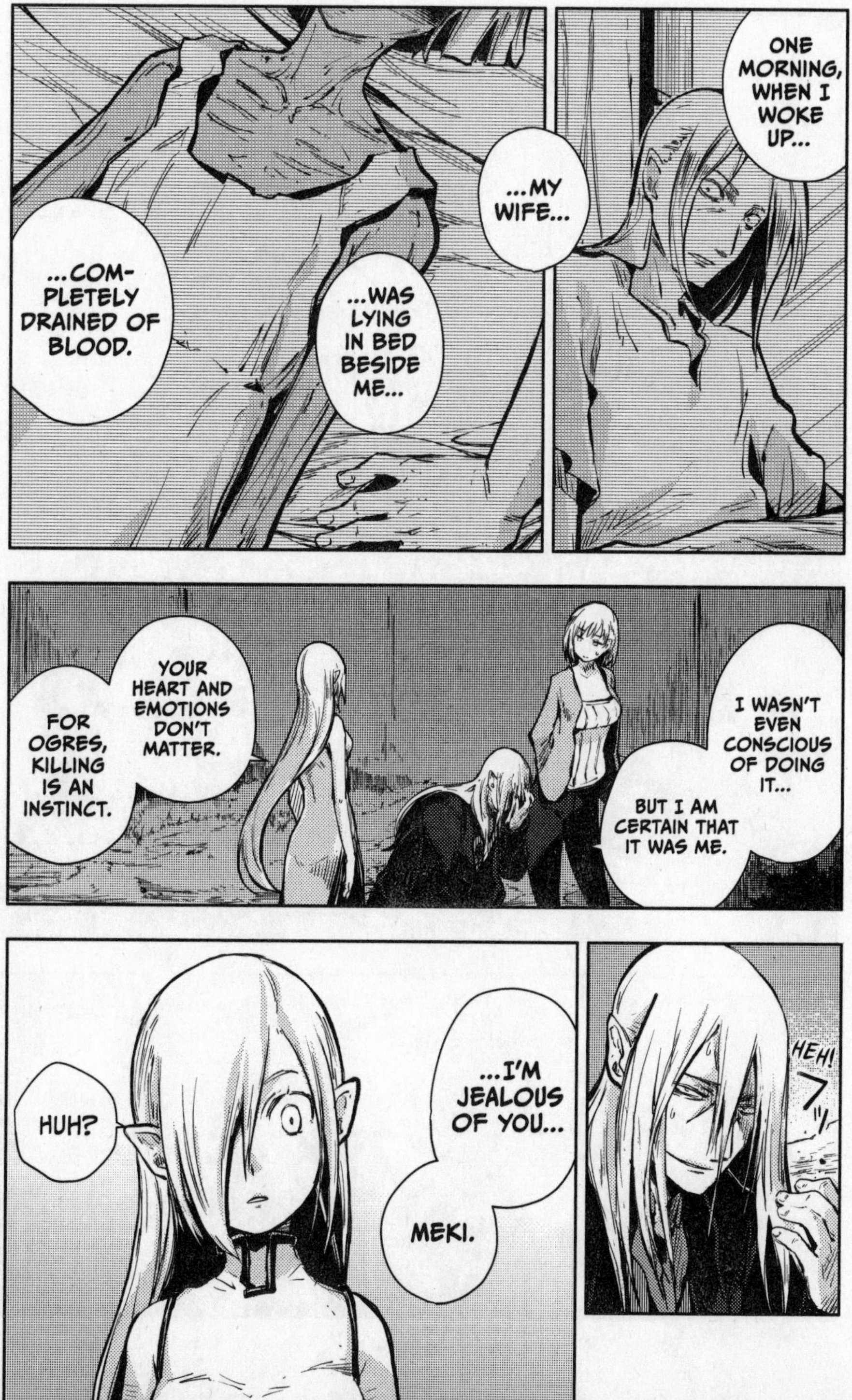
ONE MORNING, WHEN I WOKE UP...
...MY WIFE...
...WAS LYING IN BED BESIDE ME...
...COMPLETELY DRAINED OF BLOOD.
I WASN'T EVEN CONSCIOUS OF DOING IT...
BUT I AM CERTAIN THAT IT WAS ME.
YOUR HEART AND EMOTIONS DON'T MATTER.
FOR OGRES, KILLING IS AN INSTINCT.
HEH!
...I'M JEALOUS OF YOU...
MEKI.
HUH?

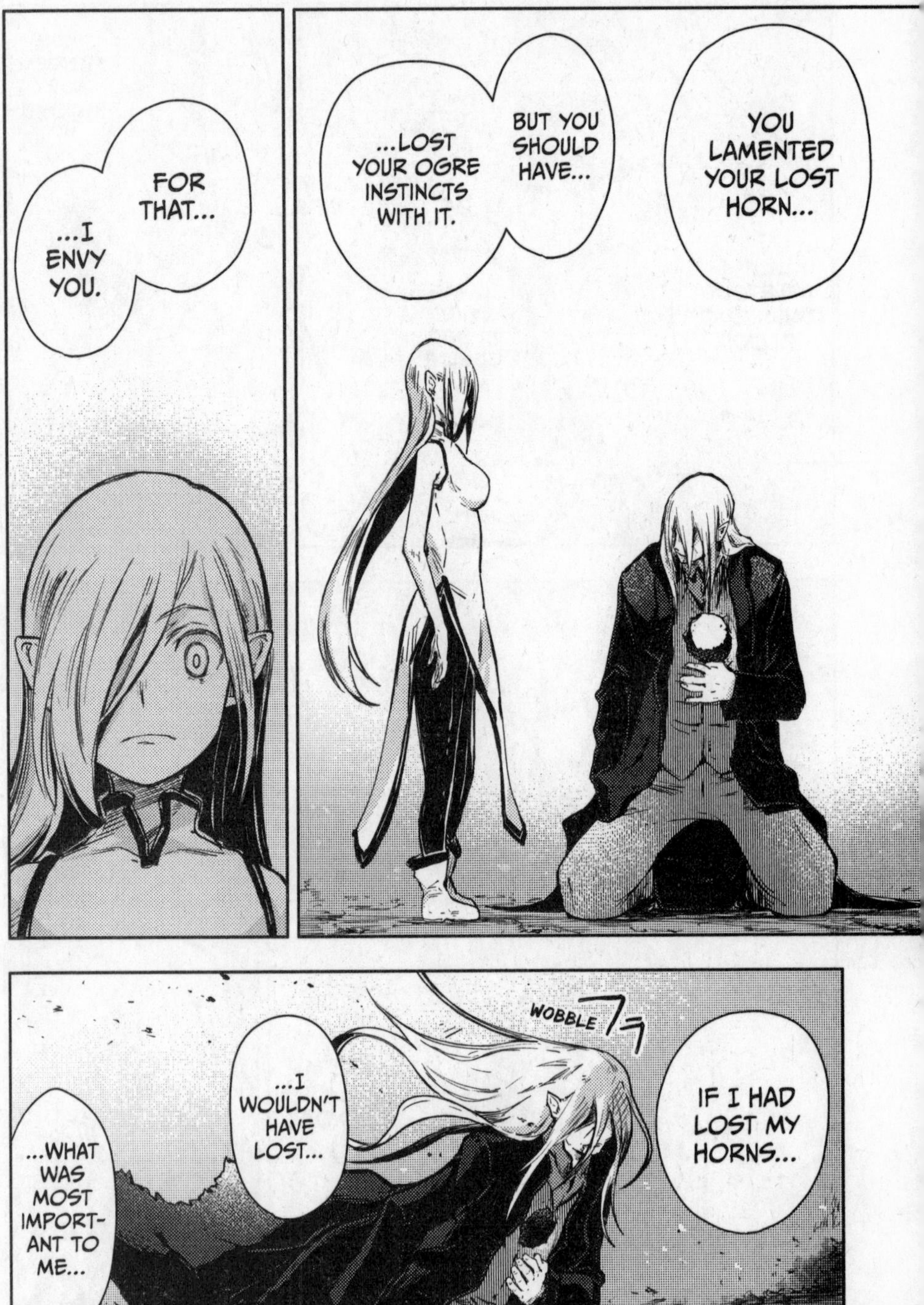
YOU LAMENTED YOUR LOST HORN...
BUT YOU SHOULD HAVE...
...LOST YOUR OGRE INSTINCTS WITH IT.
FOR THAT...
...I ENVY YOU.
IF I HAD LOST MY HORNS...
WOBBLE
...I WOULDN'T HAVE LOST...
...WHAT WAS MOST IMPORT-ANT TO ME...

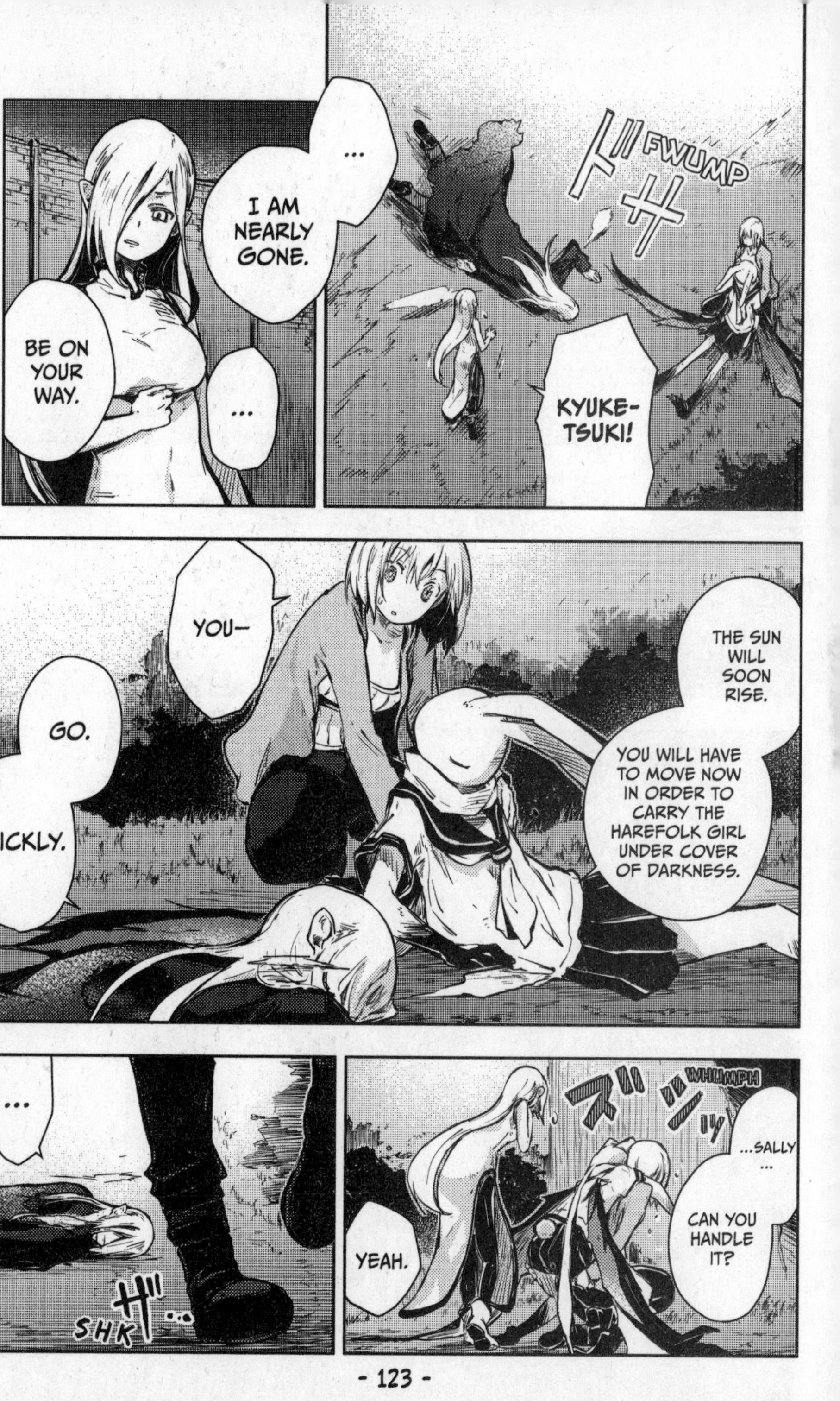
FWUMP
KYUKE-TSUKI!
...
I AM NEARLY GONE.
BE ON YOUR WAY.
...
THE SUN WILL SOON RISE.
YOU WILL HAVE TO MOVE NOW IN ORDER TO CARRY THE HAREFOLK GIRL UNDER COVER OF DARKNESS.
YOU–
GO.
QUICKLY.
WHUMPH
...SALLY ...
CAN YOU HANDLE IT?
YEAH.
...
SHK

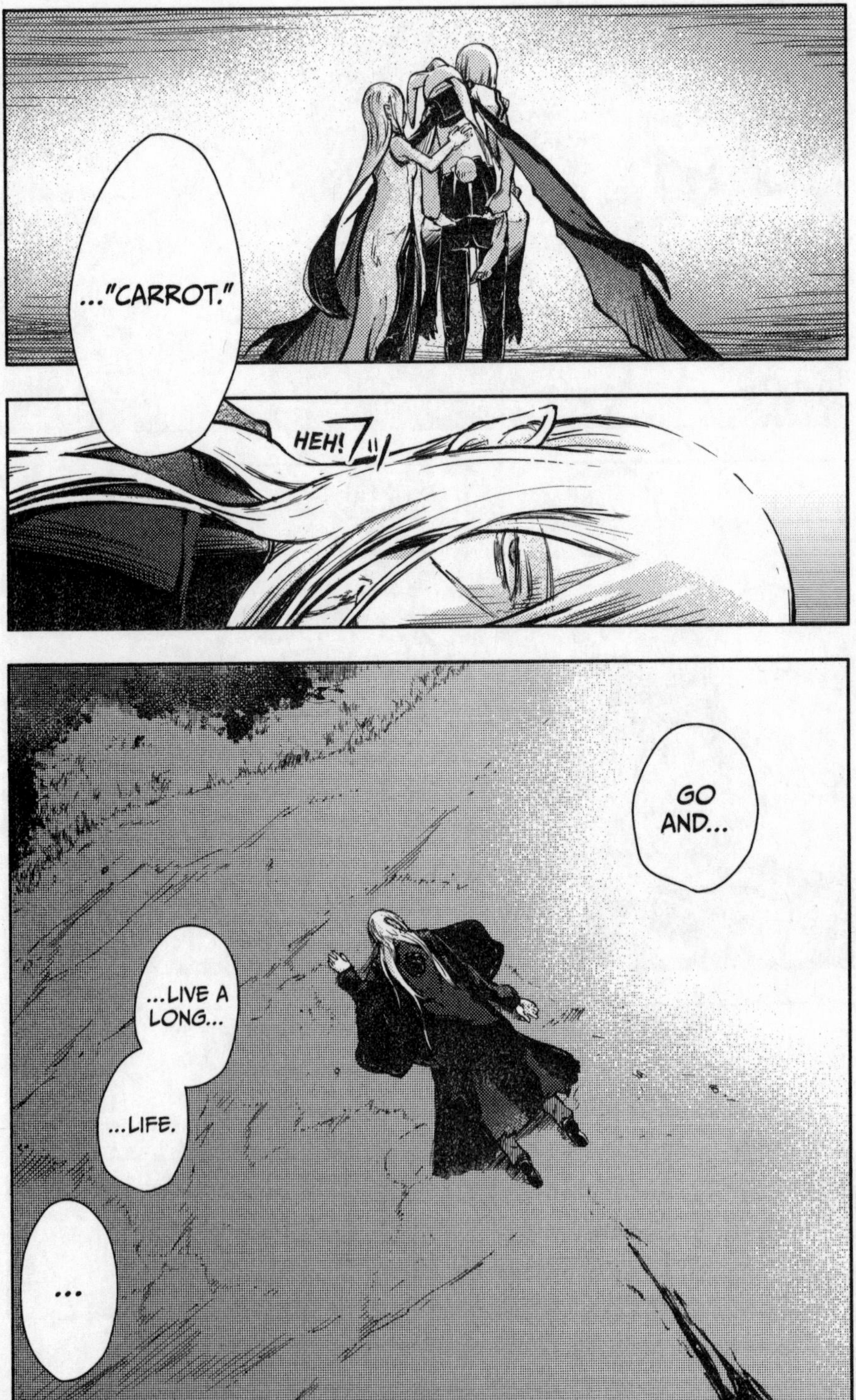
..."CARROT."
HEH!
GO AND...
...LIVE A LONG...
...LIFE.
...

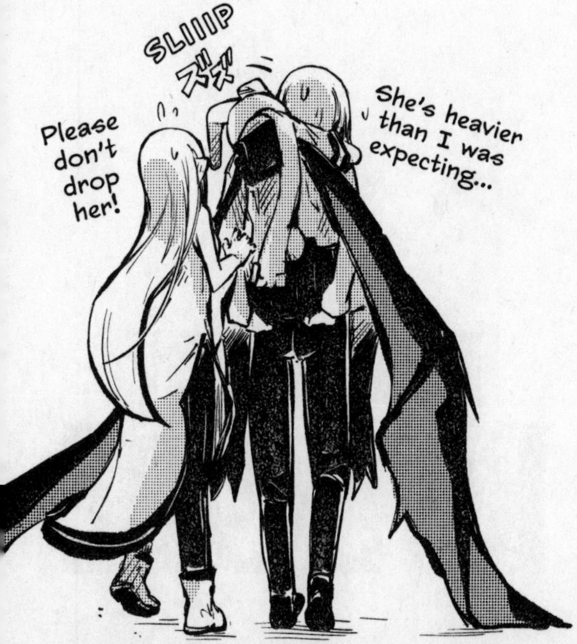
SLIIIP
ズズ
She's heavier than I was expecting...
Please don't drop her!

PEACH BOY
RIVERSIDE

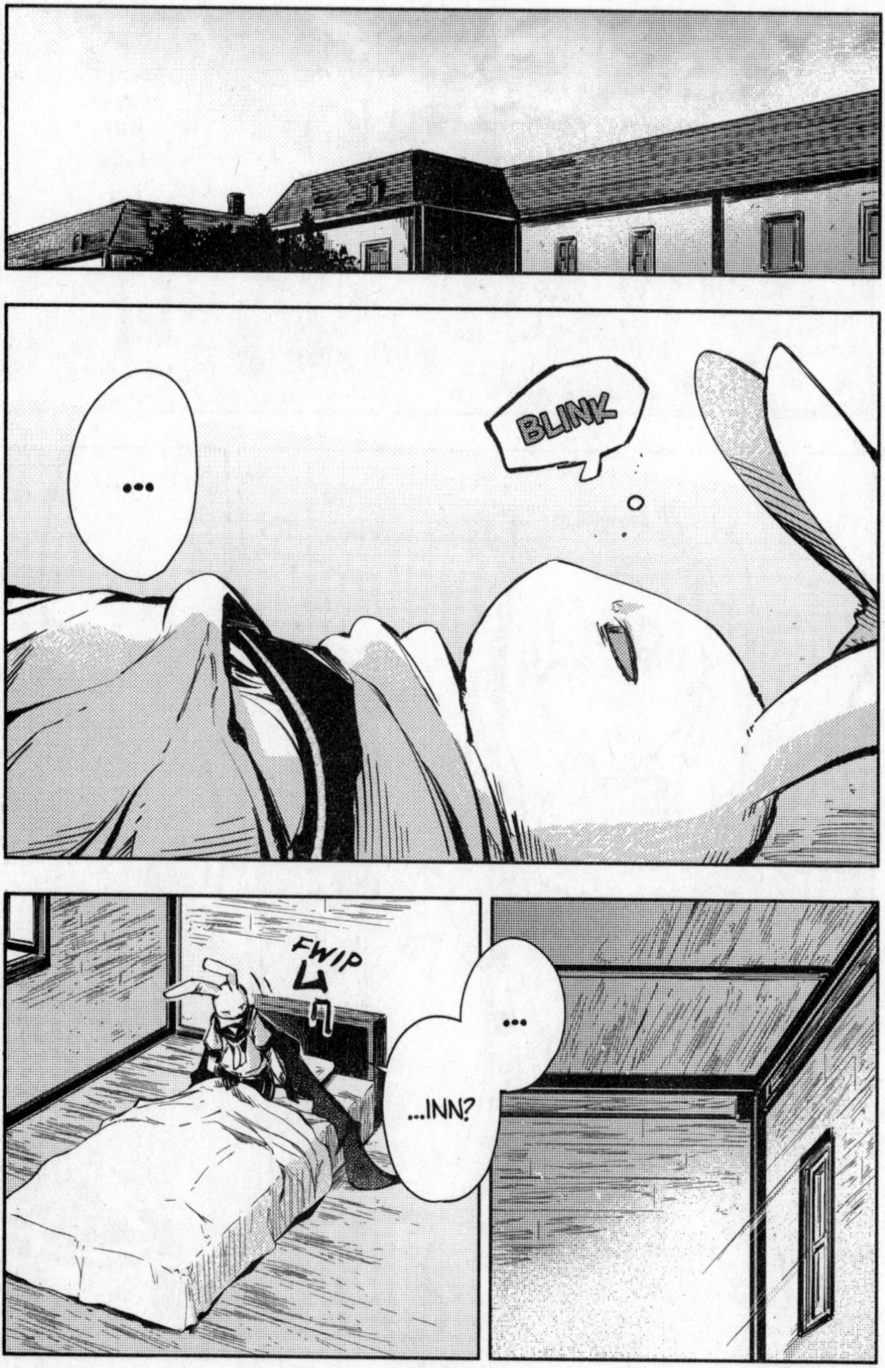
BLINK
...
...
...INN?
FWIP

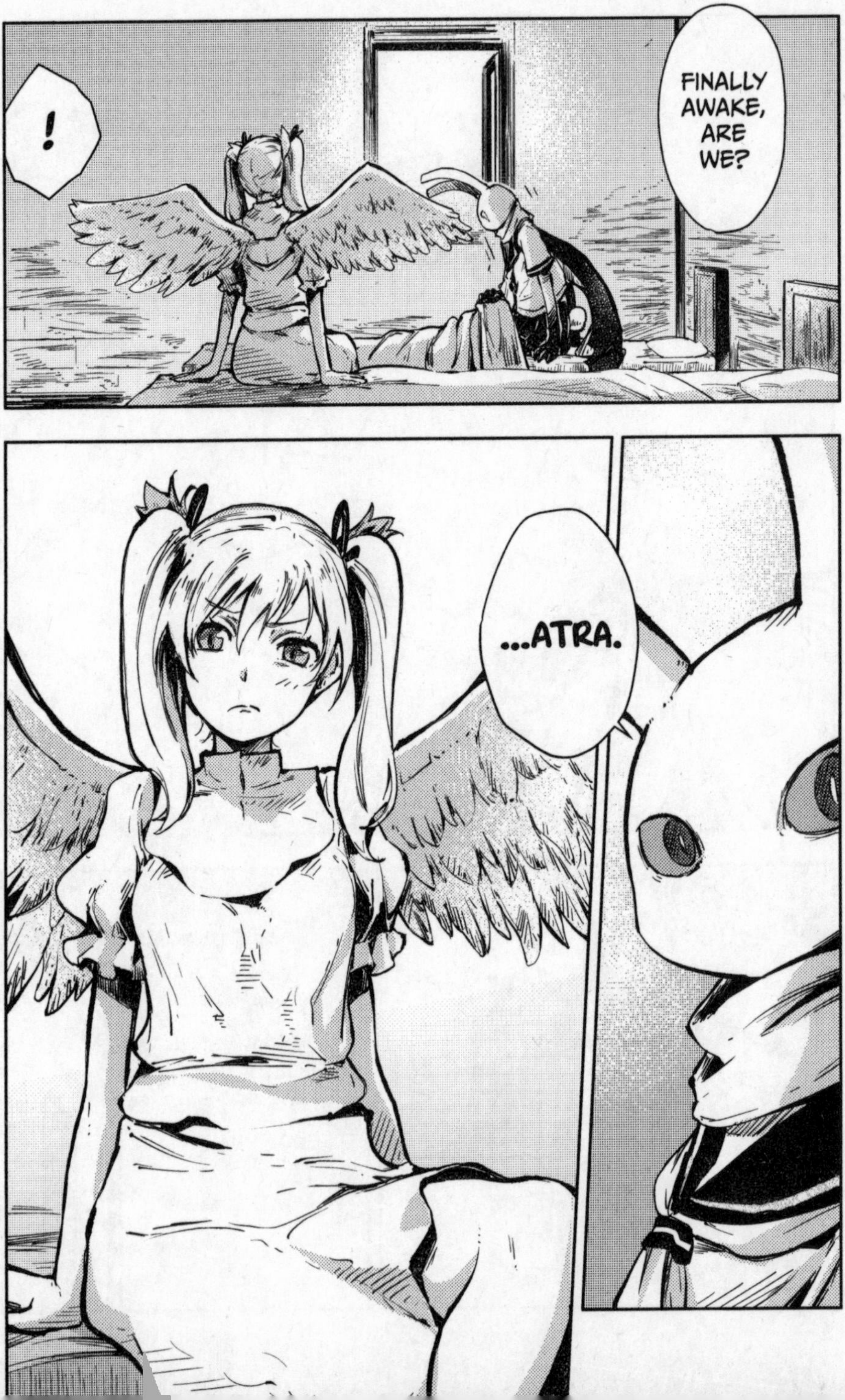
FINALLY AWAKE, ARE WE?
!
...ATRA.

CHAPTER 15: CARROT AND SALLY

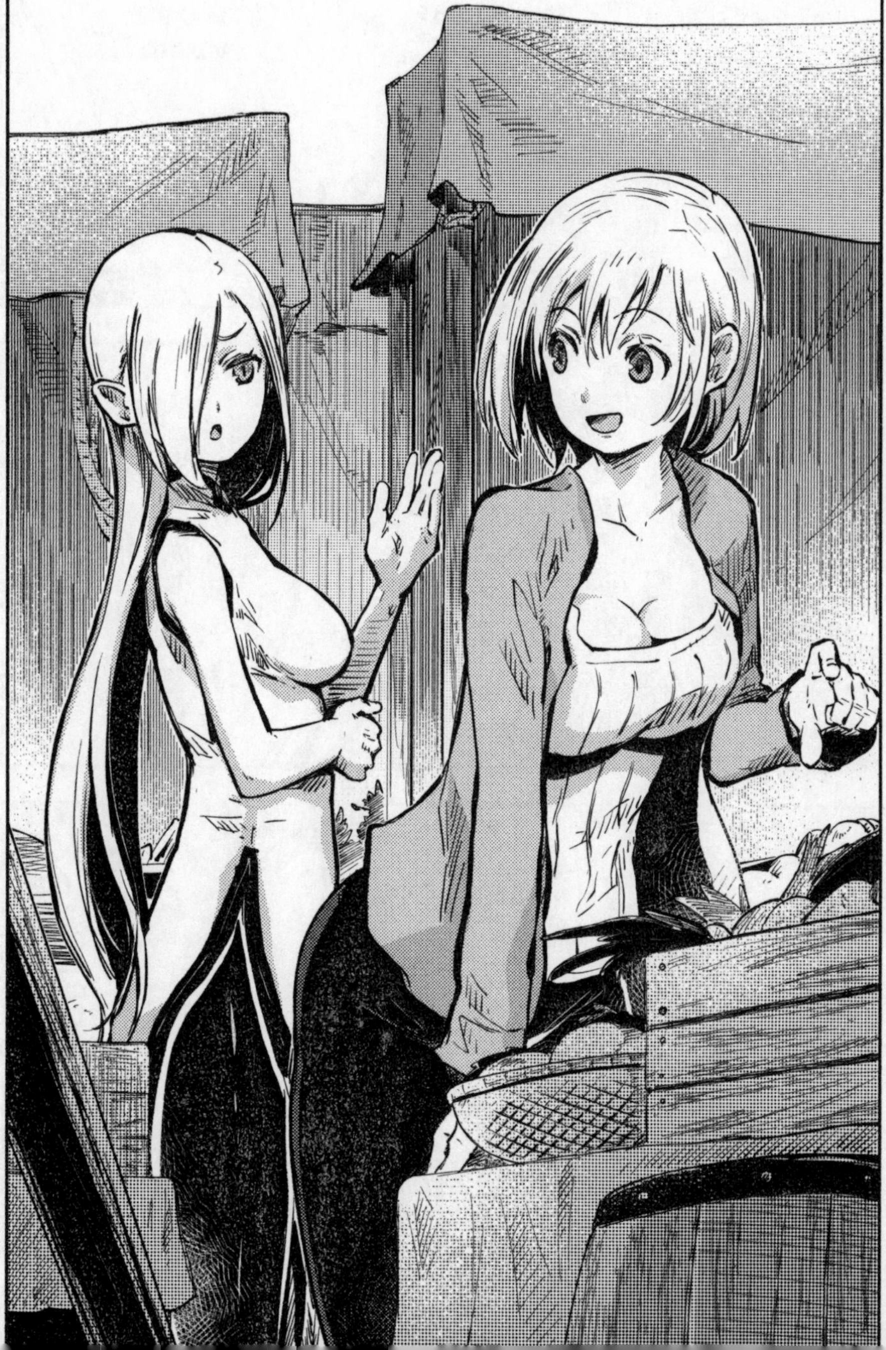

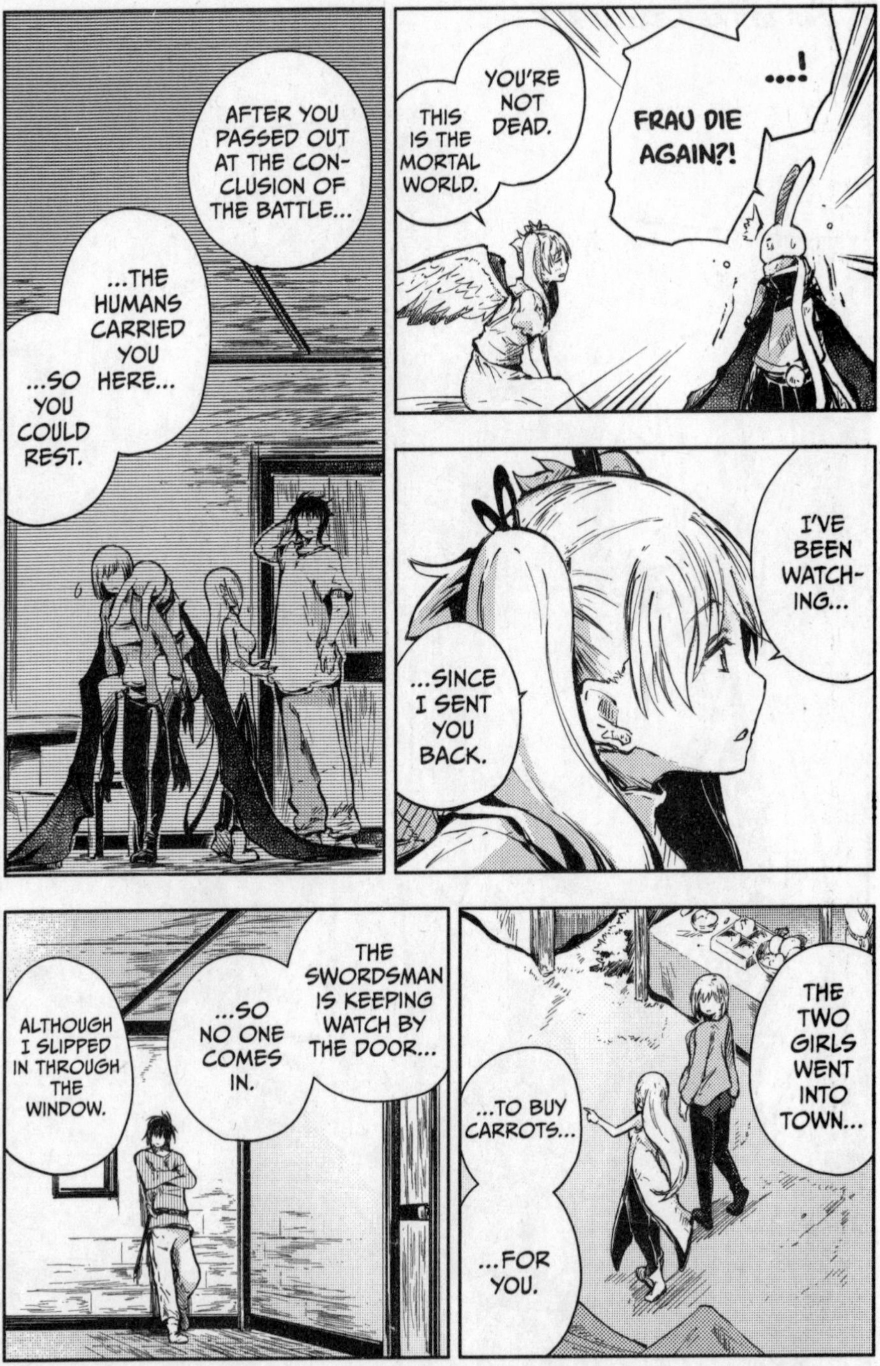
...!
FRAU DIE AGAIN?!
YOU'RE NOT DEAD.
THIS IS THE MORTAL WORLD.
I'VE BEEN WATCHING...
...SINCE I SENT YOU BACK.
AFTER YOU PASSED OUT AT THE CONCLUSION OF THE BATTLE...
...THE HUMANS CARRIED YOU HERE...
...SO YOU COULD REST.
THE TWO GIRLS WENT INTO TOWN...
...TO BUY CARROTS...
...FOR YOU.
THE SWORDSMAN IS KEEPING WATCH BY THE DOOR...
...SO NO ONE COMES IN.
ALTHOUGH I SLIPPED IN THROUGH THE WINDOW.

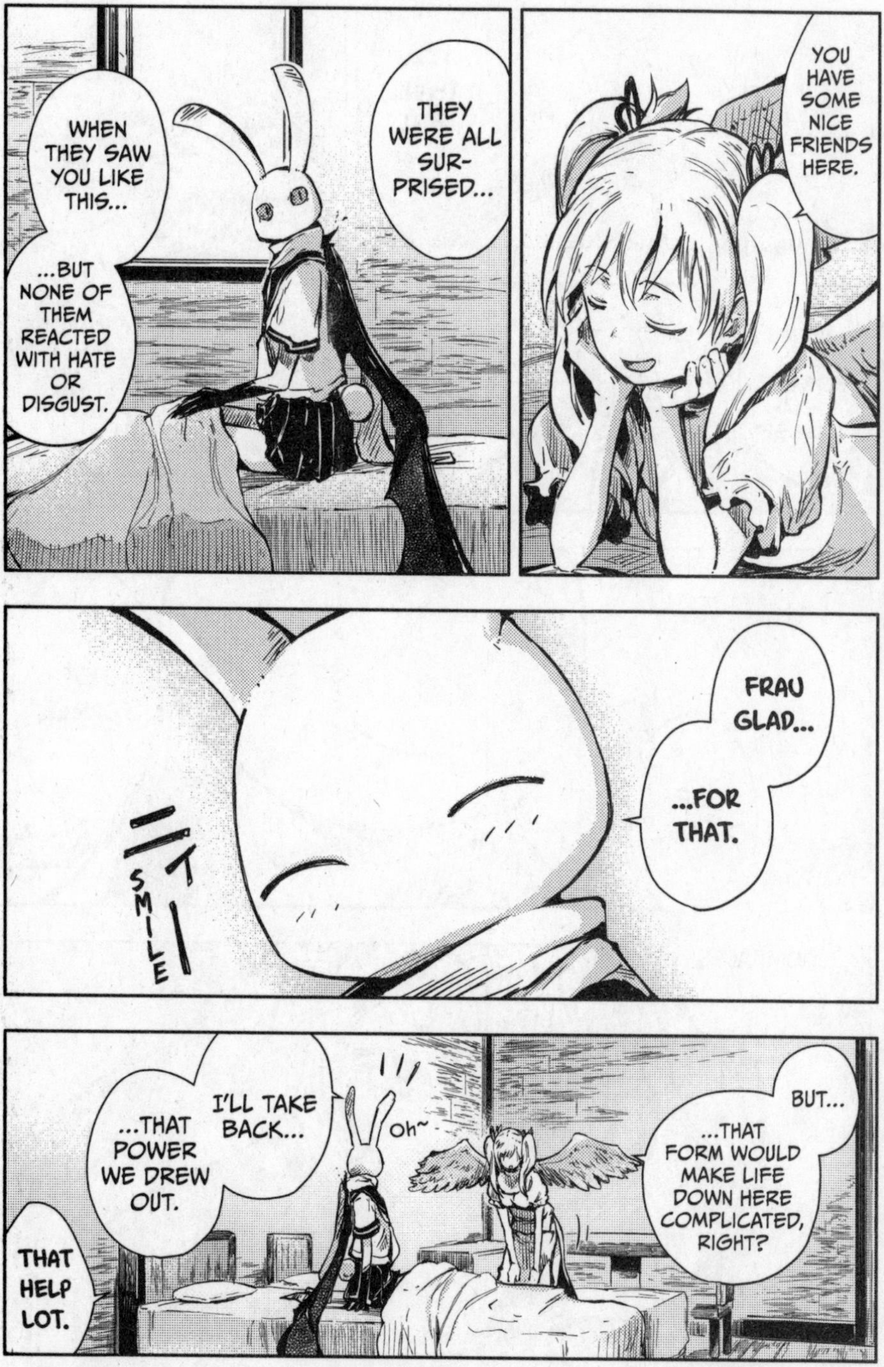
YOU HAVE SOME NICE FRIENDS HERE.
THEY WERE ALL SUR-PRISED...
WHEN THEY SAW YOU LIKE THIS...
...BUT NONE OF THEM REACTED WITH HATE OR DISGUST.
FRAU GLAD...
...FOR THAT.
SMILE
BUT...
...THAT FORM WOULD MAKE LIFE DOWN HERE COMPLICATED, RIGHT?
Oh~
I'LL TAKE BACK...
...THAT POWER WE DREW OUT.
THAT HELP LOT.

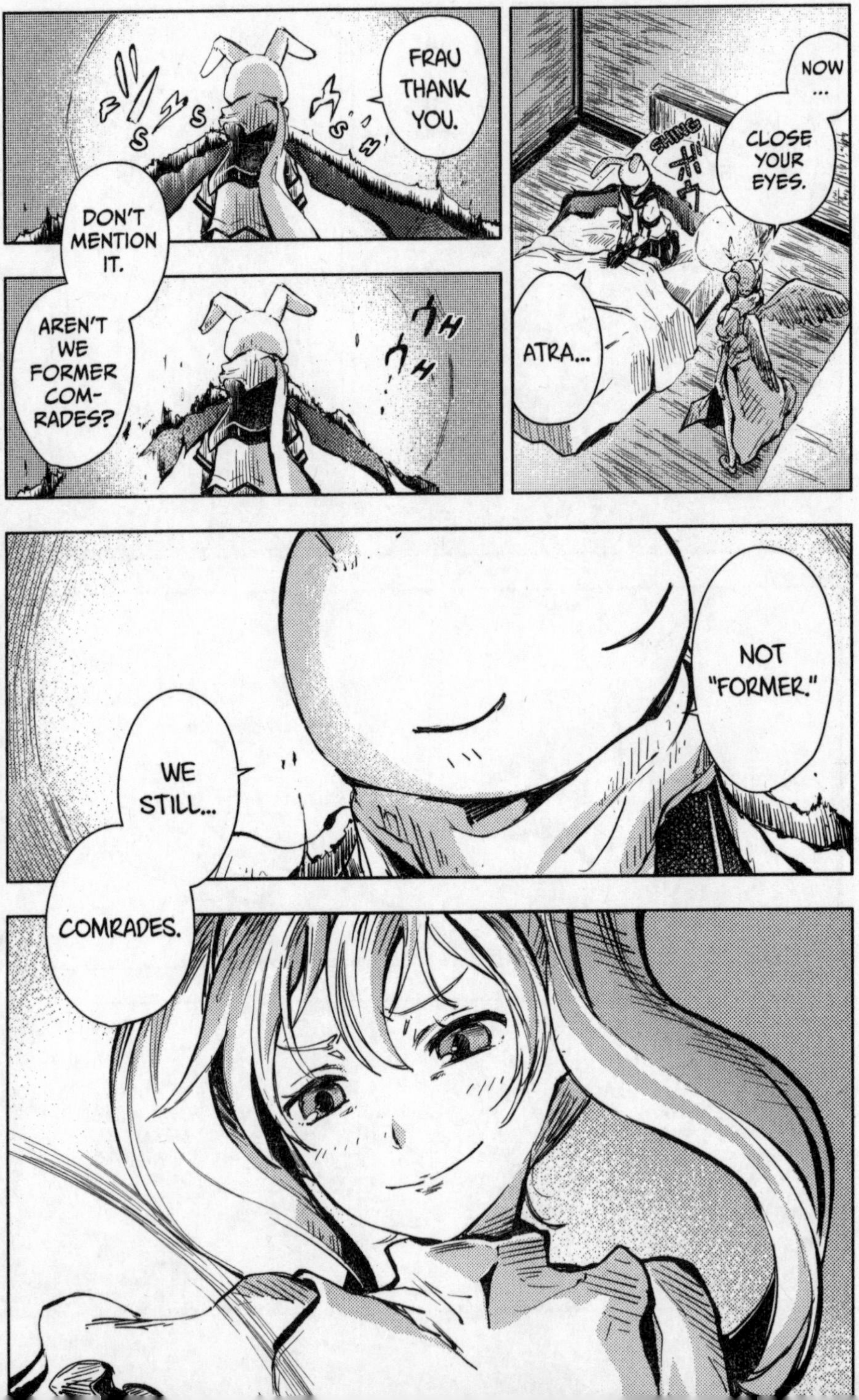
NOW...
CLOSE YOUR EYES.
SHING
ATRA...
FRAU THANK YOU.
FSSS
DON'T MENTION IT.
AREN'T WE FORMER COM-RADES?
NOT "FORMER."
WE STILL...
COMRADES.

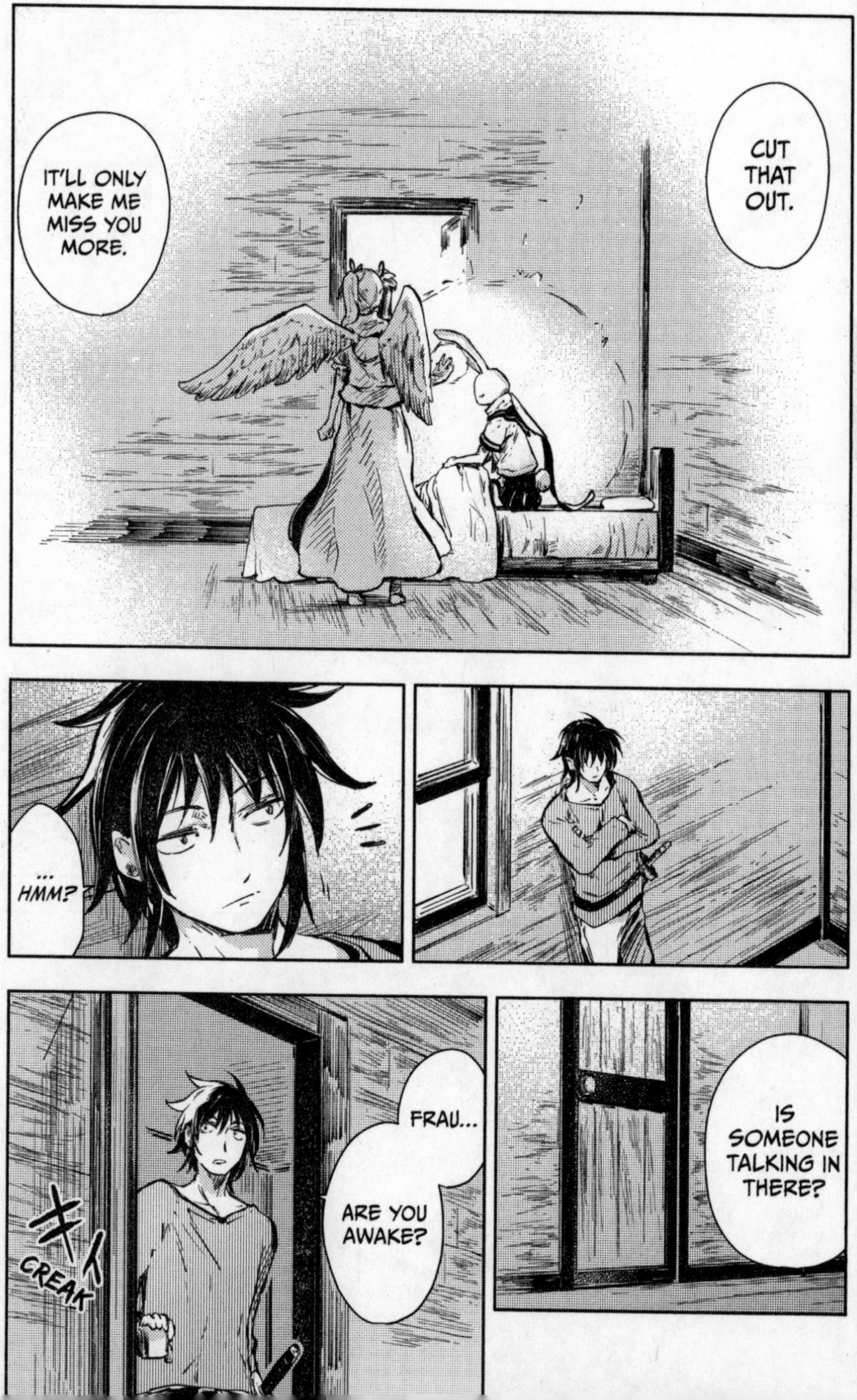
CUT THAT OUT.
IT'LL ONLY MAKE ME MISS YOU MORE.
...HMM?
IS SOMEONE TALKING IN THERE?
FRAU...
ARE YOU AWAKE?
CREAK

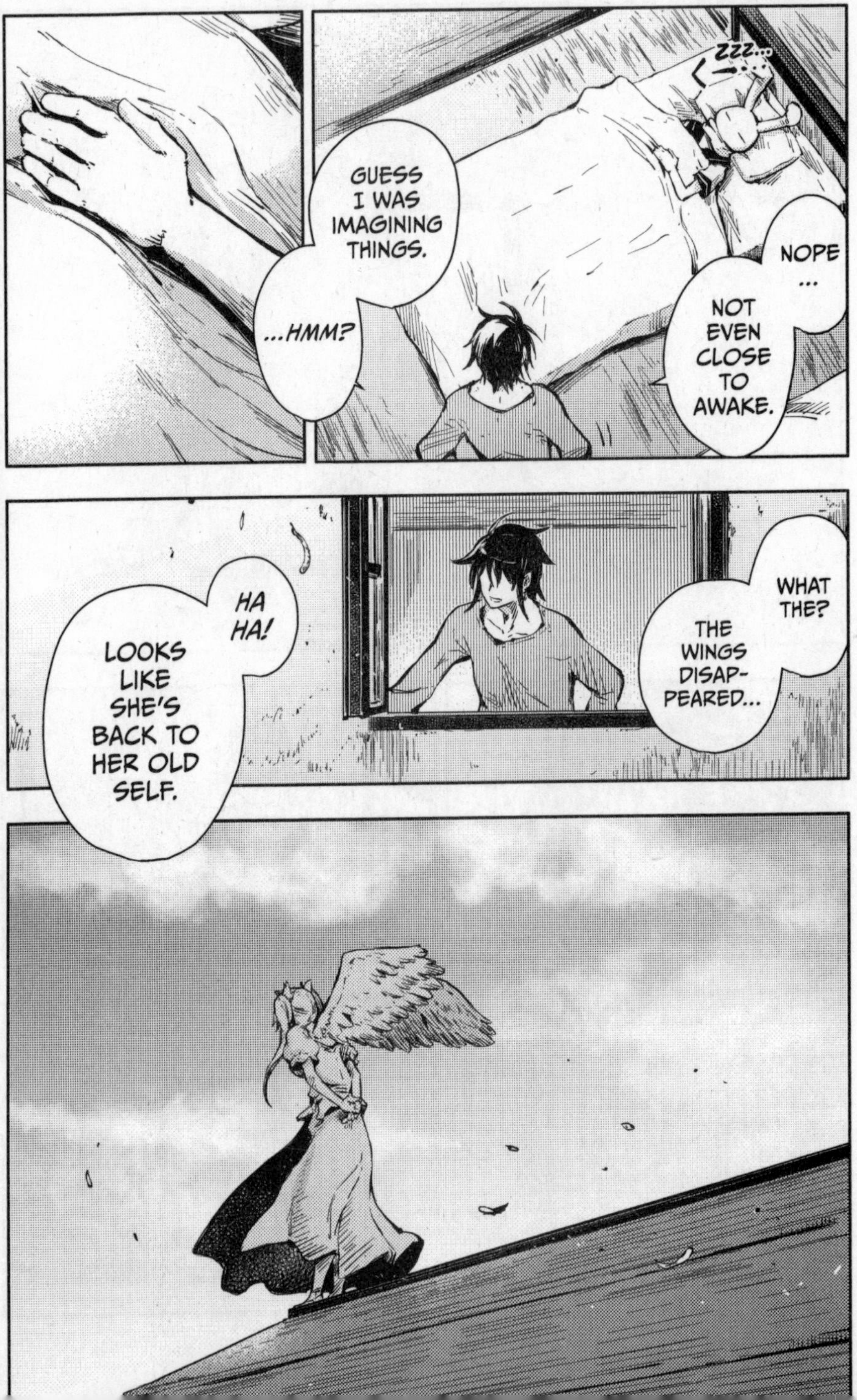
ZZZ...
NOPE ... NOT EVEN CLOSE TO AWAKE.
GUESS I WAS IMAGINING THINGS.
...HMM?
WHAT THE? THE WINGS DISAP-PEARED...
HA HA!
LOOKS LIKE SHE'S BACK TO HER OLD SELF.

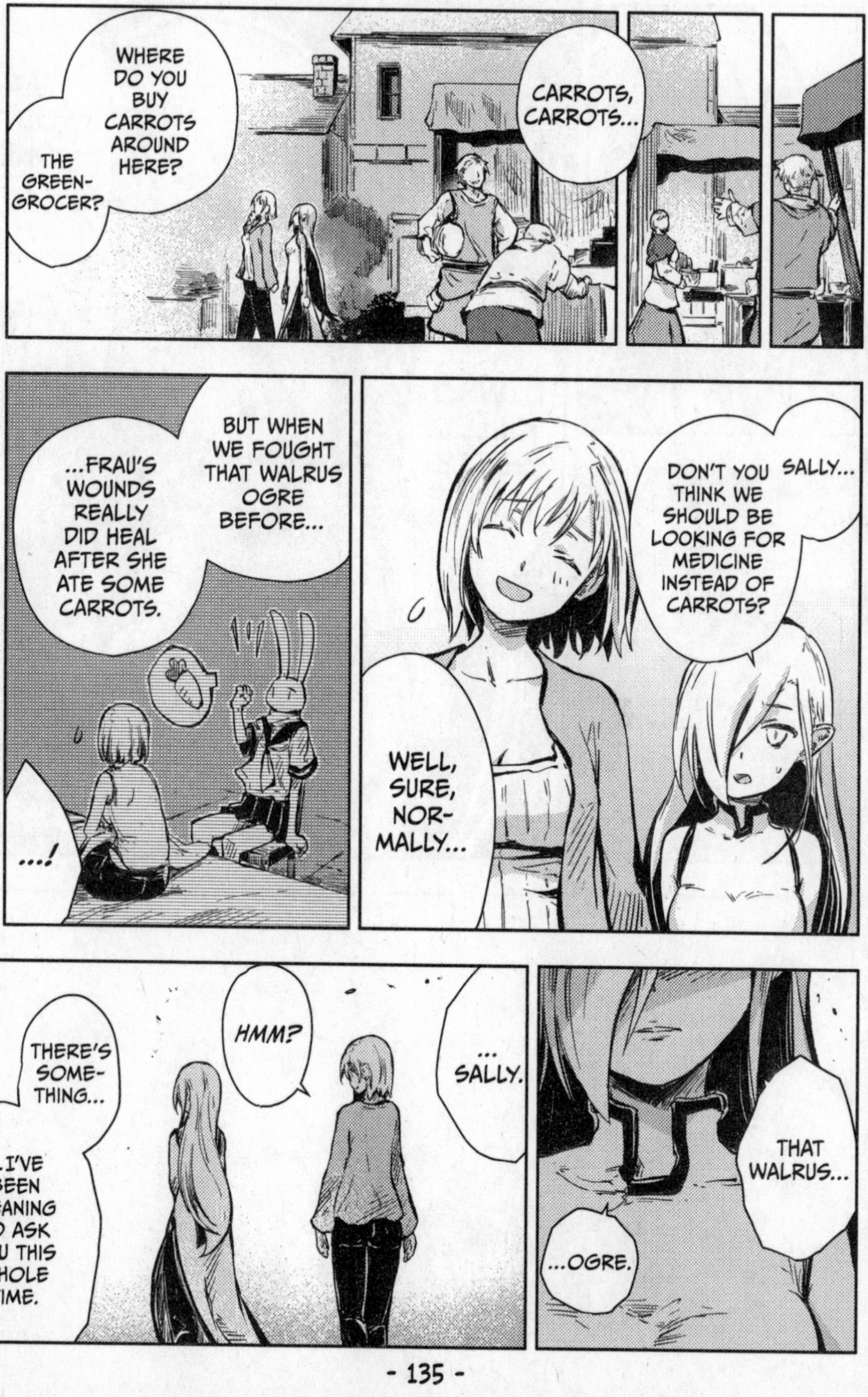
CARROTS, CARROTS...
WHERE DO YOU BUY CARROTS AROUND HERE?
THE GREEN-GROCER?
SALLY...
DON'T YOU THINK WE SHOULD BE LOOKING FOR MEDICINE INSTEAD OF CARROTS?
WELL, SURE, NOR-MALLY...
BUT WHEN WE FOUGHT THAT WALRUS OGRE BEFORE...
...FRAU'S WOUNDS REALLY DID HEAL AFTER SHE ATE SOME CARROTS.
...!
THAT WALRUS...
...OGRE.
...SALLY.
HMM?
THERE'S SOME-THING...
...I'VE BEEN MEANING TO ASK YOU THIS WHOLE TIME.

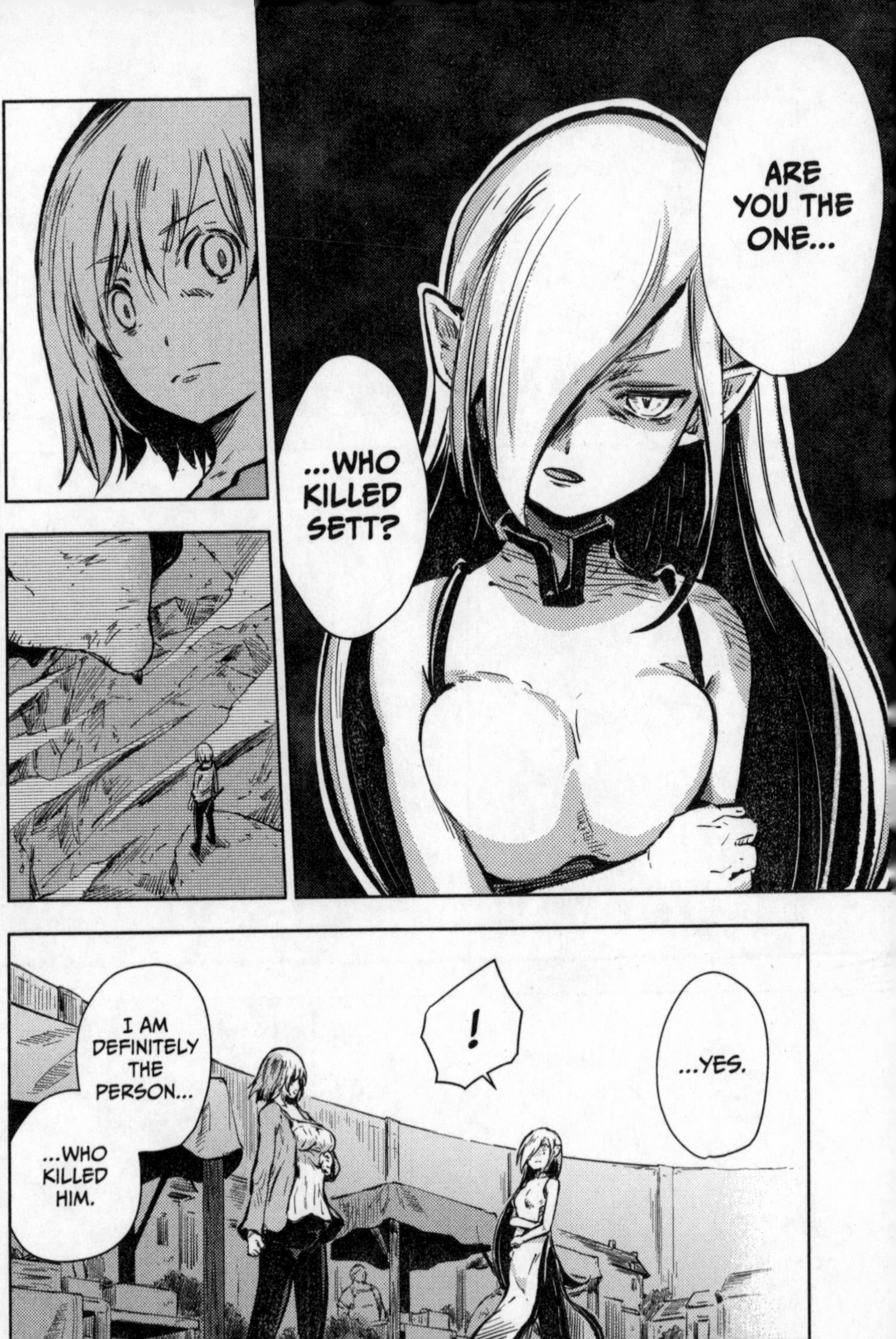
ARE YOU THE ONE...
...WHO KILLED SETT?
...YES.
!
I AM DEFINITELY THE PERSON...
...WHO KILLED HIM.

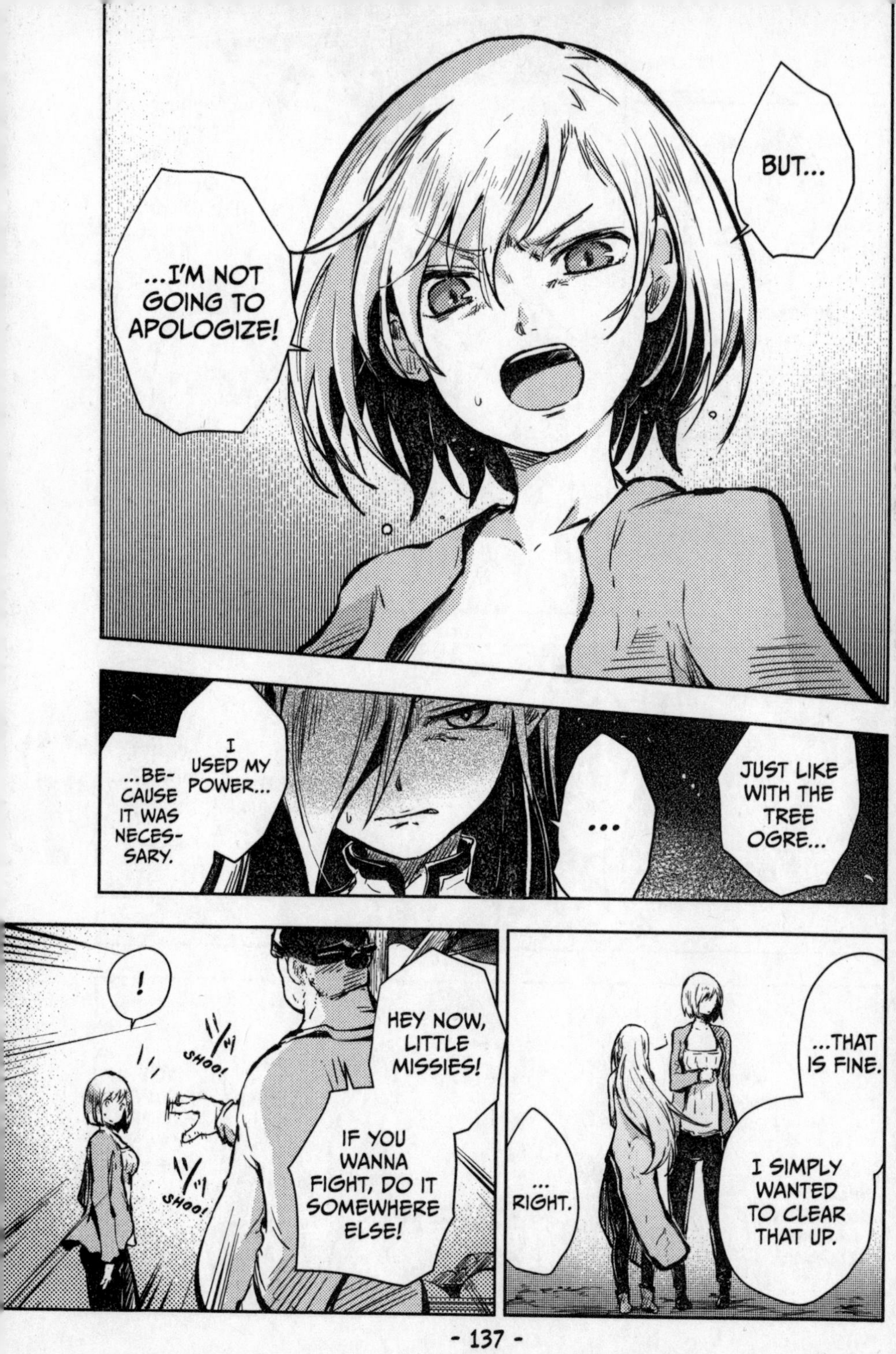
BUT...
...I'M NOT GOING TO APOLOGIZE!
JUST LIKE WITH THE TREE OGRE...
...
I USED MY POWER...
...BE-CAUSE IT WAS NECES-SARY.
...THAT IS FINE.
I SIMPLY WANTED TO CLEAR THAT UP.
... RIGHT.
HEY NOW, LITTLE MISSIES!
IF YOU WANNA FIGHT, DO IT SOMEWHERE ELSE!
SHOO!
SHOO!
!

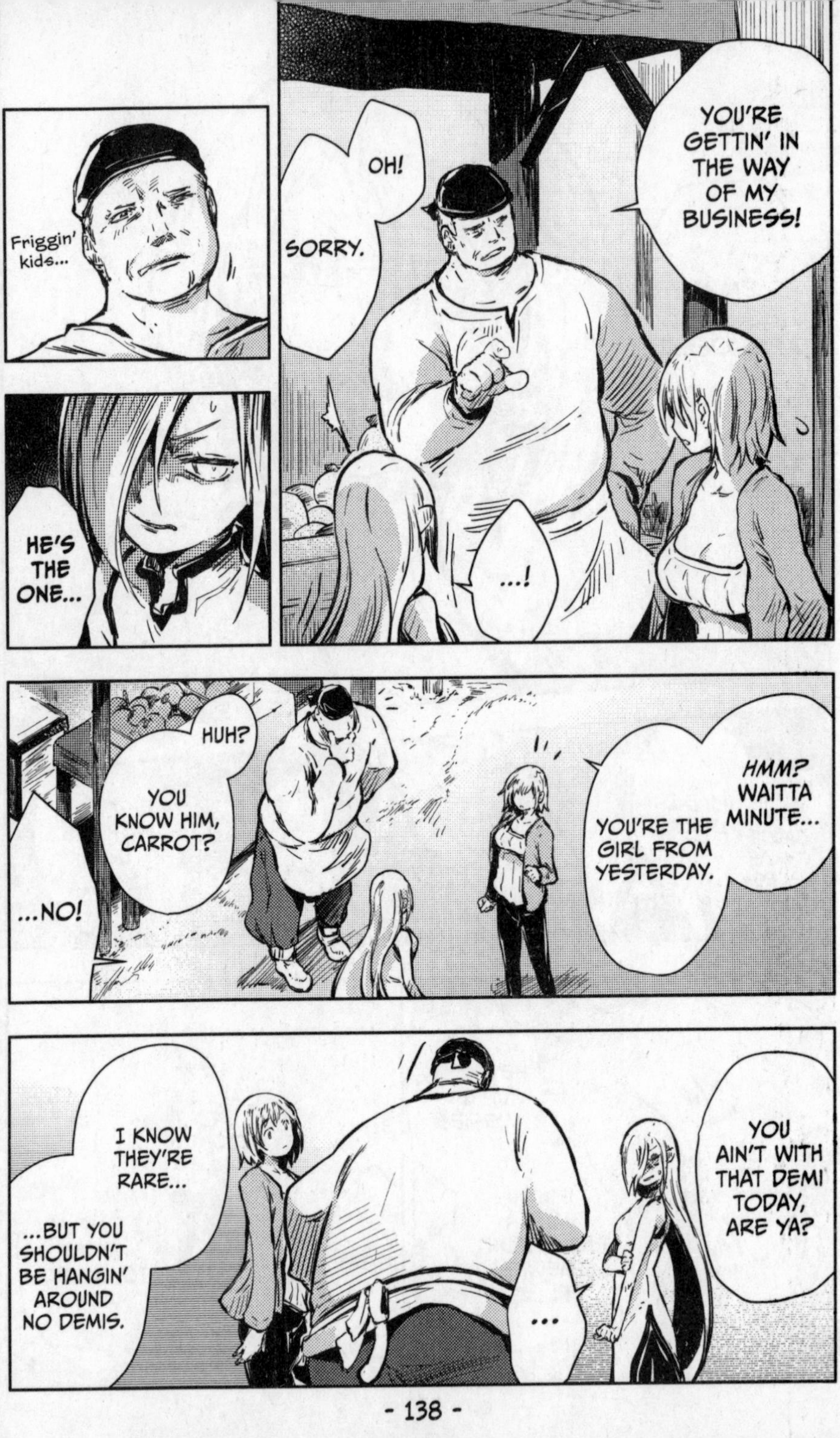
YOU'RE GETTIN' IN THE WAY OF MY BUSINESS!
OH!
SORRY.
...!
Friggin' kids...
HE'S THE ONE...
HMM? WAITTA MINUTE...
YOU'RE THE GIRL FROM YESTERDAY.
HUH?
YOU KNOW HIM, CARROT?
...NO!
YOU AIN'T WITH THAT DEMI TODAY, ARE YA?
...
I KNOW THEY'RE RARE...
...BUT YOU SHOULDN'T BE HANGIN' AROUND NO DEMIS.

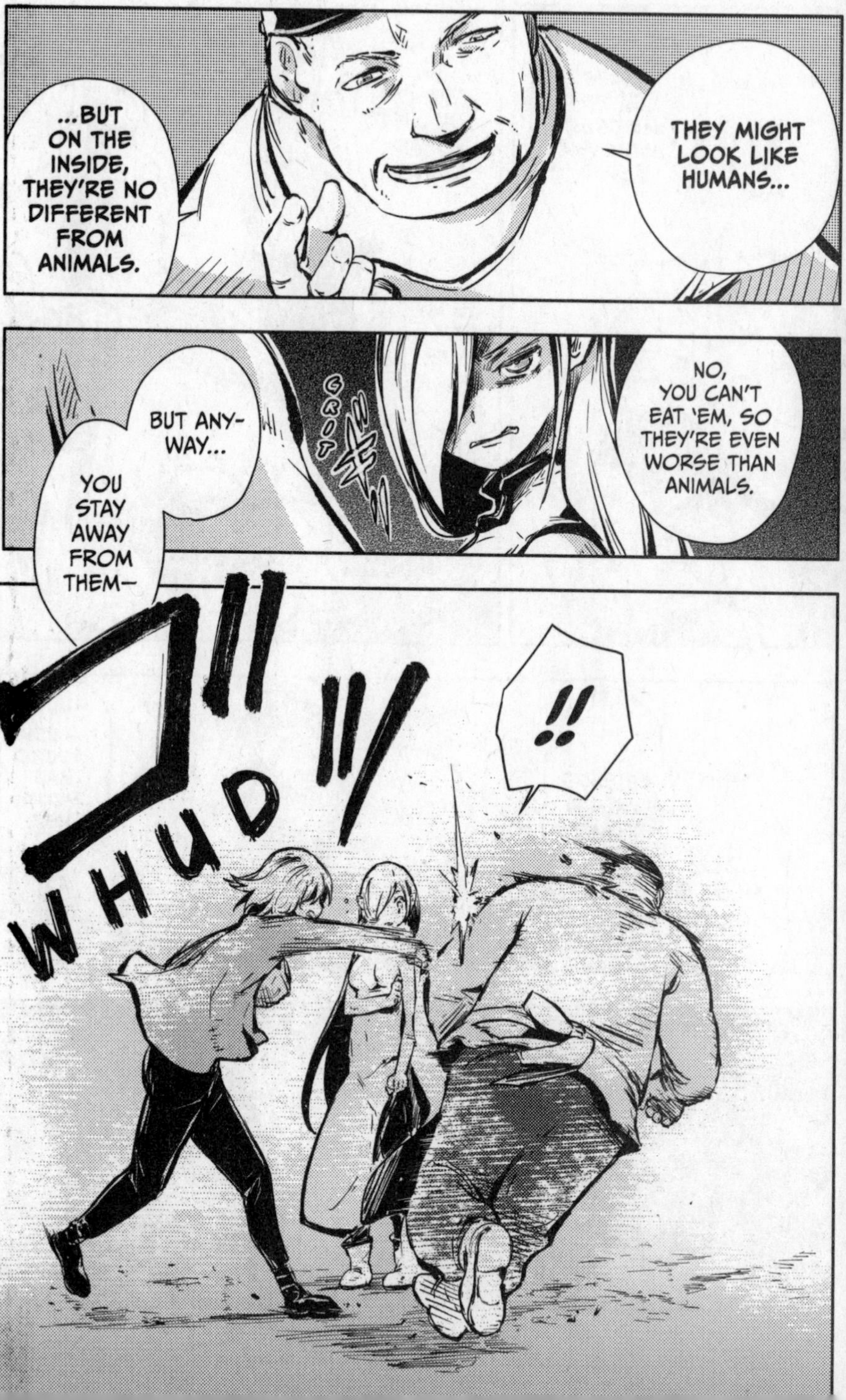
THEY MIGHT LOOK LIKE HUMANS...
...BUT ON THE INSIDE, THEY'RE NO DIFFERENT FROM ANIMALS.
NO, YOU CAN'T EAT 'EM, SO THEY'RE EVEN WORSE THAN ANIMALS.
GRIT
BUT ANY-WAY...
YOU STAY AWAY FROM THEM–
!!
WHUD

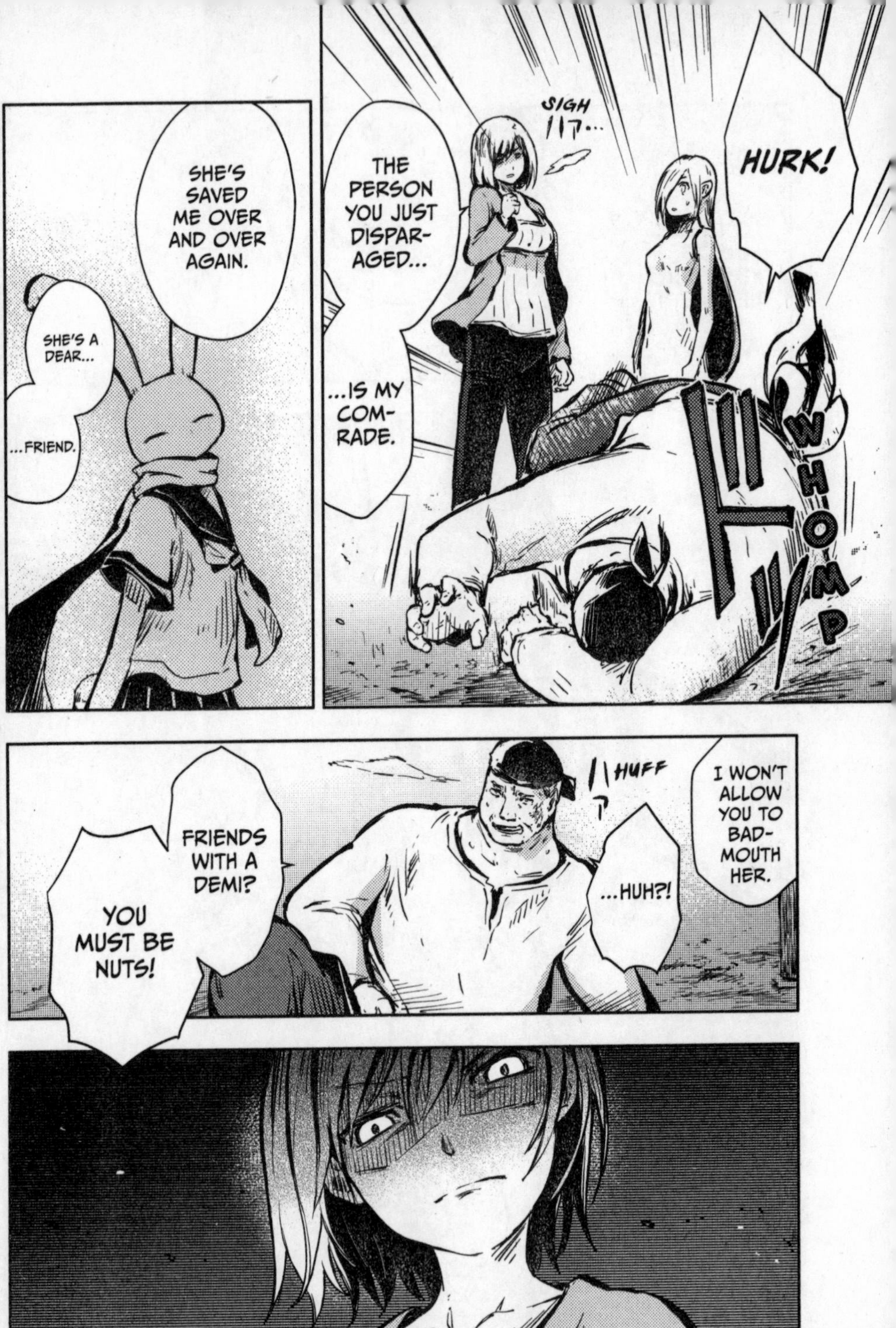
HURK!
SIGH
THE PERSON YOU JUST DISPAR-AGED...
...IS MY COM-RADE.
WHOMP
SHE'S SAVED ME OVER AND OVER AGAIN.
SHE'S A DEAR...
...FRIEND.
I WON'T ALLOW YOU TO BAD-MOUTH HER.
HUFF
...HUH?!
FRIENDS WITH A DEMI?
YOU MUST BE NUTS!

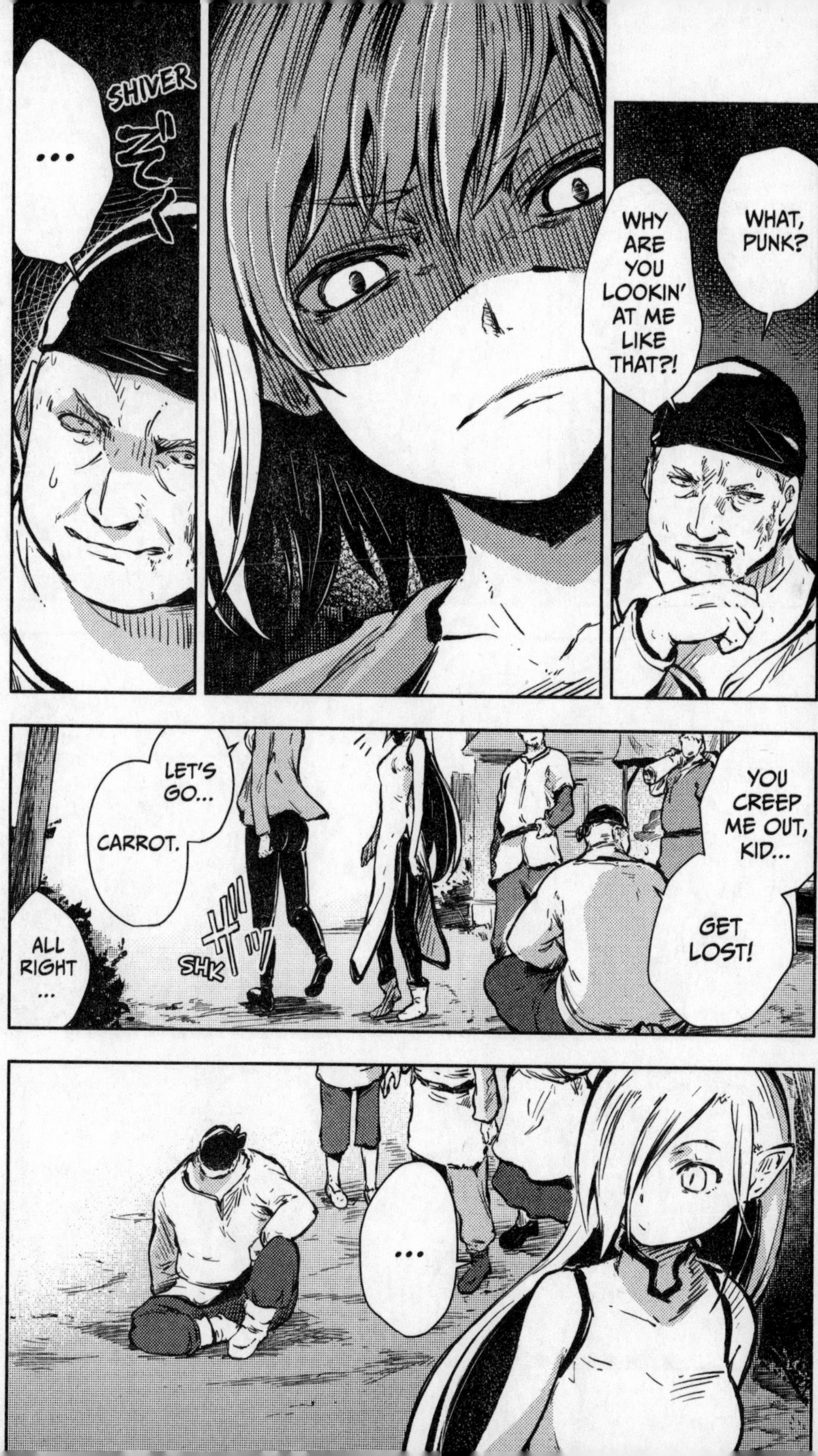
WHAT, PUNK?
WHY ARE YOU LOOKIN' AT ME LIKE THAT?!
SHIVER
...
YOU CREEP ME OUT, KID...
GET LOST!
LET'S GO...
CARROT.
SHK
ALL RIGHT ...
...

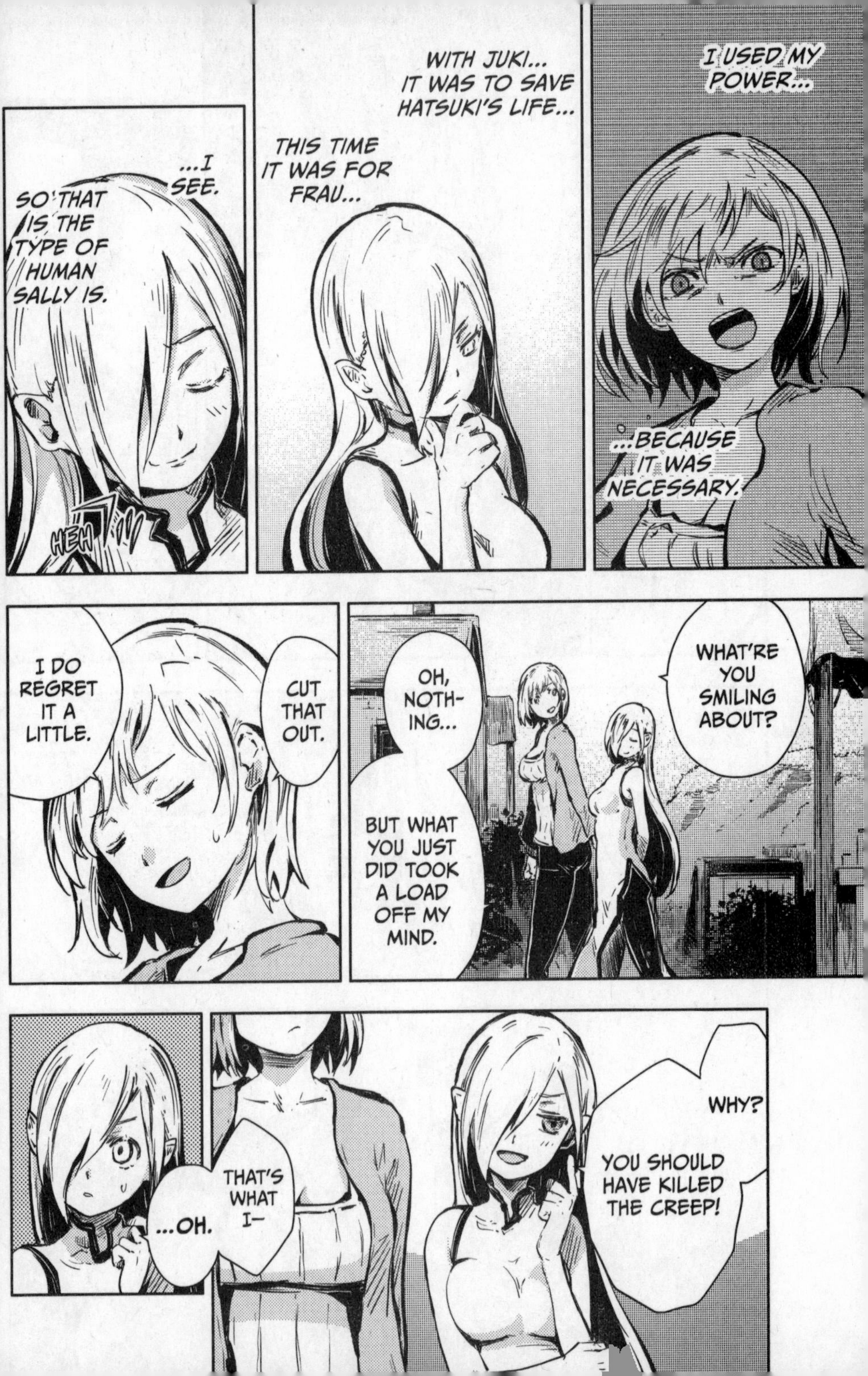
I USED MY POWER...
...BECAUSE IT WAS NECESSARY.
WITH JUKI... IT WAS TO SAVE HATSUKI'S LIFE...
THIS TIME IT WAS FOR FRAU...
...I SEE.
SO THAT IS THE TYPE OF HUMAN SALLY IS.
HEH
WHAT'RE YOU SMILING ABOUT?
OH, NOTHING...
BUT WHAT YOU JUST DID TOOK A LOAD OFF MY MIND.
CUT THAT OUT.
I DO REGRET IT A LITTLE.
WHY?
YOU SHOULD HAVE KILLED THE CREEP!
THAT'S WHAT I—
...OH.

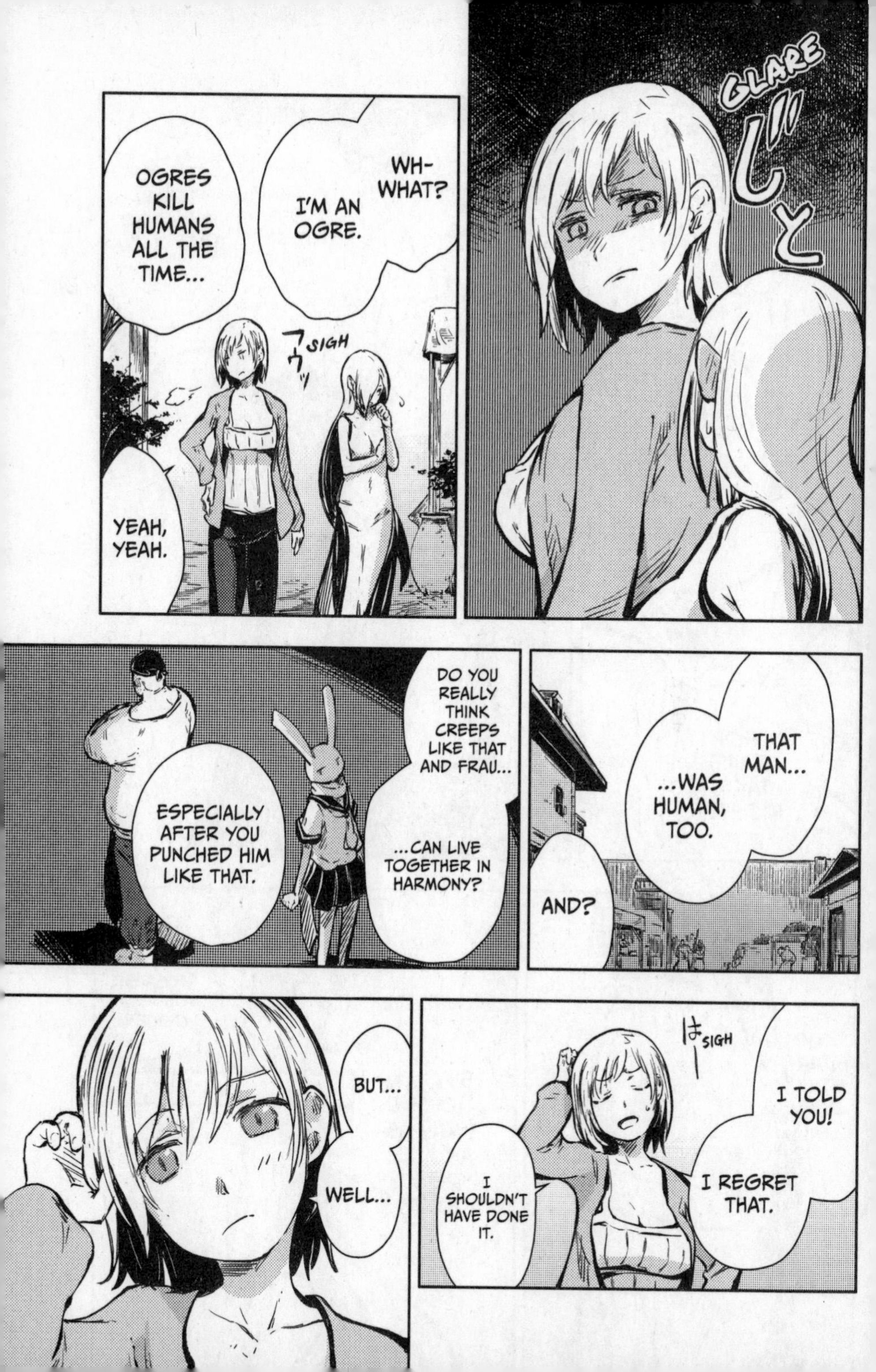
GLARE
WH-WHAT?
I'M AN OGRE.
OGRES KILL HUMANS ALL THE TIME...
SIGH
YEAH, YEAH.
THAT MAN...
...WAS HUMAN, TOO.
AND?
DO YOU REALLY THINK CREEPS LIKE THAT AND FRAU...
...CAN LIVE TOGETHER IN HARMONY?
ESPECIALLY AFTER YOU PUNCHED HIM LIKE THAT.
SIGH
I TOLD YOU!
I REGRET THAT.
I SHOULDN'T HAVE DONE IT.
BUT...
WELL...

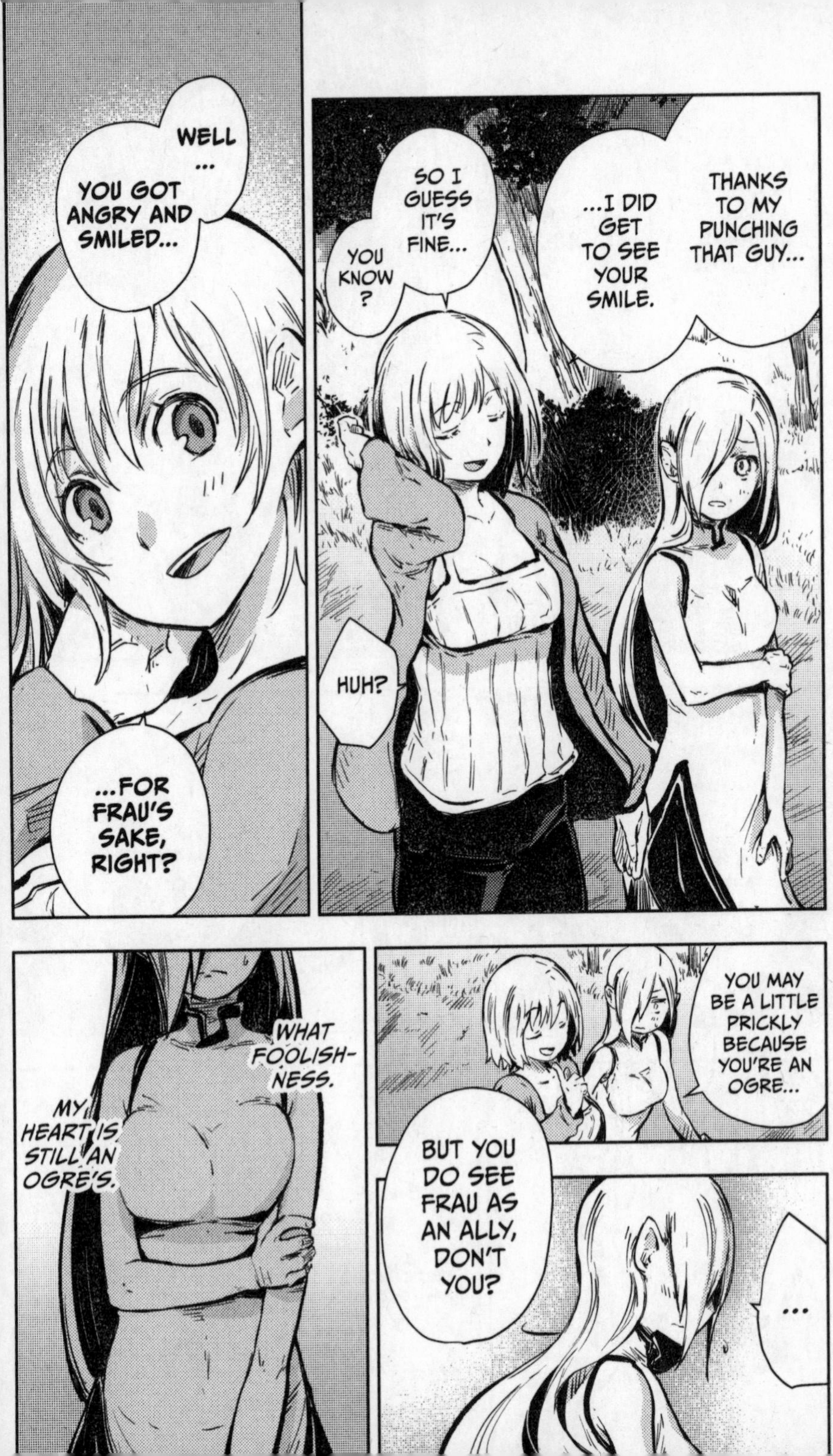
THANKS TO MY PUNCHING THAT GUY...
...I DID GET TO SEE YOUR SMILE.
SO I GUESS IT'S FINE...
YOU KNOW?
HUH?
WELL ... YOU GOT ANGRY AND SMILED...
...FOR FRAU'S SAKE, RIGHT?
YOU MAY BE A LITTLE PRICKLY BECAUSE YOU'RE AN OGRE...
BUT YOU DO SEE FRAU AS AN ALLY, DON'T YOU?
...
WHAT FOOLISH-NESS.
MY HEART IS STILL AN OGRE'S.

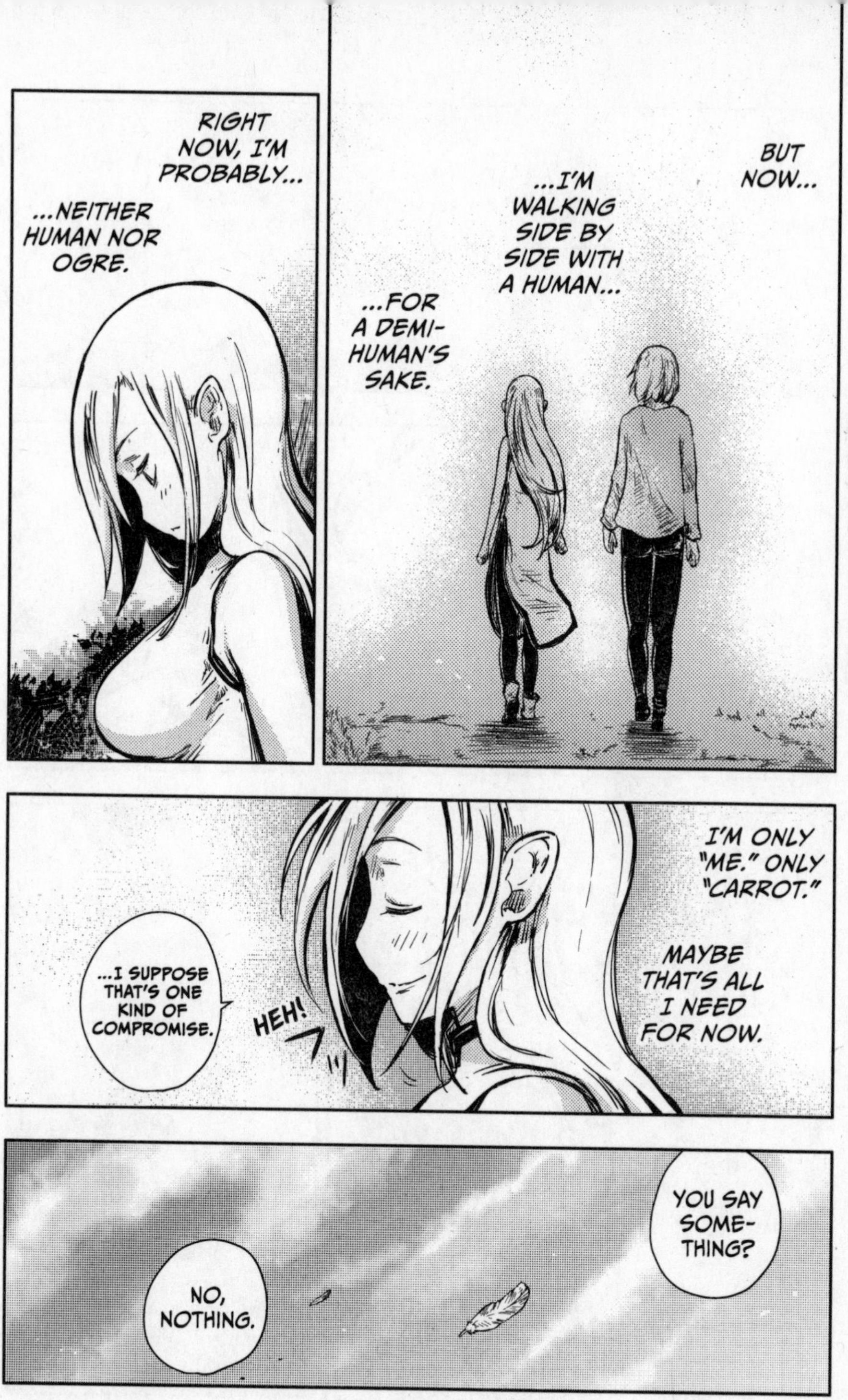
BUT NOW...
...I'M WALKING SIDE BY SIDE WITH A HUMAN...
...FOR A DEMI-HUMAN'S SAKE.
RIGHT NOW, I'M PROBABLY...
...NEITHER HUMAN NOR OGRE.
I'M ONLY "ME." ONLY "CARROT."
MAYBE THAT'S ALL I NEED FOR NOW.
HEH!
...I SUPPOSE THAT'S ONE KIND OF COMPROMISE.
YOU SAY SOMETHING?
NO, NOTHING.

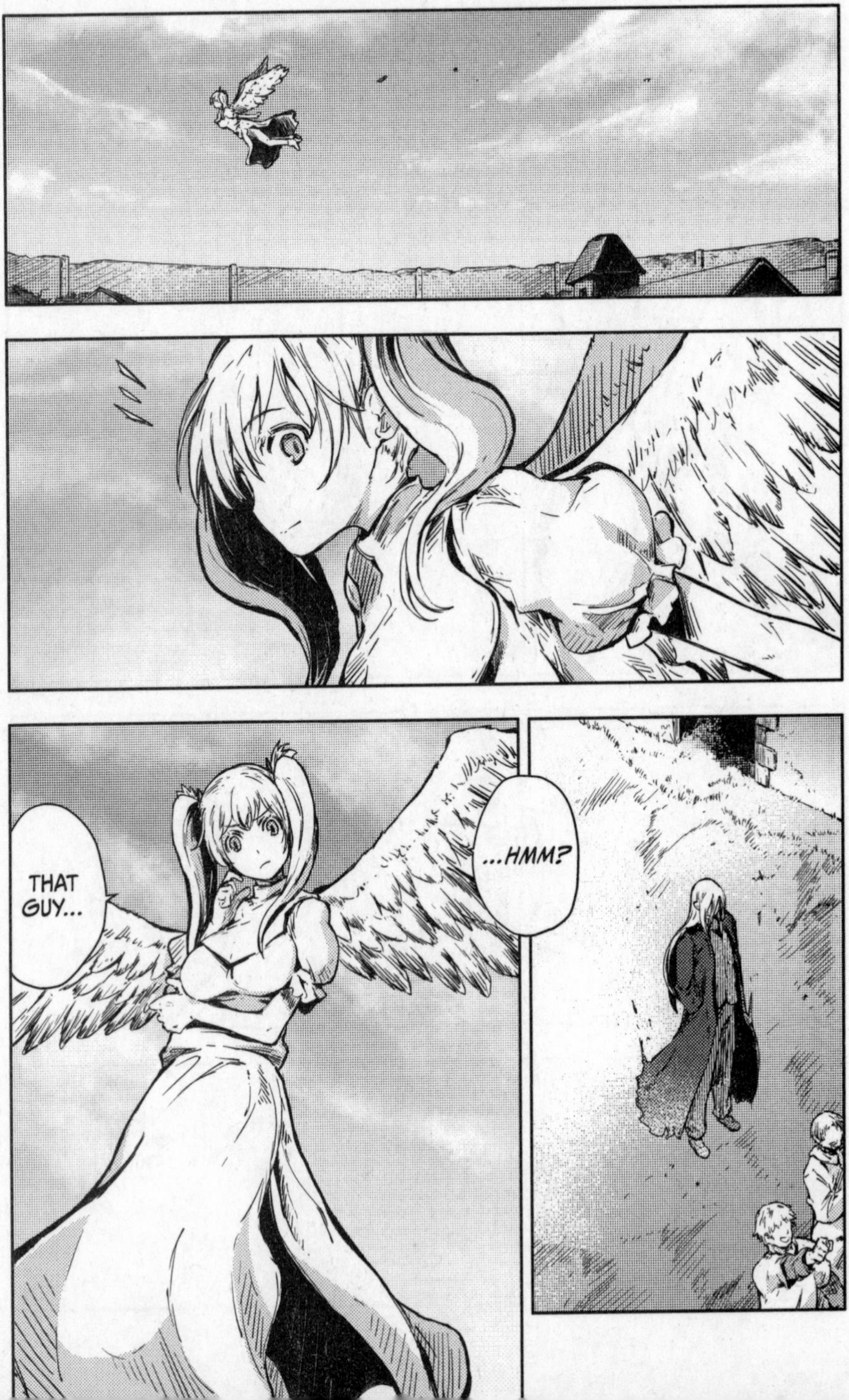
...HMM?
THAT GUY...

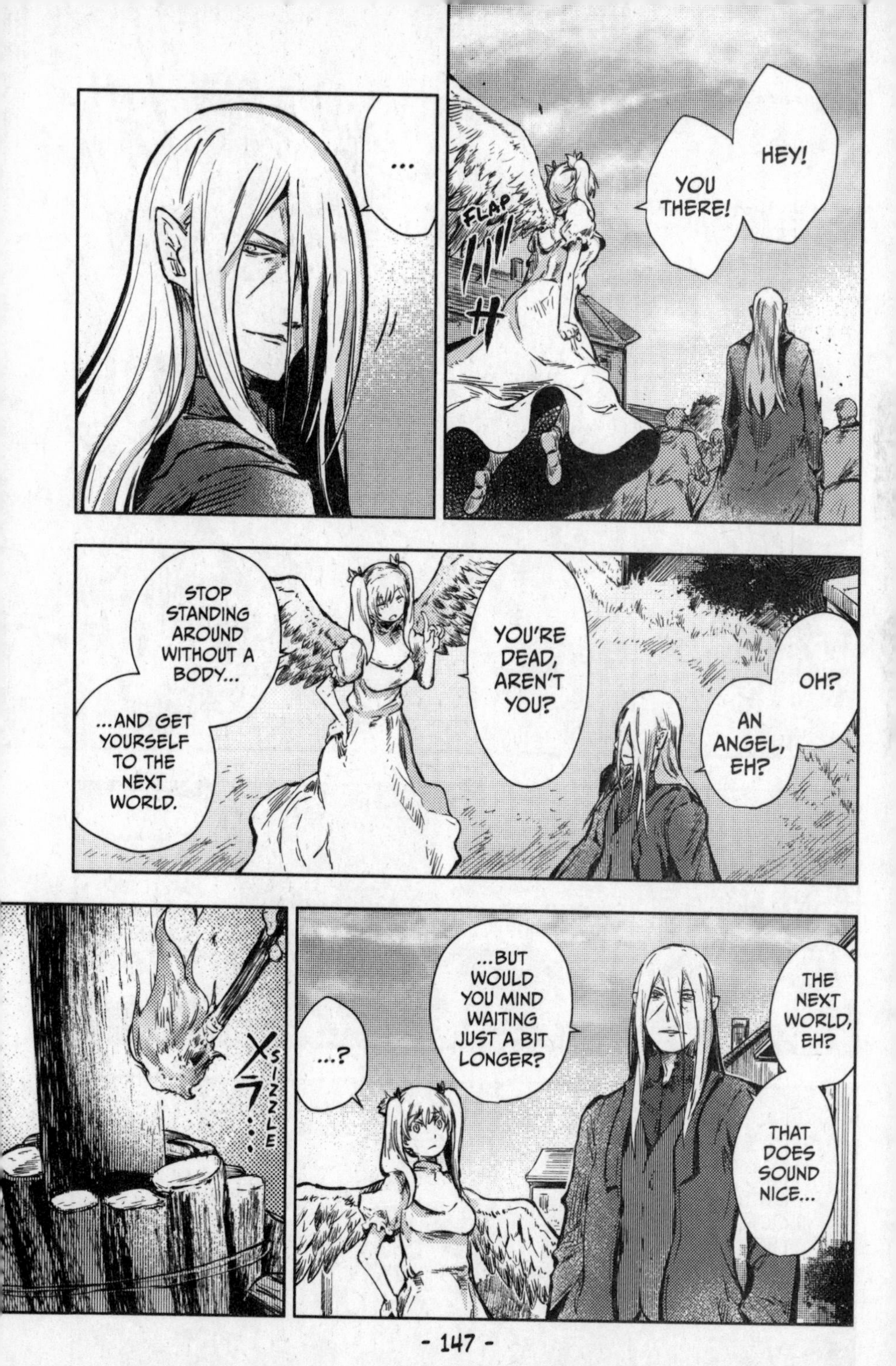
HEY! YOU THERE!
FLAP
...
OH? AN ANGEL, EH?
YOU'RE DEAD, AREN'T YOU?
STOP STANDING AROUND WITHOUT A BODY...
...AND GET YOURSELF TO THE NEXT WORLD.
THE NEXT WORLD, EH?
THAT DOES SOUND NICE...
...BUT WOULD YOU MIND WAITING JUST A BIT LONGER?
...?
SIZZLE

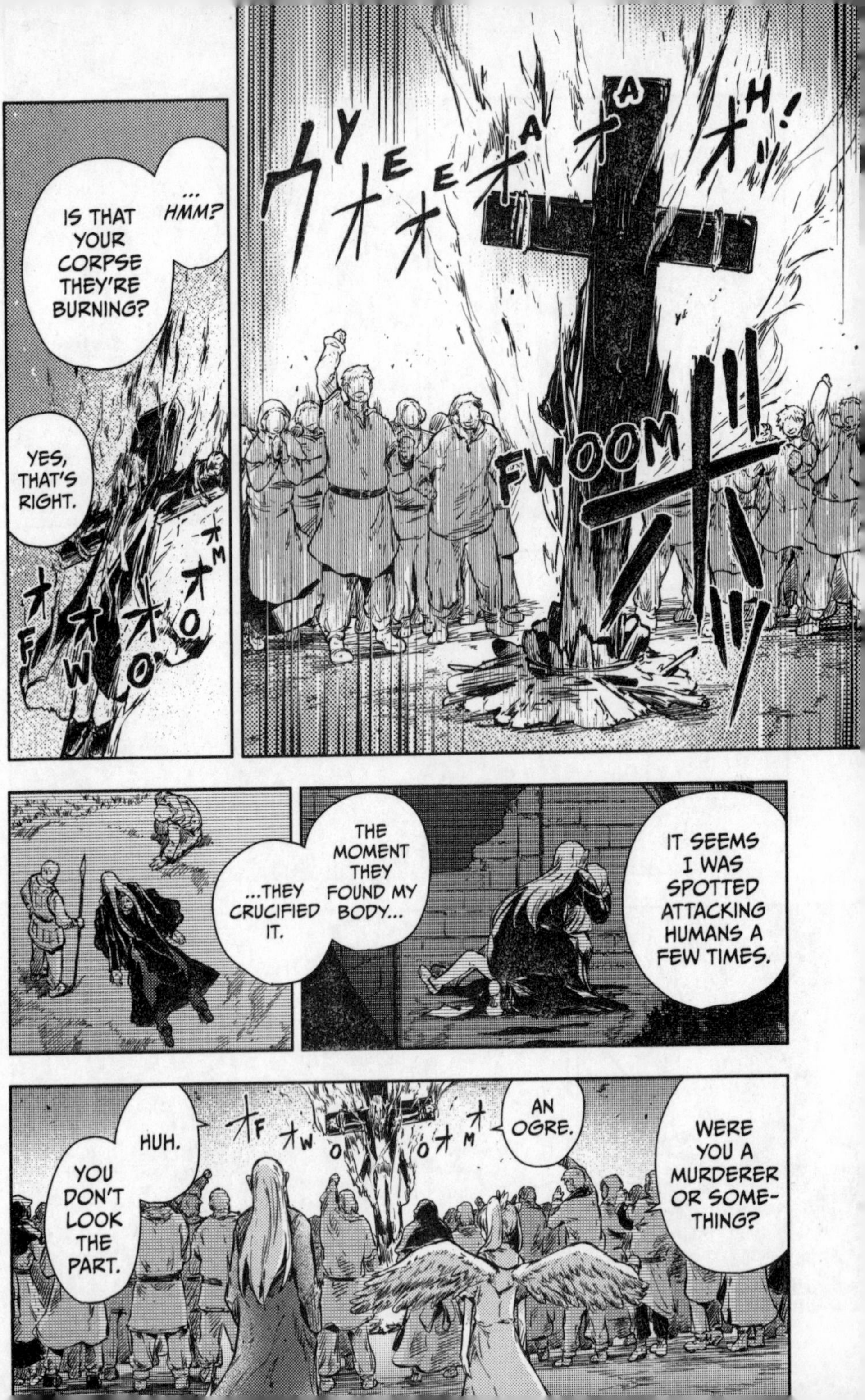
YEEEAAH!
FWOOM
...HMM?
IS THAT YOUR CORPSE THEY'RE BURNING?
YES, THAT'S RIGHT.
FWOOM
IT SEEMS I WAS SPOTTED ATTACKING HUMANS A FEW TIMES.
THE MOMENT THEY FOUND MY BODY...
...THEY CRUCIFIED IT.
WERE YOU A MURDERER OR SOME-THING?
AN OGRE.
FWOOM
HUH.
YOU DON'T LOOK THE PART.

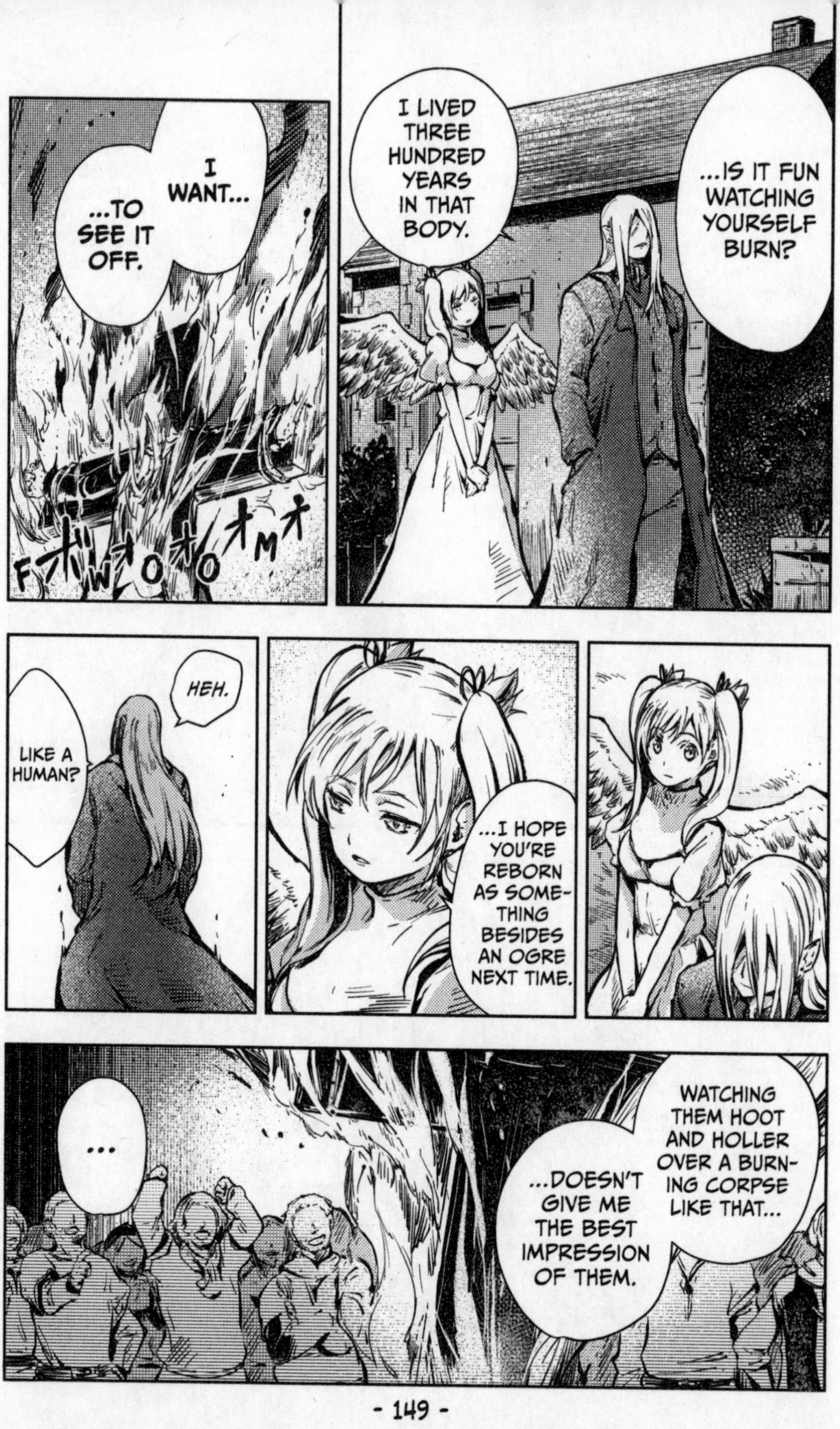
...IS IT FUN WATCHING YOURSELF BURN?
I LIVED THREE HUNDRED YEARS IN THAT BODY.
I WANT...
...TO SEE IT OFF.
...I HOPE YOU'RE REBORN AS SOME-THING BESIDES AN OGRE NEXT TIME.
HEH.
LIKE A HUMAN?
WATCHING THEM HOOT AND HOLLER OVER A BURN-ING CORPSE LIKE THAT...
...DOESN'T GIVE ME THE BEST IMPRESSION OF THEM.
...

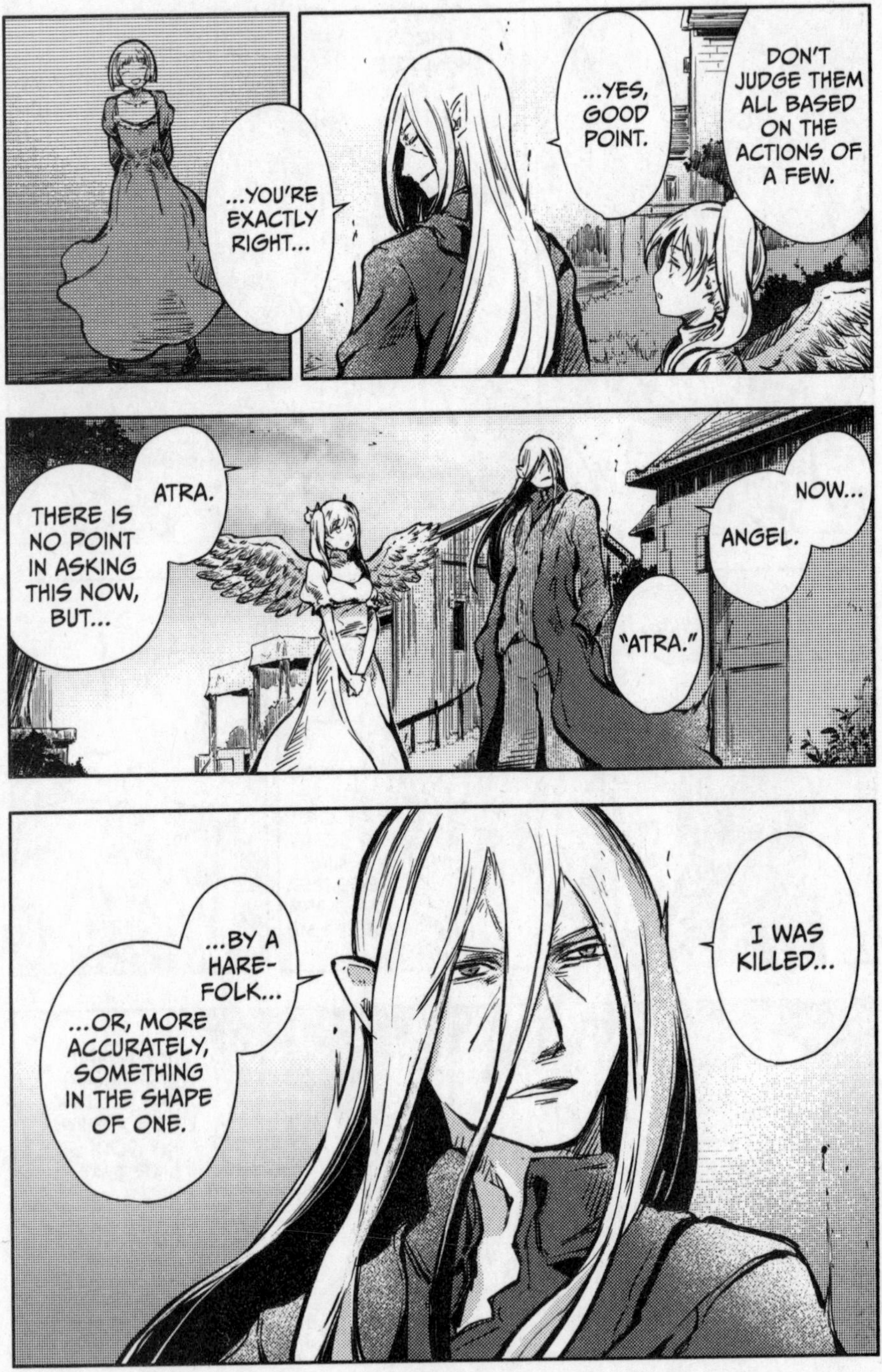
DON'T JUDGE THEM ALL BASED ON THE ACTIONS OF A FEW.
...YES, GOOD POINT.
...YOU'RE EXACTLY RIGHT...
NOW... ANGEL.
"ATRA."
ATRA. THERE IS NO POINT IN ASKING THIS NOW, BUT...
I WAS KILLED...
...BY A HARE-FOLK...
...OR, MORE ACCURATELY, SOMETHING IN THE SHAPE OF ONE.

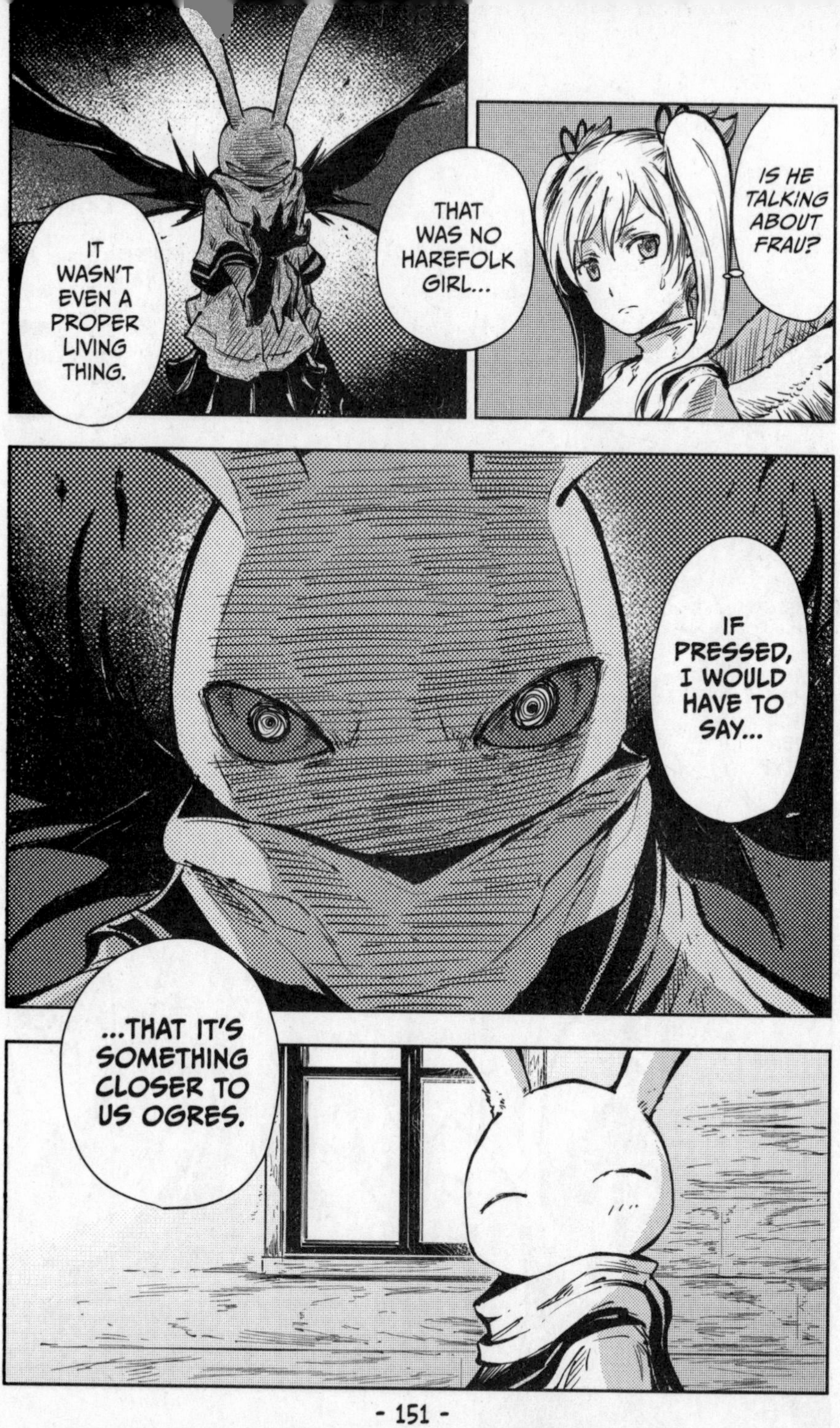
IS HE TALKING ABOUT FRAU?
THAT WAS NO HAREFOLK GIRL...
IT WASN'T EVEN A PROPER LIVING THING.
IF PRESSED, I WOULD HAVE TO SAY...
...THAT IT'S SOMETHING CLOSER TO US OGRES.

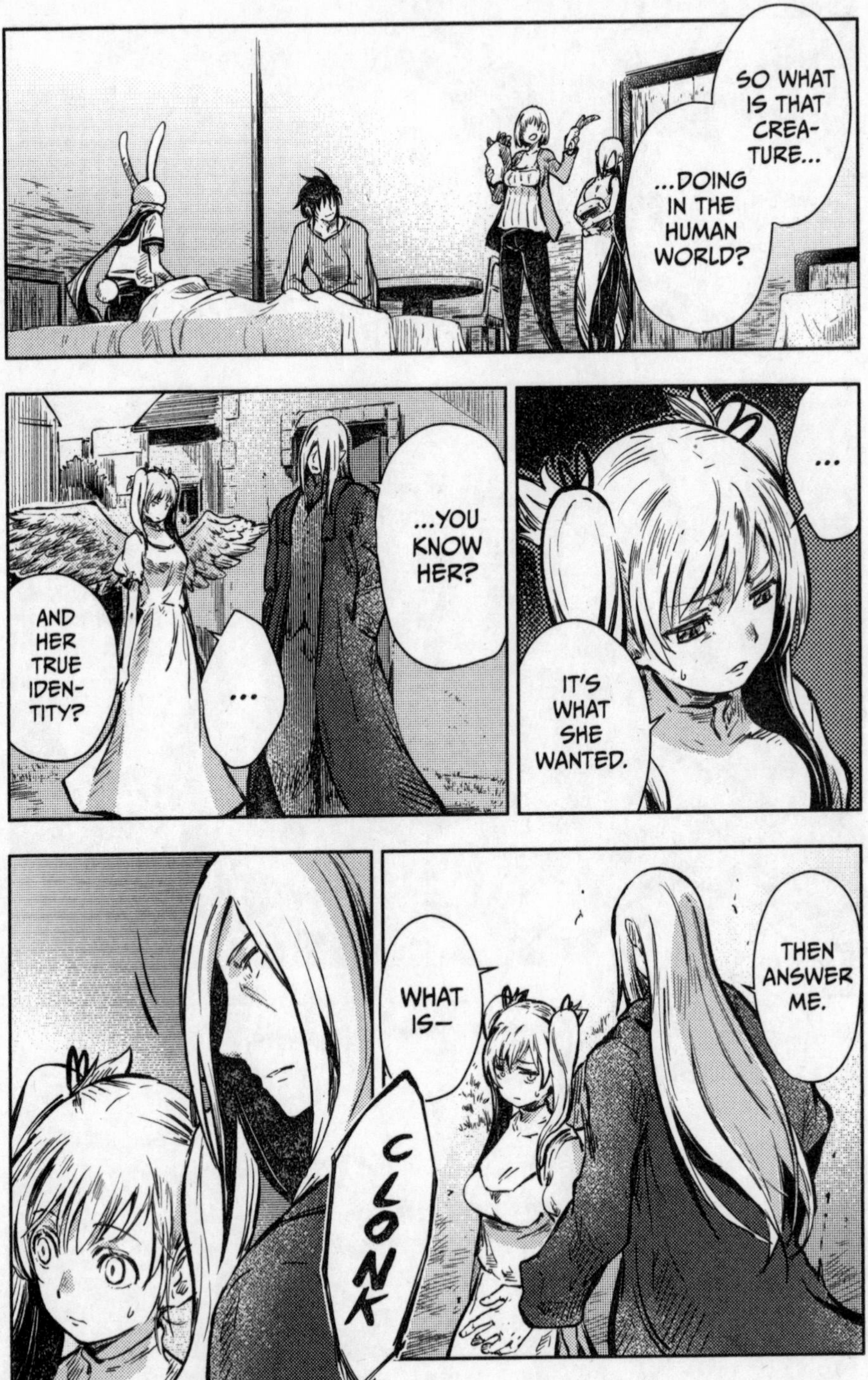
SO WHAT IS THAT CREA-TURE...
...DOING IN THE HUMAN WORLD?
...
IT'S WHAT SHE WANTED.
...YOU KNOW HER?
...
AND HER TRUE IDEN-TITY?
THEN ANSWER ME.
WHAT IS—
CLONK

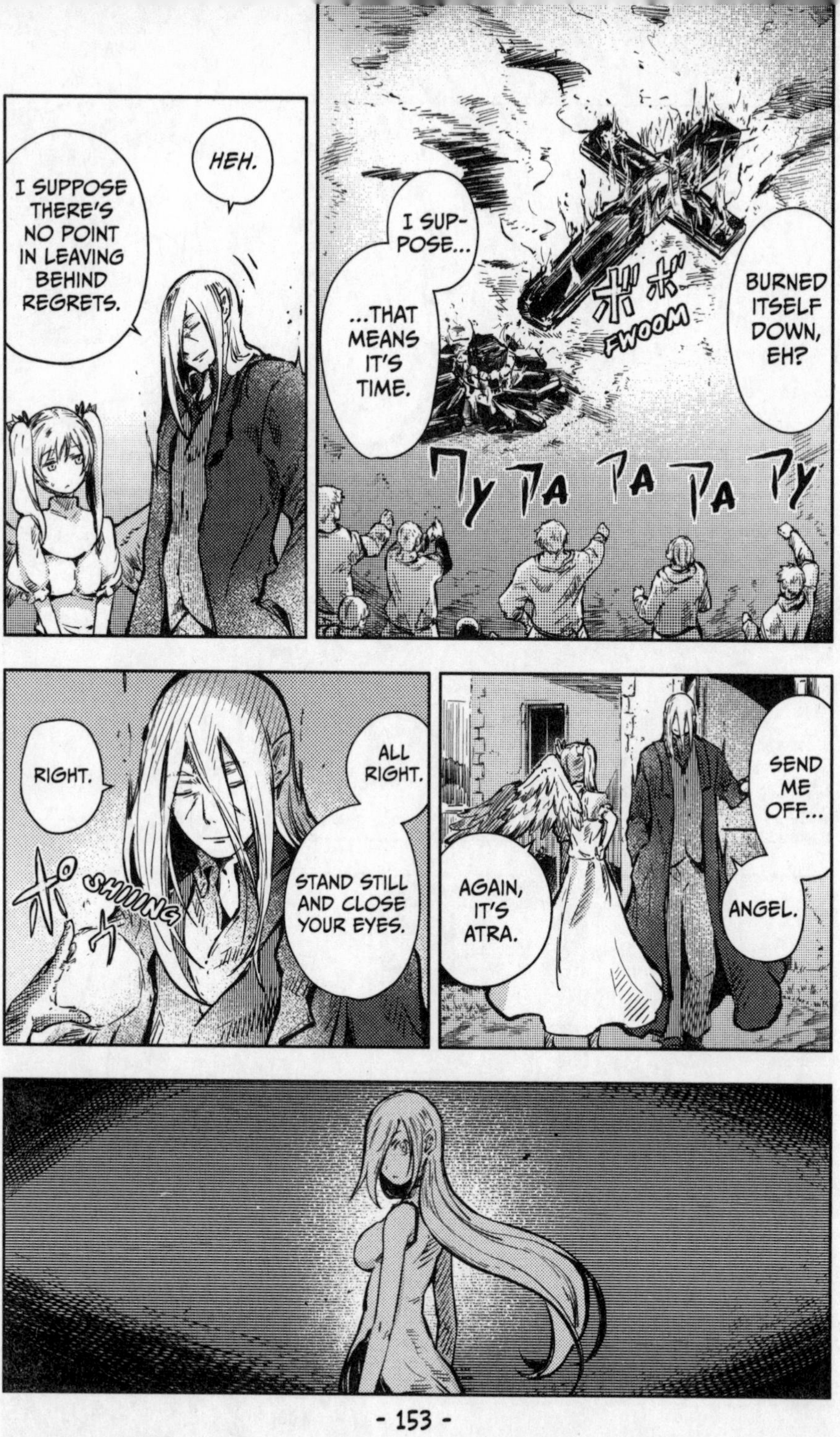
BURNED ITSELF DOWN, EH?
ボボ
FWOOM
I SUPPOSE...
...THAT MEANS IT'S TIME.
HEH.
I SUPPOSE THERE'S NO POINT IN LEAVING BEHIND REGRETS.
SEND ME OFF...
ANGEL.
AGAIN, IT'S ATRA.
ALL RIGHT.
STAND STILL AND CLOSE YOUR EYES.
RIGHT.
SHIIING

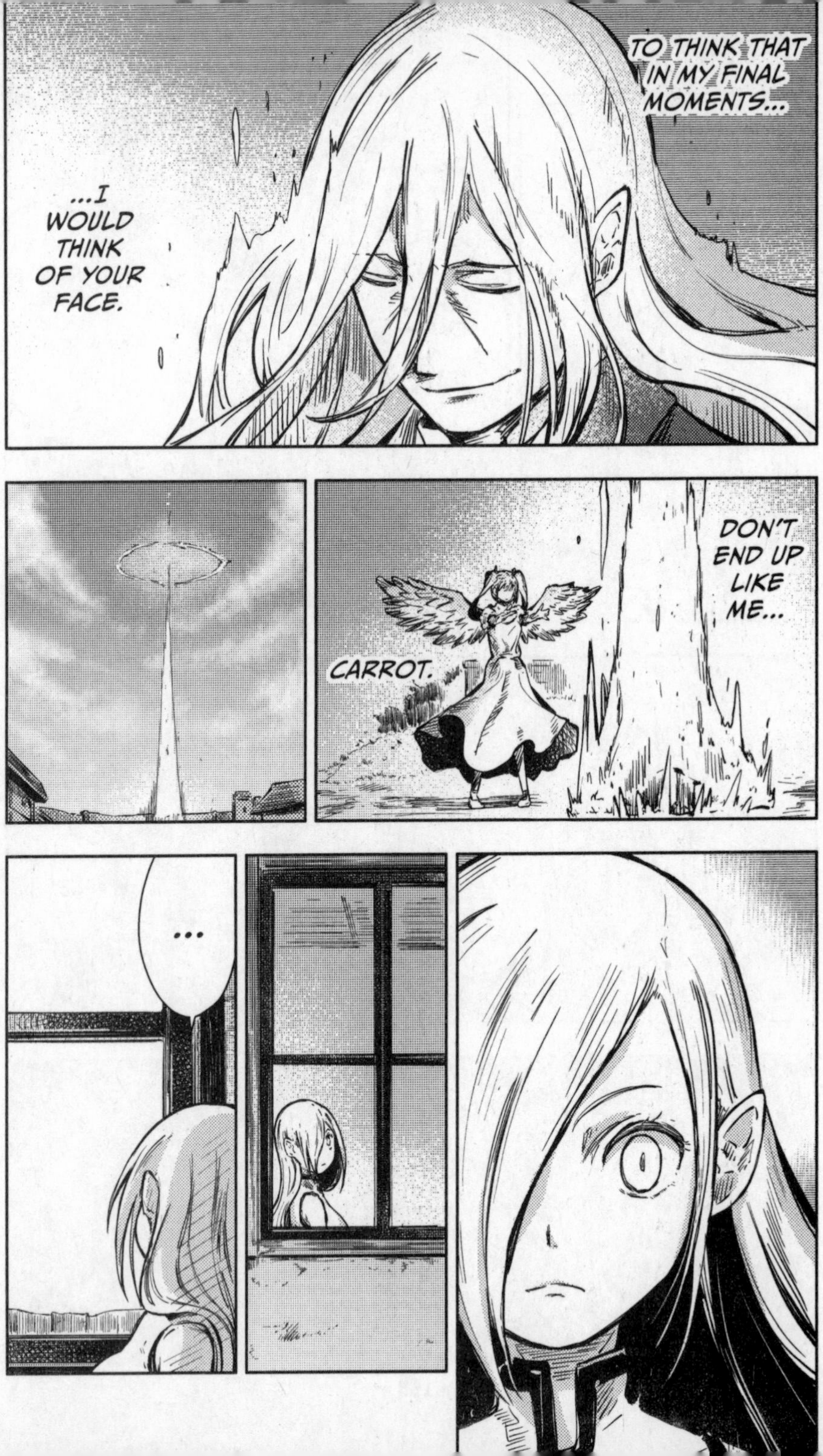
TO THINK THAT IN MY FINAL MOMENTS...
...I WOULD THINK OF YOUR FACE.
DON'T END UP LIKE ME...
CARROT.
...

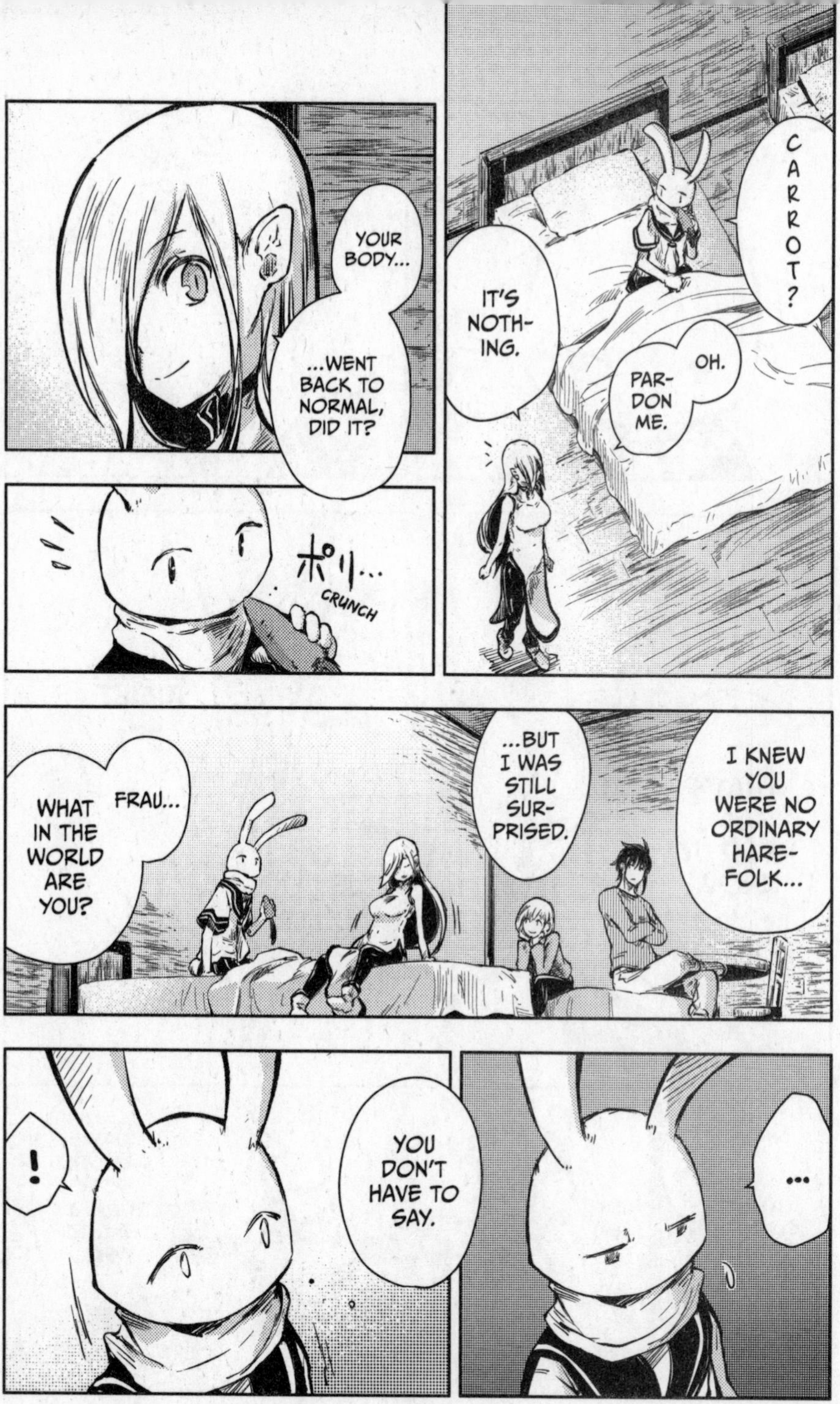
CARROT?
IT'S NOTHING.
OH. PARDON ME.
YOUR BODY...
...WENT BACK TO NORMAL, DID IT?
ポリ…
CRUNCH
I KNEW YOU WERE NO ORDINARY HARE-FOLK...
...BUT I WAS STILL SURPRISED.
FRAU...
WHAT IN THE WORLD ARE YOU?
...
YOU DON'T HAVE TO SAY.
!

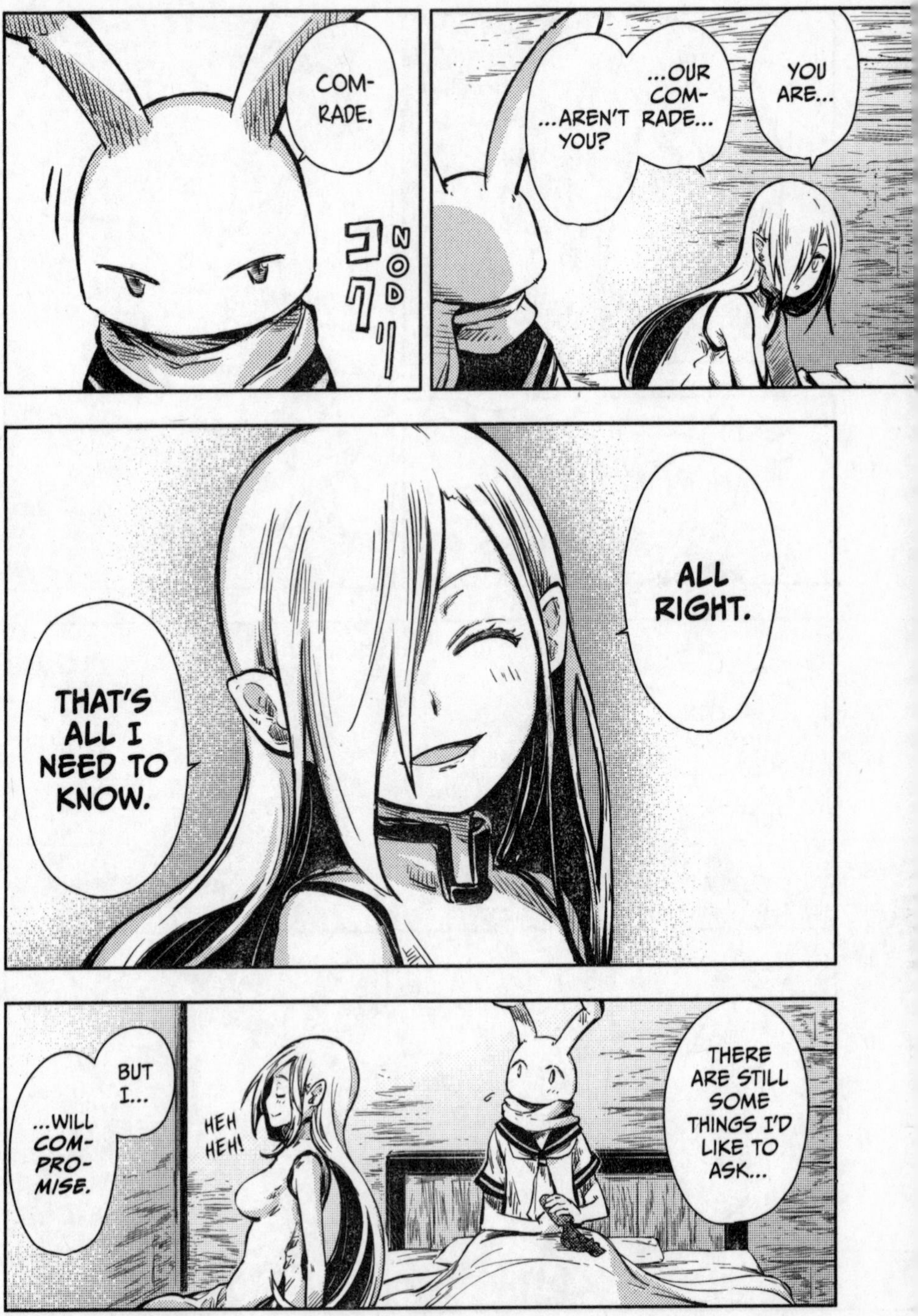
YOU ARE...
...OUR COM-RADE...
...AREN'T YOU?
COM-RADE.
NOD
ALL RIGHT.
THAT'S ALL I NEED TO KNOW.
THERE ARE STILL SOME THINGS I'D LIKE TO ASK...
HEH HEH!
BUT I...
...WILL COM-PRO-MISE.

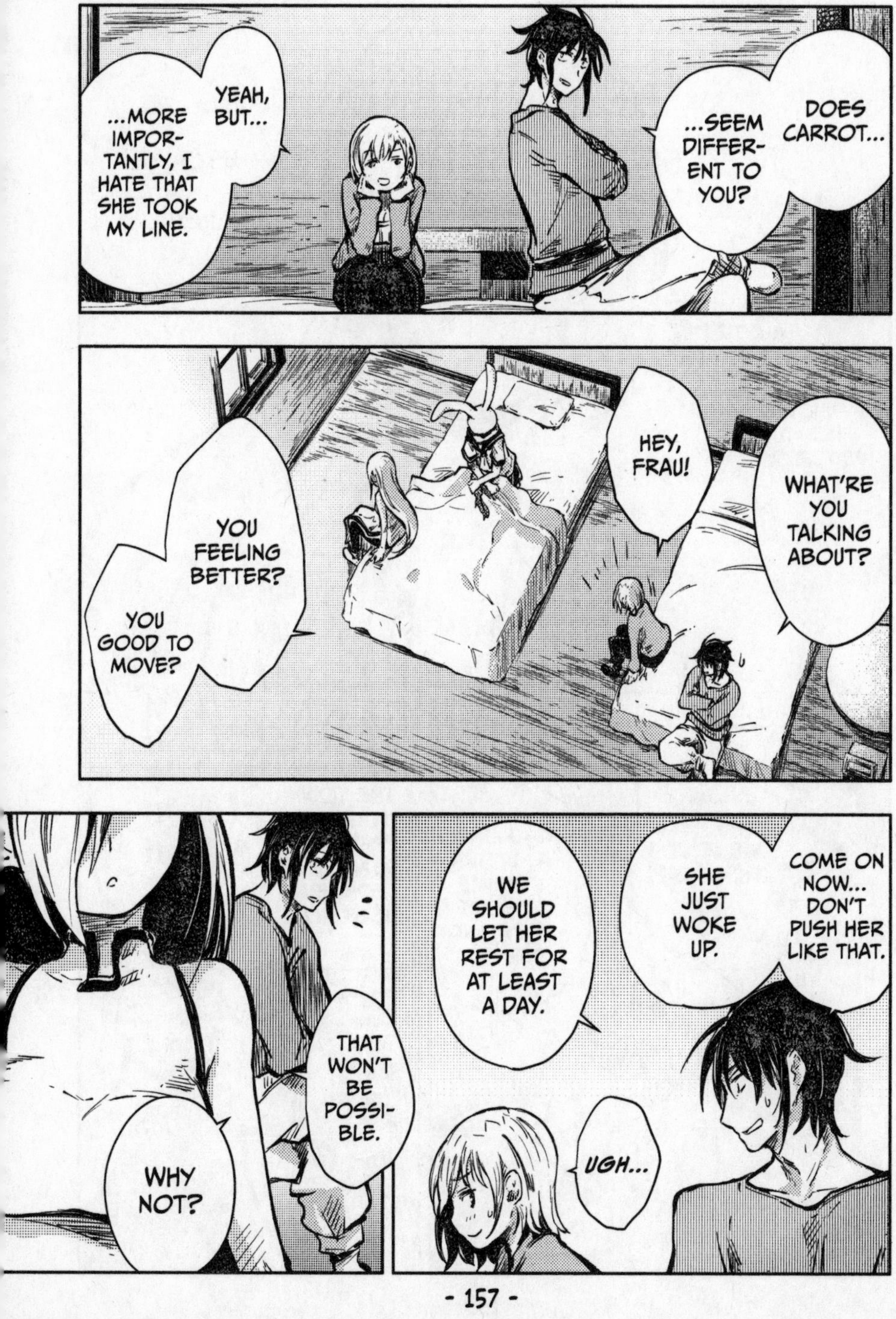
DOES CARROT...
...SEEM DIFFERENT TO YOU?
YEAH, BUT...
...MORE IMPORTANTLY, I HATE THAT SHE TOOK MY LINE.
WHAT'RE YOU TALKING ABOUT?
HEY, FRAU!
YOU FEELING BETTER?
YOU GOOD TO MOVE?
COME ON NOW... DON'T PUSH HER LIKE THAT.
SHE JUST WOKE UP.
WE SHOULD LET HER REST FOR AT LEAST A DAY.
UGH...
THAT WON'T BE POSSIBLE.
WHY NOT?

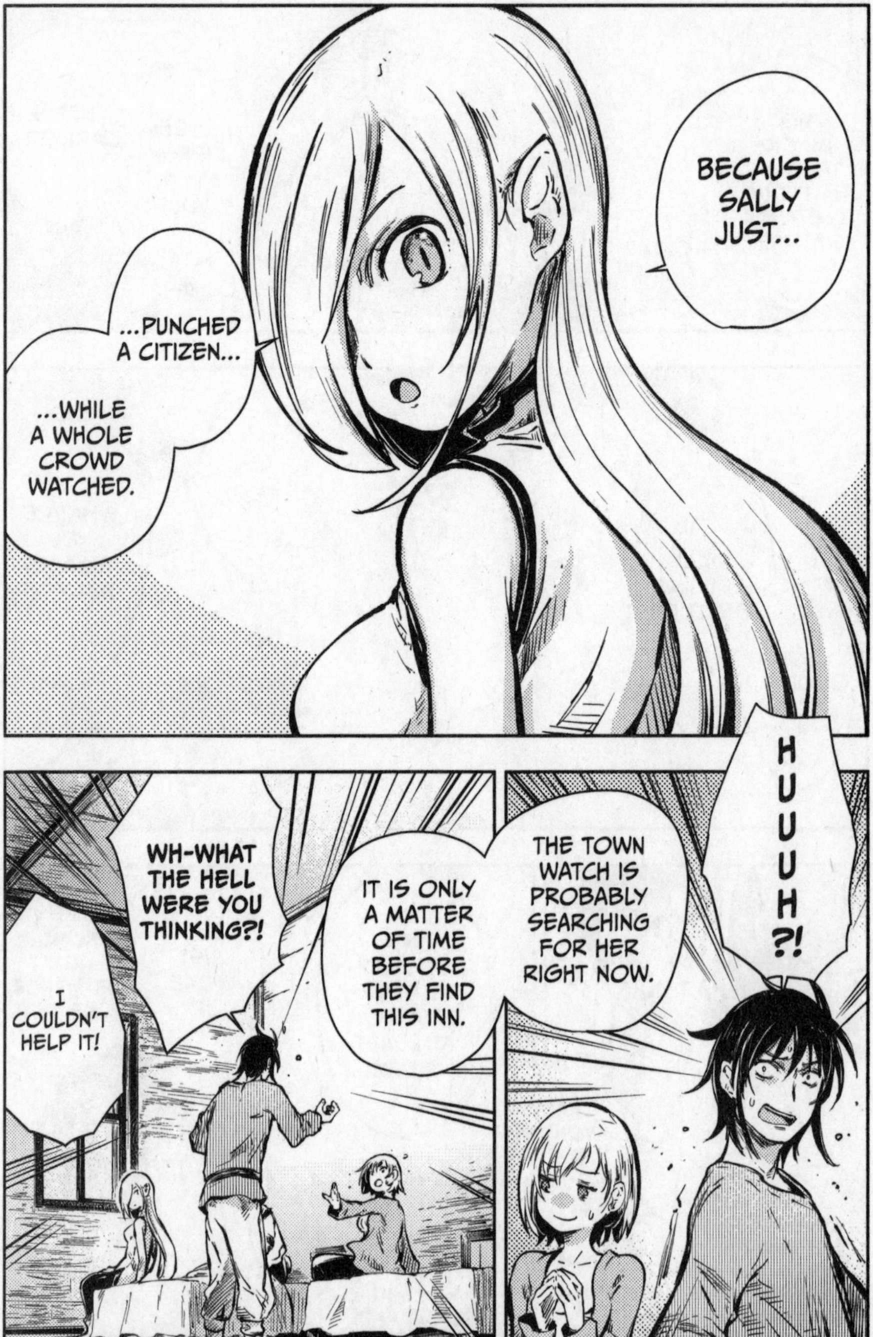
BECAUSE SALLY JUST...
...PUNCHED A CITIZEN...
...WHILE A WHOLE CROWD WATCHED.
HUUUH?!
THE TOWN WATCH IS PROBABLY SEARCHING FOR HER RIGHT NOW.
IT IS ONLY A MATTER OF TIME BEFORE THEY FIND THIS INN.
WH-WHAT THE HELL WERE YOU THINKING?!
I COULDN'T HELP IT!

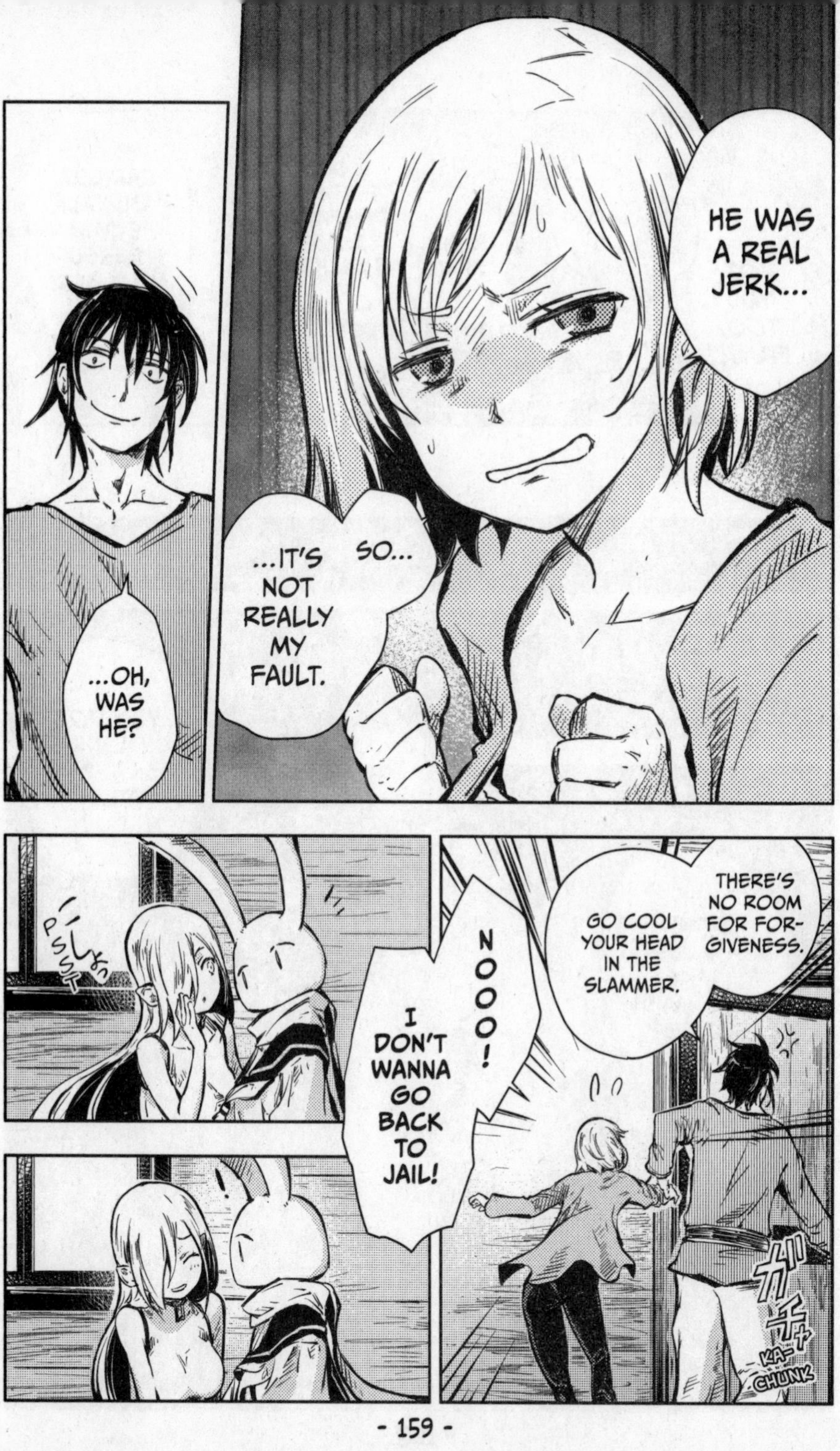
HE WAS A REAL JERK...
SO...
...IT'S NOT REALLY MY FAULT.
...OH, WAS HE?
THERE'S NO ROOM FOR FORGIVENESS.
GO COOL YOUR HEAD IN THE SLAMMER.
NOOOO! I DON'T WANNA GO BACK TO JAIL!
ガチャ
KA-CHUNK
PSST

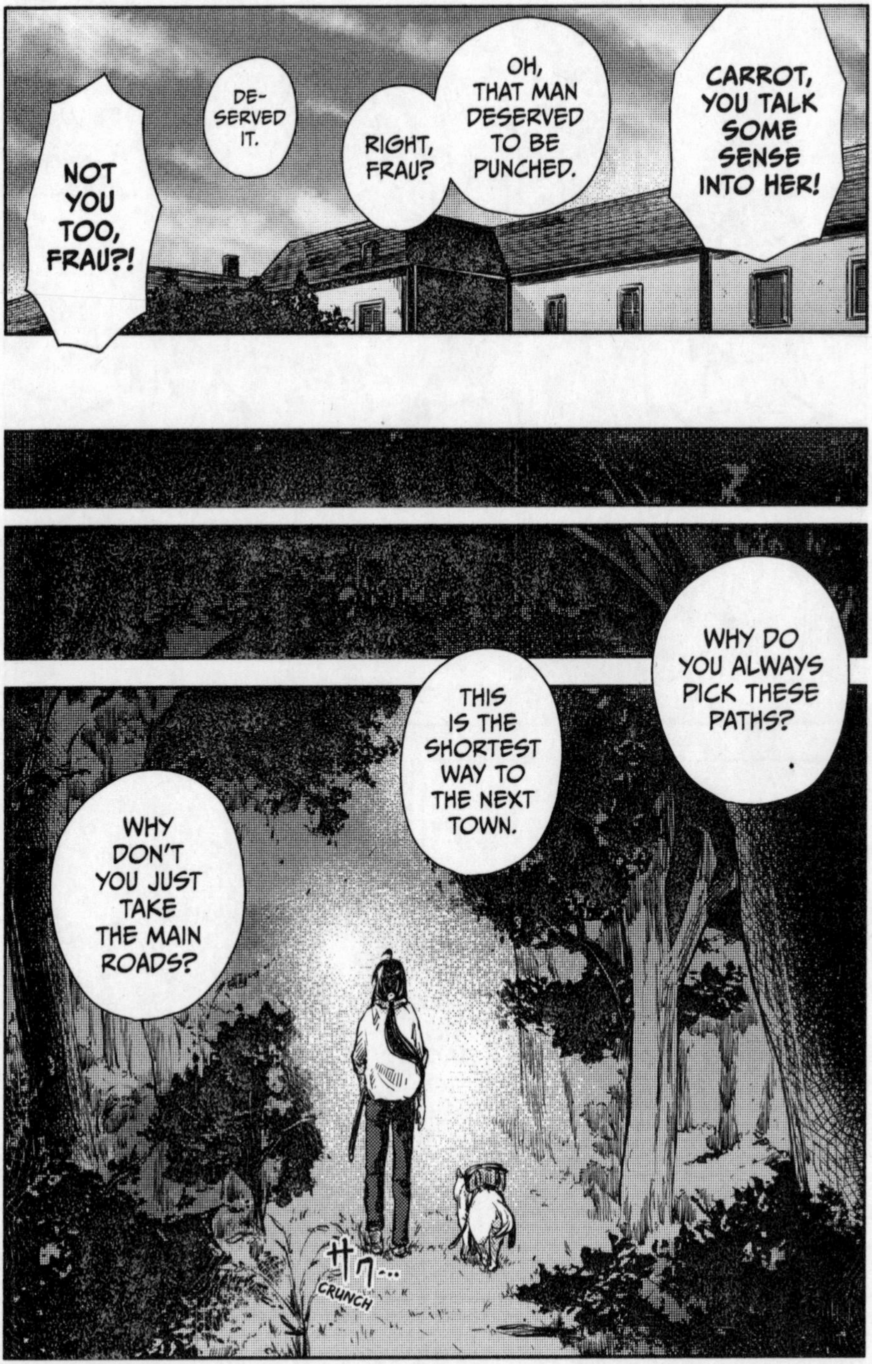
CARROT, YOU TALK SOME SENSE INTO HER!
OH, THAT MAN DESERVED TO BE PUNCHED.
RIGHT, FRAU?
DE-SERVED IT.
NOT YOU TOO, FRAU?!
WHY DO YOU ALWAYS PICK THESE PATHS?
THIS IS THE SHORTEST WAY TO THE NEXT TOWN.
WHY DON'T YOU JUST TAKE THE MAIN ROADS?
サク…
CRUNCH

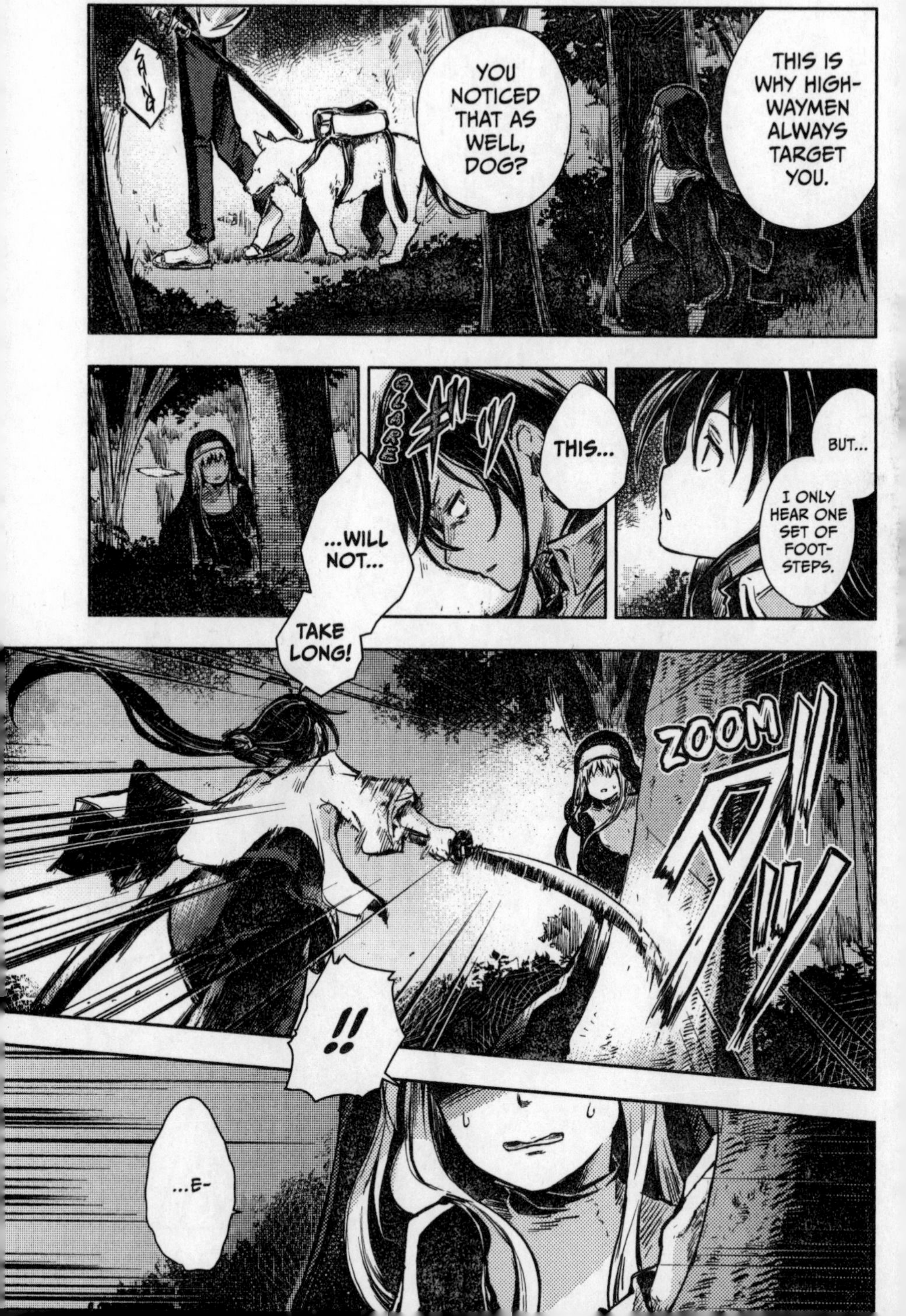
THIS IS WHY HIGH-WAYMEN ALWAYS TARGET YOU.
YOU NOTICED THAT AS WELL, DOG?
SHING
BUT...
I ONLY HEAR ONE SET OF FOOT-STEPS.
GLARE
THIS...
...WILL NOT...
TAKE LONG!
ZOOM
!!
...E-

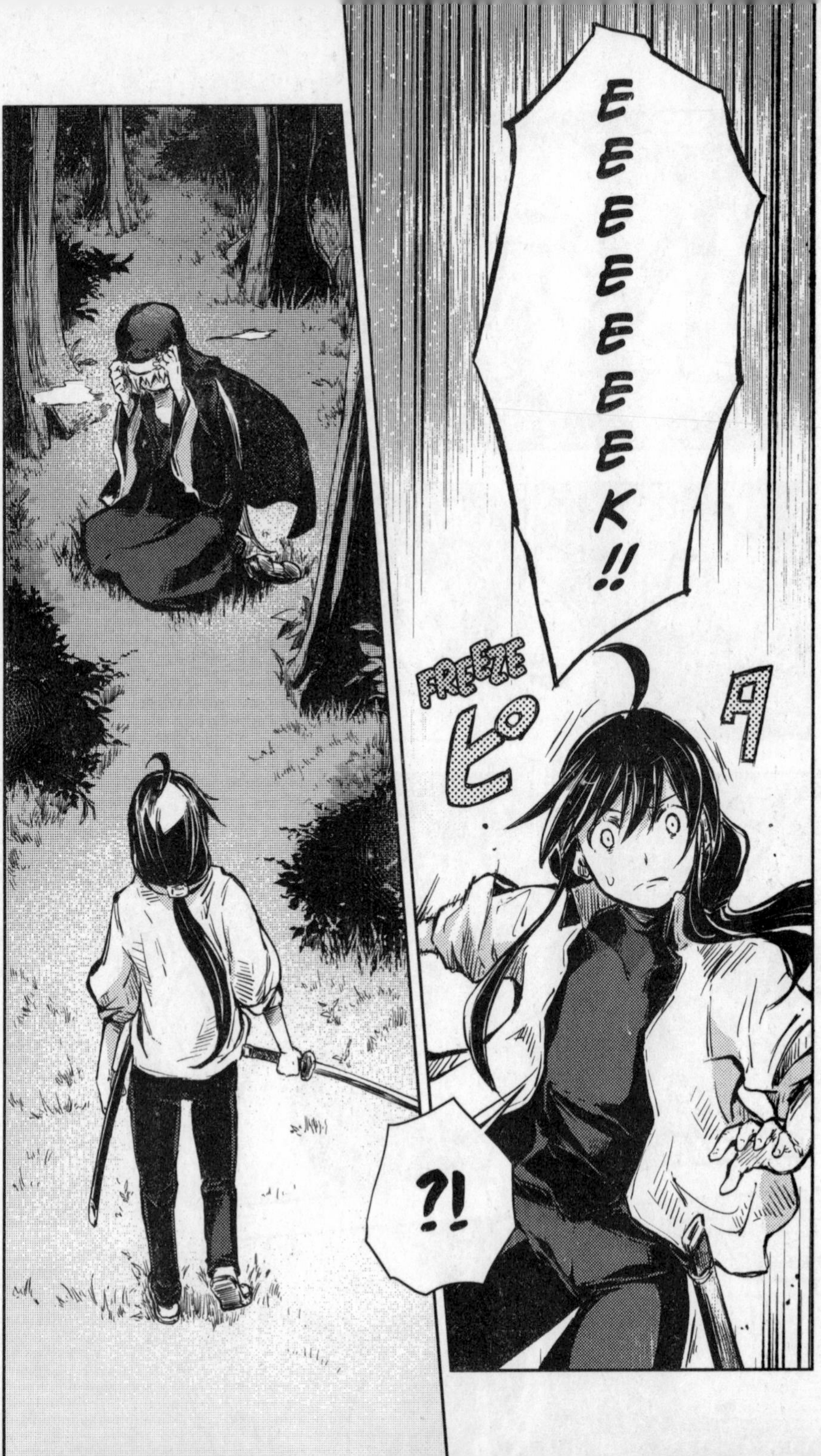
EEEEEEEK!!
FREEZE
?!

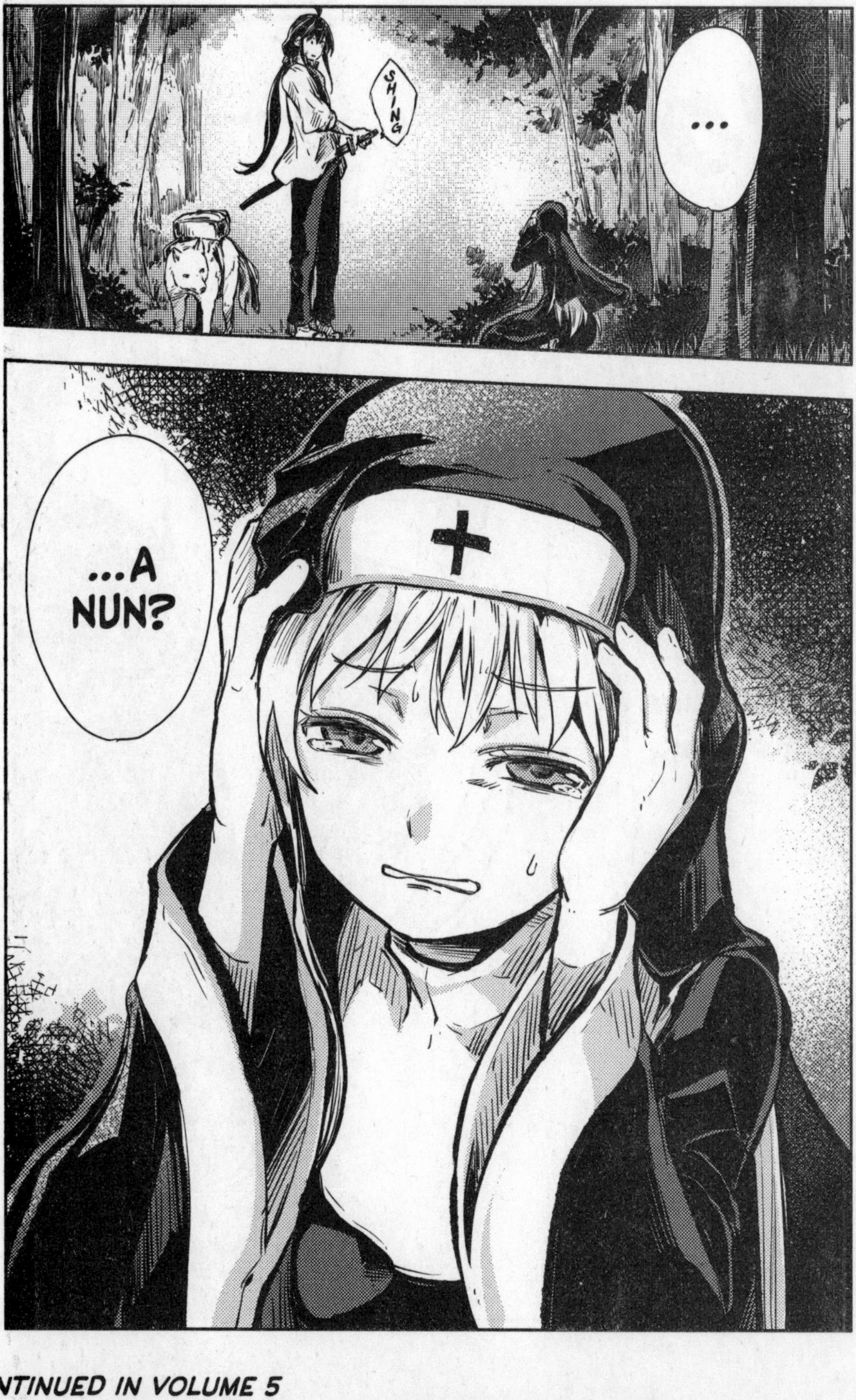
...
SHING
...A NUN?

CONTINUED IN VOLUME 5

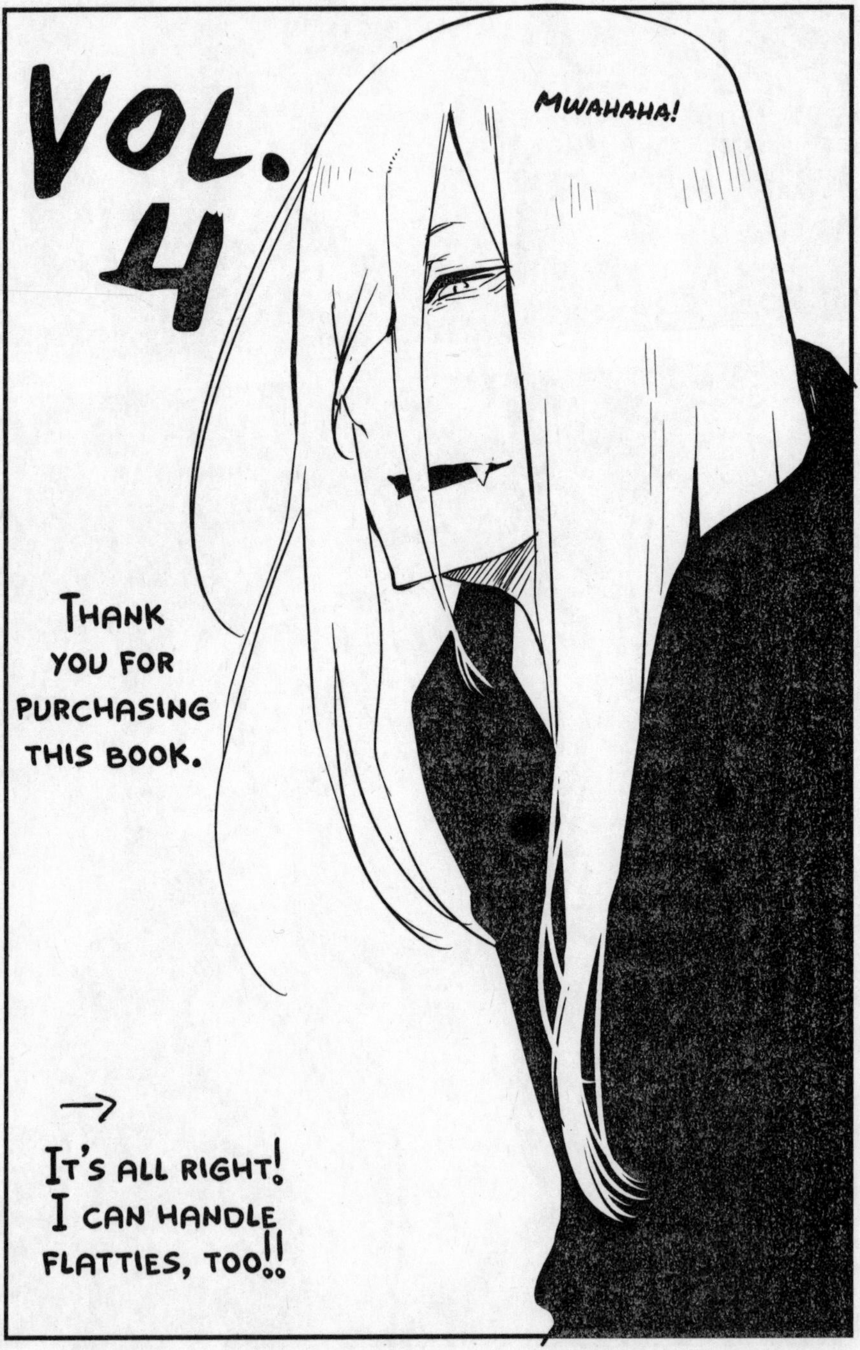

MWAHAHA!
VOL. 4
THANK YOU FOR PURCHASING THIS BOOK.
→
IT'S ALL RIGHT! I CAN HANDLE FLATTIES, TOO!!

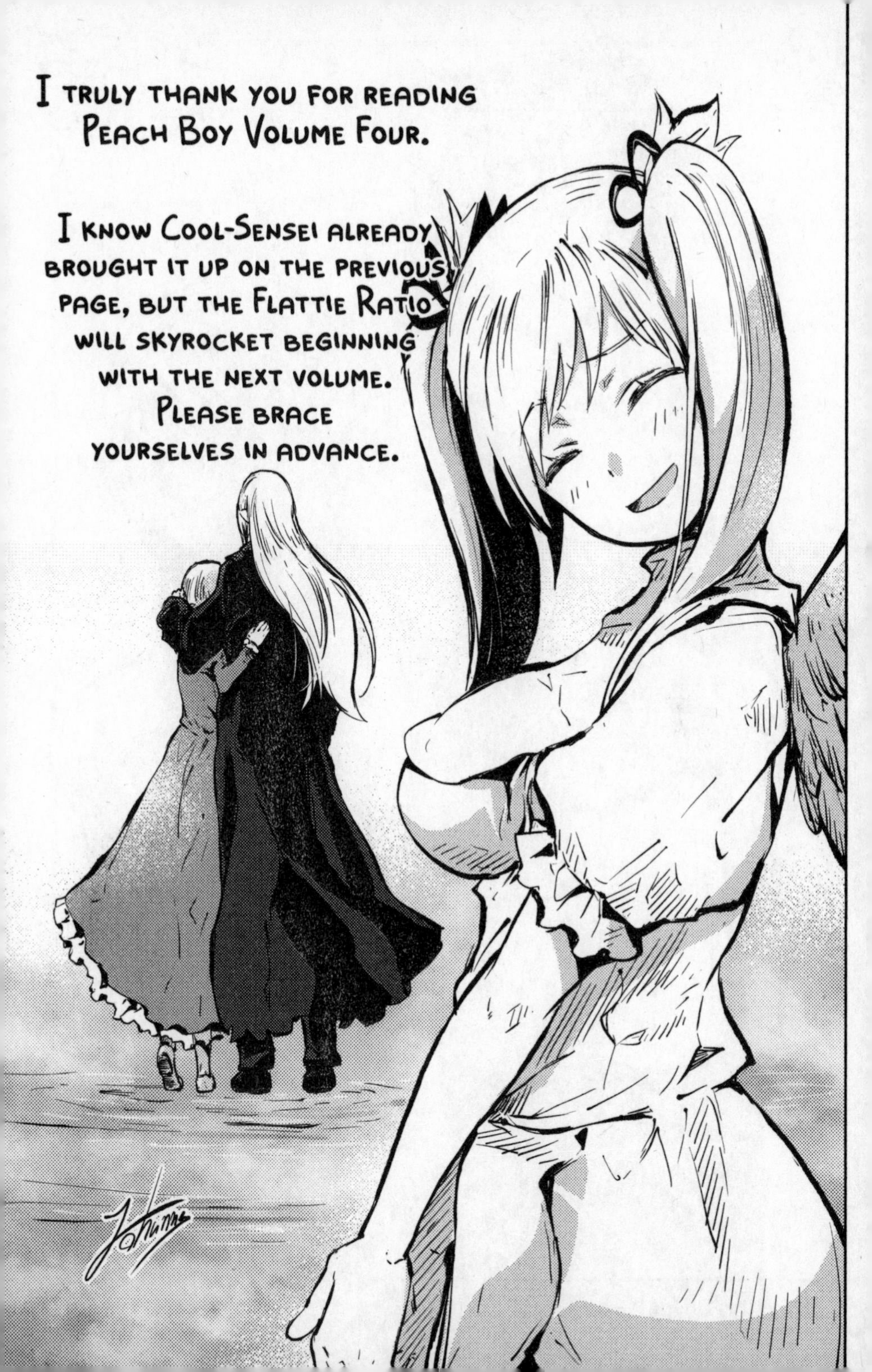
I truly thank you for reading Peach Boy Volume Four.
I know Cool-Sensei already brought it up on the previous page, but the Flattie Ratio will skyrocket beginning with the next volume. Please brace yourselves in advance.

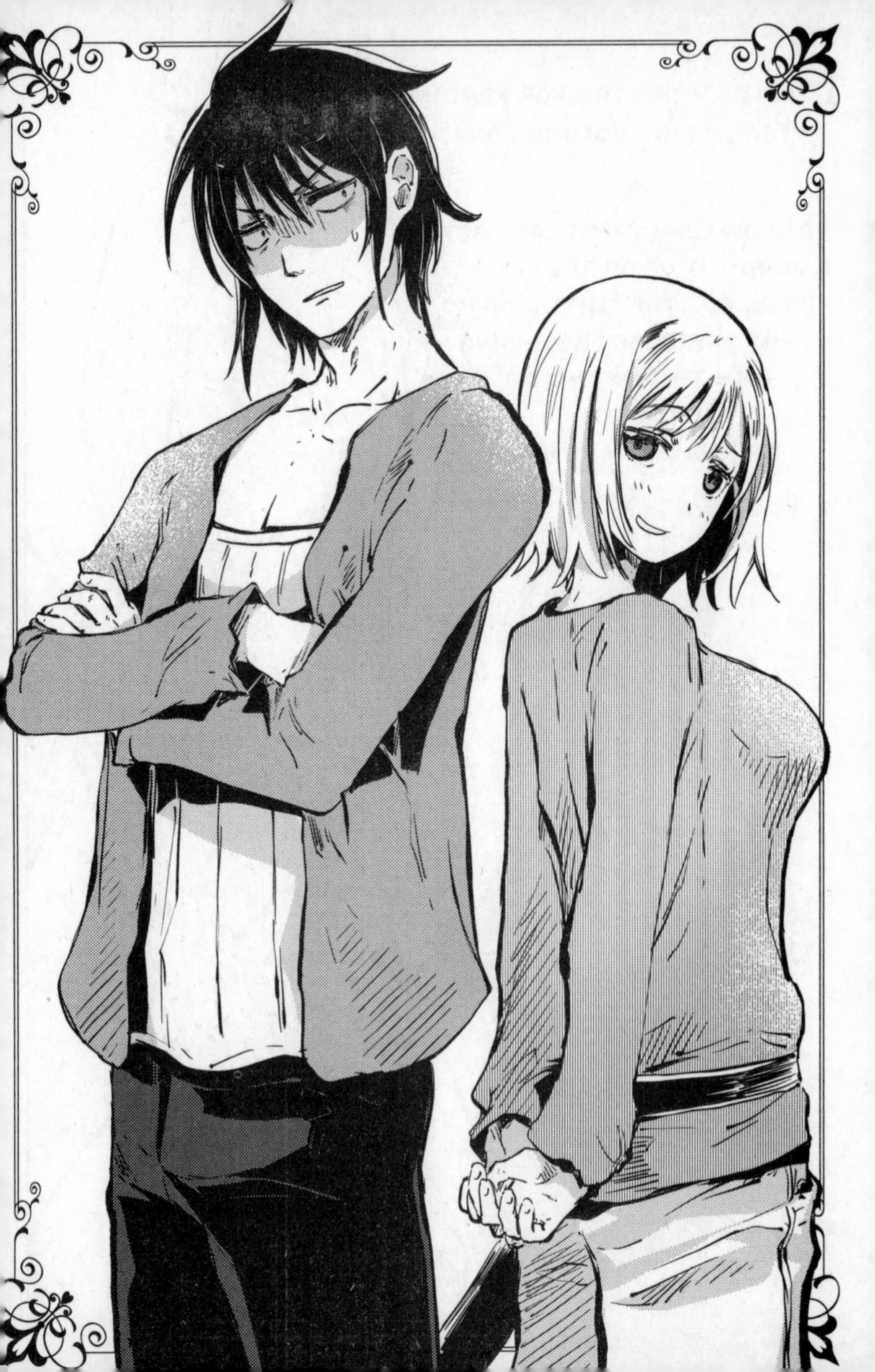

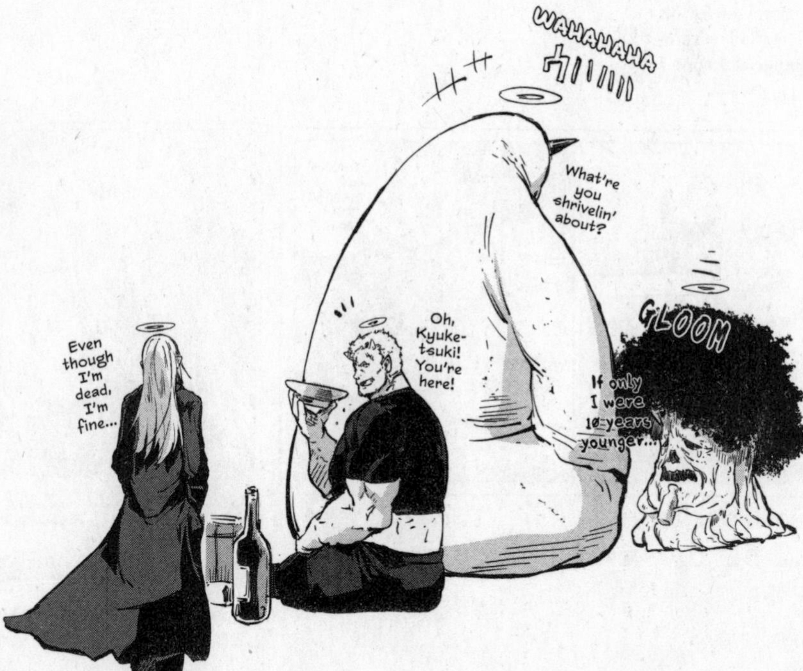
WAHAHAHA
What're you shrivelin' about?
GLOOM
If only I were 10 years younger...
Oh, Kyuketsuki! You're here!
Even though I'm dead, I'm fine...

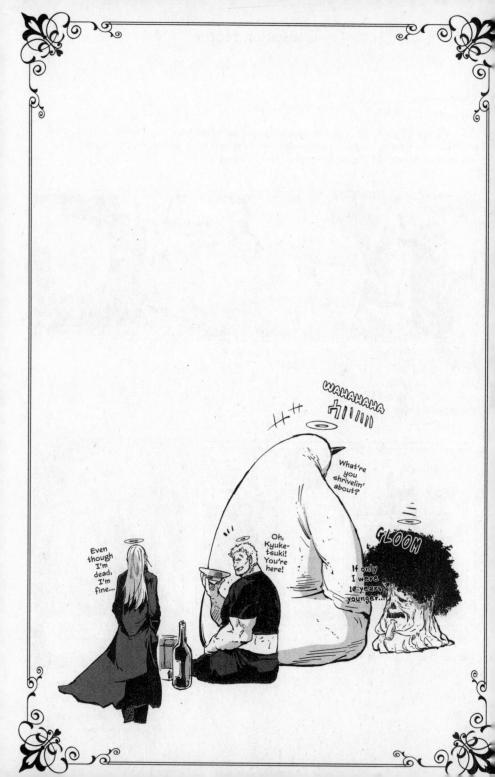

Translation Notes

Ogre names, pages 14, 15, 17, 69

The names of the humanoid ogres who have appeared thus far all follow the same formula: a Chinese character representing a defining characteristic, followed by the character for "ogre," which is pronounced "ki" or "gi." The named ogres in this volume were…

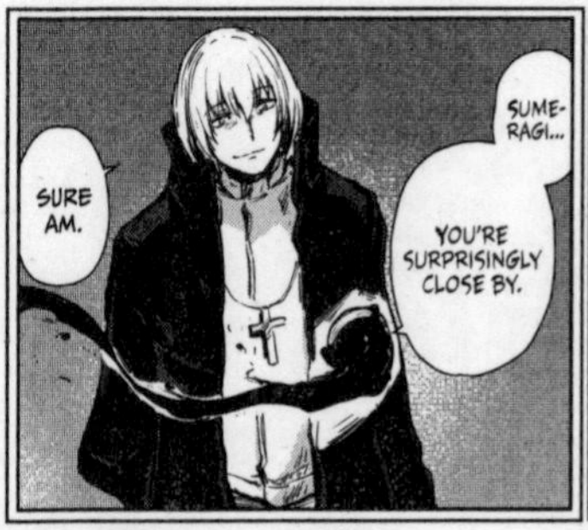
SUME-RAGI...
YOU'RE SURPRISINGLY CLOSE BY.
SURE AM.

Sumeragi: "Divine Ogre" (皇鬼)

The character for his name is used to refer to the imperial throne.

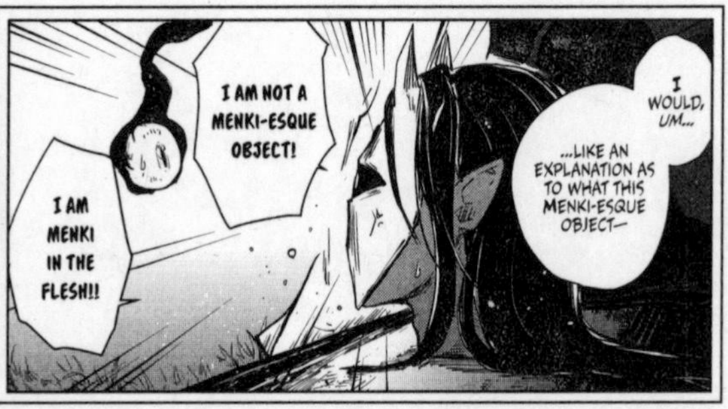
I WOULD, UM...
...LIKE AN EXPLANATION AS TO WHAT THIS MENKI-ESQUE OBJECT—
I AM NOT A MENKI-ESQUE OBJECT!
I AM MENKI IN THE FLESH!!

Menki: "Mask Ogre" (面鬼)

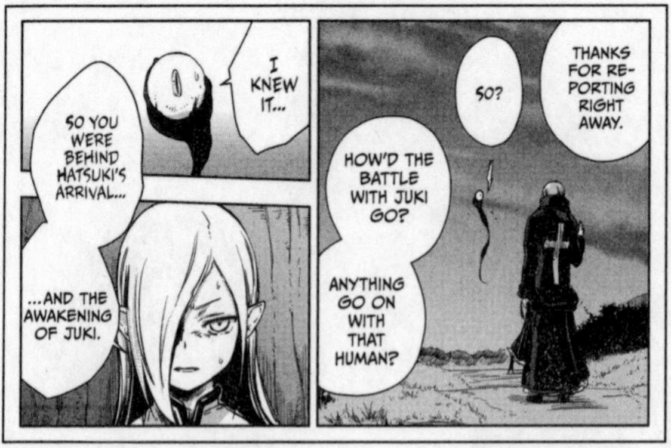
THANKS FOR RE-PORTING RIGHT AWAY.
SO?
HOW'D THE BATTLE WITH JUKI GO?
ANYTHING GO ON WITH THAT HUMAN?
I KNEW IT...
SO YOU WERE BEHIND HATSUKI'S ARRIVAL...
...AND THE AWAKENING OF JUKI.

Juki: "Tree Ogre" (樹鬼)

Hatsuki: "Hair Ogre" (髪鬼)

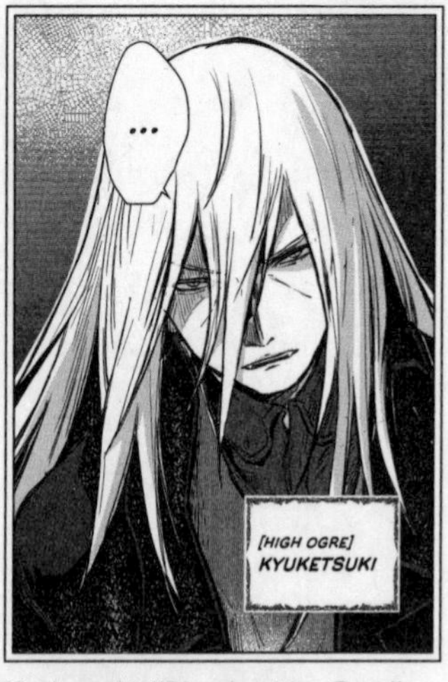
...
[HIGH OGRE] KYUKETSUKI

Kyuketsuki: "Bloodsucking Ogre" (吸血鬼)

This is the same spelling to refer to a vampire in Japanese.

The adorable new odd-couple cat comedy manga from the creator of the beloved *Chi's Sweet Home*, in full color!

Praise for Chi's Sweet Home

"Nearly impossible to turn away... a true all-ages title that anyone, young or old, cat lover or not, will enjoy. The stories will bring a smile to your face and warm your heart."

~School Library Journal

Sue & Tai-chan

Konami Kanata

Sue is an aging housecat who's looking forward to living out her life in peace... but her plans change when the mischievous black tomcat Tai-chan enters the picture! Hey! Sue never signed up to be a catsitter! *Sue & Tai-chan* is the latest from the reigning meow-narch of cute kitty comics, Konami Kanata.

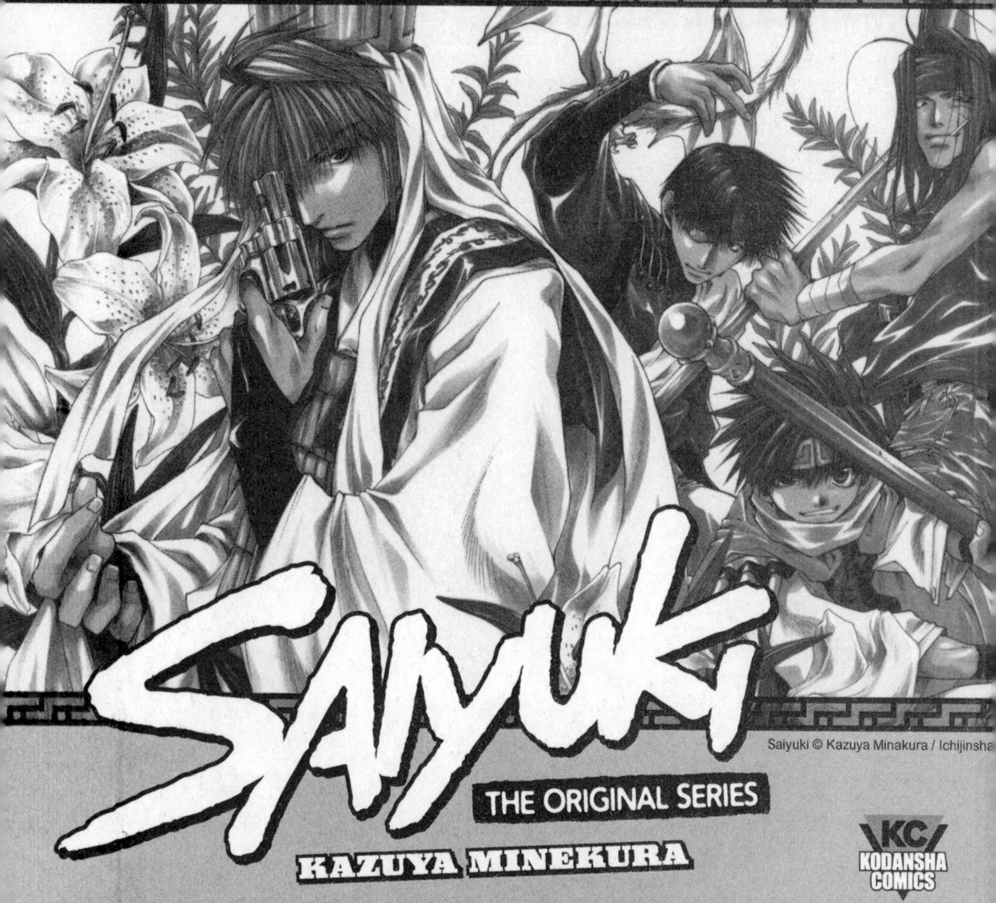

THE SWEET SCENT OF LOVE IS IN THE AIR! FOR FANS OF OFFBEAT ROMANCES LIKE *WOTAKOI*

Sweat and Soap © Kintetsu Yamada / Kodansha Ltd.

In an office romance, there's a fine line between sexy and awkward... and that line is where Asako — a woman who sweats copiously — meets Koutarou — a perfume developer who can't get enough of Asako's, er, scent. Don't miss a romcom manga like no other!

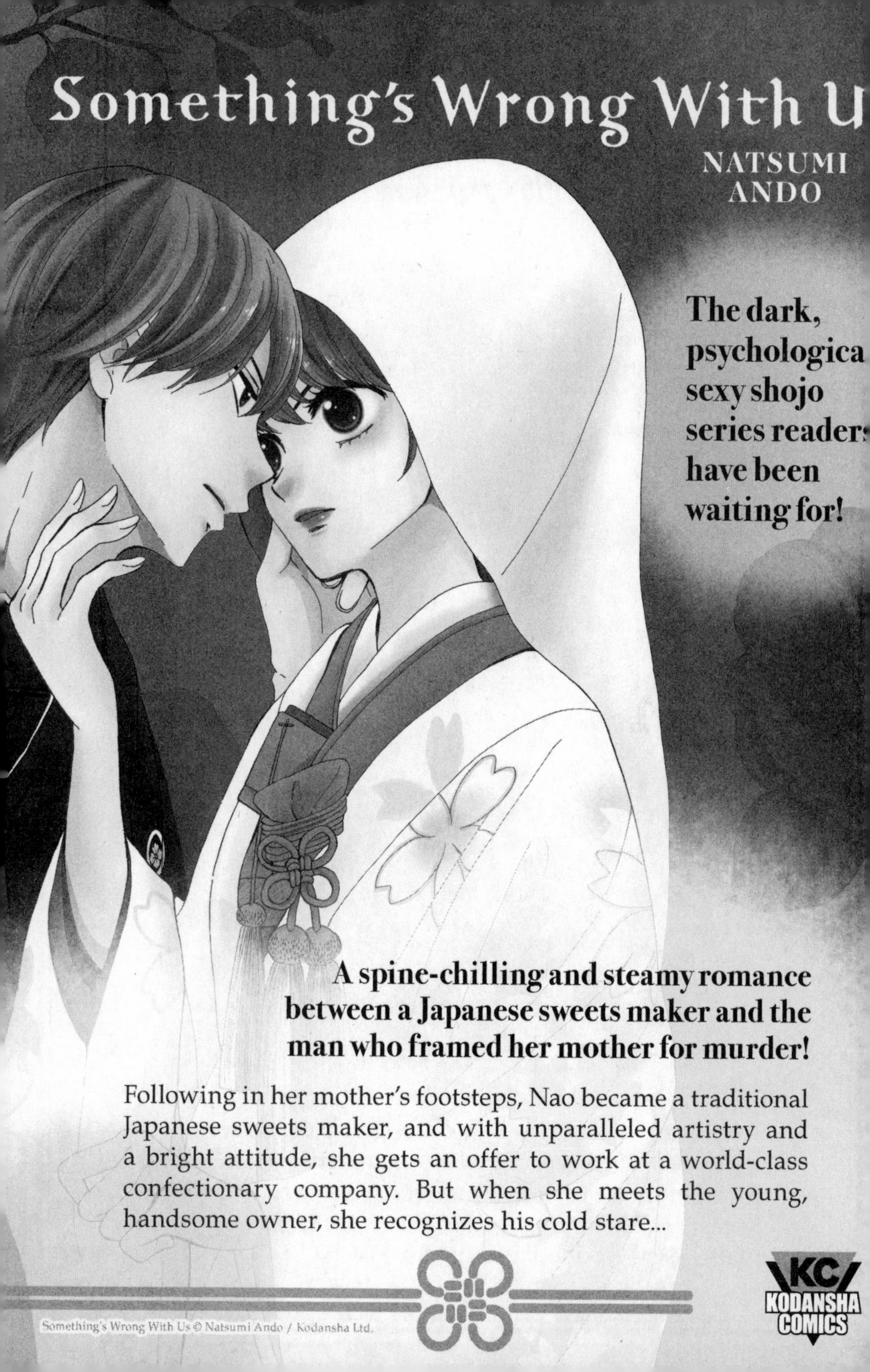
Something's Wrong With U
NATSUMI ANDO
The dark, psychologica sexy shojo series reader have been waiting for!
A spine-chilling and steamy romance between a Japanese sweets maker and the man who framed her mother for murder!
Following in her mother's footsteps, Nao became a traditional Japanese sweets maker, and with unparalleled artistry and a bright attitude, she gets an offer to work at a world-class confectionary company. But when she meets the young, handsome owner, she recognizes his cold stare...
KC KODANSHA COMICS
Something's Wrong With Us © Natsumi Ando / Kodansha Ltd.

Young characters and steampunk setting, like *Howl's Moving Castle* and *Battle Angel Alita*

A boy with a talent for machines and a mysterious girl whose wings he's fixed will take you beyond the clouds! In the tradition of the high-flying, resonant adventure stories of Studio Ghibli comes a gorgeous tale about the longing of young hearts for adventure and friendship!

A SMART, NEW ROMANTIC COMEDY FOR FANS OF *SHORTCAKE CAKE* AND *TERRACE HOUSE!*

A romance manga starring high school girl Meeko, who learns to live on her own in a boarding house whose living room is home to the odd (but handsome) Matsunaga-san. She begins to adjust to her new life away from her parents, but Meeko soon learns that no matter how far away from home she is, she's still a young girl at heart — especially when she finds herself falling for Matsunaga-san.

A Kodansha Comics Trade Paperback Original
Peach Boy Riverside 4 copyright © 2018 Coolkyousinnjya/Johanne
English translation copyright © 2021 Coolkyousinnjya/Johanne

Published in the United States by Kodansha Comics, an imprint of Kodansha USA Publishing, LLC, New York.

Publication rights for this English edition arranged through Kodansha Ltd., Tokyo.

First published in Japan in 2018 by Kodansha Ltd., Tokyo.

ISBN 978-1-64651-342-0

Original cover design by Tadashi Hisamochi (hive&co.,ltd.)

Printed in the United States of America.

www.kodansha.us

1st Printing
Translation: Steven LeCroy
Lettering: Andrew Copeland
Additional Lettering: Belynda Ungurath
Editing: Thalia Sutton, Maggie Le
YKS Services LLC/SKY Japan, Inc.
Kodansha Comics edition cover design by Adam Del Re

Publisher: Kiichiro Sugawara

Director of publishing services: Ben Applegate
Associate director of publishing operations: Stephen Pakula
Publishing services managing editors: Alanna Ruse, Madison Salters
Production managers: Emi Lotto, Angela Zurlo
Logo and character art ©Kodansha USA Publishing, LLC